Improving Leisure Services Through Marketing Action

By
Ron McCarville

SAGAMORE
PUBLISHING

www.sagamorepub.com

Interior Layout: Kenneth J. O'Brien
Cover Design: K. Jeffrey Higgerson

ISBN: 1-57167-497-7
Library of Congress Card Catalog Number: 2002107090

Printed in the United States of America

Dedication

To Marcia and Michael: my family, my friends

Acknowledgments

I wish to thank the many people who assisted me both directly and indirectly in preparing this book. First of all, this book would not have been written without the example set by Drs. John Crompton, Dennis Howard and Valerie Zeithaml. It was they who first introduced me to the world of services marketing. I thank them for their guidance and their insight.

I thank my colleagues in the Department of Recreation & Leisure Studies at the University of Waterloo for their ongoing advice and the fine example they offer me each day. I am fortunate indeed to work among these very fine scholars. Roger Mannell and Mark Havitz, in particular, are always ready with much needed perspective and direction. I must also acknowledge and thank Charlene Shannon, Monica Majewski, and Anne Ross here at the University of Waterloo for their assistance in preparing this manuscript.

I want to thank students who have worked with me in related research efforts here at the University of Waterloo. Bob Copeland, Grant Garrow, Kelly Weppler, Chris Flood, Tabatha Froats, Jen Coleman, Christina Colenutt, Ron Welch, Rylee Raymond and Colleen Bee have all assisted me with their enthusiasm and their insights over the years. This book is much improved as a result of their efforts.

I have been fortunate enough to work with many professionals who strive each day to provide quality leisure services. They are found in all levels of government, in regional and national organizations and in the private sector. I am constantly inspired by their commitment to serving their communities and to improving the lives of those around them. I hope this book offers them timely and useful insight.

Thanks to all those at Sagamore Publishing. Dr. Joe Bannon and the staff there have been remarkable both for their cooperative spirit and their equally remarkable patience.

Finally, I wish to thank Cosette Payne and the people of the Municipality of Chester, Nova Scotia. They were kind and patient enough to teach me what it was to be a leisure service provider. I thank them from the bottom of my heart and wish them well.

Table of Contents

Foreword

Think for a moment of the word "marketing." What image does the word conjure for you? For some, marketing is a much needed remedy for the ills that face leisure providers and participants alike. Its appeal is in its apparent simplicity. As John Crompton (1985) suggested, "the simplicity of the marketing paradigm has a beguiling attraction . . . [and it] is often presented as a nirvana, a cure-all and solution to all management problems" (p. 175). Link this supposed simplicity with the sheer power of marketing tools like advertising, and we begin to see the relentless appeal of marketing for many leisure managers.

For others, marketing represents a calamity for public leisure delivery systems. Leisure academics and social activists in particular have sounded the alarm over the creeping capitalism that marketing seems to represent. They believe that marketing, like commercialism, is inherently a process of exploitation. Its use will serve to objectify leisure, to make it a thing that is bought and sold. This process, they say, will diminish both the leisure experience and the opportunity for the disadvantaged to take part.

I suggest that our ambivalence over marketing arises from general confusion over the nature and function of marketing effort. This book seeks to reduce this confusion by defining and reviewing the marketing process. It characterizes marketing as a series of interrelated activities that focus on the client. The ultimate goal of this process is to discover an optimal fit between client preferences and agency capabilities, then to mobilize resources accordingly. Marketing is making people want to do business with you, to want to use the services you offer. As such, I view marketing as a tool that offers much promise for leisure providers in any sector.

Like any tool, marketing is best applied with skill. There is considerable evidence, however, that marketing effort is limited by the philosophy and skill of the practitioner. There seems to be considerable confusion in the application of rather basic marketing principles. It seems appropriate that steps be taken to reduce this confusion. One solution lies in the continued dissemination of practical information to leisure providers. That is the intention of this book.

The text guides the reader through the marketing process. It begins with an introduction to the concept of marketing, then describes how marketing is done. Two points are noteworthy as we consider how that particular job is undertaken. First, marketing is largely a circular process that begins and ends with the client. As discussed in the first chapter, this was not always so. Two generations of marketers had focused on the products they planned to sell rather than the client they hoped to serve. Eventually, however, they discovered that trying to convince clients to buy a thing they neither want nor need simply didn't work. Experience has shown that successful marketing is client— not product—driven. It is better to discover what the client wants, then mobilize resources to provide it. This process is less demanding of the provider and more appealing to the consumer.

The second point is equally critical to successful marketing. As with any complicated enterprise, marketing is comprised of many stages or steps. The order in which these steps are undertaken becomes important. The marketer must get this sequence "right" if the marketing effort is to succeed. Marketers must understand their clients before they can develop strategy. They must develop strategy before they can apply the marketing mix. The marketing mix should be established before client/staff encounters can be orchestrated. The chapters in this book are organized to reflect the sequential nature of marketing. They are provided in the order the marketer might best use to market leisure services.

The first step is one of strategy development. Strategic planning creates a blueprint for action and directs all subsequent marketing activities. The text goes on to describe the marketing mix both in its profound simplicity and its marvelous flexibility. Once the mix is reviewed, the emphasis shifts to the actual encounter between the client and the provider. Encounters between the client and staff must be managed. Nothing should be left to chance. The text describes the importance of the encounter, often called the moment of truth, and how to orchestrate that encounter. Next the text deals with the inevitability of errors. It is both possible and desirable that conflicts between clients and staff be resolved to the satisfaction of all, and an entire chapter is devoted to this purpose.

Finally, the text discusses the need for ongoing improvement in services marketing. Improvement requires two things. The first is evaluation. Marketers must constantly compare their services against meaningful standards, and these standards rise daily. It is perhaps the perversity of human nature that your marketing efforts can never be good enough. As service levels improve, client expectations will rise accordingly. If your staff is helpful on Monday, clients typically expect them to be just as helpful, or even more so, on Tuesday. As a result, to remain static is to fall behind. The second key to improvement is the ability to handle change. Successful change is difficult to achieve and remains one of the great challenges that face any leisure marketer. The text offers an overview of what it takes to make ongoing improvement and change possible.

This text displays a distinct public sector bias. Though the material provided here emerges generally from private sector sources, it focuses on public sector issues and concerns. I have taken this approach because marketing has proven most troublesome for public sector leisure providers. Though the public sector marketing literature is still in its relative infancy, we know that public sector marketers are faced with many problems unique to their sector. For example, notions of equity, which dominate public sector decision making, complicate the marketing process (Crompton & Lamb, 1986). Further, though many public sector practitioners report involvement in marketing activity, at least one national study suggested that basic marketing principles were often absent from current programming efforts in North America (Havitz & Spigner, 1993). This public sector bias notwithstanding, the insights offered here will be useful to marketers in public, not-for-profit, and private sectors.

The format adopted for this text offers several shortcuts for the marketer. A figure provided in chapter 1 outlines the entire marketing planning process. It serves to guide any marketing exercise. Further, main points offered throughout the book are reviewed at the conclusion of each chapter. These reviews can be used on their own and, when strung together, they offer a useful overview of marketing and its many steps/procedures. Taken together, the diagram and these reviews should help the beginner understand, or the more experienced user become familiar with, relevant concepts and processes.

Finally, an appendix is offered at the end of this text (see Appendix 1). It outlines one agency's efforts to serve its own needs and those of the client. Agency staff efforts were both encouraged and hampered by unprecedented budget cuts over a five-year period. The measures they adopted reflect virtually all of the discussion offered in subsequent chapters. Managers took a broad view of marketing and used every technique open to them when responding to the market conditions that faced them. The reader is encouraged to consult this appendix both during and after the reading of this text. This example may prove useful in making the leap from theory to practice.

I should offer a word on labels used in this text. I have called leisure providers marketers, planners, programmers, and decision makers. Leisure providers are all these things, and I wanted to use terms that reflect their daily reality. They use marketing tools, plan, offer programs, and make decisions on behalf of their clients each and every day. I also refer to the users of leisure programs as participants, clients, consumers, and users. They, too, are all these things. They participate, they consume, and they use leisure services. They are clients because the provider owes them a service and because the provider hopes to establish a long-term relationship with them.

David Starr Jordan once said that "Wisdom is knowing what to do next, skill is knowing how to do it, and virtue is doing it." His words should ring true to any leisure marketer. Marketing is an action-oriented process that brings together providers and users. It demands ongoing decision making and requires the skillful application of tools like the marketing mix. I hope the material offered here helps with this application. Students seeking up-to-date information on how leisure providers are actually applying these tools are encouraged to browse the World Wide Web for firsthand accounts. Sites like the Leisure Information Network (http://www.lin.ca) or the National Recreation and Park Association (http://activeparks.org) offer data sets, samples of everything from mission statements to promotional techniques currently being used in the "real world," and links to a wide variety of providers and programs.

R, McCarville

C H A P T E R

1

Understand Marketing Basics

The Evolution of Marketing Thought and Practice

In order to understand leisure marketing, one must first understand the evolution of the marketing concept. Marketing is first and foremost a tool, or more correctly, a set of tools. Like any tool, marketing was developed because of need. Marketing was first developed to meet the needs of producers. Producers needed to create desire for their products, and marketing evolved to meet this need.

Producers were being faced with a growing problem. Demand for their products was not keeping pace with their ability to produce those products. This was a relatively new phenomenon. Since the industrial revolution, society's capacity to produce goods had been increasing annually. Technology was making possible production levels unimaginable at any other time in history. Technological potential, and with it production levels, virtually leapt forward during the two world wars of the twentieth century. At the conclusion of World War II in particular, industrial and technological might that had been focused upon war effort was turned to the production

of consumer goods. Producers eventually found, however, that demand for their products was unable to match their increasingly impressive rate of production.

The increasing rate of production had created an imbalance between supply and demand. Initial efforts to address this imbalance were intended to increase demand. Marketing was created for this purpose. It became a set of activities intended to help producers sell their products. Though early marketing efforts focused on agricultural products, they soon expanded to include virtually all physical goods (Bartels, 1988). Today marketing is a pervasive activity undertaken by anyone interested in facilitating exchange with other individuals or parties.

Any tool evolves. It is shaped both by its intended use and by the demands that are placed upon it. Like all tools, marketing has changed much since its early inception. Three of these changes are particularly relevant for the leisure marketer. The first change has been to the nature of the products with which the marketer is concerned. Where once products related only to physical goods, discussion of products now includes goods, services, people, and even ideas. The second dramatic change that has occurred within marketing has been the emerging role of the consumer. Where once the consumer was considered little more than a source of revenue upon whom products were "pushed," the consumer is now considered a dominant partner in the marketing process. The third development relates to the emergent role of the workforce in successful marketing effort. The responsibility for marketing once lay with a small number of "marketing" staff. This responsibility now lies with all staff members. All are now in some way involved in marketing effort. Each of these developments has changed the practice of services marketing and all are described here.

From Goods to Services to Ideas

Early marketing effort focused exclusively on the distribution of goods. Goods are physical in nature. They can be seen, touched, and manipulated. The marketing of such goods is relatively straightforward. Goods are designed to be reproduced, reproduced to be transported, transported to be displayed, and displayed to be sold. Think for a moment of the cereal you might have eaten for breakfast this morning. The cereal producers have developed techniques and machines that enable them to reproduce the same basic product time and time again. They do so repeatedly, consistently, and efficiently. The cereal was probably placed in a sturdy case of a type that was designed to protect and transport millions of boxes of cereal. These cases were brought to your local grocer who placed the cereal in storage, either in backrooms or on the shelf, until such time that it attracted your attention and you brought it home. For the product marketer, issues of efficiency, waste reduction, packaging, and distribution are paramount. During the early days, all marketing effort was assumed to be devoted to the movement of physical goods (Fisk, Brown, & Bitner, 1993). This trend was surprisingly tenacious even as the economic landscape evolved over time.

As the U.S. began the transition from an industrial to a services economy, the development received little notice in the marketing discipline. Although the national economy was dominated by services, by the mid-1940s, some time elapsed before marketing scholars began to discuss and study the service economy and the services marketing that occurred within that economy. (Fisk et al., 1993, p. 66)

About 20 years ago, leaders within the marketing community began to explore the bounds of marketing practice. Kotler and Levy (1988) in particular reasoned that if we could market goods, then why not market ideas or people? They pointed out that politicians and their party members use marketing techniques to promote their respective platforms; that private sector companies employ marketing effort to improve their image; that nonprofit and charitable groups use marketing principles to convey their messages to the community. Why, they asked, were marketers focusing on physical goods, when marketing could be applied to "an increasingly interesting range of social activity" (Kotler & Levy, p. 38). Over the years even the most traditional marketer has come to realize that physical goods occupy only one small point along the marketing continuum. This continuum is bound by physical goods at one end and intangible ideas at the other.

New insights have been needed as marketers deal with issues located on the less tangible end of the product spectrum. For example, it became clear that intangible services varied in important ways from their manufactured counterparts. In a classic article, Berry (1984) suggested that services were different from goods in four fundamental ways and each difference presented unique challenges to the service marketer. First, services are *perishable*. Unsold services cannot be stockpiled. The opportunity to sell an empty seat in a theatre is gone forever once the show has begun. It cannot be set aside and sold later as can a manufactured product.

As a result, uneven demand may prove a considerable challenge to the service provider.

When supply exceeds demand, facilities sit idle and resources are wasted. When demand exceeds supply, clients must wait for service or are turned away. Neither condition is desirable. Further, both supply and demand may vary dramatically throughout the day, week, or season, so demand management is critical for the service provider. The provider may have to take extraordinary steps in order to ensure that supply matches demand.

Second, services are *intangible*. Unlike manufactured goods, services typically lack substance. This poses a dilemma for both the producer and the participant. Providers find it difficult to convey service characteristics to potential participants. As a result, they may struggle in their attempts to appeal to potential clients (Zeithaml, 1991). For the participants, the service is difficult to assess either prior to or following participation. They are not able to "kick the tires" before purchasing a service. Nor is the quality of a service clear even after it has been consumed. How does one judge the quality of a fitness instructor? A typical fitness class may be uncomfortable, even painful, but is it effective? It is difficult to tell both in the short and long term. How does one know if one's health is improving as a result of a program? One may feel tired, sore, and hungry after such a class. Is this an improvement over the status quo? It is often simply too difficult to say. For these reasons, one of the most difficult tasks facing any service provider is to "tangiblize the intangible"(Levitt, 1983).

This may not be an easy task. "In many cases, the only cues on which to judge quality are the service's price and the physical facilities which house the service" (Zeithaml, (1991, p. 42). This may be bad news for public sector leisure providers, because prices are often heavily subsidized, and facilities are institutional in nature. How does a potential participant judge the quality of a low-cost program held in a local school? Does it suffer by comparison to more expensive, private programs offered in relatively luxurious facilities? Public programs may offer few meaningful cues to the client regarding their unique or beneficial program attributes.

Third, services are consumed as they are produced. In other words, the client and the producer typically meet, and together they both produce and consume the service. This is called *inseparability*. Such inseparability offers several challenges for the leisure provider. It introduces an interpersonal dynamic that is lacking in manufacturing. This interpersonal component highlights the interaction between staff and the client. Such interaction has been characterized as a performance that must be repeated with each new encounter (Grove & Fisk, 1991). Like all performances, the meeting must be choreographed and managed to ensure positive outcomes.

Finally, as a result of this inseparability, service encounters are dynamic. Like all interactions, they evolve from one instant to the next, from one encounter to the next. This is called *heterogeniety*. Heterogeniety introduces an infinite variability to the service encounter. Each encounter is unique. The challenge for the service provider is to ensure that services are consistent enough to guarantee unfailing quality, but flexible enough to adjust to ongoing change.

This discussion suggests basic conceptual differences between the marketing of intangible services and of physical goods. For the past two decades, those who market less tangible products like services have begun to develop their own strategies, tools, and terminology to address their specific needs. That terminology as well as those strategies and tools are reviewed throughout this text.

The Emergent Role of the Consumer

Marketing has been hampered over the years because of fundamental disagreements over its very nature. Early definitions focused on process rather than people. For example, a 1948 definition, offered in the *Journal of Marketing*, viewed marketing as "the performance of business activities that direct the flow of goods and services from producer to consumer or user" (Alexander, 1982, p. 6). This definition is very much based on the control of process. It focuses on the mechanical flow of goods and services while ignoring the respective roles of the players or their reasons for participation. It fails to grapple with the reasons for exchange, the desires that the process is intended to satisfy.

This perspective followed logically from marketing's early focus on the provider. It was, after all, the producer who initiated the marketing process. It was the producer who had a good or service to sell and used marketing to expedite that sale. The producer was immersed in the logistics of production and brought this orientation to the study of marketing. This legacy is reflected in an early statement attributed to Henry Ford, a man once described as both "the most brilliant and most senseless marketer in American history" (Levitt, 1960, p. 47). When asked about color options for his Model T Automobile, Ford responded, "My customers can have any color they want . . . as long as it's black" (Levitt, 1983). In this case, the customers' specific desires were considered secondary to production demands for uniformity.

Within this environment, efficiencies and systems were the watchwords of the producer, and these priorities found their way into the marketing consciousness. Their legacy is a long-standing focus on the needs of production. Marketing was used typically to facilitate the movement of products from the producer's shop floor to the consumer's hand. Further to this, the consumer was often viewed as a target or even a dupe. Consumers were to be influenced and fooled if necessary. When all was said and done, the marketer's job was either to alter or sustain behavior among selected groups of individuals. Behavior thought to be problematic was altered, and behavior thought to be desirable was sustained. This very simple premise guided marketing effort, fashioned marketing tools, guided marketing terminology, and defined marketing strategy. Marketing was as simple and as complex as that. It was single minded. It operated on the premise that behavior can and should be guided. It promoted the notion that the behavior of one should be influenced by another. It accepted the idea that this can happen in systematic and predictable ways and made every effort to do so.

As a result of this long, formative period, when many of us think of marketing, we tend to think of corporate advertisers' ongoing efforts to cajole client groups into purchasing their products. Schor (1991) reports that women received particular attention from advertisers over much of this century. "Businesses subjected women to a barrage of advertising and social pressure, in order to sell more products . . . they helped spread the word that a woman who did not purchase the growing array of consumer goods was jeopardizing her family, and missing out on the best life had to offer" (Schor, 1991, p. 97). This was a time of excess bordering on outright chicanery. In *The Image Makers* William Meyers reports that advertisers often "played fast and loose with the public. They put marbles in a bowl of soup so the few vegetables it contained would float to the top . . . it's no wonder that by the 1970s advertising executives regularly appeared at the bottom of the public's 'most respected profession' list—below insurance salesmen and pawnshop proprietors" (Meyers, 1984, pp. 12-13). They perpetrated such hoaxes to encourage consumption. It is perhaps little wonder that marketing is often considered synonymous with the worst excesses of commercialism (Havitz, 1988).

Eventually, it became clear that this selling orientation was a failure for both the producer and the client. The producers learned that even the most clever sales campaign, the most useful product, the most efficient production schedule would be for naught if not supported by consumers. Clients learned that they could not trust the promises of the producer. They became cynical and opportunistic as a result. They offered loyalty to no producer but would "shop and hop" from producer to producer, seeking the lowest price. Consequently, producers were not able to develop the long-term relationships necessary to understand and respond to the needs of these consumers.

This unhappy state made clear the need to involve the client in marketing deliberations. The potential consumer expressed needs, wants, and preferences that could not be ignored by anyone hoping to develop a loyal following of consumers. The marketing concept evolved to include the consumer. The consumer was finally being offered a role in the marketing process. Note how a 1961 definition begins to address the importance of the client. "Marketing is the process in a society by which the demand structure for economic goods and services is anticipated or enlarged and satisfied through the conception, promotion, and physical distribution of such goods and services" (Statement of the Philosophy of Marketing Faculty, 1964). This definition represents a vast improvement over its predecessor. While it continues to reflect the ongoing interest in production, it introduces for the first time the twin notions of consumer demand and satisfying that demand. It was one of the first efforts that recognized the profound role of the client in the process of marketing. Just as importantly, it also suggested the importance of satisfying rather than simply creating demand.

Unfortunately, acceptance of this new thinking was slow. You may have noted that this more recent definition emerged from an academic group. It seems they may have been on the leading edge of marketing thought, because these sentiments were not widely shared within the larger marketing community. In practice, the consumer was still considered someone to be sold to, not a partner in an exchange. Too often, marketing practice continued to emphasize the commodity, the marketing organization, or the fundamentals of marketing activities like advertising or pricing (Kotler, 1999, p. xi). Real change began to occur with the publication of now classic works like Theodore Levitt's "Marketing Myopia." First published in 1960, Levitt's work questioned the traditional focus on production and process.

Levitt was one of the first to sound the alarm over the pervasive infatuation with efficiency and production while recognizing the importance of the client in the marketing equation. He rejected the selling orientation that dominated marketing thinking of the day. Levitt (1960) made a clear distinction between a selling and more contemporary marketing perspectives. He indicated that "selling focuses on the needs of the seller, [whereas] marketing [focuses] on the needs of the buyer. Selling is preoccupied with the seller's needs to convert his product into cash; marketing with the idea of satisfying the needs of the customer" (p. 46).

Levitt rejected the selling focus contending that such efforts were more concerned with tricks and techniques than with marketing. It was prophetic that "Marketing Myopia" won the 1961 McKinsey Award as the best marketing article of the year. The tide had begun to turn in the direction of the consumer.

Since that time, marketing has evolved to place increasing emphasis on the consumer. Where once consumers mattered little beyond their ability to pay for a product, they are now considered the linchpin of any meaningful marketing endeavor. As one author notes, "The paradigm has shifted. Products come and go. The unit of value today is the customer relationship" (Wayland in Kotler, 1999, p. 121). Leaders in the marketing community now view marketing as a client-centered activity. One such leader, Philip Kotler (1983), believes that the marketer's philosophy must be one of client satisfaction. "Marketing . . . activity is directed at satisfying needs and wants through exchange processes" (Kotler, 1983, p. 6).

Long-time management guru Peter Drucker (1974) agrees with Kotler, suggesting that the goal of marketing is to make selling superfluous. Drucker goes on to state that the notions of selling and marketing are antithetical. These views represent a clear client orientation. He suggests that marketing initiatives be assessed in terms of their focus as well as their results. The key question becomes, "What has been the focus of this effort?" If emphasis has been placed on developing a product in isolation of client preferences, then a product orientation has dominated. If the emphasis has been placed on convincing clients of the merits of a product without first discovering their desires, then a selling approach has been used. Current thinking holds suspect any efforts in which client preferences have been relegated to subordinate status (Lefebvre, 1992).

Definitions of marketing have changed to keep pace with the increasing focus on the client. An American Marketing Association board definition characterized marketing as "the process of planning and executing the consumption, pricing, promotion, and distribution of ideas, goods and services to create exchanges that satisfy individual and organizational objectives" (Murphy & Enis, 1986, p. 24). Clearly, marketing is now viewed as a process of satisfying the client. The client must therefore be brought into the planning and execution of leisure programs.

This emerging client orientation begs the question, what is the new role of the client? The private sector has identified three basic roles for the client (Schneider & Bowen, 1995). The first is that of a *human resource*. Given the inseparability of services, the client is often present in order to consume a service. Indeed, clients actively participate in the delivery of that service. Leisure participants fill out their own registration forms, they participate in classes and programs, they call to receive scheduling updates, and they take part in parent-tot programs. In fact, they are often asked to use every bit of skill and energy they possess when they take part in our programs. Learn to Swim programs ask them to put aside their fears, art classes force them to use both skill and imagination, and fitness classes ask them to endure discomfort bordering on pain.

We also ask them to help in the creation of the service. They must indicate their needs, their preferences and their requirements. They must provide ongoing feedback to instructors, programmers, and planners. Providers even ask them to help solve problems that arise during the service encounter. During busy periods, they are asked to wait in queue to facilitate processing. When there are problems they are asked to offer possible solutions. In this sense, clients are co-producers of many leisure services. Like staff, they represent an indispensable part of the leisure delivery process. Consequently, marketers must view clients, in part at least, as they would staff members. Clients require skill sets, specific knowledge, reward structures, and even motivation if they are to co-produce effectively.

The second role the client has adopted is that of the *manager*. Think for a moment of the role of a manager. The classic management tasks are to plan, lead, organize, and control. Clients fulfill all these tasks. For example, front-line staff are supervised by clients. Clients provide ongoing direction by asking that this program be offered, and that another

program be altered. Though they may not tell you directly, they evaluate staff and program performance with alarming regularity. They hold the entire leisure agency up to the most stringent standards. Though all agency personnel are influenced by client wishes, front-line staff are particularly open to client scrutiny and influence. Clients and front line staff work together to give life to agency programs. In doing so, staff must respond to clients' wishes. They are indeed managers in every sense of the word.

Third, clients fulfill the role of *organizational consultant* (Schneider & Bowen, 1995). For example, clients are best equipped to identify problems that face them. If marketing is a process of satisfying needs and wants, then this process begins with clients. They may feel very keenly their own unfulfilled desires. Who better to help the marketer identify opportunities for improvement or for mutual exchange? Clients are also unique in their ability to evaluate products, benefit packages, and other "solutions" developed for them by providers. From this perspective, the client is very much an advisor or consultant to the marketer.

Together, these various roles suggest that the marketer/client relationship is that of a partnership. Each must adopt various critical roles if the marketing exercise is to succeed. Together they ensure that the right service is offered to the right group at the right time for the right price. In doing so, both enjoy success. It is difficult to imagine a more appropriate basis for developing a partnership.

Such independence adds greater complexity to the task of the marketer. Bringing non-staff members into the delivery process can increase the opportunity for program failures. They may lack sufficient skills, information, or supervision to complete their tasks successfully. They may not share the goals of the leisure provider. Further, their contribution may be sporadic because of the voluntary nature of their participation.

Regardless of these many challenges, the marketer must view the consumer as a potential partner. The goals of the client and the provider must be fulfilled if marketing effort is to succeed. If either partner in the marketing exchange is not satisfied, then the exchange has been a failure. Benefits accrue to both parties when marketing succeeds. The client's requirements are fulfilled and the provider's goals are achieved. Satisfaction is actually a gift that "keeps on giving." Client satisfaction has been linked to loyalty and increased profit for the provider. As a result, there is considerable incentive to improve marketing practices so that client satisfaction can be enhanced. One of the best ways to improve those practices is to involve the entire workforce in marketing effort.

The Mobilization of All Staff in Marketing Effort

One question that continues to confound marketers relates to *responsibility*. Who, within an organization, is responsible for marketing effort? The answer to this question has changed over time. For example, Robert Keith (1988) once traced the evolution of marketing in the well-known Pillsbury company. His story, or more accurately, the story of Pillsbury is noteworthy because it mirrors the evolution of marketing thought in North America. He tells us that early marketing effort was dominated by an unrelenting emphasis on the product. As a result, their production focus (to mill the best flour) was also their marketing focus. The answer to the question "Who's responsible for marketing?" could be found in departments responsible for creating the product itself. This approach seems to have been widely shared in the production-minded era following World War I. Production-based issues were considered the sole concern of the provider.

In the 1930s, the production era gave way to a sales era. This new focus on sales brought about unprecedented expenditures on advertising and market intelligence gathering. Someone was now responsible for marketing effort but the marketer's influence was marginal at best. Companies still thought of themselves in terms of a production focus, so production received the lion's share of attention. Predictably, marketers usually existed outside the production-based organizational structure. They were typically small groups within the larger organization who had no control, or even influence, within the typical chain of command. Handmaidens to the still all-powerful production teams, they were told to "move" the products that had been created.

We continue to see vestiges of this era today within many leisure agencies. Small marketing departments are created but they operate with little input into the agency's programming efforts. They simply gather information on the agency's seasonal program schedule and promote these programs as best they can. This approach is problematic for many reasons, and they all involve focus. In such agencies, the focus continues to shine on the product. In this case, the product is a program. The program exists, and the marketer must serve that program. As we have discussed, this is an unsatisfactory state for all concerned. A revolution may have to occur in such agencies and Keith's story at Pillsbury points the way.

The third era, the marketing era, witnessed a new interest in the concerns of the consumer. During the 1950s the Pillsbury organization, for example, realized that customers, not products, occupied the center of the business universe. Keith relates how this epiphany created a revolution within the organization. Planners realized that organizational changes would have to be made if the potential of this insight was to be realized. They immediately realized that marketing was not some isolated activity undertaken by a small group designated as "marketers." The organization underwent several changes, all of which broadened the role of marketing within the company. Where once the marketers were given products and told to "sell them," Pillsbury now involved marketers in all stages of planning and production.

Responsibility for marketing at Pillsbury no longer rests with a small number of marketing staff. The organization recognized that all staff needed to be involved in marketing effort. As Keith predicted, "marketing will become the basic motivating force for the entire corporation . . . every activity of the corporation—from finance to sales to production—is aimed at satisfying the wants and needs of the consumer" (Keith, 1988, p. 37). This insight has had sweeping implications for the way corporations think about marketing activity. It suggests that everyone in the organization must accept some role in the marketing process. Indeed, Levitt (1983) tells us that every activity undertaken by a provider is a marketing activity: "The purpose of a business is to create and keep a customer. There can be no corporate strategy that is not in some fundamental fashion a marketing strategy, no purpose that does not respond somehow to what people [want]" (p. 5).

Full staff involvement in marketing is all the more critical in service industries. Because of services' unique characteristics, clients and staff typically come together to create the service. If the goal of all agency activity is to create and keep a customer, then everyone in the organization should, in some way, be supporting that effort. As one marketing adage summarizes, "If you're not serving a customer, then you'd better be serving someone who is." It suggests that all members of an organization must be involved in marketing effort.

Unfortunately, the wisdom of this adage is often ignored. Too often, marketing, the process of pleasing the client, is thought to be the responsibility of the few rather than the group. A few staff members are trained and motivated to serve the client, but they are continually stymied from doing so by policy makers removed from the actual encounter. They are frustrated by the accountants who decide that only supervisors may authorize refunds, by the managers who grant decision-making powers only to themselves, by planners who insist that changes cannot be made once policy has been set.

The typical service encounter is too complex to be controlled from above. Those in authority must support the actions of those in the front lines. Everyone must support this effort. In Levitt's terms, all staff must be involved in marketing efforts. Indeed, Gonroos (1990) actually defines marketing in terms of an activity that must be undertaken by all. He refers to marketing as "a set of ideas which must be integrated throughout the entire organization and overseen by top management" (p. 128). This final definition sets the stage for the rest of this text. Marketing is indeed an activity that revolves around ideas,

that requires complete involvement, that demands attention at the uppermost levels of the organization. Without these essential components, marketing effort is compromised.

Marketing and Public Leisure Providers: An Uneasy Alliance

John Crompton was one of the first and perhaps the most ardent champions of marketing for leisure service providers. In an early text, he and Dennis Howard outlined basic marketing processes in the context of leisure services. They and other proponents have long been advocating the application of marketing principles in the delivery of leisure services. They suggest, for example, that failure to implement marketing principles may impair leisure agencies' ability to serve their communities. "A recreation and park agency's failure often can be traced to its neglect of the basic wants and desires of its potential consumers. Indeed, it may be argued that the 'tax revolt' of the late 1970s indicated that government had failed to implement the marketing concept" (Howard & Crompton, 1980, p. 309).

Though Crompton, Howard, and others have promoted the acceptance of public sector marketing for the past two decades, support for marketing is by no means universal. Public sector leisure providers, in particular, have been slow to adopt marketing as a legitimate operational tool. This reticence arises from confusion. Confusion swirls around the topic of marketing like smoke from some eternal flame. Like smoke, this confusion both irritates and obfuscates. Some explanation seems in order.

Confusion with Advertising

There is a widespread belief that marketing is little more than promotion. This belief is fuelled by prominent, if questionable, practices commonly labelled as marketing.

Unsolicited and intrusive telephone calls from anonymous salespeople are now called "telemarketing." The term marketing has also been applied to a promotional technique used by sponsors to confuse and mislead clients. Aptly labelled "ambush marketing," this technique is used by corporate bodies attempting to benefit from promotional events without contributing requisite resources to those events. In these cases, marketing seems little more than a tool of the unscrupulous huckster. As a result, confusion often turns to irritation, and many leisure practitioners reject marketing effort as a result.

Some background may be necessary to make sense of the depth of this rejection. Peiper (1963) tells us that without "meaningful leisure" we will drift toward a slave society. Like slaves, we will idolize things and worship "know-how" while being controlled by external forces. Unfortunately, we as a society are failing to discover meaningful leisure because we have succumbed to the relentless pull of commercialism as we undertake our leisure pursuits (Scitovsky, 1992). Schor (1991) notes that we now live in homes that are about twice the size of those in which our parents were raised, yet our families are about half the size. As a result, the toiling masses have no time, energy, or resources to seek leisure, because all are devoted to chasing the economic "good life."

It is perhaps little wonder that an increasing number of social scientists report that we now feel "too rushed" to enjoy whatever leisure time that becomes available (Shaw, 1990). As a result of this sense of being rushed, we often believe that we have too little time to pursue meaningful leisure (McCarville & Smale, 1993). This endless pursuit is widely thought to be spurred by marketing. Isn't marketing responsible for the advertising that urges participants to consume? Isn't marketing responsible for the advertising that seems to encourage us to spend without reason and work ever harder to maintain a lifestyle that is personally meaningless (Hemingway, 1996)? Isn't marketing responsible for advertisers who constantly bombard clients with messages telling them that they are somehow wanting, somehow less than they could and should be? It is perhaps little wonder that some observers

believe that meaningful leisure and marketing effort are mutually exclusive.

Confusion with Commercialism

In related terms, marketing is also widely thought to be synonymous with *commercialism* (Havitz, 1988). The process of commercialism is problematic because it seeks to expropriate the means through which leisure is provided (Butsch, 1990). Providers seek to control the experience of leisure participants to ensure profit for those providers. As such, commercialization represents a process of exploitation. This process is troubling because the provider inherently controls the experience. Through commercialization "that part of our lived experience supposed to be free of domination is transformed through capitalist development" (Butsch, p. 8) to such an extent that participants may lose control over their own leisure experience. This prospect is troubling for leisure providers. They understandably reject commercialism because of its capacity to diminish the leisure experience (Schultz, McAvoy, & Dustin, 1988).

Many take the seemingly next logical step and reject marketing in the same breath. Given marketing's private sector roots, they fear that marketing is simply a tool used to promote commercialism. For example, Schultz, McAvoy, and Dustin (1988) ask, as public sector decision makers adopt marketing principles, "Who will look out for the interests of racial and ethnic minorities, single-parent families, immigrants, and the urban and rural poor? . . . Who will sustain the fight for the rights of society's underprivileged?" (p. 53). They view marketing and commercialism as being synonymous and inconsistent with the provision of meaningful leisure opportunities.

Ambivalence to marketing has also been fueled by fear among public sector practitioners. They fear that private sector methods will subvert the traditional service role of the public sector. Their argument is best represented by Jacobs in her book, *Systems of Survival* (1994). In this book, Jacobs divides the world into two basic moral systems, those of the "merchants" and of the "guardians." Agencies like municipal park and recreation departments fall under the general guardian designation. Her premise is that both systems rely on different sets of moral codes. She suggests that both groups are corrupted when they adopt the moral codes and values of the other. As a result, public sector agencies that adopt measures like marketing, risk losing touch with the values unique to caregivers. By way of example, Jacobs refers to police officers who might be tempted to assign various fines because of the resources they help accumulate. In such cases, the purposes of the police officers are subverted. Their goal becomes one of revenue generation rather than the maintenance of social order.

Jacobs (1994) goes to considerable length to establish the sheer inevitability of this corruption. In her view, participants in either system must be wary of the moral codes used by the other and adopt them only at their peril. Several opponents of the marketing of public leisure services generally support this view from an ideological as well as a practical standpoint. Tools of the merchant (like marketing) are often treated with suspicion or even reviled as "unethical." Even labels used by the private sector may be considered suspect. In one address, award-winning author John Ralston Saul suggested that the first necessary step "to regaining free speech is for people to protest whenever bureaucrats use business words such as clients or customer services in referring to citizens and the things government is supposed to do for the public good" (Simone, November 21, 1996, p. A3). These words are automatically suspect because, like marketing, they emerge from the private sector.

While Novatorov and Crompton (2001) accept the points offered by this perspective, they suggest that rejection of the marketing concept seems premature. They feel that the public sector will clearly benefit from adopting marketing tools, but simply remind public sector marketers not to embrace the goals of the private sector. Whereas the private sector marketer might use marketing to pursue the profit motive, the public sector marketer can use the same tools to pursue very different goals like the *redistribution* of wealth. The role of the public sector provider is to collect then redistribute resources in ways that benefit the larger community. Novatorov and Crompton contend that marketing can be very useful in assisting this redistribution process.

Concern over Segmentation

The marketing tenet of *segmentation* has also discouraged its acceptance by many practitioners. Segmentation is the act of dividing a community into meaningful subgroups. Marketing efforts are then targeted toward at least one of these groups. For some private sector practitioners, segmentation is problematic because they believe that focusing attention on a specific client group limits opportunity and potential profit. Why focus on one group when one can target the entire community? The public sector practitioner may make the same basic argument but for a different reason, (Havitz & Spigner, 1993). Tradition suggests that residents should receive equal treatment from the public leisure provider. Focusing on one client group over another suggests that those denied service not only fail to receive their perceived "fair" share but also suffer from the stigma that arises from this condition (Lineberry, 1977).

For public sector providers, to offer resources to a few means denying resources to the many, and public leisure providers are simply unwilling to program in this way. The logic of this argument seems profoundly compelling. A recent survey asked practitioners to whom they directed selected services. Surprisingly large numbers of public agencies reported that they targeted no one group, but instead served "everyone" with their programs. It seems that there is considerable pressure to ignore segmentation efforts and to target "all" instead of a few. Though this text makes the point that the best way to serve "all" is through segmentation, this view is not currently shared among many professionals.

Difficulty in Application

Finally, marketing has not been widely adopted by leisure providers, because it is so very difficult to undertake. Over a decade ago, Crompton (1985) warned that early marketing was likely to suffer from confusion and the inexperience of those who apply it. Events have largely confirmed his prediction. Problems continue to exist in the application of basic marketing principles. For example, in a regional survey, Johnson-Tew, Havitz, and McCarville (1999) found that many public leisure providers, while believing they were using marketing techniques in their day-to-day operation, failed to apply even rudimentary marketing principles in their operations. Few providers adapted programs or fee initiatives in order to respond to the needs of different user groups.

In a national study, Havitz and Spigner (1993) found that public agencies rarely segmented their communities according to relevant criteria like income. Neither did these agencies offer price discounts to low-income residents or coordinate efforts with official unemployment agencies. It seems that many agencies were introducing market-based initiatives (like fee programs) without applying other necessary marketing principles. These initiatives seemed to both confuse and mitigate the role and nature of marketing effort. As a result, even those public sector agencies that have embraced the marketing process may be contributing to its unpopularity.

With all this suspicion, the danger of subversion, and the potential for lost opportunity, why undertake marketing in the public sector at all? Though marketing represents an easy target for critical commentary, is it deserving of such enmity? Is it a worthy adversary to those who hope to serve the community? Proponents suggest that it represents an important ally and should be considered as such (Crompton & Lamb, 1986). I take the view that marketing represents little more than a process for mobilizing resources. Indeed, it differs little from many traditional planning processes (Bannon, 1976). Its tenets are being used to aid in social policy and planning, social marketing (Kotler & Roberto, 1989), health education (Lefebvre, 1992), and leisure programming (Crompton & Lamb). These tenets focus on mobilizing resources to meet the demands of specific

groups within the community. As a result, marketing effort may be used to good advantage to serve the larger community. To ignore or revile that process is perhaps both unwise and inappropriate.

Further, though marketing is a child of the private sector, its roots are found in traditional "helping" disciplines like psychology and sociology. Like psychologists, marketers hope to understand cognitive processes as they effect behavior. Like sociologists, marketers hope to understand the role of the group in determining individual behaviors. While its theoretical roots lie in psychology and sociology, actual marketing techniques may be traced to traditional planning and programming efforts (Bannon, 1976). It relies heavily upon insight from any profession that hopes to shape and improve society. As such, marketing tools seem appropriate for use within the public and not-for-profit sectors.

I suggest that marketing's contribution is one of strategic flexibility. It focuses on mobilizing resources to meet the demands of specific groups within the community. As a result, marketing effort may be used to serve the larger community. It might best be considered as another stage in the natural evolution of traditional planning and programming effort. This evolution may be particularly useful for leisure providers. Much of the public sector delivery system relies upon regulation and policy. Public agencies use the power of their position to ensure compliance. Residents are told to have their garbage waiting at the curb in approved containers. They must comply or lose access to garbage collection services. Residents are directed to purchase licenses for their pets, to pay taxes, to park in designated locations. Compliance with these directives is encouraged through a variety of fines and other related penalties. The agenda of the public caregiver is as often moved along as much by the stick as with the carrot.

Leisure providers live in a very different milieu, however. They cannot secure participation through decree, leisure participation is a result of individual choice. The provider cannot demand that citizens take part. The leisure provider must coax rather than coerce; encourage rather than dictate. Though this seems a relatively foreign concept to many public sector planners, it is the stock and trade of the private sector marketer. It seems likely, therefore, that marketing literature may have much to offer those in the public sector. Marketing seems a very worthwhile exercise for anyone who hopes to encourage any type of behavior. As a result, it seems an appropriate activity for any sector.

The question becomes, "How can marketing effort best be pursued?" Though potentially useful in all sectors of the economy, marketing is first and foremost a child of the private sector. The goal of the private sector marketer is to operate at a profit. The private sector marketer must focus on the financial "bottom line." The profit imperative has traditionally dominated marketing thought and practice. This imperative is not shared by practitioners within the public sector. Further, the public context is complicated by the caregiver role. The public sector marketer must be concerned with efficiency, effectiveness, and the public good.

The application of traditional marketing strategy outside its intended private sector setting will no doubt require careful thought and planning. This text suggests how this might be achieved. It explores the complexity and the simplicity of the marketing process. It is based upon a few straightforward steps that make up marketing effort. Marketing itself is viewed here simply as a tool. It represents a set of sequential stages, and each stage is made up of several steps. This process is remarkable both for its straightforward nature and its effectiveness.

While on the topic of the straightforward nature of marketing, a final clarification is warranted. In 1993, Ries and Trout published a very insightful book titled *The 22 Immutable Laws of Marketing*. One of the insights they offer is the "law of division." This law dictates that "over time a category will divide and become two or more categories" (p. 56). By way of example, they observe that the television industry began with three networks and has fragmented dramatically since those early days.

The notion of marketing itself has also revealed a tendency to divide and subdivide.

The hopeful marketer is now faced with various types of, or approaches to marketing effort.

- *Frequency marketing* is devoted to encouraging loyal consumers to consume more often.

- *Retention marketing* focuses on developing loyalty among current users.

- *Internal marketing* efforts are directed to a provider's own employees.

- *Social marketing* applies marketing principles to large-scale community issues.

The list is becoming longer with each passing year. Fortunately, whatever its label, whatever its focus, marketing effort has one basic goal. As Levitt (1983) reminds us, doing business is about finding and keeping customers. Marketing shares that basic mandate. Be neither confused nor daunted by the many names that we authors apply to the marketing process. All marketing effort is about creating and maintaining the interest of potential user groups. If those groups a marketer hopes to serve are not interested in the marketer's offerings, then the marketer has failed. Marketing, whatever its label, is about avoiding failure and creating success. The rest of this text is devoted to establishing how this success is achieved.

Overview of the Marketing Process

The process of marketing is typically coordinated around a marketing plan. This plan has many roles. It is used to discover potential and existing opportunities to better serve clients, to develop offerings that best appeal to specific client groups while building on the agency's own strengths, to identify services that are defensible against competitive or counterproductive forces, and to anticipate the effects of foreseeable occurrences or social conditions. Simply put, the purpose of the marketing plan effort is to find ways to serve clients that are different and somehow better than programs used by other providers.

All marketing plans juggle three variables: (1) agency capabilities, (2) client preferences, and (3) the capacity of competitors. Each marketing plan is developed in four stages. The first stage is one of *strategy development.* The goal of this stage is to establish a strategic baseline. This baseline helps place the agency within the larger marketplace. It answers the question, "What have we to offer?" This initial step focuses on agency capabilities, the marketplace, and potential consumers. It is concerned with deciding who to serve and how best to serve them.

The second stage is that of *planning the marketing mix.* The marketing mix is a set of activities that make up much of what we call marketing. It is comprised of the product, promotion, price, and delivery. These elements are mixed in a way that considers the provider's own capabilities, as well as the desires and characteristics of possible client groups, and the challenges of the larger marketplace.

The third stage is one of *implementation.* This stage is concerned primarily with the process of presenting the service to the client. It is this stage that demands that a provider's entire workforce become involved in marketing effort. This is a very dynamic step in the marketing process, characterized by high levels of client contact and unpredictability. As a result, considerable flexibility must be incorporated into this stage.

The fourth stage in the marketing process is that of *ongoing assessment.* This stage represents the research function that is so critical to marketing success. Though this stage is characterized here as a "final" stage, it actually takes place in conjunction with all three of the other stages. Information is gathered constantly and is used to guide ongoing decision making and improve program offerings. It is an ongoing process of discovering conditions in the marketplace so that responses can be planned or altered accordingly. This discovery may take place

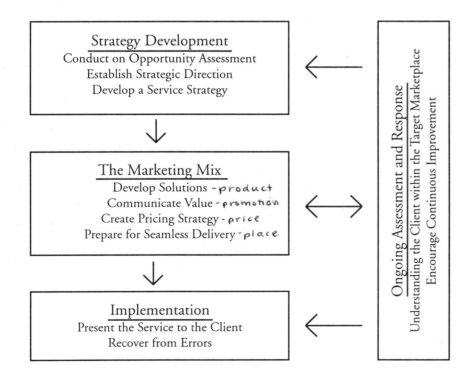

Figure 1.1: The Services Marketing Process

before an action is taken (in order to assist with planning) or after the fact (as an evaluative tool).

As Figure 1.1 suggests, marketing is essentially a circular activity. Its early stages are characterized by research hoping to identify trends and wants. It then attempts to address these trends and wants. Its final stages strive to determine how well those trends and wants have been addressed. This determination sets the stage for additional planning and implementation. The process is never complete. It is an ongoing process of identification, mobilization, and evaluation.

Main Points

· Marketing thought and practice have evolved from dealing with the production of goods to the provision of services and the promotion of ideas.

· The role of the consumer is gaining prominence in marketing thought.

· All staff members should be considered part of the marketing team.

· Public sector providers have been slow to adopt a marketing orientation.

· Though many marketing types are now being promoted, they all share the same goal—finding and keeping customers.

· The marketing process is a circular activity made up of four stages.

References

Alexander, R.S. (1982). Report of the definitions committee. In J.R. Evans, & B. Berman (Eds.), *Marketing* (p. 6). New York: Macmillan Publishing Co., Inc.

Bannon, J. (1976). *Leisure resources: Its comprehensive planning.* Englewood Cliffs, NJ: Prentice-Hall.

Bartels, R. (1988). *The history of marketing thought* (3rd ed.). Columbus, Ohio: Publishing Horizons, Inc.

Berry, L. (1984). Services marketing is different. In C.H. Lovelock (Ed.), *Services marketing* (pp. 29-36). Toronto: Prentice-Hall.

Butsch, R. (1990). Leisure and hegemony in America. In R. Butsch (Ed.), *For fun and profit: The transformation of leisure into consumption* (pp. 3-27). Philadelphia: Temple University Press.

Crompton, J. (1985). Marketing: Neither snake oil nor panacea. In T. Goodale, & P. Witt (Eds.), *Recreation and leisure: Issues in an era of change* (pp. 175-194). State College, PA: Venture.

Crompton, J., & Lamb, C. (1986). *Marketing government and social services.* New York: John Wiley & Sons.

Drucker, P. (1974) *Management: Tasks, responsibilities, practices.* New York: Harper & Row.

Fisk, R. P., Brown, S.W., & Bitner, M. (1993). Tracking the evolution of the services marketing literature. *Journal of Retailing, 69*(1), 61-103.

Gronroos, C. (1990). *Service management and marketing.* Lexington, MA: Lexington Books.

Grove, S., & Fisk, R. (1996). The dramaturgy of services exchange. In C.H. Lovelock (Ed.), *Services marketing* (3rd ed.) (pp. 97-105). Toronto: Prentice-Hall.

Havitz, M.E. (1988). Marketing is not synonymous with commercialism. *Parks and Recreation, 23*(5), 34-36.

Havitz, M., & Spigner, C. (1993). Unemployment, health and leisure: The role of park and recreation services. *Trends, 30*(4), 31-36.

Hemingway, J. (1996). Emancipating leisure: The recovery of freedom in leisure. *Journal of Leisure Research*, 28(1), 27-43.

Howard, D., & Crompton, J. (1980). *Financing, managing, and marketing recreation & park resources.* Dubuque, Iowa: Wm. C. Brown.

Jacobs, J. (1994). *Systems of survival.* New York: Vintage Books.

Johnson-Tew, C.P., Havitz, M., & McCarville R. E. (1999). The role of marketing in municipal recreation programming decisions: A challenge to conventional wisdom. *Journal of Park and Recreation Administration, 17*(1), 1-20.

Keith, R.J. (1988). The marketing revolution. In B.M. Ennis & K.K. Cox (Eds.), *Marketing classics* (pp. 33 - 37). Boston, MA: Allyn and Bacon, Inc.

Kotler, P. (1999). *Kotler on marketing.* New York: The Free Press.

Kotler, P. (1983). *Principals of marketing.* Toronto: Prentice-Hall.

Kotler, P., & Levy, S.J. (1988). Broadening the concept of marketing. In B.M. Ennis & K.K. Cox (Eds.), *Marketing classics* (pp. 38-46). Boston: Allyn and Bacon, Inc.

Kotler, P., & Roberto, E. (1989). *Social marketing: Strategies for changing public behaviour.* Englewood Cliffs, NJ: Prentice-Hall.

Lefebvre, R. (1992). The social marketing imbroglio in health promotion. *Health Promotion International, 7*, 61-64.

Levitt, T. (1960). Marketing myopia. *Harvard Business Review, 38*(4), 45-56.

Levitt, T. (1983). *The marketing imagination.* New York: The Free Press.

Lineberry, R. (1977). *Equality and urban policy.* Beverly Hills, CA: Sage Publications.

McCarville, R., & Smale, B. (1993). Perceived constraints to leisure participation within five activity domains. *Journal of Park and Recreation Administration, 11*(2), 1-15.

Meyers, W. (1984) *The image makers*. Toronto: Times Books.

Murphy, P.E., & Ennis, B.M. (1986). Classifying Products Strategically. *Journal of Marketing, 50*, 24-42.

Novatorov, E., & Crompton, J. (2001). Reformulating the conceptualization of marketing in the context of public leisure services. *Leisure Studies, 20*, 61-75.

Pieper, J. (1963). *Leisure the basis of culture*. New York: Random House Inc.

Ries A., & Trout J. (1993). *The 22 immutable laws of marketing*. New York: Harper Collins.

Schneider, B., & Bowen, D.E. (1995). *Winning the service game*. Boston, MA: Harvard Business School Press.

Schor, J. (1991). *The overworked American*. USA: Basic Books.

Schultz, J., McAvoy, L., & Dustin, D. (1988). What are we in business for? *Parks and Recreation, 23*(1), 52-54.

Scitovsky, T. (1992). *The joyless economy*. Toronto: Oxford University Press.

Shaw, S. (1990). Where has all the leisure gone: The distribution and redistribution of leisure. In B. Smale (Ed.), *Proceedings: Sixth Canadian Congress on Leisure Research*, (pp. 1-4) Waterloo, Ontario: Ontario Research Council on Leisure.

Simone, R. (1996, November 21). Free speech at risk, author says. *The Record*, pp. A1, A3.

The Ohio State University, College of Commerce and Administration. (1964). Statement of the philosophy of marketing faculty (p. 2). Reprinted in *The Journal of Marketing. 29*, (1965, January) (pp. 43-44).

Zeithaml, V. (1991). How consumer evaluation processes differ between goods and services. In C.H. Lovelock (Ed.), *Services marketing* (2nd ed.) (pp. 39-47). Toronto: Prentice-Hall.

R. McCarville

2

Conduct an Opportunity Assessment

The first and last step in any marketing initiative is that of data collection. Typically marketers begin to decide how best to serve the community by conducting an *opportunity assessment*. This assessment is a systematic search for unfulfilled need. It is a search for imbalance or gaps between the client's preferences and the marketplace's ability to fulfill those wants. Though opportunity assessments may seem somewhat long and drawn-out affairs, they are remarkably straight-forward. They simply discover what key client groups seek, then establish who can best serve those groups. Once this has been established, the marketer can develop strategy accordingly. This chapter is devoted to the many questions asked during the opportunity assessment. The

next chapter then outlines how the marketer uses this information to develop marketing strategy.

The opportunity assessment is often represented in a circular shape (Figure 2.1). The goal is to locate gaps or opportunities by discovering that which the client wants but is not being offered by other providers. The marketer does this by traveling around the circle represented in the figure answering a series of questions. If no gaps are discovered the first time around the circle, then the process is repeated but this time using different variables. For example, a marketer may wish to serve adults in a given neighborhood. After moving around the circle, the marketer may discover that other providers are currently

Figure 2.1: The Opportunity Assessment

serving this group and is doing so very successfully. The agency may then decide to target other groups who are less well served. They can then repeat the process by conducting an opportunity assessment for this second group. If they offer more potential then they may be targeted for programs and resources. If they too are now well served, a third group can be sent through the process.

The first step in making an opportunity assessment is that of identifying potential client groups that can be served by agency programs. The marketer can look to existing organizational priorities and programs to establish which client group(s) will be served. These priorities are typically expressed in terms of the *organization's mission statement, goals, and objectives*. The marketer then uses a series of audits to gather information on these clients and the marketplace in which they participate.

Using Market Segmentation

The process of breaking the community into meaningful client groups is called market *segmentation*. A segment is a group of people or organizations "that are similar in terms of how they respond to a particular marketing mix or other ways that are meaningful for marketing planning purposes" (Meyers, 1996, p. 16). Segmentation is one of the building blocks of marketing strategy. It is one of the bases upon which many marketing decisions are made. For the marketer, a "community" does not exist. A community is actually made up of many subgroups, each sharing its own priorities, interests and behaviors. As a result, segmentation divides or partitions potential clients into identifiable groups whose members share similar characteristics and exhibit common behaviors (Weinstein, 1987). In this way, agency efforts can be directed to the distinct preferences of relevant target groups.

Segmentation assumes that the marketplace should be divided into broad markets from which target groups can be selected. The leisure literature seems to support this assump-

tion. We know that considerable diversity exists among the many potential user groups within any given community. The leisure "public" is actually made up of many homogeneous groups. These groups are internally consistent in that their members share motives, preferences, and behavior patterns (Backman, 1994). For example, those who are motivated to compete may seek athletic events that pit their skills against others. Those who seek instruction may prefer non-competitive environments in which they can develop their own knowledge and skill. A competitive program may not serve those seeking instruction, just as an instructional program may not serve those seeking competition. It seems clear that all citizens are not interested in a given product or initiative, so why try to create programs that serve all? Marketers generally ignore the whole community in favor of unique groups or markets (Levitt, 1960). As Levitt reminds us, if we're not thinking market segments, we're not thinking at all.

Segmentation efforts can be client-based or product-based (Meyers, 1996, p. 17). *Client-based segmentation* efforts begin with a client group and attempt to differentiate that group from the rest of the population. For example, a leisure agency may be concerned with residents of a given neighborhood. Perhaps these residents are under-represented in existing programs and they have been targeted for additional resources. *Product-based segmentation*, as the name implies, focuses first on a product or service. In this case the leisure marketer might begin with a service in mind, say a swimming facility, and begin to segment the community in terms of usage rates or patterns. Resulting marketing efforts might be devoted to encouraging regular users to become heavy users or heavy users to try related products and services. This chapter deals primarily with client-based issues. The next chapter will deal more directly with program-based variables.

Segmenting the Marketplace

Client-based segmentation decisions are typically guided by four criteria (Payne, 1993).

Typically only those segments that fulfill the conditions imposed by these criteria will be targeted.

Responsiveness. Will the segment's members respond to the marketer's initiatives?

Identifiability. Can the members of the segment be distinguished from other segments and the general population?

Accessibility. Can the segment's members be reached by the agency's promotional and distribution methods?

Substantiality. Is the segment of sufficient size?

Given the service mandate that dominates the public sector, public leisure marketers may be faced with segmentation issues not encountered by the traditional private sector marketer. For example, segments targeted by the public sector marketer often fail the test of responsiveness, accessibility, and even substantiality (Bloom & Novelli, 1981). Sedentary clients targeted for physical fitness programs offered by the public sector may be profoundly unresponsive. Homeless children targeted for nutrition initiatives may be exceedingly difficult to locate. Small groups of residents with unique needs may fail the test of substantiality. All fail the basic criteria used by the private sector, but all must be served by the public sector.

Consequently, public sector segmentation efforts may use perceived need as an implicit fifth criterion in making segmentation decisions. Need may be expressed by members of the target market or by the larger community. Efforts to encourage voting among nonvoters, to encourage physical activity among the sedentary, to appeal to street kids and other at-risk youth, and to reduce dangerous driving activities among impaired drivers represent just a few examples of groups that, while failing several traditional segmentation criteria, often receive the attention of public agencies. They receive attention because need exists, not because they are easy to reach. The importance of need will be discussed further in the next section.

Target Market Selection

A marketer may be tempted to pursue one or several segments within a given marketplace (Kotler, McDougall, & Armstrong, 1988). This choice depends largely upon the provider's own strategy and the resources available to the provider. If, for example, the agency mandate is one of "serving the community," then several segments will likely be targeted. The actual segments selected for attention will depend upon opportunity and/or need.

Consider first the issue of *opportunity*. Recall that segments are often pursued because they will respond in predictable ways, and in sufficient numbers, to the marketer's offering. Often, groups are targeted simply because the marketer believes they will respond positively to the program offering. The marketer simply targets those who are most likely to respond in a positive manner. By doing so the marketer anticipates a higher probability of success. This is the reason so many marketers focus their efforts on heavy users.

Other groups are targeted because their wants can be addressed by existing programs. For example, a community swimming pool will continue to offer swim instruction programs to any group they think is interested simply because the pool needs to be busy if it is to fulfill its mandate. This product-based approach is common because it enables providers to build on existing strengths. It takes time and effort to gain expertise, and considerable sums of money to develop facilities. It is difficult to ignore such heavy investments, so providers are constantly trying to find new clients for old programs.

Marketers are also guided by the possibility of competitive advantage. Competitive advantage suggests that one provider possesses an advantage over a competitor. The provider in a dominant position often targets the competitor's clients simply because they are a known quantity. They are currently active, so their willingness to take part is clear. The dominant provider then attempts to lure clients away with superior program offerings.

As suggested above, *client need* may also drive many target marketing decisions. The public sector, in particular, often focuses on those groups that seem to need their program offerings. At-risk youth need constructive outlets for their energy and imagination. Sedentary adults need to discover more active alternatives, and so on. These groups are targeted for the need they display rather than the opportunity they represent. In fact, they may be especially unresponsive to such initiatives. They may consider programs designed for them to be unimportant at best, and intrusive at worst. For example, the proverbial couch potato may be content with a sedentary lifestyle and ignore pleas to change the existing activity patterns. Smokers may openly resent efforts encouraging them discontinue their smoking habits. As a result, efforts based solely on need represent some of the most difficult challenges posed to leisure marketers.

Describing Potential Market Segments

Once a target group has been selected, marketing practice dictates that the possible segment then be described in detail. Segments may be described in geographic, sociodemographic, behavioral, and/or psycho-graphic terms. The nature of most of these descriptors is self-evident.

Geographic descriptors focus on variables like location, travel time, and general accessibility.

Sociodemographic descriptors include age, stage in life cycle, gender, income, education, occupation, and ethnicity.

Behavioral descriptors relate to rate of use, level of skill, and stage of readiness.

Psychographic descriptors typically focus on activities, interests, and opinions.

Note that while the top three descriptors describe potential clients in terms of easily measurable life conditions like location, gender, age, income, or participation patterns, the last set of variables (psychographic) is concerned with the individual's lifestyle. It deals not with who clients "are" in terms of their lifestyle, but rather with who they want to be.

These descriptors are often combined to create profiles for potential client groups. These profiles are then used to understand and predict the interests and behaviors of target groups. Perhaps the most popular of these efforts has been the VALS typology developed by SRI International. VALS is an acronym for values, attitudes, and lifestyle. This typology places clients into one of eight categories based upon "self-orientation" and the number of resources they command. Self-orientation refers to the nature of the standard client's use when making decisions. For example, internally focused shoppers may look to their own values when making purchase decisions, while more status-oriented individuals are motivated to please or impress others.

Although some observers have complained about the almost astrological nature of these efforts, they are used heavily in marketers' attempts to understand their clients. All these types of descriptors are useful to the leisure marketer. We know that descriptors like age or sex may act as surrogates for a variety of important life conditions that influence leisure participation (Henderson, 1990). For example, age may influence activity preferences. It seems that in some cases, younger participants prefer more active programming opportunities (Donnelly, Vaske, DeRuiter, & King, 1996). Gender may also be a factor in determining activity patterns. McCarville and Smale (1993) found that the number of reported constraints to leisure were related to sex. Women reported more constraints than did men. Further, the number of reported constraints was negatively related to income. The greater the individual's income, the fewer the number of reported leisure constraints.

Such descriptors speak to the nature and extent of the difficulties faced by various socio-demographic groups as they pursue leisure opportunities. All can be used by the marketer to ameliorate these difficulties. Although sociodemographic descriptors offer some insight to marketers, they may fail to capture the specific needs and perceptions of these many subgroups. They must be used in conjunction with other, perhaps more profound, indicators (Howard & Sheth, 1988). The consumer behavior literature has long held that psychographic indicators, like participants' motives, preferences, and behaviors (Howard & Sheth), will enhance understanding of the client thereby improving segmentation efforts.

Fortunately, leisure researchers have traditionally been interested in these issues. They have segmented client groups in terms of (among others) motives, experience, and behavior patterns (Hollenhorst, Schuett, Olson, & Chavez, 1995); preferences (Slyvia, Sallee, & Berry, 1995); involvement profiles (Havitz, Dimanche, & Bogle, 1994); and benefits sought (Backman, 1994). All are helpful to the marketer who hopes to understand then serve a client group. The marketer must continually discover group members' preferences, behaviors surrounding key consumption decisions, and any other information that might assist with subsequent programming efforts. Programming success is largely a function of the accuracy with which these preferences can be determined.

Once the client group has been selected and described, three audits are necessary to determine how best to serve this group.

- The first audit is the *internal audit*. This audit focuses entirely on agency assets and skills. It establishes the capabilities and interests the provider can bring to the client.

- The second audit is the *environmental audit*. It considers conditions that the marketer will face but over which the marketer has no control. It asks, "What trends influence the marketplace now and in the foreseeable future?"

- The third audit is the *industry analysis*. This analysis is one of competitive assessment. It is concerned with others who provide service offerings to the same client groups. It recognizes the fundamental truth that clients inevitably shop the marketplace for options and opportunities. They compare any offering to alternatives available in that marketplace. If the client makes this comparison, then so too must the marketer.

The Internal Audit

The first step in strategy development is to understand and assess the current (and desired) role, direction, or capacity of an organization. This understanding typically emerges from an *internal audit*. An internal audit focuses on the organization itself. It demands that the agency assess its own capability to offer relevant services or benefit packages. The marketer seeks information from three levels of strategic information while undertaking the internal assessment. From the corporate strategic plan, the marketer must learn what business the organization is in and wants to be in. From the business strategy, the marketer must gather the organization's business goals and the strategy being used to pursue them. From functional strategy, the marketer assesses efforts to meet the clients' wants. What does the organization consider to be success? How well is it doing? Answers to these basic questions will direct all subsequent marketing efforts.

An example may help make this point. The marketing staff of a relatively small recreation department was considering expanding its programs in an attempt to generate both community interest in the agency and some much needed income. Unfortunately, their bosses were simultaneously deciding that the agency was going to turn increasingly to a facilitator role rather than a direct provider role. The business strategy envisioned by the top administrators was to help others offer programs rather than offer them through internal resources. There were several reasons behind this strategic move. Senior administrators believed that such measures would build the capacity of volunteer groups to provide their own programs, thereby reducing reliance on municipal government. Further, the facilitator role seemed less troublesome, at least in the short run, than did the provider role.

As you can see, while marketers were hoping to increase their presence in the community, the top level staff were planning to decrease their presence. As you might imagine, the marketers' plans to expand the agency programming profile were soon abandoned because they were inconsistent with the larger corporate strategy. The marketing team had assumed that, given the agency's need for income, any effort to generate income would be welcomed. They discovered their error only after following up on questions regarding the organization's overall business strategy.

The marketer must also be aware of the organization's strategic market position before marketing strategy can be developed. This is the position the organization hopes to hold in the mind of potential clients (Fifield, 1998). What is the role the organization hopes to play? How does it relate to other providers in the larger marketplace? The marketer's every effort must contribute to this position.

As budgets tighten and pressures to generate revenue increase, this has become no easy task. Consider the dilemma faced by virtually every public sector marketer, that of sponsorship and image in the community. Marketers may be approached by any number of private sector groups wishing to align themselves with the positive image created by recreation. Companies that sell alcohol or tobacco products, in particular, are often willing to support park and recreation initiatives in an effort to improve their own image. These groups sometimes will offer huge sums of money in return for rights of affiliation with the agency's programs. Acceptance of such funds may fulfill a few agency revenue objectives yet may undermine the positive position occupied by the entire organization. These are issues the public sector marketer

faces daily. They can only be addressed with due regard to higher level corporate strategy.

As a result, marketers must have a firm grasp of the agency's own priorities and capacities before planning can begin. They should look to three levels or types of information:

Level 1 Information: Corporate Planning Records

The highest level of information arises from *corporate planning*. Generally speaking, corporate planning deals with establishing a role for an organization or agency. Corporate planning is typically undertaken by top administrators and it directs the efforts of all employees. Perhaps the most pervasive example of corporate planning is the development of both a *purpose* and a *mission statement*.

The purpose statement sets out what the organization is trying to accomplish. This is a very abstract statement intended to establish the nature of the operation. For private sector providers this statement often focuses on survival and profit. For public sector agencies this statement typically focuses on service to the community. For example, a public leisure agency may develop a purpose statement based upon its intent to "improve the quality of life for citizens in the community through the provision of leisure opportunities."

The mission statement is a more specific effort designed to indicate how the provider plans to serve. It outlines who the agency hopes to serve and generally how this will be accomplished. In the case of a leisure provider, a mission statement typically indicates that this purpose will be pursued by providing leisure services to the client groups. Those of large, diverse organizations like cities tend to be rather general. For example, the Miami-Dade Parks Commission indicates in its mission statement that "We create outstanding recreational, natural, and cultural experiences to enrich you and to enhance our community for this and future generations." Smaller, more single-purpose organizations can develop more specific statements that even specify the types of experiences to be offered. A YMCA camp, located on John Island, Ontario, Canada offers a case in point. Their mission statement indicates that the camp is about children and those who are children at heart "daring, sharing and caring to provide lasting and positive effect on values and attitudes with a magical island as a common point."

Though mission statements may seem very abstract, they guide the marketer in virtually all subsequent decisions. They provide marching orders, as it were, in terms of who is to be served and under what conditions. The purpose and mission determine the eventual policies and procedures. For example, a mission that states that "all citizens will be served" suggests that subsequent policies will need to be introduced to ensure that target group members are not displaced if fees are instituted. If the mission indicates that the organization will serve its members, then subsequent efforts should focus on this group, perhaps even to the detriment of non-members.

When establishing a mission statement, remember that it must be both robust and compelling. It must be robust in that it offers guidance in a wide variety of settings. It must be compelling in that it offers clear, unambiguous direction to staff. It must be strong and clear (Berry, 1995). As Brown (1995) suggests, such statements become the point around which the organization rallies. They create a standard that determines whether or not a decision is a good one, an action is necessary, an outcome is desirable. They establish how business is to be done. The marketer requires a strong corporate mission statement in order to create a marketing plan. This is why an internal audit begins with an assessment of the mission statement. It asks:

a) What is our mission, what business are we in?

b) How well is this mission understood throughout the organization?

Level 2 Information: Business/Competitive Strategy

The audit then requires information on how the mission is being pursued. This is referred to as the second level of information on *business or competitive strategy*. This level of information is slightly more specific than a mission statement. It typically focuses on how the provider plans to compete within the marketplace. It is directed by various goals and objectives that together direct the activities of the organization.

Goals suggest how an organization intends to fulfill its mission. All organizations have multiple goals. They may differ according to their focus or subject matter, the organizational level to which they apply, or even the time frame within which they apply. They may relate to financial factors, the environment, the provider's own priorities, or participant groups. For example, goals might address the nature of the agency's programs (to promote and maintain physical, mental, and social well-being of [a particular client segment] through the provision of leisure opportunities) or the identity of targeted groups (to encourage youth to participate in physical activity).

The operational demands of each goal are typically clarified by several *objectives*. Objectives are less abstract than are goals. They are specific, measurable, and clearly attainable within a given time period (Kraus & Curtis, 1990). They typically focus on behavioral change and/or program implementation issues. For example, a behavioral change-based goal might dictate that "The agency will enrol 500 new participants in fitness classes over the winter months." An implementation-based objective might indicate that "a neighborhood park will be completed in District 1 by the end of the fiscal year."

Whatever their intent, goals and objectives reflect the basic philosophy of the organization. In doing so they are inevitably influenced by situational factors like legal mandates, political frameworks, wishes of residents, and practical realities. All must be synchronized so that each contributes to the organization's mission and purpose. The way in which they work together will determine competitive strategy.

The marketer must ask several questions of this competitive strategy:

1. What are our stated goals and objectives? (Goals offer general suggestions on how the organization intends to fulfill its mission, whereas objectives offer specific measurable means through which goals will be achieved.)

2. Do they lead logically to the mission? (One common problem is that of goals that focus on the needs of the organization rather than on the client.)

In terms of agency resources, the marketer must ask:

1. What are our major resources and limitations (e.g., human, financial, technical)?

2. Are resource levels and types appropriate to our goals?

3. Who are our direct competitors and partners? (It is best at this stage to describe their strategies, weaknesses, and strengths.)

4. Do we possess distinct advantages over competitors; do we offer clear advantages for partners?

5. Are changes planned that will influence resource levels? If so, is current strategy appropriate or are changes required?

True understanding of an organization comes from knowledge of its competitive strategy. This level of strategy focuses directly on how the provider plans to compete with rivals and cooperate with partners. The competitive strategies of most providers are evident to the most casual observer. McDonald's Restaurants compete through volume and consistency, Rolls Royce automakers through quality, Wal-Mart stores through low cost and selection. Even public sector providers, who may find the notion of competition troubling, must consider this level

of strategy development. They too must consider their role within the larger marketplace. The marketer must understand how the organization plans to "do business" before a marketing plan can be developed.

Level 3 Information: Functional Strategy

The third level of information, *functional strategy*, is occupied with discovering and creating value. Such value may be measured in terms of *return* for the provider or *benefit* to the participant. Functional level strategies deal with the nuts and bolts of day-to-day operation. As such, they may differ from one department to the next, from one target group to the next. Though many departments, like finance or human resources, develop functional plans, such plans are the stock and trade of the marketer. This is because functional plans are tied most closely to the provider's efforts to serve target groups (Griffin, 1984).

Several pieces of information are required if the marketer is to understand current strategy toward various target groups. The picture begins to become more complicated at this point because existing strategy may differ for each group. As a result, these questions may have to be asked repeatedly for each target market:

a) What is our key strategy toward crucial client groups?

b) Are major resource allocation decisions consistent with this strategy?

c) What are the critical factors if this strategy is to succeed (e.g., partners for distribution, facilities, etc)?

d) How are we doing? (What is our reputation? How does it compare to other providers? How are our services used? Are our promotions successful?)

These questions are concerned with the nuts and bolts of implementing the higher level strategies. Efforts to price services, develop promotional campaigns, or to deliver service to clients should all be considered if one is to understand the role adopted by a given service provider. Such data are perhaps most helpful of all in revealing how the provider interacts with clients, with other providers and with its own workforce.

One must appreciate that as questions become more specific, the audit can become very complex. For this reason, most marketers rely on a few acronyms to help them remember the types of questions they might ask at this stage of the process. One useful acronym is that of CAT. It refers to the types of questions that must be asked in order to assess functional strategy. CAT refers to *capacity, alignment,* and *the status quo.*

CAT Analysis

Consider Capacity

Capacity refers to the organization's ability to carry out its mission. Strategy is largely a process of building capacity. Capacity exists in many forms. Traditional strategic thinking views capacity in terms of *financial, physical,* and *human resources.*

Financial resources refer to the organization's ability to generate needed funds.

In the past, many park and recreation agencies enjoyed considerable certainty in their funding projections. They were allocated tax funds each year that matched or exceeded those allocated the previous year. This happy circumstance brought considerable certainty to the planning process. The past decades have witnessed a departure from this traditional model, however, forcing many agencies to look outside the traditional tax base for funding. More on this will be covered in the chapter on pricing.

Physical resources make up the physical presence of the organization and are comprised of the buildings, natural spaces, and other properties controlled by the organization. To a lesser extent physical resources are also

comprised of vehicles and other things that enhance capacity to serve. Most public park and recreation marketing efforts rely heavily on physical resources. While many agencies operate their own facilities and maintain their own natural spaces, others rely on facilities controlled by others best described as "partners." For example, in many communities, recreation departments and school boards cooperate to provide leisure programming on school property after regular school hours. Other departments rely on facilities provided by service organizations who are willing to make their facilities available on a limited basis. All these resources represent opportunity for the marketer and all must be considered in any marketing plan.

Physical resources may, however, prove both a benefit and a blight to leisure marketers. In one study, colleagues and I (Johnson-Tew, Havitz, & McCarville, 1999) discovered that leisure providers were sometimes being held hostage by their own facilities. We asked leisure programmers how they made programming location decisions. We wanted to know how willing they were to go to the client rather than force the client to come to them. We reasoned, for example, that deliberations over program locations would likely begin with the supposed location of target client groups. We thought that many programs might originate in areas, like malls, where clients gather on their own. This was rarely the case, however.

Leisure providers typically located their programs only in their own facilities. The heavy financial burden of operating these facilities forced programmers to focus all their efforts on filling these facilities. As one programmer explained, "You just can't ignore millions of dollars' worth of facilities." As a result, in order to understand capacity, one must also understand opportunities and costs of physical resources.

Human resources must also be considered in any discussion of functional strategy. Human resources refer to the organization's workforce in terms of its ability to carry out its mandate now and in the future. Elements that effect this ability relate both to the characteristics of the staff as a group (flexibility, expertise, and motivation) but also the conditions that surround them in the workplace (reward structures and working conditions).

Alignment

Alignment refers to consistency between the organization's business goals and how it is going about pursuing them. Alignment is similar to coordination but it refers, not to interdepartmental concerns, but to gaps between day-to-day operations and overriding goals and objectives. These gaps may exist between any and all of three levels of operation. For example, corporate strategy may suggest that the organization's role is one of service to the community. Its mission is to offer service to all, regardless of an individual participant's ability to pay. However, with repeated cuts to tax allocations, a new entrepreneurial spirit may come to dominate decision making. As a result, public leisure agencies may lose perspective as they bow to the demands made on them by the marketplace (Goodale, 1985). In order to maintain program levels, they may feel forced to abandon programs that offer inadequate rates of return. Free programs may be dropped in favor of fee-based programs. Disadvantaged citizens may be displaced from those program efforts as a result. A gap between mandate and practice may emerge. Such gaps should attract the attention of the marketer.

Alignment is also required between existing departments and staff members as they all seek to serve the participant. Remember that functional strategy is influenced by many players. It is usually determined by coordination between each provider along with many partners. The term *synergy* is often used to describe the ultimate alignment of that work group. Synergy refers to the creation of value through the cooperation of various units within the same organization (Aaker, 1995).

Think of how programmers' efforts could be enhanced by the efforts of others in the same agency. For example, programs could be rendered more desirable if facility managers maintained clean, modern facilities. Programs might be more valuable if accounting departments permitted flexible payment plans,

convenient refund policies, and so on. Though this requirement seems self-evident, efforts to create synergy have largely failed in the past. They enjoyed some popularity in the 1980s but have since lost favor among decision makers. There are many reasons behind these failures, ranging from strong departmental identities and management differences to differing procedures and cultures within organizations (Porter, 1985).

Whatever the cause, finding the synergy necessary to optimize functional strategy has been a tough nut to crack over the years. True cooperation is one of those notions that is acceptable to all in principle but riddled with challenges in implementation. As a result, there is often needless duplication and outright competition between departments in the same agencies. The aquatics program may have one policy on refunds while the sports program has another. Playground staff may be empowered to solve client problems while maintenance staff are not. Every department may have a different staff training regimen and many may focus only on their own respective priorities. Clients can be left dazed and confused by the variety of policies and perspectives they face when seeking help or redress. All this is fodder for the marketing strategist. Dramatic improvements can be made through the development of synergy. As a result, when making this assessment, the marketer must continually search for challenges and solutions. They can use this information later on when developing strategy.

The Status Quo

The status quo refers to how operations are currently being carried out. This is an important concept for two reasons. First, the status quo indicates the milieu in which the marketer finds herself. This is the starting point from which all new initiatives will be introduced. It is always useful to have a sense of one's starting point before undertaking a journey to another place.

Second, the status quo represents an important comparison point for all those who evaluate your efforts. The change literature makes it clear that the status quo offers a comfort point for staff and clients alike. Changes to programs are often suspect because they compete with the familiar. The more initiatives deviate from the status quo, the more suspicion and distress they may generate. It is one of the perversities of human nature that even hated routine is often preferable to potentially pleasant uncertainty. As a result, strategy must recognize *what is*, before it contemplates *what might be.* Huge gaps between the two may undermine a strategy before it can succeed.

The Environmental Audit

Once establishing the organization's position in terms of agency goals, objectives, capacity, and priorities, the marketer must decide upon the potential of this position. As suggested earlier, the marketer must seek a course of action that renders the organization and its programs unique in some meaningful way. This requires a critical assessment of the external forces that shape marketing strategy. This examination is called the *environmental audit*. This audit focuses directly on issues beyond the control of the provider. It represents a macroanalysis of the society in which the organization operates.

Again, marketers have developed an acronym to help them remember the steps of this audit. It is guided by the acronym P.E.S.T. because it focuses on *political, economic, sociological,* and *technological* issues. Consider each issue in turn.

Political issues are "concerned with the motives and the actions of governments and the way, that, via legislation, regulation and the legal/political system, they impact on [marketing efforts]" (Fifield, 1998, p. 34).

The role played by political processes is perhaps obvious. Political processes establish regulations, guidelines, and even the climate within which the marketer operates. Each

group in power places its own stamp on the mood of the marketplace. In the case of public sector providers, political issues may have considerable impact on marketing efforts. In particular, political figures may desire an active role in policy making and strategy development. This will undoubtedly influence how marketing strategy is developed and carried out.

This trend is evident as park and recreation departments have become increasingly involved in pricing their services. Though many marketers may consider pricing an internal, strategic tool, elected officials may view pricing as a political issue. As a result, there is often pressure to control pricing policy from within the political rather than the administrative ranks. The marketer may lose control of price-related decisions. For example, as part of larger cost-saving measures, several adjacent cities recently amalgamated to become one larger entity. Each of the respective cities' park and recreation departments had, over the years, adopted very different pricing policies. One city had applied virtually no fees while the others had been applying several types of fees and charges. It was clear that with amalgamation, one set of pricing policies would need to be established. A few erudite political figures saw this task as a political rather than administrative challenge and became heavily involved in the policy-making process. They imposed several policies that not only tied the hands of the decision makers in the department but also created conditions that ensured a financial shortfall of millions of dollars annually. In this and thousands of other cases, political considerations affect marketing planning. Questions the marketer might ask to establish the nature of the political environment include:

· What is the general political climate?

· What are political attitudes toward leisure services in general? What is the role of leisure services in terms of the larger political mandate?

· What are the legislative effects on organizational behavior and employment patterns?

Economic issues are those that make up the monetary climate of the marketplace.

Key economic variables include inflation rate, interests rates, and even employment levels. Together these rates suggest the amount of disposable (after taxes are paid) and discretionary (after necessities are purchased) income potential clients have available. Almost 150 years ago, Ernst Engle, the German statistician, advised that increasing disposable and discretionary income levels could lead to many happy results (Sandhusen, 1993). According to Engle, increased income ensures that families spend less of their income on essentials and relatively more on luxury items. Many types of leisure services are typically thought to fall under this luxury designation so their popularity may well be a function of economic climate.

Further, the economic climate is profoundly linked with employment patterns. What are the trends in the workplace? Stable work environments will, in turn, generate more stable economic conditions. Areas dominated by part-time or seasonal work (as is often the case in resort and rural communities, for example) may have very different leisure preferences from those where work is more reliable. Questions you might ask to get a sense of the economic environment are:

· What are current income levels?

· How is income distributed across the population? Do income levels vary systematically by sex, race, or geographic location? Are these patterns likely to change in the next three to five years?

· What is the structure of the workforce? What proportion of jobs are part-time, seasonal, or full-time? If seasonal or part-time employment dominates the work force, during what time of the week, season, or year are workers most likely to be "underemployed?"

Sociological issues focus on the values that guide the community members' motives, wants, and priorities.

Sociological values may be *core* in that they are very persistent and resistant to change. Core values might relate to community members' views on work or family. Given their stability over time, they can provide an excellent indicator of interest patterns among target markets. For example, parent and tot events are typically viewed in a very positive manner because they strike at the heart of pervasive values promoting positive child/parent interaction.

These values act as lasting guideposts for the leisure marketer. They suggest what is appropriate, what is valued, and what is not. The marketer can always be guided by these values. The trick is to identify them, then plan accordingly. This challenge is exacerbated by value diversity within any population. Not all groups share the same core beliefs. Even those that share the same beliefs may express them in different ways.

In the parent and tot example offered above, it was noted that most groups cherish the notion of family values. However, different groups in the community may express this fundamental value in a variety of ways. Visit a city park and watch how fellow visitors display their love of family in their own particular ways. For some groups, a visit to a park means gathering up several generations of family members and descending on the park en masse. For others, the park visit is an opportunity to escape the pressures of family and to visit with friends for a game of touch football. They then plan to return home refreshed and ready to take on all the challenges that families have to offer. For others, the notion of family does not involve children. Instead it is bound up in notions of close friends and close-knit groups that share their own values and ideals. All these individuals share the same basic family values but express them in their own unique ways. The leisure provider must understand these expressions so that these many unique groups can be better served.

The marketer must also be concerned with *secondary* values, which are less resistant to change (Sandhusen, 1993). Though secondary values also suggest what is right or wrong, good or bad, they are more transient than their core counterparts. For example, individuals may adopt and later drop the values of various subgroups throughout the course of life. The adolescent might adopt the sometimes reckless values of the peer group, but abandon them as adulthood approaches. Bob Stebbins's work in "serious leisure" suggests the power of second-ary values in guiding leisure behavior. He writes that participants may join leisure-based subgroups called *social worlds*. A social world is a set of networks, typical life-styles, and a central collective leisure activity (Stebbins, 1998). Group members share unique sets of special norms, values, beliefs, and moral principles that are particular to each respective group. These norms, values, and beliefs guide and direct group members' activity patterns. To understand these values is to understand and predict behavior.

Questions the marketer might ask to establish important sociological conditions are:

- What types of values guide community members' decisions to participate?

- Are these values relatively stable throughout the community, or are they shared only by subgroup members?

- What types of norms have target groups adopted?

- Who are the group leaders/role models who seem to influence the actions of other group members?

Technological issues relate to the use of various machines in the workplace.

Technology is changing the leisure landscape, and while doing so it has proven a mixed blessing. Many commentators believe that technology has tended to enslave rather than liberate those in the workplace and in the home. It has tended to increase the pace of life generally and the workplace in particular

(Garson, 1988). One has only to listen to the constant ring of the telephone, the whir of the fax machine, the continual ring of the cell phone, and the insistent buzz of the pager joined at our collective hips to observe the effect technology has had on the workplace. All serve to hasten our efforts, to alter our plans, and to demand our attention.

This trend has also made recreation participants more demanding of leisure providers. They desire more from programs and even from the agencies who provide them. They want leisure programs to provide relief from the daily grind and to provide solace in a hectic world. They want convenience, ease of payment, and empathetic staff. Given the speed with which their lives are moving, they want all these things sooner rather than later. They want to have the capacity to register by phone or over the Internet, because both provide instantaneous results. They want the convenience of using any variety of payment vehicles (credit and debit cards, cash, checks). They want staff to solve, not create, problems. They know that a single travel agent can finalize flight plans, make hotel arrangements, rent a car, and even plan the perfect meal months in advance and from a distance of thousands of miles. Technology has made this not only possible, but seem commonplace. They see it done everyday and they expect leisure staff to perform the same miracles.

Questions to ask when establishing important technological conditions:

- What is the rate of technological change?

- Can we keep up with the rate of change?

- What are our technological require-ments?

- Does our technological capacity match our clients' demands?

- How do technological costs compare to the savings they might generate?

Industry Analysis

The *industry analysis* now considers the organization's position in the marketplace. Although previous analyses implicitly considered this position, they focused primarily on the provider's own capacities. This analysis is concerned with where the provider now stands in terms of other providers. These others might be categorized in terms of suppliers, entrants, competitors or substitutes. The industry analysis represents the final phase of the strategic assessment.

Suppliers

Suppliers are the organizations that help provide programs. They may provide facilities, instructional staff, or support staff. For example, if a leisure provider operates programs through local schools, the school board should be counted among its partners because they provide needed facilities. Does the provider rely on the board's unionized maintenance workers or their teaching staff to support school-based programs? If so, they too should be considered as suppliers because they provide support staff. Sport governing bodies who certify and control instructor organizations may also be counted in these deliberations. They may dictate how much their members (agency instructors) will be paid, their work conditions, even the amount of hours their members may work.

Keeping in mind that the goal is to establish the strength and reliability of the existing delivery system, the marketer must ask several questions in assessing a relationship with these suppliers, such as the following (Fifield, 1998):

- How powerful are our suppliers? For example, would you have any recourse if a school board denied your agency access to their facilities?

- What are their mandates and strategic priorities?

- What can we offer partners that helps them offer greater value to their own clients?

Entrants

Entrants are players that have just entered or are about to enter the marketer's world of operation. It seems that several nontraditional players are now interested in the delivery of leisure services. For example, police forces around North America are becoming involved in using leisure to promote "prosocial" behavior among at-risk youth. The health profession is now interested in promoting healthy lifestyle and has identified leisure as an important element to the lifestyle puzzle. Retail outlets are now becoming heavily involved in promoting clubs, workshops, and special events in order to generate interest in their own inventory. Bookstores that organize discussion groups, public readings, and workshops now resemble community centers more than the traditional stuffy bookshop. Building supply warehouses now organize instructional workshops and outdoor retailers arrange film nights and equipment rentals.

Many nontraditional players are now exploring the possibilities that leisure provides, and each should be considered an entrant to the world of leisure provision. They are all potentially powerful players that could change the face of the leisure industry. Leisure marketers must ask many questions as they assess the role of these new entrants.

- How powerful are these entrants?

- What are their mandates and strategic priorities? If they are consistent with our own, will we treat them as partners or competitors?

- If we consider them as partners, what can we offer them that will help them offer greater value to their own clients?

- If we consider them as competitors, what can we offer their clients to gain competitive advantage?

Competitors

As the name implies, *competitors* compete directly with your own program offerings. Competitors may be friends or even partners. When this is the case, the competitive environment may be somewhat relaxed. For example, many nonprofit agencies like the YM/YWCAs offer similar programs to those offered by public leisure providers. This is a fundamentally competitive relationship, yet it is typically undertaken in a spirit of cooperation and goodwill. Both pursue the same service mandate, and the community is improved when both operate successfully.

Conversely, these providers may be unfriendly competitors. They may promote ideas or products that are contradictory to your own. For example, one municipal leisure provider learned that a private sector concern had opened a fitness studio. Preliminary analysis found that the quality of this new program was suspect and perhaps even dangerous to participants. The public provider believed that this studio posed a risk to community well-being, so management decided to compete directly with this new studio. Their goal was to provide a safer alternative so that citizens would not be enticed to join this rather dubious venture.

When planning strategy, ask this of your direct competitors:

· How powerful are they?

· What are their mandates and strategic priorities?

· What can we offer their clients to gain competitive advantage?

Competitors may also be *indirect*. Indirect competitors are also called substitutes.

Substitutes

Substitutes offer an alternative to your programs but do not offer the same benefit package. They simply offer an alternative to the potential client. The assistant marketing director of a major league baseball team was asked to identify his competition. He indicated that his direct competitors were other professional sports and teams but his greatest concern was over substitutes to his product. He indicated that every theater and restaurant in the region offered a substitute for his product because his product, like theirs, was based on entertainment. He knew how to deal with direct competitors because they were easy to identify, finite in number, and they were all following strategies that he could counter with his own efforts. His greatest concern was over substitutes.

Leisure providers too are challenged by substitutes. They must ask:

· Who offers substitutes to our programming efforts?

· What do substitutes to our programs offer?

· What is the nature of their appeal?

· What can we offer that provides superior benefit?

Once completed, these three audits will establish a baseline upon which subsequent decisions can be made. The audits may be conducted with varying levels of formality. In some cases, they may require considerable effort. This is typically the case before large-scale initiatives are undertaken or in a rapidly changing operating environment. In other cases, these audits are carried out but as a very informal assessment. They are made by staff who are already familiar with their operating environment and who carry them out almost as an afterthought. Whatever the procedure used, these audits are an essential element of marketing planning and strategy development. The next stage is one of developing strategic direction.

Main Points

· Marketing strategy begins with an opportunity assessment that identifies gaps between clients' preferences and solutions now being offered within the greater marketplace.

· The assessment begins with the provider's own goals and mandate. Once these are established, the provider can then separate and serve key groups from the larger community.

· An opportunity assessment includes an internal audit designed to establish the provider's own priorities, abilities, and capacity.

· The marketplace or environment is then assessed for threats and opportunities—the goal is to discover ways to serve clients that maximize the provider's own strengths while avoiding threats from the environment.

Case Study

A public leisure agency in a community of 20,000 is interested in hosting regional and even national-level tournaments on its many playing fields to offset the costs of operating those fields. Community members and local politicians have been quick to see the economic benefits of such tournaments because they bring new money into the community. The leisure agency has encouraged various community sport groups to bid on events and tournaments within their respective sport organizations.

One group has come to you with what its members believe is wonderful news. They believe that they can win a bid for a large, national-level tournament. This event will add thousands of dollars to the local economy. It is a softball tournament for girls under the age of

16. For an event of this caliber, fields will have to be refurbished and improvements made to the town's infrastructure. For example, additional parking will have to be created near the fields and lighting will have to be improved on all the fields. Further, about 200 volunteers will need to be recruited from the community to assist with the three-day event. Unfortunately, the national body that organizes the event dictates that it can only be held on a weekend usually reserved for the community's annual picnic. The picnic would have to be delayed or cancelled for this year.

The sport group recognizes the tremendous strain on community resources that will result from these requirements so they have been actively seeking sponsorship support from a variety of sources. One sponsor is willing to pay for the physical changes to the fields in return for free advertising at the event. Agency staff see this as a once-in-a-lifetime opportunity to have their fields improved at no extra cost to local citizens. The sponsor requires that its logo be placed on all brochures, on signage at the event itself, and that it be mentioned in all press releases surrounding the event. However, the sport group has asked the leisure agency to help it find the volunteers necessary to make the event a success. The leisure agency staff hold a meeting to discuss the nature and extent of their involvement in the tournament.

· What parties will they alienate/impress if they hold the event?

· Should they approve the request?

· If they approve the request, where might they look for assistance/ volunteers?

· Does the identity of the sponsor matter? What if it was a local software firm ... or a national beer company offering to provide resources?

References

Aaker, D.A. (1995). *Developing business strategies.* New York: John Wiley & Sons.

Backman, S. (1994). Using a person-situation approach to market segmentation. *Journal of Park and Recreation Administration, 12*(1), 1-16.

Berry, L. (1995). *On great service: A framework for action.* New York: The Free Press.

Bloom, P., & Novelli, W. (1981). Problems and challenges in social marketing. *Journal of Marketing, 45,* 79-88.

Brown, S. A. (1995). *What customers value most.* Toronto: John Wiley & Sons.

Donnelly, M., Vaske, J., DeRuiter, D., & King, T. (1996). Person-occasion segmentation of state park visitors. *Journal of Park and Recreation Administration, 14*(2), 96-106.

Fifield, P. (1998). *Marketing strategy* (2nd ed.). Oxford: Butterworth Heinemann.

Garson, B. (1988). *The electronic sweatshop.* New York: Penguin Books.

Goodale, T. (1985). Prevailing winds and bending mandates. In T. Goodale & P. Witt (Eds.), *Recreation and leisure: Issues in an era of change* (pp. 195-207). State College, PA.: Venture.

Griffin, R.W. (1984). *Management.* Boston: Houghton Mifflin Company.

Havitz, M., Dimanche, F., & Bogle, T. (1994). Segmenting the adults fitness market using involvement profiles. *Journal of Park and Recreation Administration, 12*(3), 38-56.

Henderson, K.A. (1990). The meaning of leisure for women: An integrative review of the research. *Journal of Leisure Research, 22*(3), 228-233.

Hollenhorst, S., Schuett, M., Olson, D., & Chavez, D. (1995). An examination of the characteristics, preferences, and attitudes of mountain bike users of the national forests. *Journal of Park and Recreation Administration, 13*(3), 41-51.

Howard, J.A., & Sheth, J.N. (1988). A theory of buyer behavior. In B.M. Ennis, & K.K. Cox (Eds.), *Marketing Classics* (pp. 105-123). Boston: Allyn and Bacon, Inc.

Johnson-Tew, C.P., Havitz, M., & McCarville R.E. (1999). The role of marketing in municipal recreation programming decisions: A challenge to conventional wisdom. *Journal of Park and Recreation Administration, 17*(1), 1-20.

Kotler, P., McDougall, G., & Armstrong, G. (1988). *Marketing: Canadian edition.* Englewood Cliffs, N.J.: Prentice-Hall.

Kraus, R., & Curtis, J. (1990). *Creative management* (5th ed.). Toronto: Times Mirror/Mosby.

Levitt, T. (1960). Marketing myopia.. *Harvard Business Review, 38*(4), 45-56.

Lipsky, M. (1980). *Street-level bureaucracy: Dilemmas of the individual in public services.* New York: Russell Sage Foundation.

McCarville, R., & Smale, B. (1993). Perceived constraints to leisure participation within five activity domains. *Journal of Park and Recreation Administration, 11*(2), 1-15.

Meyer, A., & Westerbarkey, P. (1996). Measuring and managing hotel guest satisfaction. In M. Olsen, R. Teare, & E. Gummesson (Eds.), *Service quality in hospitality organizations.* (pp. 185-203). New York: Cassell.

Meyers, J.H. (1996). *Segmentation and positioning for strategic marketing decisions.* Chicago: American Marketing Association.

Payne, A. (1993). *The essence of services marketing.* New York: Prentice-Hall.

Porter, M.E. (1985). *Competitive advantage: Creating and sustaining superior performance.* New York: The Free Press.

Sandhusen, R.L. (1993). *Marketing* (2nd ed.). Hauppauge, New York: Barron's Educational Series, Inc.

Stebbins, R.A. (1998). *After work: The search for an optimal leisure lifestyle.* Calgary, AB: Detselig Enterprises.

Sylvia, G., Sallee, C., & Berry H. (1995). Determining leisure program formats based on participant preferences: A case study in nature-based education. *Journal of Park and Recreation Administration, 13*(2), 55-72.

Weinstein, A. (1987). *Market segmentation.* Chicago: Probus Publishing.

R. McCarville

CHAPTER

3

Establish Strategic Direction

Strategy development begins with the discovery of opportunities. The opportunity assessment discussed in the last chapter identified gaps and challenges that might exist within the marketplace. In the most general terms, the audit answered four basic questions:

- Who are my customers?

- How are they different and what are their needs?

- What products or services will I offer to meet those needs?

- How are my offerings different from competing products/services (Meyers, 1996)?

Once the opportunity assessment has been completed, the marketer can begin to decide how to pursue opportunities identified during this assessment. The goal is to use *distinctive capabilities* to offer *special value* to *target segments* or *markets*. This is the process of developing *strategy*. Strategy seeks to pursue these opportunities. It determines *who* can best serve a client group and *how* this might be accomplished.

Developing Strategy

The word strategy originates from the Greek word *strategia* meaning "generalship." Originally, strategy referred exclusively to the making of war. It was concerned with the movement of troops, maneuvering for advantage, and generally planning for victory on the battlefield. Its martial origins are evident even today. Strategists from many walks of life continue to read and gain insight from Sun Tsu's *The Art of War* written about 500 B.C. Despite its militaristic roots, the word strategy now refers to any planning procedure for the deployment of resources. It might be defined as "the overall plan for deploying resources to establish a favorable position" (Grant, 1998, p. 14). As such, strategy has become accepted procedure in any complicated enterprise.

In many ways, the principles of strategy have changed little over the centuries. In order to be effective, any strategy must have three basic characteristics. First, it must provide *clear, unambiguous direction*. Strategy should offer vision to everyone in the organization. It must ensure what Edwards Deming referred to as "constancy of purpose." Deming, the father of the modern quality assurance movement, offered several tenets of quality management, and this notion of "constancy of purpose" was first among them. Uniform effort toward a common goal ensures cooperation while breaking down barriers between departments and individuals. Without such uniformity, any enterprise is doomed to failure. For some, failure will come sooner, while for others, later. But come it will; of this Deming was convinced (Gitlow & Gitlow, 1994).

Second, strategy must be *flexible* and *responsive*. The marketplace is dynamic. It is a sea of changing priorities, players and plans. Trends come and go, and strategy must have the capacity to adjust accordingly. For example, during the last two decades of the twentieth century, a powerful tax limitation movement dramatically changed the economic landscape for many public leisure providers. Proposition 13, a landmark tax limitation bill in California, changed overnight how public leisure agencies pursued their respective mandates. This same period witnessed increasing interest by the private sector in activities that had historically been the domain of the public sector. Private sector providers were anxious to replace or supplement the activities of many public leisure agencies. Many public providers struggled with finding a new role in the shifting sands of the marketplace. Strategy can and should help with finding and maintaining this role.

Third, strategy must be *sustainable*. Sustainability refers to the long-term viability of a given course of action. If a given strategy cannot be sustained, then it is typically considered a failure. In the past, public sector leisure providers created strategies that were sustainable only with the ongoing and heavy infusion of tax dollars. With the growing strength of the tax limitation movement, surveys reported public providers were often dubious regarding their ongoing ability to offer quality programs to their communities (Brademas & Readnour, 1989).

Sustainable strategies establish a balance between the needs of the provider and the wants of the consumer. This balance must be maintained if the relationship between the two is to continue. The private sector seeks the balance so that its members might continue to profit. The public sector seeks the balance so that it might continue to serve. Whatever the

motive, the balance must be assured if the relationship is to be sustained.

Deciding How Best to Serve

Marketing strategy focuses on the provider's ability to serve a client group. Effective marketing strategy springs from doing what clients want done (Fifield, 1998). The goal is to discover the provider's own unique skills and assets, then to use them to provide specific target groups with valued services better than does the competition. The strategic blending of these multiple priorities creates a competitive advantage.

There are three possible competitive strategies the marketer might adopt. In his classic work on competitive advantage, Harvard professor Michael Porter (1985) suggested that strategy may focus on cost leadership, differentiation, or focus.

Cost Leadership

A provider who adopts a *cost leadership* strategy attempts to offer the least expensive services in the industry. The ability to maintain a cost leadership position is typically built on ability to reduce production costs. For example, Wal-Mart is able to make each store more profitable by reducing the amount of space needed to warehouse inventory. A sophisticated ordering and distribution system ensures that items are ordered and delivered only when they are needed on the sales floor. As a result, each store is often more profitable than competitors, because more of its space is available as sales floor. Selection increases, sales volumes rise, and profits increase. Wal-Mart is then able to keep prices down and maintain cost leadership.

Public leisure providers have traditionally adopted this strategy. They have done so, not through efficiency or cost reductions, but through access to tax revenues. As suggested above, however, this access has been strained over the past several decades. As a result, many public leisure providers are now exploring (at least for some of their programs) other strategic directions. One of the most popular has been that of differentiation.

Differentiation

A *differentiation* strategy demands that the provider be unique along some service dimension that is valued by participants. The provider "selects one or more attributes that many buyers ... perceive as important, and uniquely positions [the agency] to meet those needs" (Porter, 1985, p.14). While it is difficult to create a truly unique program, many providers differentiate themselves from the competition by offering that is superior to that of other providers.

In *Power Retailing*, Stevenson, Shlesinger, and Pearce (1999) suggest that retailers may all differentiate along four dimensions: selection, customer experience, price, and convenience. They believe that each of these dimensions is valued by customers and recommend that a differentiation strategy be built around providing them. For many years, municipal leisure providers have attempted to compete, at least partially, through convenience. They have traditionally distributed parks, facilities, and programs throughout the neighborhoods of their communities. They developed this strategy in order to ensure access, rather than to compete with other providers, but it represents a competitive strategy nonetheless.

Focus

A strategy based on *focus* is one that selects a group or groups of potential partici-pants and delivers programs to them to the exclusion of others. For example, many clubs and retail outlets surrounding a university focus their strategic efforts directly on the student population. They offer food, drink and other services that might appeal to many groups, but they focus their effort by appealing to the sometimes unique interests of student groups.

Although some strategists believe that only one strategic option is possible, others believe that the three strategic options are not

at all mutually exclusive. The latter believe, for example, that a focused strategy might also rely on cost or differentiation techniques to increase its appeal to prospective customers. A fitness club focusing on university students will likely offer a variety of price incentives to capture students' interest. The same club might also use a differentiation strategy to ensure that its offerings are superior to other providers who might target the same group. Indeed, it may be unwise to sacrifice one option for another. A focussed service provider who hopes to be a price leader must still maintain quality levels that are close or on par with those of the industry if he hopes to succeed. For this reason, many strategists now reject the notion that the best strategy is to pick one option or another. This either/or approach seems needlessly restrictive and potentially ineffective.

Taken together, Porter's (1985) insights suggest that strategy can really only take two directions. The first is that of charting a new path. This new path typically involves offering something that is unique. The second direction is to follow the path set by others; to offer something they are already offering but to do so in a different or improved way (Fifield, 1998). Conceptually, that's really all there is to strategy. Success, however, is found in the details. Marketers must always find a way to be superior to other providers but do so in a way that serves both the client and the provider.

Making Program-Based Decisions through Portfolio Analysis

Leisure providers typically serve their clients through the provision of programs. Programs thought to serve important client groups are developed and enhanced, while less successful alternatives are dropped. Program development often begins with *portfolio analysis*. Portfolio analysis is the process of classifying programs in terms of their potential, then deciding which programs should receive additional resources. There are several program

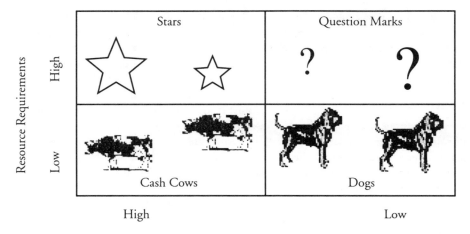

Figure 3.1: Basic Program Types

types that should be of interest to the marketer. All have strategic implications. These types were first developed by the Boston Consulting Group (BCG). The BCG suggested that strategic planning include a portfolio analysis in which programs are considered in terms of their ability to capture market share and their capacity to generate revenue. In their terms, there are four basic program types (Figure 3.1).

The first program type is the *star*. Think of a shooting star and you'll get the idea of a star's performance. These programs burn brightly, capturing much attention, but they also burn resources at a sometimes alarming rate. They need to be fueled with staff, facility time, and ongoing attention. In return for these resources, the star can be very rewarding for the client and the provider. For the leisure participant, they offer an interesting leisure alternative. For the provider, they capture both interest and market share. Like a shooting star, as they burn out, their growth slows. With luck they will become cash cows.

Cash cows are beloved among marketers. They are low-growth programs that require little additional funding but continue to produce positive returns. Think of a milk cow that asks for little more than grass and shelter but continues to provide high-quality milk. The key to a cash cow is that it provides much more than it requires from the producer. During the last decade, aerobics programs were often recreation departments' perpetual cash

cows. Hundreds of clients could be directed, coached, and otherwise cajoled by a single instructor. These programs served thousands of clients while bringing in handsome profits for many providers. These profits were often used to finance more speculative ventures called question marks.

Question marks are those programs that, while requiring considerable support from the provider, bring in few resources. They exist within a high growth marketplace, so they possess considerable potential if the conditions are right. Think of the world of the movie studio as Christmas approaches. Executives know that holidays are very popular among moviegoers, so as Christmas draws near, they may spend millions of dollars to promote the projects for which interest has been slow to build. Only time will tell whether or not they will receive adequate returns from these efforts. These are the programs that keep marketers up nights. They require many resources, and there may be little return at the end of the day. Conversely, they exist within high growth areas, so their potential is high. If they fail to live up to this potential, however, they will eventually be classified as dogs.

Dogs are programs that possess little market share, and there is little prospect that this situation will improve. With due respect to our canine friends, this is a program type generally avoided by strategists. It is generally being shunned by clients, and hopes are dim for any improvement in that situation. Think of a leisure facility devoted entirely to roller skating. Interest in traditional roller skating has been falling for years, and the advent of new in-line skates has taken skating out of these single-purpose facilities and onto the streets and pathways of the city. It is unlikely that future generations will be enticed back into the roller rink of the past to circle endlessly on the same rather primitive skates. This is a classic "dog." Such enterprises may generate enough money to support their own operations but they generate little in the way of additional funds. Their long-term survival is uncertain at best.

Classic portfolio analysis suggests that a cash cow is preferable to a dog. It generates more revenue and requires fewer resources. As a result, many dogs are abandoned, while cash cows and stars are favored. However, as with most things, even obvious decisions are sometimes difficult to make. Strategy may dictate that selected dogs are maintained just as assiduously as cash cows. It may be necessary to retain a dog that is not self-supporting because it adds value to a cash cow or a star.

In Praise of Dogs

A *loss leader* is a product that is purposely priced at a loss in order to generate additional volume or interest. In effect, it represents a dog in terms of its profit potential. The introduction of loss leaders is a common practice in both the public and private sectors. Private sector marketers use loss leaders to increase traffic in their facilities, to generate interest in their programs, and to highlight their services. In effect, they forego profit in one area in order to increase profits in another. Public sector marketers will operate at a loss for many of the same reasons. They too want to generate interest and increase participation, but often this proves to be an end in itself. They are not interested in profit margins or financial return on investment. Both are willing to support a dog because it fulfills long-term goals that extend beyond the viability of a single program. The effectiveness of the loss leader suggests the importance of taking a very broad view when developing strategy.

Further, the public sector may not be able to abandon dogs simply because they cannot afford to ignore the interests of select client groups. There are many instances in which public leisure facilities or programs lose money but continue to play an integral role in the larger program offering. Traditional swimming pools, for example, rarely turn a profit, yet few are abandoned because of their importance to the community. Other programs may appeal to only a few members of the community and will never turn a profit, but they too will receive support from the public agency. This suggests the importance of viewing strategy in terms of the big picture. Establishing strategy one program at a time is both wasteful and short-sighted. Each program must be considered as part of the strategic whole. Its value can only be established as part of that whole.

Building Strategy with the Ansoff Matrix

These basic product types suggest that the marketer may pursue a variety of outcomes through program selection and development (Kotler, McDougall, & Armstrong, 1988). Leisure providers who hope to increase the number of clients they now serve may aggressively pursue stars and question marks, while ruthlessly dropping programs they believe to be dogs. This represents a *building* strategy which uses today's resources to improve services in the future. A more conservative strategy is called a *holding* strategy. This strategy, one of maintaining the status quo, is typically undertaken in times of instability or uncertainty. A final option, that of *harvesting*, focuses exclusively on drawing resources from cash cows. This choice enables the provider to build cash reserves. It does so at the expense of long-term planning, however.

A very useful tool, called the *Ansoff* matrix, is typically used to describe available strategic options. Igor Ansoff, one of the founders of modern strategic planning, suggests that strategists place important

		Program	
		old	new
Market	old	market penetration	service development
	new	market development	diversification

Figure 3.2: Sample of an *Ansoff* Matrix

variables (like target market and product type) on a basic two dimensional grid when making strategic choices. This process suggests how strategy might be developed and options pursued. For example, a marketer concerned with growth options might create a very useful *Ansoff* matrix by focusing on client groups (old/new) and/or program types (old/new). The resulting options are displayed as shown in Figure 3.2.

This rather simple matrix is at the heart of marketing strategy. It outlines all possible growth strategies. Let's review these basic strategic choices.

Market penetration is the process of appealing to existing client groups with the same basic program. The marketer who adopts this strategy hopes to increase participation by encouraging existing participants to take part more often. This is a common strategy. Marketers know that, within the community of potential users, loyal customers are likely to be most responsive. Loyal participants are familiar with the benefits the program has to offer, with the demands of participation, with administrative requirements, and so on. They have already made the commitment to take part. The marketer simply appeals to this commitment in hopes of encouraging more regular participation. This strategy is appropriate when latent or surplus demand exists among current users. It may be ineffective if interest in a program is declining or if providers hope to reach new client groups with their efforts. In the former case, the status quo is simply inadequate, and interest will continue to falter. In the latter case, this strategy continues to ignore the wants of unserviced groups.

Service development appeals to existing client groups but with a variety of program

offerings. For example, a marketer might decide that participants in physical fitness programs would also enjoy related services ranging from bicycle maintenance to low-fat cooking classes. This strategy has many advantages. First and foremost, it helps build value for the participant. Ancillary programs like these help the client better enjoy the original program (fitness), while offering new insights, building new skills, and developing related talents. They also help combat boredom or "menu fatigue." Menu fatigue is the inevitable result if a provider offers too much of the same thing. Even the most loyal participants can become tired of the same old offerings.

Market development uses existing program offerings in hopes of appealing to new client groups. This strategy is typically used when existing target markets have been exhausted, while existing service offerings have potentially broad appeal. For example, pool operators who traditionally target children for open swims may decide to target adults with those same programs. To do so typically requires a few changes (e.g., the swims may be held in the late evening and be renamed "moonlight swims" and so on), but the basic product remains the same. This is a popular alternative to providers who are bound by the limitations of facilities like pools and single-use play areas (tennis or squash courts). Marketers for these facilities have very little flexibility in changing their basic product so they must focus on bringing in more and different user groups if they hope to increase their client base.

Diversification is the option most riddled with risk and uncertainty. This choice involves targeting new client groups with new programs. The provider has perhaps developed a new program offering that is so revolutionary and offers so much potential, a complete change seems appropriate. This is seen as an opportunity for diversification. Unfortunately, this option is not for the faint of heart. It purposely seeks new strategic ground so the marketer cannot use past experience as a guide. As a result of this uncertainty, few leisure marketers choose this option. It is simply too laden with risk.

Those who do use this option often do so as a last resort and hedge their bets by simultaneously retaining more tried and true offerings. These provide a fall-back position should the new strategy fail. For example, a fitness club chain may become involved in an "active wear" clothing line or the sale of vitamin supplements, because such ventures are seen to have tremendous growth potential. It is unlikely, however, that the chain would abandon their original fitness orientation in doing so.

The Role of Positioning

Whatever approach is adopted by a leisure provider, that provider must then consider the challenge of *positioning*. A market position is "the place the [service] occupies in consumers' minds relative to competitors" (Kotler et al., 1988, p. 40). Positioning refers to a provider's effort to establish a clear, unambiguous location in the mind of the client. A provider's position often determines the fate of any given marketing initiative (Ries & Trout, 1986). If this position is ambiguous, potential clients will have no compelling reason to select that provider. Why would potential participants choose a leisure provider that seems to have no clear identity? A badly chosen position is just as counterproductive as one that is ambiguous. Why would participants seeking high-quality programs frequent a facility they believe offers poor-quality alternatives?

Think of the client's mind as a complex arrangement of ladders. Each ladder has many rungs. On any given issue (or product at-

tribute) the client's favorite provider occupies the top rung while the least favorite provider occupies the bottom rung. Consider, too, that there may be several ladders clustered together to form a sort of pyramid. Each ladder represents an attribute that is valued by the target market. Important attributes will be placed higher than less valued attributes, but all contribute to an overall assessment of the marketplace.

Clients will place a provider on a rung depending upon how well they think the provider performs on that attribute. If they value price and the provider offers the lowest price, they will probably place that provider on the top rung of the "price ladder." If they value convenience but they believe other providers provide more convenient programs, that provider will be placed on a lower rung of the "convenience ladder." In this way, each provider's overall position is determined. This position establishes the overall appeal of a program or provider in the mind of potential clients.

Marketers have traditionally responded to the challenge of positioning through communication. They have focused almost exclusively on positioning their products through advertising and promotion. "This reflects the widespread use of advertising in packaged goods marketing to create images . . . so as to give them a special distinction in the consumer's mind. This approach is sometimes known as copy positioning" (Lovelock, 1991, p. 110). Lovelock goes on to encourage service marketers to consider positioning as more than simply imagery generated through creative communication. He suggests that market position is a function of price, availability, and performance, as well as promotion. Image matters little if the service is inferior. Indeed, copy positioning is only likely to be important when the client knows nothing of the product or when "competing services are perceived as being identical on performance, price and availability" (Lovelock, p. 111).

Positioning requires a thoughtful, integrated strategy including issues like service quality, pricing, and distribution. These are best integrated within a larger positioning strategy. The nature of this strategy flows naturally from an opportunity assessment. If the assessment makes it clear that your role is one of providing low-cost leisure opportunities, that your clients want and expect such alternatives, and that no one else in the marketplace is willing to provide similar program options, then your positioning strategy becomes straightforward. You will likely focus on the provision of low-cost programs.

This notion of positioning may be applied at many levels in the organization. The whole agency may adopt a given position, while different programs or facilities can adopt different but complementary positions. For example, a leisure provider may position the entire agency as a comprehensive program provider, but a given pool facility may focus on general swims in its positioning efforts. Another pool may focus on instruction and lifeguard training. Though the two pools have positioned themselves as single-purpose facilities, together they support the comprehensive position adopted by the umbrella agency.

Positioning Strategy

Positioning strategy should answer the following three basic questions (Lovelock, 1991, p. 225):

1. What do we plan to offer?

2. What are its distinguishing characteristics?

3. To whom will we direct this service?

There are several positioning strategies that a leisure provider might pursue. The first is based on *attributes*. The provider focuses on service characteristics thought to be valued by the client. Some leisure providers (e.g., white water rafting companies, bungee jumping operations, etc.) focus on adventure, while others focus on relaxation (e.g., spas, cruises, etc.) The position they seek influences the programs they offer and the training and

appearance of staff, as well as the nature of their advertisements. For example, staff on a white water rafting trip are expected to appear rather rough around the edges while spa staff might drape themselves in clinical garb. In both cases, staff are donning uniforms consistent with the attributes-based positioning strategy.

The second strategy is based on *price*. Clients tend to categorize providers in terms of the prices they charge because price tends to be the first (and often only) piece of information sought for a given service. As a result, the providers use the pricing tool to differentiate themselves from others. For leisure providers, this strategy typically focuses on low price levels. Unfortunately, this focus may suggest poor quality to many prospective clients. As a result, this strategy often requires additional promotional effort to assure the client of excellent quality in spite of the low price.

Many marketers attempt to adopt both attribute- and price-based positions. One popular advertisement once displayed a long list of facilities and programs. It asked readers if they would like to join a private club that offered tennis facilities, swim pools, golf courses, instructional programs, and so on. After providing this long list, the advertisement informed readers that the club was now accepting members for only pennies a day. This club was their very own municipal parks and recreation department. The reader was then encouraged to join the club. This advertisement was using both an attributes- and a price-based positioning strategy.

The third positioning strategy is that of making *comparisons to competitors*. As Ries and Trout (1986) suggest, for every attribute the market leader provides, other people will value the opposite attributes. As a result, these positioning strategies focus on what the provider doesn't offer as much as what it does offer. Remember when the soft drink 7-Up worked so hard to be called "The Uncola?" This was an effort to appeal to those who failed to appreciate the leaders' (the colas') strengths. This was a truly inspired strategy. It turned weakness into strength and created virtual partners of rivals. Not being a cola was deemed an asset, and each time the colas advertised, which was constantly, they were reminding 7-Up drinkers that they longed for something else . . . the uncola.

The fourth strategy is based on *product class*. This strategy is similar to that of making comparisons to competitors, but it does so on a much broader scale. One product is not compared directly to another product. Instead, providers try to position themselves as the alternative to an entire set of options or products. Bus companies advertise that they are preferable to commuting by private car. Tropical resorts position themselves as being preferable to winter winds and snow. Leisure providers offer themselves up as a healthy alternative to the couch and a bag of chips. This technique is often used by umbrella organizations to promote its members. For example, state or provincial governments use promotion to position their regions as preferable alternatives to other tourist locations. In these cases, the individual providers in these respective regions must still position themselves in terms of their own competition.

A fifth strategy is built around the *user*. Sub-groups have interests and priorities that are particular to those groups. Providers may position themselves so that these groups identify with the provider's efforts. For example, with its "Just Do It" advertising campaign, Nike positioned itself as a product for the active individual. When participants take part in physical activity, they are likely to think of Nike's encouragement and perhaps purchase Nike products accordingly.

A final strategy focuses on *use-related* variables. Use-related variables refer to the way a product is consumed. Restaurant owners know that patrons are more likely to eat out on special occasions, so the hospitality industry often focuses its efforts on reminding clients to celebrate. Restaurateurs offer free birthday cakes, balloons, special rooms for large groups, and so on. All their efforts are intended to create a destination for special events, a place for celebration.

Like the municipal recreation department advertisement described above, providers can adopt several strategies at the same time. When doing so, Ries and Trout (1986) offer a few words of advice. First, they suggest that

marketing is a battle of perceptions. The actual quality of a program matters little if potential clients are uncertain or ignorant of this quality.

Second, they suggest that copy positioning efforts, in particular, are most successful when providers associate their services with a word that is already valued by clients. Can you name the automobile manufacturer that has positioned itself to stand for "safety" (Volvo) or the toothpaste brand that stands for "cavity protection" (Crest)? These companies are relentless in their efforts to associate their products with words already important to our collective psyche.

Third, the positioning strategy you adopt is typically determined by the position or rung you occupy on clients' cognitive ladders. You cannot pretend that yours are premium offerings when your clients know they are not. Recently an airline used promotional copy to claim that it was paramount in its industry, yet published reports consistently assessed its service levels as being below average. Their flights were often late, they were losing luggage faster than others in the industry, and their customer service ratings were lackluster. No one believed their claims as they tried to position themselves at the top of the airline ladder. Ries and Trout (1986) advise that it's better to acknowledge your position and work from there. Like 7-Up, it's to your advantage to turn weakness into strength. If your agency is positioned second best, then promise to try harder. If your programs are more crowded than your competitors', tell your clients about the friends they will make. If your fitness class offers a heart-pounding workout, tell clients they'll scream for mercy and love the class.

Finally, according to Ries and Trout (1986), positioning strategy is determined by the market leader. You cannot compete for a position that a superior provider already occupies. It is rarely wise to compete head-to-head with someone who is viewed as superior to you. When faced with this condition, it is best to adopt what is called a *contrary position*. Again, like 7-Up, you must stand for something the other provider does not offer. If the other provider offers inexpensive classes, then your agency might focus instead on improved service quality. If the other provider is known for program variety, then you might focus on program depth. Where the competitor might offer many introductory classes, you might provide in-depth instruction in selected programs. Again, contrary positions appeal to prospective clients who either do not value or appreciate the qualities offered by the market leader.

Perceptual Mapping

Strategic planning requires that the marketer adopt a position in the marketplace. This process is enhanced when providers have some idea of the position they now occupy in the minds of their clients. This position is typically determined through *perceptual mapping*. Perceptual mapping plots program and agency location in terms of important attributes and relative to other providers. It's a very simple process. Marketers simply choose attributes thought to be important to their target market (two attributes are typically chosen) and then place these attributes on a two-dimensional grid. This grid creates four possible quadrants, each indicating a possible

position they might occupy in the mind of a client. Marketers then compare their own position to that of their competitors on the grid.

An example might help make this concept more straightforward. Let's assume that a volunteer neighborhood association board decides to expand the services now offered by the board. Board members hope to offer minor sports in a local park on a year-round basis but know that many other providers offer similar services on a community-wide basis. Will they be able to gain the support they need to expand their program? Perceptual mapping might help establish their relative place among other providers. They might determine through surveys and group discussions that the two attributes most valued by parents in the neighborhood are quality of play fields/facilities and location/convenience. As portrayed in Figure 3.3, the association park is well positioned in terms of location because it controls a playing field in the middle of the neighborhood. The quality and location of the site are also superior to fields maintained by nearby community groups.

However, the association falls behind several city and minor league-operated fields of quality. The association has several choices and

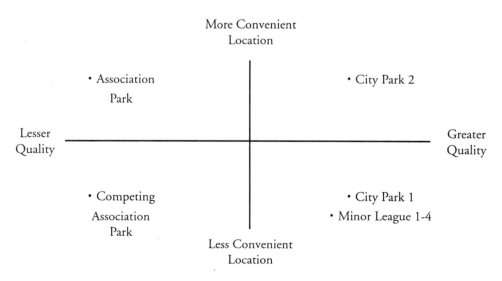

Figure 3.3: Positioning Map of Quality vs. Location

this perceptual map makes these choices very clear. It can choose to improve its own facilities or focus on the strengths of its own site. For this group, the latter choice seems strategically advantageous and financially less expensive. The strength of the association's seemingly inferior site is its location. How might this be exploited? Its advertisements might play on nostalgia ("Remember the good old days when you could play baseball in your own backyard? Those days are back. . . ."), convenience ("Why travel across town when you could stay at home and play with us?"), or even the flaws in the existing facilities ("It's easier to get a home run on our ball fields!").

This very simple perceptual map is a very useful planning tool. However, the quality of the map (and the plan) is a function of the accuracy with which your position has been determined. Ongoing effort must be devoted to establishing the place you occupy in the minds of your clients. This is quite a challenge because your position will invariably change over time. It is created though personal encounters with the agency, word of mouth and impersonal communication like advertising. As these variables change so too will your position.

The Dynamics of Repositioning

No discussion of positioning would be complete without reference to *repositioning*. Repositioning is a process of changing your existing position (Lovelock, 1991) when it is deemed to be inadequate or inaccurate. Perhaps there has been a shift in direction and your position must be changed accordingly. For example, many smaller park and recreation agencies have changed the way they serve their communities over the years. They may have started out as direct providers of services, but as demand increased they often reverted to the role of program facilitator. In the facilitator role, they focus more on helping others, such as community groups and associations, offer programs and less on direct program provision.

This role requires fewer resources from a single provider but can ensure that a wide variety of programs and services are offered. This is quite a change in direction, and when it takes place, repositioning is necessary.

Another common problem leading to repositioning is that of client confusion. For decades municipal park and recreation departments were viewed as the public providers of activities leading to a productive, healthy lifestyle. Other public providers are now becoming involved in these same activities. Ries's and Trout's (1993) observation that "over time a category will divide and become two or more categories" (p. 56) certainly applies in the field of recreation. Libraries are now providers of "entertainment" for example. They plan puppet shows, story telling, and even costume parties to encourage participation among young people. In many ways a public library now resembles a community center. Law enforcement agencies are now keenly interested in recreation as a way of appealing to at-risk youth. Church groups too have become very interested in promoting family recreational activities.

This trend is certainly not restricted to the public and not-for-profit sectors. As suggested in chapter 2, private sector providers are also offering a wide variety of leisure-based programs. Bookstores arrange public readings, discussion groups, and how-to sessions. Outdoor stores organize paddling days and camping trips. Building supply chains offer workshops and seminars on everything from improving your lawn to building a deck in the back yard. These organizations aggressively promote the opportunities they provide. As a result, the public may become confused over the role and the position of the park and recreation department. Repositioning may become necessary.

There are several ways to reposition an agency. The marketer may offer new programs, discontinue existing efforts, or even target new client groups. The marketer may also adopt a new strategy, perhaps move from a price-based strategy to one focussing more clearly on service attributes. Whatever the strategy, marketers cannot ignore the positions they and their competitors now hold in the minds of clients. It is best to establish the new position by remembering the past but building on the future, to focus on your own unique capacities and strengths. These existing qualities will help carry your agency to the new, more desirable position.

Learning from Others

The leisure marketer need not develop strategy from scratch. Leisure providers may seek insights from any number of service providers. For example, hospitals may discover that they can learn from hotels or that swimming pool operators can learn from movie theatres. Marketers may look to any source that faces similar conditions and priorities to their own (Lovelock, 1996). The challenge is to think creatively as to where these sources might be found. Although there is considerable temptation to look to others in the same industry for insight, the most innovative and helpful ideas may come from unusual sources.

An example might help make this point. An airline was unhappy with the amount of time it was taking to fuel its planes. Additional minutes on the ground created expensive delays, and management wanted to speed the process. Logically, they looked to other airlines for insight. To their disappointment, they found that other airlines were experiencing the same problem. They had to break out of their own industry's policies and procedures for real insight. They finally looked to the pit-stop procedures in the auto racing industry for a solution to their problem. Pit crews had developed procedures to virtually blast fuel into their cars during pit stops that lasted only seconds. The airline adopted and adapted this technology to improve their own procedures. They now exceed their own industry standards for fuel stops by several minutes.

The trick is to find other and perhaps non-traditional providers who might offer meaningful insight. The best way to begin this search is to describe your own service in terms

of its fundamental characteristics. You might define your services in terms of

- the nature of the service act (tangible vs. intangible)

- the level of contact between the producer and the client,

- the object of the service,

- the use of goods to enhance the exchange, and

- the nature of the relationship (member vs. no formal relationship) between the client and the provider (Lovelock, 1996; Vandermerwe & Chadwick, 1991).

You can then search for other providers who share these same basic characteristics. Leisure counselors, who offer very intangible services, might look to providers like insurance professionals for insight. Both face the daunting task of rendering their services tangible. Painting classes, where level of client contact is high, can improve with insights from lawyers or medical professionals. The staff of both must project an image of caring, knowledgeable professionalism if they hope to succeed. They must be willing and able to respond to the unique desires and requirements of each client, and they must do so quickly and efficiently.

Services like skate sharpening or racquet stringing focus on an object, while fitness classes or swim classes focus on an individual. This suggests that a fitness class planner might learn from hair salons or health spas because all of them work with the client's own body. Further, a food concession at a recreation facility serves the client through the provision of goods. It uses "things" to help create its service. Concession operators can look to others who share this approach as they serve their clients. The food concession may learn from movie theatres or grocery stores as much as from another food concession.

Main Points

· Strategy evolves from the insights gathered during the opportunity assessment. It establishes who gets what.

· Three competitive strategies are possible: cost leadership (compete through cost), differentiation (being unique), or focus (select a group or groups of potential participants and deliver programs to them to the exclusion of others).

· Strategic thinking might be enhanced through use of portfolio analysis and application of the ANSOFF matrix.

· The marketer must establish a clear, unambiguous position in the mind of the consumer. This is done by promoting tangible variables like service attributes or price, by comparing services to those of other providers, or by focusing on particular user groups or product classes.

· Perceptual mapping helps marketers understand the position they occupy in relation to other providers. Repositioning activities may be necessary if the current position proves unsatisfactory.

· Leisure providers can look to many other service providers for useful insights regarding marketing strategy.

Case Study

A municipal park and recreation director has discovered that her agency has developed a reputation for being "second-best" in the community. Though citizens widely congratulate the agency for offering inexpensive leisure programs, all but the very poorest members of the community avoid public leisure programs, preferring instead to frequent privately offered programs.

The director is troubled by this discovery for two reasons. First, she believes that perceptions among community members are simply incorrect. Her agency offers some of the very finest programs in the area. Citizens are (incorrectly) assuming that the private sector is able to offer better quality than the public sector. Community members are paying premium fee levels for private offerings while missing out on quality publicly provided programs.

Second, the director is astute enough to know that she will need widespread community support each year she returns to city council for funds to support her many programs. She fears that the political will to support her programs may falter unless she can show clearly that the entire community benefits from her agency's efforts. She simply must change attitudes toward her agency and her programs.

· What is the most pressing perceptual issue the director faces?

· How might she change community members' views of her agency?

References

Brademas, D., & Readnour, J. (1989). Status of fees and charges in public leisure service agencies. *Journal of Park and Recreation Administration, 7*(4), 42-55.

Collis, D.J., & Montgomery C.A. (1999). Competing on resources: Strategy in the 1990s. In *Harvard Business Review on Corporate Strategy* (pp. 33-62). Boston: Harvard Business School Press.

Fifield, P. (1998). *Marketing strategy* (2nd ed.). Oxford: Butterworth Heinemann.

Gitlow, H.S., & Gitlow, S.J. (1994). *Total quality management in action.* Englewood Cliffs, NJ: Prentice-Hall.

Grant, R.M. (1998). *Contemporary strategy analysis* (3rd ed.). Oxford: Blackwell Publishers Ltd.

Kotler, P., McDougall, G., & Armstrong, G. (1988). *Marketing: Canadian edition.* Englewood Cliffs, NJ: Prentice-Hall.

Lovelock, C.H. (1991). Creating and delivering services. In C.H. Lovelock (Ed.), *Services marketing* (2nd ed.) (pp. 223-235). Toronto: Prentice-Hall.

Lovelock, C.H. (1996). *Services marketing* (3rd edition). Toronto: Prentice-Hall.

Porter, M.E. (1985). *Competitive advantage: Creating and sustaining superior performance.* New York: The Free Press.

Ries, A., & Trout, J. (1986). *Positioning: The battle for your mind.* New York: Warner Books.

Reis, A. & Trout, J. (1993). *The 22 Immutable Laws of Marketing.* New York: HarperCollins Books.

Stevenson, L.N., Shlesinger, J.C., & Pearce, M.R. (1999). *Power retailing.* Toronto: McGraw-Hill Ryerson.

Vandermerwe, S., & Chadwick, M. (1991). The internationalization of service. In C.H. Lovelock (Ed.), *Services marketing* (2nd ed.) (pp. 48-58). Toronto: Prentice-Hall.

S. Czekus

4

Develop a Service Strategy

Once target markets have been identified, agency capabilities have been assessed (in terms of the competition and the desires of the target groups), and conditions that exist within the industry and the general environment have been established, the next challenge is to use this information to create a blueprint for action. This blueprint is often called a *service strategy*. A service strategy establishes how the provider plans to give value to the client (Berry, 1995). In developing a strategy, "leaders must define correctly that which makes the service compelling. They must set in motion and sustain a vision of service excellence" (Berry, p. 62).

The service strategy fulfills two very important roles. The first is a call for action. It makes clear the goals that all are pursuing. This call provides an emotional basis for action. The second role is that of a road map. It guides and directs efforts to serve the client. The importance of such a blueprint cannot be overstated. Decision makers exist in a hectic world of too many decisions and too little time. The average manager moves from decision to decision every few minutes. How can we ensure that each decision contributes to the same fundamental goals? How can we ensure that these goals are even worth pursuing? A service strategy is the key.

Front-line staff members have even less time to ponder the solutions to problems they face. They are confronted with new clients almost on a minute-by-minute basis. Every new encounter presents its own challenges. How can they possibly hope to make decisions that contribute to the same goals, and move the organization in the same, useful direction? Again, a service strategy is the key. Strategy is needed to guide these thousands of decisions.

Value: The Building Block of a Service Strategy

Recall that one goal of service delivery is differentiation. If you are to build interest among potential clients, your service offering must be different in some way from that of competitors. It must be different in some important way; in a way that offers value to the client and the provider. As a result, discussion around service delivery strategies typically focuses on the notion of *value*.

Strategy is built upon value, value for the client, and value for the provider. Think of any delivery system as a chain. It is made up of links that, when strung together, provide value to the client and the provider. As with any chain, links will vary in strength. The chain may fail anywhere along its length as a result of weak links. It will certainly fail if it offers inadequate value to the client or poor return to the service provider. The goal of strategic planning is to remove sources of weakness along the chain. It becomes important, therefore, to understand how value is created, then to build strategy around the value creation process.

Creating Value

The marketer typically focuses on two types of value. The first *is value for the client.* This type of value "is based on the assumption that delivering what customers value is at the center of the company's corporate strategy. Value creation is the ultimate customer strategy, because it draws on the multiple perspectives of all the company's functional areas and brings them together to work toward the common goal of creating and delivering value to customers" (Band, 1991, p. 21).

The second type of value focuses on the provider. It is the notion of *competitive value.* Competitive value relates to competitive advantage. How well can the service compete against counter offerings provided by competitors? Competitive value establishes the relative costs and benefits of offering a given program and service. The goal is one of establishing a niche in the marketplace that is defensible against competitive forces. Several steps may be taken to assure the competitive value of any given program or service. These steps are outlined later in the chapter.

Value for the Client

Value is a function of both benefits and costs. It is typically defined as the perceived benefit generated by a given transaction, moderated by the perceived costs incurred to enjoy that benefit (Monroe & Petroshius, 1981). Thus increased benefit or reduced costs can both enhance value levels. The service provider offers two types of benefits. The first is *product*-based. It represents the benefits the product itself offers the client. Clients seek benefits from leisure participation, ranging from spiritual enlightenment to physical fitness. Product-based benefits help fulfill those basic desires.

The second type of benefit that should gain the marketer's attention is *service*-based. Service-based benefits arise from the way in which the service is offered to the client. A service provider's efforts to improve service delivery may provide considerable benefit to the client. They, too, add to the value of a service. They do so by increasing benefits and reducing convenience-related costs. It is the service-based benefit that receives much of the attention in this chapter.

Treacy and Wiersema (1995) have combined the notions of product- and service-based benefits to generate several types of value the service provider might offer. They are:

> *Operational excellence*—Operational excellence refers to low-cost, reliable service delivery with products that are easy to use.
> *Product leadership*—Clients want to know that the services and programs you offer are of good quality, employ the latest insights, and adopt the most advanced approaches.
> *Customer intimacy*—As Lovelock (1991) reminds us, products provide benefits but services provide solutions. Clients seek solutions, to their own unique problems, from service providers. Finding and providing these solutions is only possible if the provider develops a relationship with individual clients.

Determinants of Service Quality

It is to marketers' advantage to discover what clients like and dislike so that staff can provide the former while avoiding the latter. Though specific likes and dislikes of various client groups can only be determined through market research, the marketing literature suggests that several generalizations are possible. In a series of studies Zeithaml,

Parasuraman, and Berry (1990) sought to discover how clients evaluate service quality. They considered what the client looked for when attempting to evaluate the quality of a given service. Their findings suggest that clients look for many things from service encounters, however, five in particular seem to stand out. Zeithaml and her colleagues call these the determinants of service quality and suggest they form the basis of any effort to provide benefits to clients.

Tangibility—Tangibility refers to the appearance of physical facilities, equipment, personnel, and even communication materials (Zeithaml et al., 1990). Given that services are themselves intangible, clients will often look to objects (called *tangible cues*) in the service setting to establish the quality of the program or provider. These cues will be used to establish the relative quality of a service provider. Cues like paint peeling from the walls, dirty staff uniforms, or even the appearance of other clients can be used as hints of poor service. It matters little that none of these variables may actually impact directly on service levels. The client will use them to judge the quality of the provider so they must not escape the attention of the marketer.

Reliability—Does the provider offer the promised service dependably and accurately over time? Leisure providers make many implicit promises to their clients. They promise that programs will begin on time. They promise that client concerns will be handled fairly and quickly. Does the provider follow up on these promises? Are they fulfilled with each and every encounter? This consistency is the essence of reliability. Clients crave predictability and quickly notice failures to provide it.

Empathy—Empathy is caring, individualized attention offered by staff to clients. The need for empathy can

vary dramatically from context to context. It is unlikely a spectator at a sporting event would often require much empathy from grounds keepers. However, empathy is highly prized in instructional programs where the client may need ongoing assistance and understanding.

Responsiveness—Responsiveness represents staff willingness to provide prompt attention. Clients simply wish for staff to be willing to help out and to assist where necessary. Though all clients prefer responsive staff members, the desire for responsiveness typically rises with situational urgency. A parent who has lost a child in a facility will experience greater urgency than another who simply wishes a refund. A client who wishes a refund will experience greater urgency than another who is simply asking for directions. Though all will place different demands on the staff member, all will be seeking responsiveness that matches the demands of the situation.

Assurance—Clients want staff to be knowledgeable and courteous in a way that inspires both trust and confidence. Again, the importance of assurance will vary with urgency. Patrons at a swimming pool will have only fleeting interest in the expertise of lifeguards on duty until they require that expertise. The demand for assurance is often low until it is called upon. Many demands for assurance are procedural in nature. Clients seeking a refund will hope that staff can complete the required steps quickly and efficiently. Hikers looking for a trail will hope that park staff can offer accurate and helpful directions. Program participants hope that those completing registration forms will do so without error.

As suggested, the relative importance of each determinant may change from setting to setting. Those using sport facilities like playing fields or arenas may place considerable value on tangible elements. Conversely, others enrolled in art classes may value empathy far more than tangibles (Crompton & MacKay, 1989). The same individual may even focus on different determinants over time. For example, clients who typically value empathy may focus more on responsiveness on days when they are running late or, focus more on assurance when they have questions of personal concern.

Reducing Costs to Enhance Value

Recall that value can be enhanced if perceived costs are reduced. As discussed in chapter 9, costs represent more than monetary expenses. Costs reduce either the desire or capacity to participate. Band (1991) tells us, for example, that clients become discouraged by what he calls a "defensive attitude." Indicators of a defensive attitude are:

- cumbersome or complex complaint procedures,

- a slow and grudging approach to refunds and repairs,

- numerous exceptions in warranty policies,

- an adversarial approach to dealing with customer complaints, and

- delays in making necessary changes in products or services (Band, 1991, p. 28).

Reducing these defensive indicators can reduce costs to the client, thereby improving value. Though these issues are addressed directly in chapters 9 and 10, a few comments are appropriate here because they relate directly to the creation of value. Defensive measures like those listed by Band often represent standard operating procedures. Many providers seem more willing to introduce them to their own procedures than to remove them. There is perhaps a natural hesitation to offer unlimited refunds or warranties, to deal freely with

"complainers," or to respond to complaints with program changes. They are perhaps fearful that clients will take advantage of them. These are often the reasons given for becoming defensive, but they seem to fail the test of value creation.

Remember that such measures, though reassuring to the provider, steal value from the client. Sewell and Brown (1998) offer some useful advice on this issue. They recognize that some clients will gladly take advantage of a provider. They acknowledge that, as a result, providers can become cynical over time. They also advise, however, that they must fight against such cynicism (as well as the defensive posture cynicism creates) because:

> 99 percent of the people are just as honest as they can be . . . if we start trying to figure out who's lying to us, invariably we'll guess wrong and alienate a good customer. We're far better off assuming that if a customer tells us he has a problem he really does have a problem. (Sewell & Brown, p. 58)

Whatever your views on the accuracy of Sewell's assessment, his views are shared by other top service providers. These providers assume that the vast majority of clients are treating service providers in a fair, honest manner. As a result, they refuse to treat these clients with suspicion and a defensive attitude. A more friendly approach seems to be to remove many unwanted costs for the client thereby increasing value.

The perspective taken here is one of maximizing value. Successful marketing seems inextricably tied to providing "customer driven, superior value" (Stevenson, Shlesinger, & Pearce, 1999). Indeed, it seems that the strategies used by many of the most successful service providers in North America are based on value maximization. To this point the text has focussed on value maximization for the client. The provider also needs to receive value from a given encounter. The provider too must be able to discover value if success is to be assured. The planning literature refers to this as creating *competitive value*.

Competitive Value: Value for the Provider

The second type of value that is important to strategy is *competitive value*. Competitive value refers to a service or program's capacity to create competitive advantage in the marketplace. Though a common topic among private sector providers, the issue of competitive advantage has proven problematic for public leisure providers. When O'Sullivan (1991) discussed the notion of competing for market share, McLean and Johnson (1993) admonished her. They suggested that the role of the public sector was not to compete but to complement. They, and others, believe that public leisure providers should back away gracefully from any program that generates interest from private operators.

The logic behind this view is straightforward. The public sector is intended to serve the larger community and is funded by that community. As a result, it operates outside the capitalist sphere. It cannot serve by competing with its own community members. However, this characterization seems to ignore the inherently competitive nature of the larger community. Many powerful forces conspire against public providers' efforts to serve the community. Public exercise programs compete with sedentary life-styles. Programs for at-risk youth compete with the lure of the street gangs. There are few, if any, instances in which leisure providers are not competing with someone or something for the attention of potential participants. All leisure marketers must, in some way, compete, and their strategies must reflect this. As a result, competitive value is an issue that must be addressed by all leisure providers.

Marketers typically address competitive value by asking the following five questions about resources, services, or programs (Collis & Montgomery, 1999):

1. inimitability—is the service easily copied?

2. demand durability—can the service sustain competitive advantage over time?

3. appropriability—who captures the proceeds the service generates?

4. substitutability—can other services replace this one?

5. competitive superiority—is the service really better than those offered by others?

These terms may sound like hopeless jargon, but they are at the heart of competitive value. Consider each in turn.

Inimitability: Is the service easily copied?

Inimitability relates to the unique nature of a service. Logically, if a service is unique, it will offer more competitive advantage than a second program that is easily copied. There seem to be four tests of "inimitability." The first is *physical uniqueness*. This typically applies to a product and its ability to be copied. Experience tells us that few, if any, products and virtually no services fall into this category (Chakrapani, 1998). All are easily copied. This is the bad news. In fact, many private sector companies no longer even try to make their products unique. Their products are virtually identical to those of their competitors. Their products are made in the same factories by the same people using the same tools, machines, and materials. Their products differ only in the advertising program that promotes them. A few of the very large sportswear companies fall into this category. They spend millions of dollars each year creating an image around an often mundane product hoping to render it unique. Though the long-term viability of this seemingly dubious approach is in question, it can be successful in the short term.

Another way to enhance uniqueness is to render mundane programs unique by surrounding those programs with excellent service quality. This approach suggests that though the program is common, the way in which it is delivered can be uncommon. This approach is gaining growing acceptance in the service industry. The heavy advertising of the approach noted above can be incredibly expensive and focuses on perception rather than value. Conversely, private sector firms have found that an emphasis on service quality costs only about three percent of sales revenue (Band, 1991) and actually helps create value. As a result, programmers hoping to create unique services are encouraged to do so by supporting existing programs in ever new and unique ways.

The second test of inimitability is *path dependence*. It takes many steps to create a leisure program. Can other providers duplicate these steps with ease or only with great difficulty? If it is difficult to recreate this production path, then it is difficult to recreate the program itself. In this way, programs can become very difficult to copy. This may well be the case for many localized leisure programs. Many leisure providers, and particularly those in smaller communities, have developed extensive neighborhood-based networks of volunteers and programs. These networks are uniquely suited to discover and respond with surprising speed to local priorities. They are often inextricably linked to local power structures so they are able to gain access to facilities and resources not available to outside organizations. They are knowledgeable of local expertise that they can draw upon as needed. These networks can be remarkably responsive to the demands of the neighborhood. It takes years of ongoing effort to duplicate this type of organization, so it is high on the inimitability scale. It is unlikely that other providers could easily copy such extensive delivery networks.

A third test of inimitability is *causal ambiguity*. Can competitors actually establish what it takes to make the service successful? We all know of community centers that are more popular than their competitors. They seem to be more fun, and visitors seem to relax the moment they enter them. It is reasonably

simple to copy their pool facilities, their lobbies, their activity spaces, but how can that sense of fun and belonging be duplicated? It is this undefinable component to many services that adds to both their value and their unique nature. Competitors may be hard pressed to discover the secret formula to their success.

The fourth test of inimitability is one of *economic deterrence*. It may be a straightforward process to duplicate a service, but due to limited economic return potential, other providers choose not to do so. This is often the case for public sector programs. Their fee levels are typically low and their client groups often disadvantaged. In other words, there is little existing profit, and it is unlikely that profit potential will increase in future. Private sector competitors are unlikely to target such programs in their own competitive strategies so the programs remain free from direct competition. Other informal competitors may also find it difficult to compete with the public sector. Though street gangs have many resources to draw upon, they cannot provide their members with a community center or a swimming pool. As a result, due to economic factors, public sector providers are often ideally positioned between informal and private sector competitors.

Together, these tests offer a measure of inimitability. They suggest the degree to which a program is unique within a community. Strategy is typically developed around strength, and unique programs offer such strength. Remember, that no program is truly unique. The marketer does not look for perfection. This is a relative assessment at best. There are common themes in all programs, but each may possess unique elements, elements that discourage participant defection. (Defection refers to abandonment of the program by existing participants.) The marketer's task is to discover these elements and build strategy around them. If these elements are not present, the marketer should look elsewhere for strategic advantage.

Demand Durability: Can the service sustain its competitive advantage over time?

Demand durability relates to a program's appeal over time. Will a popular program be equally popular a year from now or even in a few months? The notion of the product life cycle suggests to us that no program will be popular indefinitely. Interest in a program or service will ebb and flow as it does in all things. Further, durability will vary from one program to the next, from one period to the next, and from one group to the next. Programs categorized as fads gain popularity very quickly then drop off just as quickly. Dance crazes can come and go within weeks. Teens and preteens often tire of a program much faster than their older counterparts do. It is difficult to build strategy on the basis of programs with little demand durability.

Marketers are keenly aware that rapid advances in anything technological often change demand dramatically. Technology often hastens the introduction and even decline of programs. The popularity of downhill skiing fell dramatically among teens with the introduction of snow boards. Roller skating programs were made obsolete with the development of in-line skates. Touring bicycle sales dropped precipitously with the introduction of mountain bikes. Interest in bike-touring programs was replaced virtually overnight with trail-riding workshops and events. The trick is to understand the forces that either inhibit or enhance demand and plan strategy accordingly.

Appropriability: Who captures the proceeds generated by the service?

Appropriability refers to the direction in which the profits from a given service flow. There are any number of partners, intermediaries, or even clients who may wish to share in the proceeds of any given initiative. A program may require facility rental, the hiring of instructors, contracting of custodial staff, and

so on. These incidental costs may render a seemingly excellent program unprofitable once all the bills are paid.

Appropriability is not as simple an issue as it may first appear. Though most private organizations hesitate to bargain away profits in order to offer the service, they may, on occasion, decide that they are willing to "lose" resources so that important partners will benefit. This is the basis upon which philanthropy operates. Many businesses offer programs that benefit charities. For example, several national chains donate proceeds from selected programs to local, regional, and national charities and they lose profits while doing so. Appropriability is still served because these organizations are making a conscious decision to help a deserving partner. Each must decide whether these strategies are viable given their competitive context.

For the public sector provider, it may appear inappropriate to be concerned with profit when service to the community represents a more important issue. Public sector programming decisions is guided by more than the profit motive. If profitability becomes the standard for success, then the public sector has abandoned its service ethic in favor of pure capitalism. As a result, some argue that appropriability is simply irrelevant to the public sector provider.

Appropriability, however, deserves at least some attention from public sector providers. Appropriability suggests that providers must answer the question "who benefits" from any strategic initiative. This is a question that is equally relevant for the public and not-for-profit sectors. Public sector agencies are consistently deciding if they are willing to absorb operating costs to benefit participants. They too may be willing to "lose" profits by funneling proceeds to worthy or needy partners and clients.

Substitutability: Can other services replace this one?

Substitutability refers to a service's potential to be replaced. History is strewn with the debris of unsuccessful providers who erroneously believed that their services could not be replaced. Railroad barons thought trains could not be replaced by other forms of transportation. Conventional watchmakers didn't foresee the coming dominance of digital watches. Corner grocery stores did not anticipate the growth of supermarkets. Each of these examples reflects how easily an existing approach or program, however dominant, can be overwhelmed by an alternative.

Strategists have always developed competitive strength by focusing on services they thought were irreplaceable. In the hospitality industry, for example, location was often thought to make a facility irreplaceable. The hotel with the best view literally held a place of power. No one else could gain that same spectacular view so the location was considered unique. Though this logic holds true to a degree, a single program component (like view) cannot carry an entire facility. Though the hotel with the best view may have one advantage, the rest of its service offerings may be infinitely substitutable. The beds, the food, the linens may all be copied with ease.

As a result, few strategists now rely on developing programs that are irreplaceable. Instead, they fully expect that their programs will be replaced. They gain strategic advantage by being the first to improve and replace their own offering. For example, when so-called "hi-tech" products are developed, the producer often creates three teams around the new product. The first team is concerned with that product as it now exists. Team members focus their attention on making it in a cost-efficient, user-friendly way. The second team immediately begins work on the second generation of that device. They look at what it could become, not what it is. The third team deals directly with the issue of substitutability. Its role is to render the device obsolete, in effect to substitute it with the company's own product. They do not wait for competitive forces to knock them from their place of advantage. They do it themselves, thereby maintaining that advantage.

Although few leisure providers have the resources to create multiple teams around single programming initiatives, they can all gather insight from this strategy. For example, no program should be considered in terms of

what it "is." Instead it should be viewed in terms of what it could be, in terms of what might be done to improve it. Any team assigned to the task of programming might be assigned three objectives.

The first objective is to develop a program that is as desirable as they can make it. The team's second objective is to improve that same program. If the program itself cannot be improved, perhaps procedures used to support the program can be enhanced. It's third objective might be to improve the program and support services to such a degree that they are no longer recognizable or even necessary. For example, a team might be assigned the task of establishing a coordinated registration system. Team members might begin with the traditional mail-in and tele-phone-based programs that dominate many agencies' registration efforts. They could coordinate these efforts to ensure that they work both efficiently and effectively. They might then seek to improve these efforts by increasing the number of payment options, the number of open hours, or even the methods of payments. Finally, they could seek to render these procedures obsolete by creating new procedures such as on-line registrations or on-site kiosks. These changes will eventually replace the slower mail or more limited telephone procedures.

Competitive Superiority: Is the service really better than those offered by others?

This final issue is one of *competitive superiority*. Collis and Montgomery (1999) suggest that one of the greatest mistakes planners make "when evaluating their compa-nies' resources is that they do not assess them relative to competitors. Core competence has too often become a 'feel good' exercise that no one fails" (p. 45). No one wants to admit that a favorite program or service is second best. This infers that it is second-rate, and providing second-rate programs is not the way to success or promotion. It is rare that a marketer will attend a management meeting claiming that her programs are clearly inferior to those of other providers.

Collis and Montgomery (1999) recommend that any effort to establish resource superiority should be a "harsh external assessment" of those things the provider does better than competitors and vice versa. Managers are probably the worst suited group to evaluate their own programs in terms of the competition. They simply have too much personal investment in the way the program currently operates. External evaluators are a much more appropriate group to make this assessment. Participant evaluators, for example, are probably familiar with several providers programs and can offer insights superior to those of any manager.

Those assessing resource superiority often operate at a level that is too abstract to be useful. For example, they might discuss superiority at the division level of operation: Our fitness programs are among the finest in the city (p. 45). Though this is a common enough claim, it may speak more to the naiveté of the claimant than the actual quality of the program. Superiority, like many good things, is best judged in terms of details. One agency's programs may be superior in terms of facility location, but inferior in terms of instructor quality.

The issue of abstraction can be addressed through *disaggregation*. Disaggregation is the process of becoming increasingly specific (Collis & Montgomery, 1999). Divisions may be broken down by departments. Departments may be broken down by facility. Facilities may be divided into program units. Programs may be discussed in terms of their specific attributes. The key is to make the assessment meaningful. In order to be meaningful, the level of discussion must address the fundamental question, "what makes this resource worthy of our clients' attention?" Once this is established, the secondary question of advantage can be asked—"What makes this resource superior to those offered by other providers?" Together, these questions will help determine the competitive value of any given resource. They will establish the importance of a program or service. Asking these many questions will help marketers estimate the value of a resource in terms of its capacity to serve the client while creating competitive advantage.

Establishing a Culture of Value

The term *culture* represents the many organizational norms and procedures that direct and influence employee actions and decisions on a day-to-day basis. The importance of culture is a common theme in the service quality literature. Culture guides the way in which employees treat each other and their clients. A culture based upon strict interpretation of rules and written policies will value regulations over responsiveness. A culture based on value provision is more likely to promote client interests over its own internal priorities.

Though culture emerges from a complex interaction between various organizational and interpersonal conditions (Schneider, 1988), two management strategies seem to aid in a culture based upon value. If the marketer can ensure that these strategies are implemented in a way that stresses value to the client, a value-based culture can emerge in any organization. These strategies focus on a *clear service vision* and the development of *service principles*.

The Service Vision

A service vision is a statement of how the provider plans to compete in the marketplace. This statement is concerned with how the service will be rendered "valuable" to the client. Vision statements are generally shared with both staff and customers so that all are aware of how the provider plans to "put the customer first."

"The power of the service vision is the guidance it offers . . . the stronger the vision—the greater its clarity and emotional buy-in, the thinner the company service policies and procedures manual" (Berry, 1995, p. 11). This emphasis on vision rather than rules when making programming decisions is now being popularized by a few leaders in the mail order industry with dramatic results. One primarily mail order supplier, tells its employees that they can be fired for only two reasons. The first is showing disrespect for a customer. The second is stealing from the company. Other than that they are free to serve the customer and ensure that every purchase is "completely satisfactory." They rely on this service vision, not rules; they use procedures not policies. As a result, staff are free to focus on value rather than worry about following policy.

Another provider Land's End, lists in its catalogues a few cardinal rules that guide their own vision of customer service. The rules are: "1. Make your merchandise as good as you can, 2. Always price it fairly, 3. Make it a snap to shop for 24 hours a day, and 4. Guarantee it. Period." These few rules provide explicit instruction to their staff and notification to their clients about the service they intend to provide. These types of service vision statements are now being copied throughout North America.

Service Principles

Service principles, which are consistent with the service vision, can then be established. These principles are critical because they guide all subsequent decision making. In establishing service principles the marketer is determining the following:

1. The business the provider is in.— Disney theme parks base their entire operation on a few guiding principles. Among these principles is one that indicates that the parks are intended to put on a show to entertain their guests. Everything else they do is based upon this type of basic principle. Staff uniforms are called costumes, their encounters with clients are heavily scripted, and the parks themselves are managed not as traditional parks but as large stage settings.

2. How good the provider wants to be at that business. —In the Disney example, their guiding principles also

indicate that the parks are about being safe, friendly, and efficient. These principles are intended to establish the level of care they provide their guests. Every decision is judged against these operating guidelines.

3. How the provider plans to go about fulfilling its mandate. —Disney's theme park guidelines also include words like courtesy, management support, cleanliness, under-promise/ over-deliver, product knowledge (interpreted as mission of agency), and training. Notice how these principles outline those things the corporation values as well as how to go about addressing these priorities. All programs, policies, procedures, and responsibility assignments are based on these principles.

The principle of "assertive friendliness" is of paramount importance to the Disney theme park operations. Assertive friendliness dictates that employees (the cast) will not wait to be asked. They will go out of their way to ensure that guests are enjoying their stay. If they notice a confused look or an unhappy child, they are encouraged to help out without being asked. This is a great example of a guiding principle that truly guides interactions between the cast and the client. It helps establish a positive mood in the workplace for staff and clients alike.

Any leisure provider would benefit from adopting a few guiding principles then judging success in terms of how well they are accomplished. Principles that might be considered in a leisure context include convenience, value, safety, opportunity, choice, satisfaction, and so on. In order to help staff remember these important guidelines, several providers now adopt principles that might be represented by some sort of meaningful acronym. For example, one coffee shop chain states its principles in terms of the acronym F.A.I.R. (family, achievement, integrity, respect). Their slogan is "always fresh, always f.a.i.r." (Tim Hortons, job application, 2000). These acronyms are useful because they are easy to commit to memory and to explain to both staff and clients.

These principles should be used to establish procedures for all manner of staff actions. In the Disney example provided above, the notion of assertive friendliness is used to guide recruitment procedures, hiring decisions, and even training and staff reward programs. Consider a typical interview in which a leisure provider is looking for summer staff members. If the provider is looking for potential staff who are actively friendly, then job interviews can watch for this tendency among applicants. Interviewers might ask candidates to tell them a funny story; perhaps to relate one of life's embarrassing moments. If the candidates enjoy telling the story, are outgoing and comfortable in this interaction, then they have fulfilled one of the basic criteria for employment. They will be at ease in their efforts to be assertively friendly.

Virtually any decision made by a service provider should be guided by these basic service principles. The marketer must use them as the ultimate litmus test for every decision and for every policy. What kinds of programs should be offered if the service principles focus on safety? How might training be carried out in order to fulfill the requirements of these principles? If the staff member is to "respect" the client, how should the client be greeted? What insights does this principle offer in terms of designing encounters between staff and clients? What steps should be taken if the client is unhappy? These are the questions that often dominate the professional life of the service provider. Each question demands that decisions be made and choices taken. These choices are too important to leave to chance or to decide one question at a time. Guiding principles must be developed to direct each and every decision, to solve each and every problem, to please each and every participant.

Main Points

· Service strategy is often built around the provision of value to both the client and the provider.

· Competitive value for the provider is enhanced when services that are not easily replaced by other providers can be offered reliably and profitably.

· Value for the client may be enhanced either by improving service levels or by reducing costs that clients would rather not bear.

· Clients seek varying degrees of empathy, reliability, assurance, responsiveness, and even tangible cues when they assess service offerings.

· Marketers are charged with creating a value orientation in their respective organizations.

· A value orientation arises from a clearly articulated service vision and the development of principles that guide and direct daily interactions with clients.

Case Study

A fitness studio owner is worried. Five years ago, he was the first entrepreneur in his community to open a facility devoted entirely to cardiovascular fitness. Business was all that he had hoped for in those early days. He simply had to open his doors and the studio filled. Weekends were particularly busy as his 20- to 35-year-old clients dropped by to workout. His goal was to create a very dynamic fitness facility that offered an intense workout format. He was proud of his motto, "We'll get you fit because we'll never let you sit." He trained his staff to keep the clients moving and even removed traditional chairs and couches from his facility.

Recently new studios have opened in the community, and his business has been declining. Last year he tried dropping prices and business again picked up but it didn't last. Competing clubs quickly matched his new low prices, and his customers again began to drift off. He now realizes that his new low prices have failed in two ways. First, they failed to rebuild his falling membership levels. They attracted price-sensitive users but they were soon lured away by other low prices across town. Second, they have cut deeply into his own profit margins. He had hoped that increased volume would make up for the lower prices but the higher volumes have failed to materialize.

This year he tried bringing in new equipment. This too worked for a few months, but competitors soon copied his efforts. He's worried that his clients will soon begin to drift off to other clubs again. He has to provide reasons for his clients to stay with his facility and not be lured away. If not, he may be forced to close the studio.

The owner recently attended a seminar in which he learned that competitive advantage can only be achieved through a clear and appropriate service strategy. He's begun to

think that his operation is more than simply a place to get in shape. It is also a place where clients seek peace of mind, friendship, and perhaps a bit of excitement. This realization has opened up tremendous possibilities for the club.

· What might the owner and staff do to expand their existing (and rather limited) service strategy?

· What unified vision might guide his deliberations and actions?

· How might he create value for his clients?

· What kind of services might he provide that offer more long-term competitive advantage than low prices or new equipment?

References

Band, W.A. (1991). *Creating value for customers.* New York: John Wiley & Sons.

Berry, L. (1995). *On great service.* New York: The Free Press.

Collis, D.J., & Montgomery C.A. (1999). Competing on resources: Strategy in the 1990s. In *Harvard Business Review on Corporate Strategy* (pp. 33-62). Boston, MA: Harvard Business School Press.

Crompton, J.L., & MacKay, K.J. (1989). Users' perceptions of the relative importance of service quality dimensions in selected public recreation programs. *Leisure Sciences,* 11, 367-375.

Lovelock, C.H. (1991). Creating and delivering services. In C.H. Lovelock (Ed.), *Services marketing* (2nd ed.) (pp. 223-235). Toronto: Prentice-Hall.

McLean, D., & Johnson, R. C.A. (1993). The leisure service delivery dilemma: The professional versus the marketing model. *Journal of Applied Recreation Research, 18*(4), 253-264.

Monroe, K., & Petroshius, S. (1981). Buyers perception of price: An update of the evidence. In H. Kassarjian & T. Robertson (Eds.), *Perspectives in consumer behavior* (pp. 43-55). Dallas, TX: Scott, Foresman & Co.

O'Sullivan, E.L. (1991*). Marketing for parks, recreation, and leisure.* State College, PA : Venture Publishing Inc.

Schneider, B. (1988). Notes on climate and culture. In C.H. Lovelock (Ed.), *Managing services: Marketing, operations, and human resources* (pp. 352-358). Toronto: Prentice-Hall.

Sewell, C., & Brown, P. (1998). *Customers for life.* Toronto: Pocket Books.

Stevenson, L.N., Shlesinger, J.C., & Pearce, M. R. (1999). *Power retailing.* Toronto: McGraw-Hill Ryerson.

Treacy, M., & Wiersema, F. (1995). *The discipline of market leaders.* Reading, MA: Addison-Wesley Publishing Company.

Zeithaml, V.A., Parasuraman, A., & Berry, L. (1990). *Delivering quality service: Balancing customer perceptions and expectations.* New York: The Free Press.

City of Waterloo

5
Product Basics

The leisure marketer must now decide what will be offered to the target market. This introduces the first "P" in the marketing mix, that of the "product." A *product* is any benefit package that can be offered to a client. Products may be comprised of either goods or services. Products often receive more attention from clients than do any of the other elements of the marketing mix. Distribution operates below clients' awareness levels; price represents an imposition rather than a benefit; and promotion offers little of direct value to them. Indeed, the client makes sense of the provider through the provider's product offerings. For these reasons, most marketers believe that product quality sets a provider apart from competitors.

The Product Life Cycle

Deliberations over products typically begin with the concept of the program life cycle. The life cycle concept assumes that, over their lifetime, products move through several distinct phases or stages. These phases are marked by the popularity the product enjoys. More than that, the phases "describe a product's sales, competitors, profits, customers and marketing emphasis from its beginning

until it is removed from the market" (Evans & Berman, 1995, p. 312). The life cycle concept is a compelling idea. It borrows from life the rather inescapable notion that to all things there is a beginning and an end. The rates of growth and decline may vary but the pattern is clear. Introduction leads to growth, growth leads to maturity and maturity leads, in turn, to decline and eventual death.

The notion of the product life cycle is not without its problems and has fallen out of favor as a result. Primarily, the cycle has been criticized for its simplistic nature. Like any sweeping idea, it is well suited to helping conceptualize the problem but ill suited to making specific predictions. The life cycle "length, shape, and even stages entered into by products is determined by the product type and the diversity of external factors that are difficult to predict, such as the inflation rate, legislation, changing consumer life-styles, and the extent of competitive response" (Sandhusen, 1993, p. 302). In other words, one cannot make accurate predictions when relying on the cycle. There are simply too many unknown variables that influence the size and shape of the cycle to render any predictions as accurate as one would like.

Further, it is difficult to establish where any given program sits on the cycle. If interest levels dropped off, will they plateau, fall or rise again with renewed vigor? It may be impossible to say without the benefit of hindsight The life cycle is best observed after the fact. Only then are trends discernible and patterns obvious. Regardless of these limitations, however, the life cycle represents an important concept. No marketer can ignore either its implications or its insights. The product life cycle can help with general planning decisions. When used as a general guide, the concept of the cycle is as robust as it is compelling. Its properties, however vague, help the marketer envision and plan for changes in demand for a product.

The concept of the product life cycle can be applied to individual programs, entire brands, and even communities and geographic regions. Countries and empires have succumbed to its relentless rhythms and predictions. All are subject to the logic of the cycle. The tourism industry has long understood that the popularity of various tourism locations will grow then decay over time. They spend vast sums attempting to speed acceptance of a

location then slow its inevitable decline. For the private sector marketer, the goal is one of ensuring the program life cycle is as predictable and profitable as possible over the long term.

The goal is not much different for public sector providers. They too desire predictability, for predictability is the bedrock of planning effort. They need some sense of upcoming demand so that they might allocate resources accordingly. Though the public sector may not be interested in profit, it is interested in a related concept, that of participation. The program life cycle offers some insight in this regard.

There are several basic shapes that the product life cycle might assume. These shapes all track the relative popularity of the program over time. Each shape reflects the variable nature of client response. Response patterns no doubt rely upon the nature of the program type. Some leisure programs are likely to last longer than others. Those that tap basic interests are likely to last longer than those that

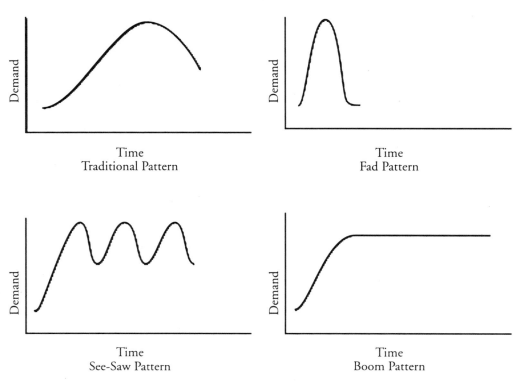

Figure 5.1: The Many Shapes of the Product Lifecycle

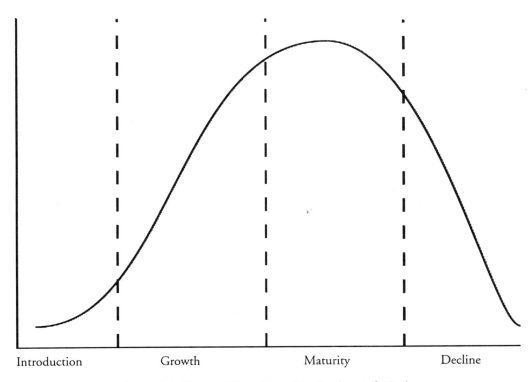

Introduction   Growth   Maturity   Decline

Figure 5.2: Demand Over Time: The Product Life Cycle

appeal to faddish concerns. For example, swim classes seem to outlast skateboard programs. Other programs might be seasonal in their appeal. The pattern of demand for these types of programs might see-saw over time (Figure 5.1).

Whatever its shape, the life cycle moves sequentially through a series of phases. Together, these phases create the cycle. Typically, the cycle follows a path characterized by slow then rapid growth, followed by stability then decline (Figure 5.2).

Introductory Phase

This initial phase is one of considerable uncertainty. The marketer is introducing a product that offers promise but success is never guaranteed. Indeed, various industries publish statistics on the ratios of hits (those products that survive beyond introduction) to misses (those that fail to gain sufficient popularity to survive beyond introduction), and these figures are never encouraging. In the leisure industry,

dozens of programs may be introduced before one actually succeeds. The introductory phase is characterized by low but (hopefully) growing levels of client interest. At this stage, conventional wisdom suggests that only the adventurous few individuals are willing to try the product. It's simply too new and too unfamiliar to attract the interest of the mainstream user.

Growth Phase

The cycle generally assumes that successful programs will begin to experience increasing demand. If supply can match this demand, a growth phase will begin. This growth phase is characterized by growing interest in and demand for the program. As interest increases and as positive word of mouth spreads, new clients will be drawn to the program. This stage is difficult to plan because growth rate varies widely from one product to the next, from one setting to the next, and even from one sector to the next. For example, fads grow in popularity very rapidly, but their fall in popularity is just as precipitous. Other programs may begin slowly but, thanks to positive press coverage or a successful special event, interest may blossom overnight. In the marketing world, they talk of the "buzz" that might accompany a new program. This buzz is comprised of positive word of mouth. Often, the louder and more persistent the buzz, the more rapid the growth process.

Maturity Phase

Growth begins to slow during the maturity phase. The length of this phase establishes the "shelf life" of the product. Shelf life represents how long interest in the program lasts and is a function of many variables. For example, changes in technology can render a program obsolete. Lawn tennis courts were once very popular until artificial surfaces replaced them by the thousands. Traditional swimming pools were popular until the leisure pool with its slides and beach-like atmosphere arrived. Shelf life is also influenced by the target market. Young teens are more likely than perhaps any other age group to adopt then quickly abandon products. The life span of a teen idol's popularity is typically measured in months, whereas older adults may favor an artist for decades.

Decline/Extension Phase

Interest in all programs eventually begins to slip. Participants tire of the activity or move on to alternative offerings. The rate of decline varies from one product to the next, from one sector to the next. For example, fitness-based activities have shown considerable resiliency over the years and demand seems unabated. Walking has been called the single most popular leisure activity. Marathon runs have ebbed and flowed in their popularity, but they continue to attract millions of participants annually. Fitness and health-related programs form the backbone of many park and recreation department offerings. For other programs, the decline may be more rapid. As noted earlier, dance crazes create dramatic demand for instruction but by the time instructors have been trained and programs

developed, the craze has often passed, and a new dance form or craze has gained precedence.

The Tactics of the Program Life Cycle

There are actions the marketer can take to manipulate the shape of the life cycle. Marketers use a variety of tactics to hasten acceptance of a program, to extend the growth stage of the life cycle, or to delay the onset of decline. *Tactics* are activities undertaken to achieve short-term objectives. Whereas strategy focuses on nonspecific issues, like positioning or long-term planning, tactics are concerned with details and specificity. Tactics deal with techniques, programs, and implementation.

The Tactics of Introduction and Growth

At the introductory phase, the challenge is one of creating interest in and support for the product. Preferred techniques typically attempt to generate positive word-of-mouth communication through contests, free trials, and special events. During the growth stage, the marketer is faced with two dominant challenges. The first is that of meeting the demands of potentially rapid growth. Marked increases in demand create myriad problems ranging from staffing to product reliability. It might be easy to provide excellent service when managing 25 encounters a day, but what happens when demand grows to 500 encounters a day? How will staff handle the added pressure?

A second problem at this stage is the growth of copycat programs. Others will see the success of a program and decide they want to be part of it. They may use the same program idea, the same program names, and even attempt to lure away key staff. Further, these copycats have not used organizational resources to research and develop the new program. As a result, they may be able to offer the program at costs less than your own.

The Tactics of
Mature Services

The next phase, that of maturity, often lasts longer than the previous phases so it also introduces a greater sense of predictability to the marketplace. This offers a bit of respite for the provider. However, the maturity phase is also characterized by a very competitive environment. This can be a time of increasing competitive pressure. The provider often has many rivals in the mature marketplace. The more successful the program, the more competitive that environment will be.

Maturity is also characterized by a slowing of the growth of or even a reduction in sales. As growth slows and even drops off, the provider may be faced with the problem of *overcapacity*. In other words, providers are able to provide more services than are being demanded in the marketplace. This trend may be exacerbated if clients are lured away by rival providers. The tactics of the mature product and of overcapacity are straightforward. The marketer can either change the product in some way or seek new client groups.

In the former case, marketers have two basic alternatives. First, they can improve the quality of their *service delivery*. Such quality initiatives often focus on improving convenience and reliability, because these issues seem to have universal appeal. Now that rapid growth has slowed, the provider can begin to fine-tune the delivery process. With stagnating sales comes the opportunity to step back and reassess operating procedures and the process of service delivery.

Second, marketers can improve *service features*. These new features improve the service's value in the mind of the participant. Many such efforts focus on price reduction, because marketers prefer to enhance the appeal of successful programs without having to make any dramatic changes in standard operating procedures. However, efforts to improve services should never be restricted to simple price reduction. More useful efforts actually improve the solution offered by the service itself.

The decision to seek new client groups is infinitely more complex than the decision to alter delivery or product features. There are simply more unanswered questions when the marketer begins to look outside traditional client groups. What does this new group seek? What do its members care about? How can they be reached? The marketer must undertake a new opportunity assessment in order to discover a new group to consume an existing program offering.

This approach can prove very rewarding. It can rejuvenate a failing program by introducing it to an entirely new group of potential participants. For example, martial arts classes, once the domain of young men, began to wane in popularity so they were reintroduced as self-defense classes for women. This move breathed new life into a mature program offering. As this offering to women matured and growth slowed, it was again reintroduced to children (and their parents) as a positive way to develop mind and body.

Note that each reintroduction required more than a redirection of focus. Each time the sport changed client groups, it was forced to make minor modifications to delivery and program features. A martial arts class for adult males will differ in form and intensity from that offered to 10-year-olds. A self-defense class for women concerned over their own security will differ from that organized around a competitive club.

The Tactics of Decline

As aging programs begin to decline in popularity, marketers are faced with three options (Kotler, Armstrong, & Cunningham, 1999). The first option is that of *maintenance*. In other words, they may decide to maintain the service in its current form. They may believe that there is sufficient interest to keep the program "on the books." They may also believe that other providers will soon abandon that same program. As other providers leave the scene, they may hope that old clients will return and that demand will be rejuvenated.

The second option is one of *harvesting*. A harvesting approach demands that the provider begin to draw resources from the service. In some cases, this withdrawal may free up additional resources to support "stars" currently being introduced. In other cases, the provider simply uses the additional savings to enhance profits. In either case, the provider hopes that interest in the program will continue long enough to make this option worthwhile.

The third option is one of *retrenchment*. Retrenchment is the act of withdrawing resources from a program. Though it seems obvious that programs will eventually decline and be discontinued, there seems remarkable resistance to retrenchment in the marketing world. The reasons for this resistance seem to emerge generally from *uncertainty* and *attachment*. Consider first the issue of uncertainty.

Retrenchment typically "kills" a program. Many marketers hesitate to take this dramatic final step. They are simply uncertain over the consequences of their actions. Interest in the program may be declining, but is this decline permanent? Will the program recover? Perhaps it is about to experience a jump in interest. For example, who could have predicted that the yo-yo would gain such interest now, decades after its initial introduction? Will displaced participants be angry over cancellation? These questions tend to create hesitation bordering on paralysis among even the most action-oriented marketers.

Attachment adds to this paralysis. Leisure programmers have considerable attachment to their own programs. They remember a time when now-failing programs were vibrant and alive with potential. They developed many of these programs from scratch and nurtured them over the years. It is emotionally difficult to eliminate such programs even when elimination is the only option available. As a result, the decline stage is long and lingering for many programs. This topic will be discussed in more detail later in this chapter.

Program Life Cycle and the Diffusion Process

The program life cycle assumes that individuals differ in their willingness to try new products. A few adventurous souls will try a new product but most will wait until the product has proven itself in the marketplace. This assumption is best explained by the process called *diffusion of innovation (DOI)*. Everett Rogers (1983) explored individuals' willingness to adopt new ideas or products. He was interested in the speed at which new ideas were adopted by or diffused through a population. His results suggested that willingness to adopt change placed individuals into one of five "adopter categories." These categories varied in terms of socioeconomic characteristics (i.e., education, literacy, and social mobility), personality variables (i.e., empathy and dogmatism), and communication behavior (i.e., social participation and being connected to social systems).

Rogers found that *innovators* were the first to try new ideas and programs. They form the leading edge of any adoption process. From a program life cycle perspective, these first few will determine whether or not a new program gets off the ground. Promotional efforts for new programs are typically directed to innovators. The style and nature of these efforts are determined by the preferences unique to the innovator category. They are venturesome by nature and can deal comfortably with uncertainty. They enjoy the company of others who share their innovative spirit and tend to be more educated than their less innovative counterparts. As a result, promotional efforts tend to be social in nature, upbeat in tempo, and intended to encourage positive word-of-mouth communication. This group is attracted and well suited to such message formats.

The second category members, *early adopters*, are critical to the eventual success of a program. The program's appeal must soon extend beyond the small group of innovators if it is to succeed. Early adopters must now pick up the baton. These individuals have many of the characteristics of innovators. They have the ability to deal with abstraction and enjoy innovation, and they actively seek contact with those outside their immediate social circle. They have considerable exposure to media and are regarded as opinion leaders. This final role is noteworthy. New programs cannot succeed if they do not receive the endorsement of opinion leaders. For this reason, many promotional programs specifically target early adopters in their efforts to generate positive word-of-mouth communication.

In one case, marketers, hoping to generate such communication over a new "wave" pool, organized pool parties "by invitation only" (Sherman & Havitz, 1991). The goal was to create word-of-mouth communication before the doors officially opened, so staff focused their efforts on innovators and early adopters. "The pool complex functioned by invitation only during its first six weeks of operation. ... The district invited hundreds of companies, civic groups, schools, clubs and organizations" (Sherman & Havitz, p. 37). The goal was one of creating the best possible impression among this select group of people. As the authors noted, "The invitation-only parties assured that visitors' first impression of the pool would be one of a popular, people-filled place rather than a lightly attended cavernous facility" (p. 38). From all reports, the effort succeeded beyond their most optimistic hopes.

The next two categories, *early* and *late majority* represent two sides of the same coin. Members of these groups are progressively slower to adopt innovation than are their innovator or early adopter counterparts but they are just as important to the long-term success of a program. As the term "majority" suggests, they represent a very large part of the target market. Once they begin to support a program, growth can be dramatic. However, before they adopt, they want to hear consistently positive reports about the program from current users. They do not take new purchases lightly and are troubled by innovation for the sake of innovation. They seek change only when it offers clear advantage.

The final category is that of *laggards*. This name has been criticized because it has a very negative connotation. The reason for this can be traced back to John Locke. In the seventeenth century, Locke set forth a theory of labor that tried to describe the "order of man." He believed that the earth was a divine gift—common property to all. In order to fulfill the promise of this gift, he advised all to convert or subdue the earth to personal property through personal toil. Personal property gained through toil was the very basis of society. Consequently, he believed, people become naturally segregated. Those who were hard workers became, through the fruits of their labors, the elite (property owners), and those who failed to gain property (from sloth) were known as laggards. These laggards were suspect because they were social and economic failures. They were so suspect, in fact, that Locke suggested the role of government was to protect the industrious few who owned property from those who did not. Laggards were not to be trusted.

Rogers (1983) does not use the term "laggards" in this lamentable manner. He uses it only to suggest that group members lag behind their more innovative counterparts. Laggards are slow to accept change. They welcome the status quo, so they are typically the last to adopt an innovation. Rogers notes that, as a group, they are suspicious of change, preferring to rely on tried and true products. They are described as "backing into the future," because they are more comfortable with the past than with the future. Their cautious approach is often motivated by a general lack of resources. They cannot afford to experiment with new products and are therefore unwilling to do so.

The Attributes of Innovation

The diffusion of innovation literature also offers insights regarding how the leisure marketer might best encourage participation in programs. Rogers (1983) found that several product characteristics facilitated diffusion. He referred to these characteristics as the "attributes of innovations." Although Rogers was concerned only with innovations, these attributes seem useful to anyone hoping to encourage leisure participation. Programs that exhibit those characteristics are more likely to be supported than are those lacking these same characteristics. These characteristics seem to both encourage and ease acceptance of new programs. This is good news for the leisure marketer.

Programs, and their many components, can be held to these standards. Do they exhibit these attributes? If so, then acceptance and participation is more likely. If not, then changes are required. The attributes are trialability, complexity, relative advantage, observability, and compatibility.

Trialability

Trialability is "the degree to which an innovation may be experimented with on a limited basis. New ideas that can be tried out on an installment plan will generally be adopted more rapidly than innovations that are not divisible" (Rogers, 1983, p. 231). Think about test driving an automobile and you get the idea. If shoppers cannot kick the tires, sit behind the wheel, and take the auto for a drive, they are unlikely to purchase the auto outright. The greater the risk associated with the purchase, the more important becomes trialability. No one wants to incur high costs, only to find out the product is unsuitable. The consumer behavior literature makes it clear that most consumers will decide not to purchase rather than risk "mispurchase" (buying services they discover they neither want nor enjoy).

Consider how this might apply to a leisure program. Participation in a leisure program is riddled with costs. The low prices that characterize many public sector programs reduce only monetary cost. For many participants this represents the least important among many more onerous costs. The real costs arise from insecurity, embarrassment, uncertainty, and inconvenience. Participants in fitness classes, for example, may be filled with doubts and fears over their participation (Reid & Crompton, 1993). They ask themselves, "Will I look silly? Will I be able to handle the physical demands of the class? Will the class make me feel better? Will I enjoy myself? Will the class itself offer the benefits promised in the brochure?" One of the best ways to deal with these uncertainties is by making programs more trialable.

Standard procedures in most agencies determine that participants pay in advance and restrictions are then applied if they decide to withdraw. Brochures tell them that "satisfaction is guaranteed," but they must come to some central office during regular working hours and fill out several forms if they want a refund. This practice reduces the trialability of these programs. They are told that they must pay an administration fee or accept fines if they have actually participated in a class or two before asking for that refund. Again, this practice reduces the trialability of these programs.

The leaders in the service industry offer unconditional refunds to their customers so that trials are encouraged. As L. L. Bean tells its clients in each and every one of its millions of catalogues:

> Our products are guaranteed to give 100% satisfaction in every way. Return anything purchased from us at any time if it proves otherwise. We will replace it, refund your purchase price or credit your credit card, as you wish. We do not want you to have anything from L. L. Bean that is not completely satisfactory. (Source: virtually any L. L. Bean catalogue.)

Leisure marketers might adopt this approach if they hope to increase the trialability of their programs.

Complexity

Complexity is the "degree to which an innovation is perceived as relatively difficult to understand or use ... the complexity of an innovation, as perceived by members of a social system, is negatively related to its rate of adoption" (Rogers, 1983, pp. 230-231). In other words, if potential users think the program is complicated or difficult to undertake, they will hesitate giving it a try. It's clear that innovators are less troubled by complexity than are laggards, but the problem of complexity is an issue for virtually everyone. If participants are uncomfortable with the difficulty offered by a program, it is unlikely they will try that program.

This point is perhaps best made by a story told by talk show host Jay Leno. He once told the story of buying his parents a new television. When he returned home, he found that they had tucked the remote control away in a closet drawer and were continuing to push buttons on the set by hand as they always had. When he asked why they weren't using the control, they told him they were afraid it would start a fire. He reported his exasperation while reminding them it was a remote control and not a "death ray," but they refused to use it. It was simply too complicated for them, so they were unwilling to adopt what for them represented a complicated innovation.

Relative Advantage

The concept of *relative advantage* asks the question, "Is the program a clear improvement over the existing offering?" Does the program make the client's life easier, better, or more enjoyable? Rogers (1983) defined the term as the "degree to which an innovation is perceived as being better than the idea it supersedes" (p. 213). The improvement may be cost-based or may be based upon performance. If a program offers the same benefits but at reduced costs, then advantage is improved. If program components are enhanced, relative advantage is gained.

In some cases, a simple change is considered synonymous with improvement. "New" is often viewed as "better." A new menu item at a restaurant is welcomed because it offers another choice. Hotels will refurbish their lobbies simply to create a feeling of renewal. The fashion industry thrives on seasonal and annual changes that are undertaken for the sake of change. This trend undoubtedly applies, at least to some extent, to leisure programming. New offerings often create a sense of anticipation and excitement. New furnishings in a facility or new equipment in a gym all create a sense of progress and success.

While virtually everyone seeks change, they may do so within a framework of predictability. A few innovators welcome change, but many others prefer stability. As a result, leisure providers must pursue balance in their programming efforts. Coca-Cola™ learned only after changing its old formula that millions of their customers preferred the old taste. Coke was forced to offer both the old and the new tastes. Clearly most clients prefer improvements to be offered within familiar contexts and surroundings.

Another challenge arising from the issue of relative advantage is uncertainty. Many improvements are not at all obvious. For example, an arena may purchase new ice-making equipment or an instructor may gain new qualifications. These may all represent improvements in an objective sense, but are they considered enhancements by the client? When changes are obvious they may be considered as problematic by some users. Those who have been with a program the longest seem most resistant to program changes. They have come to expect a certain level and type of service, and departures from the existing pattern are often viewed with suspicion. They may see changes as offering anything but relative advantage.

Observability

Observability is the "degree to which the results of an innovation are visible to others" (Rogers, 1983, p. 240). This attribute relates directly to the issue of relative advantage. How can the benefits of adopting the innovation, of participating in a program, be made clear? This is a difficult task because it actually involves predicting the future. Providers cannot promise that the individual will enjoy the program. They cannot promise that the individual will live longer, better, or more happily because of the program. Even if these promises were true, how can these rather intangible benefits be made more tangible? How does one make "a better life" observable? These questions strike at the very heart of the challenge of service provision.

Services are intangible so they are difficult to observe, and their results are even more difficult to communicate. Indeed, results or benefits from participation may not be at all obvious to the casual observer. Many marketers now take for granted that benefits of participation are hidden completely behind uncertainty and doubt. They then develop promotional programs that make this benefit more clear, that make results more observable. These marketers must then make benefits clear and results obvious. In particular, they cannot leave clients' appreciation of results to chance. Their marketing efforts remind clients of the benefits of participation both before and after they have taken part. This topic will be covered in more detail in the upcoming chapters on communication.

Compatibility

Compatibility refers to whether or not the innovation is generally consistent with current practice. Rogers (1983) defines compatibility as "the degree to which an innovation is perceived as consistent with the existing values, past experiences, and the needs of potential adopters" (p. 223). There is a natural comfort zone that surrounds the status quo. We all seek the predictability that accompanies familiarity. Staff and clients alike compare new programs to other, more familiar offerings. They compare programs to their existing hopes and desires. Programs that "fit" these criteria are likely to be accepted, whereas those that fail the test of compatibility are likely to be rejected.

The compatibility issue is complex. It tells us that consistency is prized among participants. It suggests that clients compare programs to a reference point created by existing offerings. While this is undoubtedly the case, this comparison point is actually a moving target. Even popular leisure programs may become incompatible with client expectations as the world advances and they remain the same. Leisure providers must constantly ask the question, "Do we operate in a way that our clients have come to expect?"

Consider a typical registration procedure. Registration is often a tedious experience comprised of waiting in queues hoping to get into programs that may or may not be available. In many cases, a potential participant may register for a course today and discover weeks later that the course is not being offered due to insufficient registration. Surprisingly, advanced leisure providers sometimes use

seemingly archaic registration procedures because that is the way they have always done them. To the leisure provider, these procedures are indeed compatible with their own current practice, but they may be falling behind the practices of the rest of the modern world. Irritation and dissatisfaction may result.

Clients are increasingly being exposed to other, better registration systems. Anyone who has used a travel agent is accustomed to making all arrangements at one point in time through one individual. Travelers are able to make arrangements by phone or on the Internet. When doing so, they receive immediate feedback on the status of their arrangements and can make changes to their plans with little difficulty. They can make payment with any credit card, can make payments over time, and can even arrange substantial discounts if they agree to travel during periods of reduced demand. Can leisure registration procedures offer the same level of convenience, reliability, and flexibility? If not, leisure providers face problems with compatibility, not because of their own innovations, but due to those of other providers.

Expanding the Notion of a Product

In the early days, deliberations over products were most concerned with the basic physical item or service. In a classic article called "Marketing Myopia," Levitt (1960) described the rather severe limitations of this focus. He suggested that this limited view focused attention on the product itself and not the consumer. Producers focused on the product they produced and not the client they hoped to serve. This orientation is currently alive and well in many leisure agencies. When asked about the nature of their business, pool directors often respond that they are in the pool business, athletics coordinators believe they are in the sports business, and so on.

Levitt (1960) went to great lengths to discourage this type of thinking by relating the story of railroads at the turn of the century. At that time, the railroad industry believed it was in the railroad business and not the transportation business. Even though the need for freight and passenger transportation continued to rise, railroads declined rapidly because owners failed to see how other providers could better fulfill the wants of their own clients. If product-oriented leisure providers are to escape the fate of the railroads, they too might benefit from a more expansive notion of product.

Over time, most marketers have come to recognize the limitations of an emphasis on the physical product. It has become clear that the product itself is unimportant if it fails to satisfy needs and offer desirable results. The marketer's emphasis has shifted from a product orientation to a client orientation. Marketers now view their primary task as one of pleasing the client and a product as simply one means of fulfilling that mission. In making this point, Nylen (1990) refers to a product, not as a thing, but as the "total needs-satisfying benefit provided to consumers" (p. G-248). This benefit is created through the coordination of many program elements. How well is the client treated during each phase of participation? Are staff willing and able to assist where necessary? Are programs offered at convenient times in convenient locations? Is delivery seamless without flaws and interruptions? These program characteristics, when offered together, create what is now being called a product bundle. Bundles represent all the things a provider might do to please the client.

The Product Bundle

The service marketer is concerned with satisfying the client. This is often a complicated process and far beyond the means of a single program or service. As suggested above, service marketers rarely refer to the product. This is a limited term that makes one think of a single, unidimensional thing. Rather, they discuss the *product bundle*. The logic behind this becomes clear once you understand the complexity of a program offering.

A product possesses three distinct levels. The first is the *core* product. It represents that which the client seeks from the leisure experience. Later in this section this notion is described as a primary need. Core or primary leisure, relates to a remarkable array of individual and collective priorities, ranging from affiliation to the desire for mastery (Mannell, 1999).

The next product level is the *actual* product. It represents that which the marketer provides the client. The actual product may take the form of information, programming efforts, or other forms of client assistance. Unfortunately, there is an understandable desire to focus programming efforts on the actual product. Participants desire exercise, so providers offer aerobics classes. Participants desire to cool off on a hot day, so providers build swimming pools.

This tendency is unfortunate because inevitably gaps exist between the product sought by the adopter and that which is provided by the marketer. For example, Scott (1993) suggested that many traditional product characteristics actually inhibit participation. Traditional programs require a commitment of time and energy that client groups may be unable to devote to leisure activity. Participation levels are diminished as a result.

This is a common problem in services marketing so marketers have added a third level to the product bundle. It is called the *augmented* product. This product level has proven a critical indicator of program success. It represents any additional services and benefits designed to help the client overcome the constraints posed by many traditional programs. Augmentations are intended to aid the client in both consuming and enjoying the actual product.

Consider a golf course program. It offers an obvious blend of core, actual, and augmented products. In terms of a core product, like any leisure activity, golf offers a context for personal expression. It may be used by the participant to pursue a wide variety of personally relevant goals ranging from enhanced life satisfaction to increased physical and emotional well being. Its actual product is little more than a green space equipped with small flags, sand-pits, and water holes. You no doubt recognize the profound gap that might exist between the core product and the actual product in this case. Product augmentations are required to fill this gap. They bring the golf course to life for the typical user. Instructions are made available for the neophyte, golf carts for the sedentary, concessions for the hungry, and so on. They fill the gap between the core and actual products.

Though the role of product augmentations has received little attention in the leisure programming literature, they offer considerable potential for leisure participants and marketers alike. Augmentations enable clients to virtually customize each leisure encounter to their own specifications. Participants can choose between available augmentations to meet their own individual wants and concerns. Augmentations also offer pricing options for public sector marketers. In order to maintain their service ethic, public sector providers may continue to offer basic programs at little or no cost. However, they may charge varying rates for augmentations. Those unable or unwilling to pay related fees may continue to enjoy the basic program at low traditional fee levels. Those who wish to enjoy more personalized/augmented service levels can pay for that option (thereby helping subsidize more price-sensitive participants).

Augmentations are best considered *before, during* and *after* the leisure encounter. Clawson and Knetsch (1966) suggested that the on-site experience represents only the tip of the iceberg of any given leisure episode. The entire episode is comprised of several sequential steps: *anticipation* (imagining and planning), *travel to the recreation site, the on-site experience, travel from the site*, and later *recollection of the on-site experience* . The leisure marketer must devote considerable energy to design augmentations to move the client from one stage to the next, and to enhance the experience at each stage.

An example might help make this point. The author once took part in a study that explored the marketing efforts of charter boat operations in the Gulf of Mexico. Many of those who chartered these boats travelled thousands of miles by automobile to do so. One operation found that most of its clients originated in Michigan and Minnesota. Their clientele consisted almost exclusively of "snowbirds" who hoped to escape winter weather and enjoy a few days on the water.

After reviewing their marketing efforts, the research team found that the operator gave only one line of directions to those who drove over a thousand miles to that operation. That one line indicated that clients should meet the boat "at Dock A in Berth 12 by 6:00 am."

A better augmentation might be to help with the whole trip-planning process. How might the entire trip be made more enjoyable? The planning phase would be a great start. The charter operator could recommend clothing to wear, food to bring, or even cures for motion sickness. A detailed map of how to find the state, the city, and the dock would also be useful planning tools. Does the client know where to stay while in the area? Could the operator provide suggestions on nearby hotels, restaurants, or trailer parks? The operator might also take pictures of clients during the charter and send them out free of charge a few months after the conclusion of the experience. This picture would remind clients both of the fun they had and to make reservations for the next year.

One park and recreation department in Illinois applies this "before, during, and after" concept to the way leisure programs are organized. Staff found that the agency offered a great many leisure programs in local schools. They knew that adults often had bad memories of their time in school so staff wanted to put clients at ease as soon as they entered the school facilities. Staff also knew that school buildings could be confusing places for first-time visitors. They decided to employ "meeters" and "greeters" to wait at the doors of the schools during the first few nights of programming. Their job was to put clients at ease and to direct them to their program locations. This was a great idea but its true genius was revealed at the end of the night's programming.

Staff knew that clients worry about security as they look for their cars in dark parking lots. They arranged for the greeters to return at the end of the evening to escort clients through the parking lots to their cars. These greeters were the ideal choice, because they had met with the clients earlier in the evening so a sense of trust had already been established. Staff were able to discontinue the program after a few nights because, by that time, friendships had grown in the classes, and friends were escorting each other to their automobiles. This program is a great example of augmentations to improve the experience before, during, and after the actual leisure encounter.

Lovelock (1994) characterizes augmentations as the petals of a flower. Each petal helps to add beauty to the flower, to improve its quality and appearance. Six of these petals or categories are of interest to leisure marketers. Each helps improve the service concept and the value offered to the client. The first augmentation category is that of *information*. As Lovelock (1994) advises, "to obtain full value from any good or service, customers need relevant information about it, especially if they are first-time users" (p. 183). Relevant information may relate to how the client can reach the provider (e.g., maps, phone numbers, hours of operation) conditions of sale/consumption (e.g., price, required skill or fitness level, warnings), and confirmation of activity (e.g., receipts, tickets, confirmation numbers).

The second augmentation category or petal is that of *consultation*. Consultation includes any effort to advise or counsel. This is more than the simple provision of information. The consultative process is iterative in that information is shared between the two parties and together they attempt to solve the problems of the client. The solution is customized to the specific requirements of the individual client.

The third augmentation category is that of *order taking*. Order taking occurs after the individual has decided to do business with a provider. Clients want the provider to be accessible, then once access is gained, they want their wishes dealt with quickly and accurately. Think about program registration. Clients want the process to be convenient and virtually instantaneous. Once they have registered for a program, they want records to accurately reflect their wishes and requirements. They want to be certain that their names are not dropped from program lists or waiting lists, they want to be notified if

programs are delayed or canceled, they want registration forms to be clear and easy to follow. They want fee payment procedures to be straightforward and convenient.

The fourth augmentation is that of *hospitality*. Hospitality refers to treating clients as a host treats a guest. This is typically considered one of the most important augmentation categories. It focuses on courtesy and consideration for the client. There are several elements within the category. The first deals with greetings. From birth we are taught to greet friends when they enter our home. We do so promptly and with sincerity. As a result, we all expect to be greeted when we enter a service provider's facility. The second refers to fees. Karl Sewell (Sewell & Brown, 1998), a leader in customer service, offers this rule of thumb: "You never charge clients for services that you would offer free to a friend." A local store owner currently offers free juice and soft drinks to clients as they visit his shop. In his view, he always offers a drink to friends when they drop by his home and would never think of charging them for it, so he treats his clients the same way.

Hospitality extends to the facilities offered to clients when they enter leisure facilities. Clients apply a very high standard when they evaluate the bathrooms and eating facilities offered by service providers. They expect bathrooms to be clean and well equipped, lunch counters to be spotless, lounges to be comfortable, and magazines to be current. These are all part and parcel of hospitable service. They notice when providers have failed to meet their very high standards. The best program in the world will be compromised if the change room is dirty or the chairs in the waiting area are damaged.

The fifth category is that of *care taking*. Lovelock (1994) suggests that care taking refers to how well we take care of the client's possessions. How well do we take care of their coats during our concert series, their bags that are stored in our lockers, their boats that float in our marinas? Will we help them care for their equipment? Will we rent them a larger locker if they ask? Do we provide a covered area in which they can lock their bicycles? They may not even own the objects that we care for. For example, they may be very picky about the quality of the golf clubs they rent from you or the towel you provide in the locker room.

The sixth category is that of handling *exceptions*. "Exceptions involve a group of supplementary services that fall outside the routine of normal service delivery. However, astute managers anticipate exceptions and develop contingency plans and guidelines in advance. In that way, employees know what to do, and so do not appear helpless and surprised when customers ask for special services" (Lovelock, 1994 p. 186). Exceptions fall into several subcategories. They include special requests in which a client may demand a customized response from staff that is not usually offered. For example, a client may ask that staff hold places in a program for him and his family until he can pay registration fees at the end of the month. A group with physical disabilities may request that a program be altered in order to facilitate their participation. Another group may ask that weekend leagues be altered so that they could participate without violating their own religious practices. These are all examples of special requests that must be addressed with sensitivity and flexibility. Other exceptions may arise from complaints or requests for restitution. These issues will be dealt with in considerable detail in chapter 13.

The Value Proposition

Product bundles require a theme around which they can be created. Each bundle is comprised of many components, and the provider must decide the nature and appearance of any given bundle. The theme now being used by many programmers is the *value proposition*. The value proposition outlines the clients' wants that are to be satisfied, as well as how they are to be satisfied. For example, many retailers now believe that clients seek value in selection, customer experience, price, and convenience (Stevenson, Shlesinger, & Pearce, 1999). Others have suggested that clients search for security, esteem, and justice (Schneider & Bowen, 1995). Whatever the needs the provider hopes to fulfill, the value proposition offers a "detailed description of what is to be done for the customer (what needs and wishes are to be satisfied) and how this is to be achieved" (Edvardsson & Olsson, 1996, p. 149). This concept needs to be both clear and compelling.

A great example is that offered by L. L. Bean back in 1912. He advised his employees to "sell good merchandise at a reasonable profit, treat your customers like human beings, and they will always come back for more" (L. L. Spring Collection Catalogue, 2000, p. 1). This small, profound statement has guided most of their efforts since that time. Every decision they make, every policy they generate, and every product they sell has been compared against that simple proposition. Once the proposition is clarified, the actual product bundle can be planned accordingly.

The notion of the value proposition suggests that the provider must take every opportunity to "add value" to the service offering. For this reason, a product must be considered as more than a simple physical thing or a single service. It is a coordinated set of services and augmentations designed to satisfy the client. The author recently had the opportunity to linger in a hotel in Halifax, Nova Scotia, while waiting for transportation. While there, he observed the great lengths to which staff was willing to go to create solutions for their clients. For example, when valets returned cars from the hotel parking lot, a staff member reached for a squeegee hidden unobtrusively behind a planter located in the lobby. He then cleaned the car's windows before their owners arrived to claim the car. This same hotel used a large, revolving door as its entrance. Revolving doors can be intimidating and even dangerous if the unwary user isn't careful. Staff was aware of this, so the door staff person continually aligned the door each time it was used to ensure easy access.

One must ask, why would this hotel place such emphasis and allocate the resources to provide these little services; services that clients probably never notice? They were attending to invisible services because such services make life easier for their clients. These measures render life less hectic, more seamless. It's this attention to detail that helps marketers create better programs to offer improved value propositions.

Linking Products through Product Families

The value proposition may also be enhanced through the development of *product families*. Product families or product lines are made up of related products that are marketed to the same (or similar) target groups (Nylen, 1990). A YMCA might offer a full range of fitness classes as part of their product family. A travel company might target ecology-minded travelers with a full range of eco-tours ranging from backpacking trips to kayak adventures. Again, these represent a family of services. Linking services has several advantages. First, by creating service groups or families, you are increasing choice alternatives for your clients. Remember that you are offering these programs to the same basic group. A more comprehensive line of services will undoubtedly better serve that client group. It also combats *menu fatigue*. Menu fatigue rears its head when clients become tired of the same old offering. How often can a budding artist take the same old class in oil painting? It is likely that this same artist could also be interested in other mediums or in other painting styles. Product families offer a popular way of planning for service variety.

Second, product families overcome a rather natural hesitation to try new offerings. Many clients fail to consider taking part in new programs. There are many good reasons for this and chief among them is uncertainty. They may be unaware of the benefits a program offers or they may wonder if they have the skills or talent needed to enjoy the program. Consequently they often choose to participate in the same old programs or decide not to take part at all. Linking products into recognizable families brings a certain familiarity to new offerings so trial participation is more likely.

The best way to create product families is to consider how programs are consumed by clients. The marketer can then create product families in ways that are consistent with these consumption patterns. For example, one product family might be created around the expertise of the clientele. The programs might offer a progression of options, ranging from those with beginner status to those who qualify as advanced participants. Another family program might be based on interest patterns. Think how one type of program might piggyback on another. How might one program complement another? Perhaps a bicycle maintenance course might be offered to runners who hope to form a triathlon club.

Main Points

• All products evolve along a life cycle that begins with an introduction phase and concludes with eventual decline and death.

The rate at which this evolution proceeds varies from product to product and from setting to setting.

· A product's location within the life cycle traditionally determines the tactics adopted by the marketer.

· The rate of a product's acceptance by leisure participants will be influenced by the product's own characteristics, as well as by the personal idiosyncrasies of those participants.

· Products most likely to succeed offer a bundle of benefits; together these benefits offer meaningful solutions to prospective clients.

· Establishing a value proposition (a statement of what is to be done for the customer) helps leisure providers decide how to best create and offer meaningful solutions.

· Products may be linked together to create program choices.

Case Study

Two recent graduates from a leisure studies program have developed what they believe is the ideal business start-up idea. They have decided to open a bicycle touring company. They both love to tour by bicycle and believe that such a company would prove the ideal blend of work and leisure. They have little capital with which to start a business but believe that their idea will require little investment beyond their own ideas and hard work.

They have been thinking of targeting retired adults as their primary clientele and organizing cross-country bike trips for groups of twenty clients. The trips will move from the west to the east coast and take several weeks to complete. They will advertise on the Internet, so little advertising budget is necessary. They plan to work from home, so no office rental expense will be incurred. Finally, they know

that anyone interested in cycle touring would provide all their own equipment. Yes, it seems to them that this is the ideal venture.

You have been asked by these young entrepreneurs to act in an advisory capacity.

· What benefits package might they create for this client group?

· Develop a list of product characteristics that might ease acceptance within the target market.

· Can different programs be linked together to make this program more palatable for prospective clients?

References

Bitran, G., & Pedrosa, L. (1998). A structured product development perspective for service operations. *European Management Journal*, 16(2), 169-189.

Chakrapani, C. (1998). *How to measure service quality and customer satisfaction.* Chicago IL: American Marketing Association.

Clawson, M., & Knetsch, J. (1966). *Economics of outdoor recreation.* Baltimore: The Johns Hopkins University Press.

Edvardsson, B., & Olsson, J. (1996). Key concepts for new service development. *The Service Industries Journal,* 16(2), 140-164.

Evans, J.R., & Berman, B. (1995). *Marketing.* Englewood Cliffs, NJ: Prentice-Hall.

Kotler, P., Armstrong, G., & Cunningham, P. H. (1999). *Principles of marketing* (4th ed.). Scarborough, ON: Prentice-Hall Canada Inc.

Kotler, P., McDougall, G., & Armstrong, G. (1988). *Marketing: Canadian edition.* Englewood Cliffs, NJ: Prentice-Hall.

Levitt, T. (1960). Marketing myopia. *Harvard Business Review,* 38(4), 45-56.

Lovelock, C.H. (1994). *Product plus.* New York: Prentice-Hall.

Mannell, R.C. (1999). Leisure experience and satisfaction. In E.L. Jackson & T.L. Burton (Eds.), *Leisure studies: Prospects for the twenty-first century* (pp. 235-251). State College, PA: Venture Publishing, Inc.

Nylen, D. (1990). *Marketing decision-making handbook.* Toronto: Prentice-Hall.

Reid, I.S., & Crompton, J.L. (1993). A taxonomy of leisure purchase decision paradigms based on level of involvement. *Journal of Leisure Research,* 25(2), 182-202.

Rogers, E.M. (1983). *Diffusion of innovations.* New York: The Free Press.

Sandhusen, R.L. (1993). *Marketing* (2nd ed.). Hauppauge, NY: Barron's Educational Series, Inc.

Scott, D. (1993). Time scarcity and its implications for leisure behavior and leisure delivery. *Journal of Park and Recreation Administration,* 11(3), 51-61.

Sewell, C., & Brown, P. (1998). *Customers for life.* Toronto: Pocket Books.

Sherman, J.S., & Havitz, M.E. (1991). Introducing an innovative recreational facility: Lessons from a success. *Journal of Park and Recreation Administration,* 9(3), 29-40.

Stevenson, L.N., Shlesinger, J.C., & Pearce, M.R. (1999). *Power retailing.* Toronto: McGraw-Hill Ryerson.

R. McCarville

C H A P T E R

6

Develop Solutions

Service marketers are beginning to view the notion of programs and products in very broad terms. They now think of products as "bundles of satisfactions" (Edvardson, Thomasson, & Ovretveit, 1994) made up of thousands of little things that please and delight the client. Whereas the marketing mix typically deals with single products, the leisure provider cannot be content to focus on programs. Thinking in terms of single programs leads inevitably to a product orientation in which the program becomes an end in itself. In order to be effective, the marketer must focus instead on solutions that satisfy the client (Lovelock, 1991).

The Customer Relationship Life Cycle

As marketers plan solutions, they typically do so with the *customer relationship life cycle* in mind. Like its product life cycle counterpart, the relationship life cycle assumes that relationships progress along a predictable path (Gronroos, 1990). The speed and distance the participant travels along this path has important implications for both the participant and the provider. It is often considered optimal

that the participant move through the relationship cycle sooner rather than later. For example, the banking industry has realized that the longer clients stay with a given bank, the more deeply immersed they become in that bank's service offerings. They may begin by opening an account, then several accounts, eventually expanding their investment in that bank by arranging mortgages or car loans. As the relationship matures, clients may rent safety deposit boxes and open credit card accounts.

Banks know that their profits rise as the client adopts each new service. They are no longer willing to wait for several years for the relationship life cycle to mature on its own, so they have adopted several measures to accelerate the process (Reichheld, 1996). When a client arranges a mortgage, the bank may offer a free safety deposit box for a year. If a car loan has been arranged, the client may receive free checks for several months. Few clients abandon these additional services at the conclusion of the complimentary time period because they come to appreciate the advantages they offer.

Leisure providers may also benefit from this insight. They may wish to encourage potential participants to become involved in a variety of leisure programs. They may not be motivated by profit, as are the banks, but by the desire to improve clients' life-styles. They may offer new clients free lockers in their facilities for a year. They may offer complimentary passes to ancillary programs when the client registers for a class or program. For example, a client who registers for a fitness class may receive a free swim at the agency pool. This may encourage the client to become more involved and perhaps more attached to that provider. The client benefits and the provider is helping fulfill its own service mandate.

It is important, therefore, that the marketer understand how the customer life cycle develops. The process begins with *client awareness,* at which time the client becomes aware of the program offering. The individual may be actively seeking information on program options or may learn of program opportunities by chance. This introduction to the program and provider begins the life cycle process. A *decision* is then required to move the relationship forward. The client will decide to participate, delay, or not to participate at all. If a decision is delayed or a negative assessment occurs, the provider has lost the opportunity to serve that individual. If, however, the decision is positive, *consumption* may occur. If this is the case, the client begins to formalize a relationship with the provider. As the relationship progresses, participants become more deeply involved in the program or activity. Participants become more knowledgeable about their own requirements, as well as the provider's capacity and willingness to fulfill them.

Throughout the process, participants will reflect on the quality of their interaction with the provider. They will ask, "Did I enjoy myself? Did the program offer the benefits I sought? Could my time and resources have been better spent by participating in another activity?" This is called *post participation evaluation.* During this evaluation stage, participants decide whether or not their interactions with the provider have fulfilled their original goals. The relationship develops if these questions are answered in positive ways and deteriorates with negative assessments. If the goals were satisfied, then *repurchase* is

likely. This extends the life cycle. If the goals remained unfulfilled, then *abandonment* will likely occur. This formally ends the life cycle.

Unfortunately, the relationship may be derailed at any step in the process. The individual may never be made aware of the provider. As a result, the potential relationship fails to get off the ground. The individual may be familiar with a program but is unimpressed with that offering. Again, the relationship fails before it can develop. Perhaps the individual participates in a program but does not enjoy this involvement. The relationship will fail and the participant will look elsewhere for leisure opportunities. None of these scenarios is desirable. Remember, the goal of leisure marketing is to attract and retain leisure participants. To do so requires that a strategy be developed in a way that moves the client from one stage in the relationship to the next. The relationship cycle suggests how this strategy might best be developed. It suggests, for example, that the relationship can only begin when the client believes the provider is able to provide a useful solution to an important problem or concern. This indicates that the provider must fully understand the priorities of members of the target group (Assael, 1984). As a result, building relationships with clients begins with research to establish client preferences and desires.

Further, in order to begin the relationship, the client must be aware that the provider offers a meaningful solution to a relevant problem. This suggests the importance of effective communication programs to ensure clients are made aware of the marketer's program offerings. Once the client is aware of a service offering, a decision is either made or delayed. A positive decision is typically followed by some effort to contact the provider. As a result, programs and services must be within easy reach of the prospective client. This has implications for the way in which programs are distributed, phone numbers and web sites are communicated, and how staff are trained to deal with inquiries.

Establishing Client Requirements

Services must address clients' *primary* and *secondary* requirements (Edvardsson & Olsson, 1996). Primary requirements are those that motivate a given behavior. If prospective clients hope to exercise, they may wish to attend a fitness class. If they plan to learn a skill, they might join a painting class. If they are interested in some sort of athletic spectacle, they might decide to attend a professional basketball game. Their wishes, hopes, and interests represent primary requirements that must be fulfilled. Their actions help address these primary wants. However, each of these decisions raises a second set of questions. If they decide to attend a fitness class, can they find one that matches their current fitness levels or that fits within their daily schedules? Will they need particular skills to enjoy a painting class? Will they know others in their class? These questions represent secondary requirements that also must be addressed if these individuals are to enjoy the class.

Success in programming is determined by the degree to which leisure providers focus on solutions to both primary and secondary requirements. Success begins with identification of both *rational* and *emotional* requirements the client might identify (Bitran & Pedrosa, 1998). Rational requirements arise naturally from both primary and secondary preferences. If a client seeks fitness opportunities, the program should possess characteristics that will logically enhance fitness levels. If clients identify time and convenience as requirements to participation, the programming schedule should be planned accordingly.

Emotional requirements are not so easy to fulfill. Clients seek a kind of intimacy from their service providers (Treacy & Wiersema, 1995). This intimacy takes many forms. It may involve personalized solutions to clients' problems. It may, as Zeithaml, Parasuraman, and Berry (1990) found, take the form of knowledgeable staff willing to provide prompt attention. Whatever the form these emotional requirements take, it is essential that marketers discover what the clients seek before creating the service offering. This is the role of market research. This topic is covered in greater detail in chapter 14.

A final word on client requirements. Not all requirements are created equal. Some represent minimum standards established by the client. If the program offering does not fulfill these basic standards, the client is unlikely to take part. Others represent preferences more than standards. They encourage participation but are not considered critical by the individual. For example, several natural park areas recently conducted surveys asking clients about the importance of different programs and park features. It should come as no surprise that sanitation was considered an absolute requirement in some areas but less so in others.

The park user surveys discovered that cleanliness was extremely important in washrooms and restaurants, but not as important in other facilities (e.g., scenic lookoffs, etc.). Park managers wisely decided to improve their sanitation program in the areas considered most critical by their clients. Other programs, like interpretative services, were desired but not essential to clients' requirements. As a result, park managers decided to use the interpretive programs to "add value" to the visit. In this way, the managers began to design a program offering that responded to the subtleties of their clients' preferences.

Establishing Design Requirements

Once client requirements are understood, the marketer can begin to establish basic *design requirements*. Design requirements lay down guidelines for developing the product bundle. They are typically developed to address both agency priorities and client preferences. Once these guidelines are established, the provider can then develop program elements or features that the program must possess if it is to succeed. There are four basic design requirements (Juran, 1992) that apply to virtually all leisure programs. They relate to search properties, service demands, packaging, and conformance potential.

Search Properties

A service must exhibit *search properties* to help the client search for and select from different service options. Two pieces of information play a critical role in the search process. The first is price. Price tends to be one of the first, rather than the last, pieces of information clients seek regarding a program. It seems to play an accept/reject function. If the price is consistent with expectations then purchase is more likely. If the price violates expectations by being too high or too low, then likelihood of purchase declines. This issue will be discussed in considerable depth in chapters 9 and 10.

The second piece of search information is that of the program name. Names may represent one of the most important product features. Names are also among the first pieces of program information gathered by a prospective client (Jacoby, Szybillo, & Busata-Schach, 1977). As a result, they, too, play a key role in helping potential participants evaluate a program prior to consumption. In one experiment, researchers offered students a series of names for a hypothetical fitness program (McCarville & Garrow, 1993). They found that name selection altered subjects' price expectations by as much as 46 percent and willingness to pay levels by as much as 47 percent. A name focusing on benefits generated the highest price expectations and willingness to pay levels. It seems that participants look to names as a sort of short cut in their search for benefits. If the name suggests the benefits the program offers, and the participant seeks those same benefits, then participation is more likely.

Service Demands

Service demands relate to how the program will be used or consumed by the client. Note that these requirements arise from how the product *will* be used, not how it *should* be used by participants and intermediaries (like parents who perform registration-

related tasks, etc.). The difference between "will" and "should" creates significant problems for leisure programmers. Programmers often assume that participants will use programs as intended, will read instructions as advised, and will follow directions as instructed. Unfortunately this is not always the case. We have all heard the saying, "When all else fails, read the instructions." This saying is considered a key bit of conventional wisdom for good reason. Clients tend to struggle through, relying on experience and instinct instead of directions and instructions. This causes untold grief to programmers, because they assume that potential participants will read directions before acting.

Leisure marketers often prepare long and detailed brochures outlining various procedures on the intricacies of registration, refunds and program offerings with all the relevant dates, times, and locations included. They then assume that participants will read these publications in detail before taking part. This is one of the great myths in leisure programming. In keeping with this myth, programmers often develop elaborate policies and procedures in order to ease the programming process. Unfortunately, they soon learn that they seem the only ones who study or understand those same policies. They must constantly remind clients of what they should be doing, and how they should be acting in order to enjoy leisure programs.

It is better to design features that focus on how clients *will* use rather than *should* use program offerings. These features will make the program more user friendly and safer for clients. Assume that the client will begin to take part without the requisite knowledge or preparation. Features must be designed in order to build solutions into program design. Many providers are now providing "help" lines where well-trained staff are on hand virtually 24 hours a day to aid frantic callers with some program-related emergency. Others pre-test new procedures or programs on complete neophytes, those who have no experience with the program or the agency. If the new initiative works for these uninitiated few, it can work for anyone.

It is now commonplace to provide a brief, to-the-point fact sheet or list of what the client will need in order to enjoy the program. This list might include when to arrive, the equipment to bring along, or any preparation that might be needed to take part. Organizers of large events like fun runs know this. Most provide participants with a sheet of helpful tidbits (e.g., where to start, the location of water stops, and so on) at each event. These instructions are helpful precisely because they are simple and direct.

Packaging

The notion of packaging arises from traditional goods marketing. Packaging represents the way in which the product is presented to the client. It reflects the way in which a program's many *features* are combined to offer benefit and create solutions. Features are comprised of program elements ranging from price to the number of classes being offered.

When creating packages, the marketer must repeatedly go back to the way in which the client will use or consume the program. For example, cereal boxes are intended to be opened and closed repeatedly. Their packaging is conducive to this use pattern. They are intended to be used and reused over time, so they are designed to fit snugly on any cupboard shelf. Cereal producers know that while eating their favorite cereal, consumers often take time to read the box. As a result, they provide messages on the box, ranging from upcoming contests to dietary information. These features all arise from the use requirements of the intended user.

What might the leisure programmer learn from a box of cereal? Well, it's clear that all clients desire flexibility. There are times when they want an "individual serving" and other times when the whole family becomes involved. This is the case with leisure participants as much as with cereal consumers. Many leisure agencies recognize this by offering a full range of participation options for any given program. Clients may participate in one of many offerings and do so by the day, week,

month, season, or year. This type of flexibility creates a great program feature.

A cereal box also offers convenience, because producers know that virtually all clients crave convenience. The leisure provider can build convenience into any and every program by simplifying registration procedures, offering easy payment plans, and providing timely and relevant program information. These are all features that enhance the program package. This focus on convenience is perhaps most evident in the case of fitness classes. Various types of fitness programs have been wildly popular over the past two decades, and programmers have been improving them over the years to help maintain this popularity. One of the great improvements has been in terms of program flexibility. For example, many programs are offered simultaneously throughout a given community. The same program might be offered twice daily at five or six facilities. There are programs at 6:00 a.m. and 7:00 a.m. in one facility, at 10:00 a.m. and 11:00 a.m. in another, and at 7:00 p.m. and 8:00 p.m. in another. Each time period appeals to a different client group. Those with traditional jobs may opt for the early morning or evening classes, while those who are available during the day may frequent the mid-morning classes. Without fail, however, someone who usually attends one time period will ask if she can attend another time period. An early morning participant has the day off and would prefer to sleep in just this once. Is the program flexible enough to permit her to participate at 10:00 a.m. instead? Others might have slept in even later this morning. Can they take part in the evening session?

One popular fitness program offers flexibility by simply issuing punch cards to registrants. These clients are then free to attend any regularly scheduled class whenever and wherever they like. The card is punched by volunteers (who get to participate free of charge) each time they attend. This is a brilliant idea. Clients pick and choose the time and location of the program they visit. Programmers know that, once people get settled into a program, they rarely deviate from that schedule. As a result, participants are given the flexibility they desire but almost never exercise it. This represents a win/win opportunity for all concerned. The client is offered flexibility, and the provider is offered predictability for planning purposes.

Several providers add even more flexibility to the program by altering the length of possible registration periods. Generally, those who plan to participate on an irregular basis can pay only for those sessions they attend. Those who plan to drop by on a more regular basis are rewarded with lower overall costs but they, too, are accommodated. For example, those who simply wish to sample a given program might come out for one night only. They might pay $5.00 for the opportunity, but consider this money well spent because they enjoyed having the chance to test themselves and the program. A couple, planning a hiking trip in the near future, might wish to register for the same program for a month in order to improve fitness levels before their hike. They might participate in eight classes then discontinue as they leave on their trip. They would pay more overall but less per visit than those who dropped by only once. Finally, other participants may be committed to these same classes and prefer to register annually each year. They pay much more in total than the others we have mentioned but pay less per visit because of the extent of their commitment. Again, these types of features ensure that flexibility is available on demand.

Conformance Potential

Conformance potential refers to the program's ability to reduce the gap between promised and delivered service. Is there an adequate fit between the provider's capacity and the requirements of service provision? Program features must be created to minimize slippage between what is promised and what is actually provided. There are several gaps that might emerge as we offer leisure programs.

Gaps often arise from two related sources. The first source is that of *operational demands*. An apartment dweller recently contracted a local mover to relocate her furniture. The mover was owned and operated by a man who seemed dedicated to service

quality. When he and his team arrived, he asked if he could videotape staff members as they moved the various pieces of furniture. He planned to use the video to train new employees. As the videotaping began, his team donned white gloves to protect the furniture and placed mats on the floor to protect the floor they moved across.

The client was impressed with the mover's attention to detail throughout this exercise. Just as the move was getting into full swing, the owner/operator finished up the taping and left his staff alone to complete the move. To the client's consternation, upon the owner's departure, his staff immediately removed the gloves and mats because they were too cumbersome. These features were a nice idea, promised by the owner, but the staff refused to use them unless the owner was supervising them directly. They were features that staff refused to provide on a consistent basis.

There are many operational conditions that might create problems for conformance potential. Staff may be unmotivated or poorly trained. Funding may be limited so that resource levels never match program demands. One of the most prevalent of these conditions is actually created by management, however. It is that of restrictive operating procedures. The agency may plan to offer quick and easy refunds, but their efforts are hampered by other departments who demand that complicated and time-consuming procedures accompany any cash refund. Slippage may also occur due to uncertainty in the general operating environment. A provider may promise an outdoor festival, but be confronted with high winds and rain on the appointed day. The agency may plan ice sculptures at a winter carnival, only to be foiled by unseasonably warm temperatures. These problems arise from uncertainty. Such uncertainty is always present but is never more dangerous when dealing with the weather or with any complicated enterprise.

The second source of gaps between promised and actual service levels is that of the provider's own *communication* efforts. Communication can introduce gaps because it may establish unrealistic expectations among users.

In a sense, it may promise features that the provider cannot provide. All consumers have fallen victim to promises that the provider cannot hope to fulfill. Assured that a product will arrive shortly or that staff will be delighted to assist, these consumers soon discover that the missing part may be delayed for weeks or that staff are unsure how to install it. This is known as *over promising* and *under delivering*, and it is a common approach in business. The provider fears that by telling the truth about waiting times, the client will become discouraged and shop elsewhere. In order to forestall this loss of business, the provider makes promises that cannot be kept. The over promise/under deliver approach is problematic, because the promise establishes an expectation. Subsequent performance always fails to meet the standard the provider has set. Disappointment and dissatisfaction are inevitable. As a result, a product bundle can only be successful if it is consistently and reliably "deliverable" to the client. It must be planned to ensure that what is promised is also possible. This is the essence of conformance potential.

Generating Program Ideas

Once clients' program requirements have been established, the next step in creating programming solutions is that of idea generation (Sandhusen, 1993). Ideas for solutions may come from several sources. As in all good marketing efforts, the process should begin with clients. The goal is to meet or exceed their expectations, so the best ideas tend to come from watching and listening to the clients themselves (Kotler, Armstrong, & Cunningham, 1999). There are many ways to do this.

Asking Clients

Leaders in service provision like to identify participant requirements/preferences by exploring clients' notions of customer service and service quality. They typically use a broad brush at this stage. They don't focus on details but try to get a sense of what is important and what that means in terms of program features. These leaders look first to information readily at hand. Client complaints, suggestions, and comment cards are considered essential in identifying problems and possible solutions.

Unfortunately, many public or private sector marketers ignore these sources of information during program development (Murdick, Render, & Russell, 1990). In a recent study, researchers surveyed municipal leisure providers about program development (Johnson-Tew, Havitz, & McCarville, 2000). In particular, the researchers were interested in how leisure providers planned their newest, most innovative programs. Few agencies looked to their clients for ideas or suggestions when developing their programs. They relied almost exclusively on staff for ideas. This rather inward-looking approach could be improved by greater client involvement.

While it is true that staff meet regularly with clients and can appreciate the requirements of these clients, it is worrisome that programs emerge so often from staff and staff alone. Staff have priorities that are different from those of clients. It matters not that staff are well intentioned, well informed, or well trained. They have a perspective that is different from their clients. They are concerned with efficiency, whereas the client is concerned with effectiveness (Lipsky, 1980); they are concerned with policy, whereas clients are concerned with play. If providers fail to ask clients on an ongoing basis, they risk losing touch with client priorities and concerns. This is a concern for all providers, and it is amplified with the passage of time. As Albrecht (1994) reminds us, "The longer you've been in business, the greater the probability you don't really understand what's going on in the minds of your customers" (p. 138). The only way to combat this trend is to "ask, ask, ask" your clients for help (Sewell & Brown, 1998).

Using Internal Sources

Leisure providers are not alone in their reliance on staff for program ideas. Murdick, et al. (1990) suggest that providers in all sectors typically use staff evaluation committees, rather than a formal processes, to develop and evaluate new program ideas. While this approach was discouraged in the last section, it must be recognized that there is some merit to this approach. Indeed, staff may represent an excellent source of program ideas. As Schneider (1988) indicates, front-line staff members may meet with hundreds of clients in the course of carrying out their duties. They are undoubtedly familiar with the requirements and the preferences of these same clients. Staff are also aware of competitors' offerings and have a sense of what is happening in the marketplace. Most providers are constantly scanning the environment for program ideas. As a group, staff represent an impressive resource for program development. As suggested above, however, their input is best considered in conjunction with that of clients.

Asking Other Providers

Marketers often look to other providers, partners, and even government agencies for program ideas. As the concept of the product life cycle suggest, programming success breeds imitation. A successful program idea will soon be copied by others hoping to capitalize on this success. Program ideas can be gathered from many sources. First, marketers look to other providers' advertising. Most leisure marketers have a complete file on the brochures and advertising copy of providers they hope to emulate. Second, they may also "mystery shop" other providers' programs. Mystery shoppers participate in other providers' programs, hoping to gather insights and ideas that will improve their own service offering.

Third, they may look to official industry meetings and publications. Leisure professionals organize regular meetings like conferences and workshops in order to share success stories. The goal is to gather and eventually copy these ideas once they return home. Professional associations spend much of their time facilitating the exchange of program information. For example, most professional associations provide newsletters and/or magazines to their members. These magazines often highlight award-winning programs or review new insights that

are emerging from various research initiatives. These are great sources of program information.

Develop and Choose Between Conceptual Program Alternatives

The next step in creating solutions is one of developing conceptual alternatives. Many program alternatives may be created to "solve" client problems. Service marketers begin to formalize their thinking about these solutions by developing a *program concept*. The program concept is simply a basic program idea stated in terms that are meaningful to the eventual client (Kotler et al., 1999). All program concepts address the same four basic questions (Kotler et al.):

· To whom is the program directed?

· What primary benefit should the program provide?

· How does this offering relate to existing offerings?

· When and where will the program be consumed?

The program concept suggests how the provider plans to mobilize resources to create client-friendly solutions. Various concepts are developed then evaluated. For example, leisure agency staff recently decided to celebrate the children in their community through the organization of a children's festival. Several festival concepts were developed.

Concept 1: A family day would be proclaimed within an existing music festival held during the summer months in a large, community park each year. On that day, prices charged to children would be waived, and children's entertainers would highlight the day's entertainment.

Concept 2: A festival would be organized during the school year. Schools in the community would be asked to invite their students to prepare posters and reports on "Being a Kid." The focus would be on developing a personal sense of pride and accomplishment for the participants. A competition would then be held, and winning submissions would be posted in city hall. A special day would be set aside so that all school children could visit city hall, review the winning submissions, and receive an official welcome from the city mayor.

Concept 3: A festival would be organized by children for children. The children themselves would use the school year to develop potential activities and events that might take place throughout the summer months. The theme would be one of "Kid Power," in which children could discuss and celebrate ways in which they could improve their own community. Although several potential activities were suggested by staff, the actual festival would be developed by committees of children in consultation with staff. The parks and recreation department would then coordinate these events through community groups, school board representatives, and, of course, the children.

All three of the concepts were evaluated in terms of the agency's own mandate and service strategy. As staff evaluated the options in terms of their own stated goals, they soon realized that the first two options were unsatisfactory. Both were "easy" for the service providers but failed to provide meaningful benefit packages to the ultimate users. The first option piggybacked on an existing event that was frequented by adults who typically purchased multi-day passes for the music festival. It was unlikely that many such adults would be interested in purchasing the same pass if one of the days of the concert was devoted to children's entertainment. It was feared that this option would alienate much of the existing festival's clientele.

The second option failed to offer much benefit to the children. Only a few would "win" the proposed contest, and even fewer would be tempted to visit city hall for a dry welcome offered by some unknown (to them, at least) politician.

The third option was thought to offer the greatest amount of challenge because it required considerable coordination and offered much uncertainty, but it was considered the optimal program solution. This final option was the unanimous choice of the programming committee. Once various alternatives have been evaluated and the program concept finalized, the task becomes one of translating the many design requirements into a series of program features.

Develop Program Features

As suggested earlier, program features represent the many elements that comprise the actual solution offered to the client (Juran, 1992). They might include level of complexity, program duration, meeting time, or price. These features are critical to the success of any given program because they help the client

- search for and select from alternative services,

- experience the service, and

- assess that service once it has been consumed (Zeithaml et al., 1990).

Features also shape the architecture of the entire service system (Bitran & Pedrosa, 1998). They establish the nature and level of the demands that will be placed on those delivering the service. If program features focus on reliable service, then staff training and support systems must also focus on reliability. If features focus on low cost, the provider too must focus on achieving those same costs. As a result, these features must be chosen with great care.

Program features are typically described in a type of hierarchy. The first level of features, *fundamental features*, deals with issues that are basic to any program offering. They are determined by legislated mandate, safety concerns, and ethical considerations. For example, public leisure programs must be delivered in ways that are consistent with public policy, they must be safe, and their pricing should be fair. Program features must, first and foremost, reflect these fundamental requirements.

A second level, called *primary features*, must address the core desires of the participants. Recall that primary requirements are those that motivate a given leisure behavior. Primary features address these requirements by focusing on program type and facility design. For example, if clients seek the opportunity for quiet reflection, the agency might provide contemplative spaces within their parks and facilities. If they hope to learn new skills, the provider might arrange instructional opportunities. These features provide a reason for the client to take part. While necessary, however, they are not sufficient to ensure participation. Participation is often determined by issues related to convenience, cost, or advertising appeal. As a result, a final level must be added to this hierarchy.

The last level of the features hierarchy focuses on *secondary features*. They address issues that arise once the client has decided to fulfill those primary desires. They can relate to scheduling, instructional techniques, and even the design of various advertisements. Secondary features often determine the relative success of any program. They help the potential client solve the many dilemmas posed by participation. Is the program offered at a convenient time? Is the program likely to be entertaining? Have promotions done an adequate job of informing clients of the program characteristics?

Whatever their place in the hierarchy, all features must receive due attention. "For design purposes, this hierarchy must be subdivided or broken down to the very lowest level. Every feature, however tiny, requires [attention]" (Juran, 1992, p. 174). The provider must decide which features will receive priority, then performance specifications can be developed.

Develop Performance Specifications

Once the program features have been established, providers must determine how the programs will actually be created for clients. The marketer must now establish *performance specifications* that ensure that the desired features are indeed offered. They are typically developed around the single question, "How will this program serve the client?" There are many answers to this questions, but they all focus on what the program is intended to do. For example, a travel program concept might be built around worry-free travel in which the agency completes all planning and coordination. Resulting features might focus on choice, flexibility, and low cost. Performance specifications would then focus on how the agency plans to make such travel possible.

Establishing performance specifications is actually a process of translating customers' primary and secondary requirements into program characteristics (Erma & Kniper, 1998). In doing so, these specifications may relate to both the technical and functional aspects of delivery. *Technical components* relate to what the client receives in interactions with the agency. In terms of the travel program example offered above, technical aspects might include an easy-to-remember phone number (1-800-Itravel), travel planning services, and perhaps discount coupons for airport parking. Technical specifications receive a great deal of attention, because they are easy to monitor. Ease of monitoring helps providers track the success or failure of their measures. They can count how often the phone number is being used, if travel itineraries are being planned, if discount coupons are being offered, and so on. They can track how many trips are booked and how many coupons are redeemed.

Functional components focus on how the service is provided. They relate to efforts to enhance the client's emotional reaction to the service encounter. These components are not easily measured because they relate to interpersonal dynamics. They are a function of variables like attitudes, behavior, appearance, personality, and general approachability (Edvardsson et al., 1994). Many service providers try to deal with functional components by choreographing staff response during encounters with clients. These procedures ensure that communications between staff and client are based on a mood of cooperation and compromise. For example, some providers focus on visual cues during the encounter. They ask that staff adopt the "5 and 10 rule". This rule demands that clients who approach within 10 feet are acknowledged with a nod and smile, while and those within 5 feet are greeted with a warm "hello." Other retail chains now insist that staff members simply smile as they greet shoppers. Telephone operators at one large mail order business are not permitted to say "no" to a client without the permission of a supervisor. In other words, staff are encouraged to comply with the wishes of their clients until authorized to do otherwise. Management knows all too well that clients judge the quality of an entire retail chain by the friendliness of their staff.

Efforts to measure the delivery of functional components have received a rough ride. It is difficult to mandate that staff be pleasant or helpful. For example, one retail chain built the "smile factor" into their staff evaluation procedures. Staff were instructed to smile at clients as they passed them in the aisles of their stores or face disciplinary action. Staff judged to be inadequate in their efforts to smile are penalized by supervisors. Staff members have been disciplined because their smiles were not "broad enough" or lacked "warmth." The employees' union is officially grieving this policy, not because they hesitate to smile at customers, but because of seemingly inadequate measurement techniques. When is a smile judged to be cold? What separates a warm smile from a cold smile? What does it take to be "helpful?" These types of questions often dominate discussions of functional program components.

Whatever the problems that arise from these functional performance specifications, they must be addressed. Recall that services are intangible; they are difficult for clients to understand or even evaluate. As a result, clients often judge the quality of a service encounter by the quality of the relationship developed with staff members. Earlier this was termed as "client intimacy." Whatever its title, this interpersonal element seems a pervasive and important factor in the determination of service quality.

Discussion of performance specifications leads quite naturally to program delivery processes. If specifications dictate, for example, that staff should be able to correct errors as soon as they are reported by irate clients, then all staff members should be given the resources to make such corrections. Does each staff member have immediate access to record keeping systems? Can all staff make monetary refunds without their supervisors' approval?

Testing the Concept

The program is still not ready for general distribution. Before being tested against the demands of the marketplace, new programs should be exposed to select groups of users. Marketers often use focus groups for this purpose. The goal is to determine

- · if the programs are likely to be supported by the target markets;

- · if problems exist, to determine their nature and how they might be remedied; and

- · if several new programs are being tested, which ones are likely to receive the greatest support.

The questions asked in a typical concept test are pretty standard. The marketer first wants to establish if participants understand the program being considered (Do you understand the program concept?). The second point is one of value (Does this program offer the solution package you had hoped for?). The third point probes their assessment of the program's competitive potential (What benefits do you think this program offers over similar programs?). In a related question, the marketer might ask in what way the new program is preferable to existing alternatives (Under what conditions might you prefer the new program over existing alternatives?).

Once the relative appeal of the program has been established, the marketer can then ask for improvement suggestions (What improvements in the program's features would you suggest?). The next question refers to price (What is a reasonable price to pay for this new program?). The penultimate question is one of the decision process (What would be involved in your decision to participate in the program?). Finally, the marketer might ask about the individual's intentions (Would you register for such a program?) (Kotler et al., 1999, p. 319). Together these questions help the marketer understand and predict reaction to the program idea.

This is one of the few times that service providers have an advantage over those who sell tangible goods. Those who sell goods often have to test complicated offerings that do not yet exist. As a result, they may have a difficult time making their product seem tangible to the testers. They must create prototypes or somehow create detailed images of the product to be tested. Computers have been a great asset in this endeavor. They can be used to create virtual realities to place drivers behind the steering wheels of cars that have not yet been built or place potential home owners in homes before a brick has been laid.

The testing process is not so difficult for leisure service providers. It is often relatively easy to reveal a new program concept to clients and to gather their impressions. One park and recreation department likes to target existing groups that might be interested in the new offering. They simply discover the time and location such a group meets, then arrange to drop by with pizza and a trial run of the new program. They then run the test and gather ideas for improvement as well as a sense of its potential popularity. Enthusiasts are willing, and even eager, to try new activity formats and ideas. The agency takes full advantage of the interest and generosity of these groups when testing new program ideas.

Program testing can even help agencies discover the best ways to deliver existing programs to unresponsive user groups. For example, a municipal agency hoped to involve a group of at-risk youth in some sort of late night recreation program. They asked an activity coordinator to meet with the group and expose the group to a variety of activities until they found something that seemed to generate interest. They finally settled on street basketball with a few rule changes that suited the informal nature of the group. Once they succeeded with this group, they used the lessons learned to involve other youth groups in the community. This original test helped them come to a better understanding of the group dynamics so that the program (and process) could be altered accordingly.

Supporting New Programs

A marketer can never be certain that a new program will succeed. In fact, many more programs fail than succeed. Failed programs are to be avoided for obvious reasons. They fail service providers by wasting resources, and they fail clients through their inability to meet their service requirements. The key is to develop new programs that have the very best chance for success. Up to this point we have discussed program development in terms of the program itself. We have focused on understanding client needs then developing program components that satisfy those requirements. Successful programming requires more than excellent program ideas, however. It also requires considerable organizational commitment and preparation. We now know that success relies on adequate organizational preparation as much as on program fundamentals. The best programs receive the organizational support necessary to introduce and maintain them in the marketplace.

Marketers who work with tangible goods have honed this process down to a fine edge. New initiatives are expensive to develop but profitable when they succeed, so marketers take great pains to support product introduction and development. One study tracked several successful products from their inception to their introduction to the community. These success stories all shared several traits that seemed to ensure their success (Edgett, 1994). They first emerged from a preliminary *market assessment* that judged the need within the marketplace. This preliminary assessment helped the providers develop a clear, specific target market. By the time of introduction, providers understood their potential customers' requirements for the product. These new programs were tested to ensure that they could be delivered consistently.

Further, there were high levels of *awareness* within the organization that the new product was being developed. The development process was characterized by considerable *coordination* among people and departments. The product seemed clearly *superior* to competing products in terms of meeting customers' needs. The delivery system was *ready* for, and supportive of, the product launch. A strong advertising, promotion, and marketing *communication effort* supported the launch. This communication effort was directed toward the target group.

Program development resembles a large, complicated puzzle that must be assembled piece by piece. If pieces are missing, the assembly cannot succeed. The flaw becomes obvious and the image ruined. The key seems to be one of coordination. Coordination demands that both the client and the agency work together toward a common, valued goal. New products must arise from a specific need within a clearly defined target group. They require support from clients and staff alike and this support is created through awareness campaigns. Success is the product of planning, preparation, and precise execution. These processes must involve more than the program itself. They result from the sum total of the organization's efforts to perfect and introduce a new offering.

A program may possess the right features, but without organizational support, it is doomed to failure. The Colgate organization feels so strongly about supporting new products that they have developed a concept called the " bundle book." This book deals with uncertainty and confusion over marketing practices surrounding new brands and prod-

ucts (Kindel, 1996). The bundle book, which is created centrally, provides front-line managers with "all they need to know about the brand, down to the smallest detail; includ[ing] product attributes, market research, pricing objectives, even advertising, public relations, and point-of-sale materials" (Kindel, p. 27).

The question becomes, "What might leisure service marketers learn from product marketers?" From the outset, we must recognize that leisure marketers often deal with conditions that are very different from those of product marketers. These conditions extend far beyond the basic differences between services and goods. Whereas goods marketers deal with relatively few products, leisure providers may offer virtually thousands of programs. They offer camps, instructional programs (on land and in the water), sport leagues, and any number of special events. The breadth and depth of their program offering are sometimes staggering.

These differences notwithstanding, leisure marketers can gather some insight from the coordinated efforts of the goods marketer. For example, it remains axiomatic that programs be given the attention they require to succeed. If the agency as a whole is unwilling to do so, the marketer can influence program introduction through a concept like Colgate's "bundle book." When new initiatives are planned, leisure marketers can develop a promotional piece that outlines the program concept behind any new offering, how the company plans to promote the product, and even describes the market group to which the product is being targeted. This piece can be circulated to staff who are expected to carry out any facet of the organization's marketing strategy.

Any organization can adopt the notion of the bundle book. The marketer might develop a coherent, focused marketing strategy, then use the book concept to communicate the strategy with other staff members. Such efforts can direct and guide staff, thereby ensuring consistency, maximizing resource allocation, and focusing the attention of staff members. Marketing efforts and the ultimate client will benefit from such initiatives.

Program Retrenchment

Retrenchment is the process of removing resources from an existing service (Crompton & Lamb, 1986). Because retrenchment involves the removal of resources, it often leads to the termination of programs. On the surface, retrenchment appears to be a very natural act. All programs must eventually come to an end. This seems a straightforward and inevitable conclusion for every program. It seems logical and even desirable that programmers would actively retrench so that resources could be allocated in more effective ways.

Unfortunately, there is a very natural hesitation to permit programs to die. There is an even greater hesitation to actively terminate programs. Instead, marketers often try to resuscitate programs long after meaningful life has left them. There is perhaps fear that clients will complain or the hope that the program might experience a turnaround. There is also distaste for the additional work that change creates. For all these reasons (and hundreds more), marketers resist terminating regular programs.

There is actually quite a large and informative literature on why humans resist change. It is comforting that this tendency is not isolated to managers or marketers or programmers or even, the leisure profession. It is a predisposition that all people share in spite of compelling reasons to let change happen. As O'Toole (1996) suggests in his book, *Leading Change*, "the puzzle is that people resist [changes] that are clearly in their self-interest" (p. 233). Even programs that should be eliminated are extended time and time again. Managers often ignore program changes that must be made, hoping that somehow the condition will improve.

Retrenchment usually takes place in three stages:

Step 1: *Identify* candidates for retrenchment (Crompton & Lamb, 1986). Typically programs are compared to some standard, and those failing that test are considered as possible candidates. Have sufficient numbers of people taken part in the program? Has it generated sufficient income? Is there an acceptable balance between the resources required to offer the program and the benefits enjoyed by the target population? Are participants satisfied with the service as it now exists? Programs might be earmarked for automatic assessment at some specified point in the future. A new program might be evaluated on its first anniversary. Has it lived up to expectations? What is the long-term prognosis for the program? A few agencies rely almost exclusively on this step to meet their retrenchment needs. They automatically discontinue programs on a designated anniversary unless programmers can find a compelling reason to keep the program in their family of offerings. Other standards arise from various measures of the program's popularity.

Step 2: *Evaluate* candidates once they have been identified. Among those programs that might be retrenched, which ones top the list? Again, this is a process of comparing the program's performance to some agreed-upon standard. The validity of this decision is determined by the quality of the established standard. It may be that while programs fail to meet the established standards, they may still offer some potential to benefit to the community. Strict reliance on arbitrary standards may cause effective programs to be retrenched unnecessarily. For example, a not-for-profit agency decided that its programs should generate their own operating costs. Programs that were unable to meet this arbitrary standard were targeted for retrenchment. Several beneficial programs were lost as a result.

Step 3: *Take action*. Two types of action are possible. First, programs can be *altered* rather than eliminated. These alterations may be designed to create new interest in the program or may simply represent efforts to reduce the costs of operating the program. The marketer may create renewed interest by changing the program and/or the target market. A failed program that was once directed to teens may have to be completely revamped in order to appeal to other, perhaps younger, client groups.

On other occasions, the program may continue to be offered but with fewer resources. For example, an oil painting class that failed to generate sufficient interest may be placed within another class devoted to a variety of mediums. In both cases, the programmer continues to capitalize on the resources of existing instructors while reducing the cost of each program. In this way, the program continues to be offered, but resources are also liberated to develop or improve other offerings.

Programs can also be *eliminated*. This is the second alternative when taking action. For many programs, closure is the only viable option. Those programs that generate the highest costs while offering the least benefit are typically selected as candidates for retrenchment. The first programs to be retrenched are those that create the most undesirable costs. Some costs are simply more difficult to bear than others. For example, a municipal park and recreation department had, for several years, been offering a summer concert program in one of its parks. The park itself was a popular location, and apartment complexes began to rise up around its periphery. These new tenants began to complain about the noise and traffic congestion generated by the concert series and the concerts were soon canceled. The series program was a success by many standards, such as popularity and attendance, but it failed those of the dreaded "complaint" costs.

Program elimination may take place in a variety of ways. A program may be reduced gradually over time. This is a great alternative if the program offers several stages or phases of participation. For example, a swim program might continue to offer upper-level classes (to ensure that those currently in the system can proceed through the various skill levels) but stop offering entry-level classes. In this way, all participants will gradually work their way through the program, and interest will fall off as they do so. The program can then be discontinued without displacing current participants.

Another solution is to announce a future date upon which the program will be discontinued. This technique has the advantage of creating a transition period during which any existing clients can find alternative program offerings. The canceled concert series cited above, for example, might have functioned for another full year but then have been discontinued. This option would have satisfied existing concert goers, because they would have been given one more opportunity to take part in the series. It would have satisfied organizers because it would have offered an extended grace period during which they could make alternate plans, communicate directly with their clients (at the final series), and perhaps even generate additional funds to facilitate a move to another site. This choice would also have been relatively painless for nearby residents, because they could be assured that this was the final concert series, so resulting noise and congestion was temporary.

The goal is to carry out retrenchment in a way that encourages acceptance from all those affected by that retrenchment. As suggested earlier, retrenchment is inherently troubling. Both providers and clients seem attached to the status quo and deviations from that standard are often considered as "losses" by participants. No one wants to lose resources, to receive less than is now being received. When threatened with such losses, people tend to resist. As discussed more fully in the final chapter of this book, such resistance is reduced by the nature of the change *process*. Those affected by change need to feel they have taken a hand in creating and directing that change. Before taking part in the change process, however, some education is required. Those involved in the change process must understand why change is being undertaken, why this program in particular is being targeted, and the types of goals being pursued by the change initiative.

One agency brings together participants and programmers involved in any program they have identified as a retrenchment candidate. They discuss the goals for the program and the managerial realities they now face (perhaps reduced budget or inadequate return on investment in the program). They then ask the group to develop recommendations on how the program might be improved. There are agreed-upon goals and procedures that must be followed, and time lines are attached to any of their program choices. Retrenchment may be implemented immediately, if no viable alternatives are available, or new program options may be pursued. The important point is that the affected individuals actively create and implement these options. They are not being imposed by the agency, so greater acceptance is likely as a result. The quality of the solutions is also superior, because they arise from the individuals who know most about the program.

Main Points

· Successful relationships with clients evolve as clients come to know and value leisure providers' offerings.

· Successful relationships are only possible if providers fulfill clients' primary and secondary requirements.

· Program design must balance both the clients' and providers' requirements.

· Program ideas are gathered from clients, staff, and other providers.

· New programs progress from ideas to concepts. They are then assigned features and performance specifications to help bring them to life.

· New programs require both emotional and technical resources if they are to flourish.

· All programs must eventually be retrenched (retired). The retrenchment process is as difficult as it is necessary.

Case Study

A community volunteer group was casting about for ideas to encourage teens to take part in organized leisure programs. They were particularly concerned with troubled youth who were being drawn into gangs and activities that were creating havoc in the community. Recent fires and even a train derailment had been blamed on youth who were seeking a break from the tedium they experienced during their leisure time.

The volunteer group decided to organize a series of dances, beach parties and youth festivals during the summer months. All events were sponsored by local businesses and a radio station and chaperoned by adult volunteers. Unfortunately, they all fell flat. Few teens came out to the events. At one low point, only two teens attended one of the beach parties. The community group has come to you for assistance.

Your first piece of advice is that while adults often seek structure, rules, and schedules in their programming efforts, youths prefer to develop their own schedules and activity patterns. You offer the favorite activity of "hanging out" as an example. To adults, this seems a mindless and purposeless activity, yet to youths it represents a complex activity full of nuances and rules imposed by the participants themselves. You then suggest that very different and nontraditional programs may have to be offered to this target group.

· Walk the group through the program development process.

· Who should be involved?

· What characteristics might the new programs possess?

References

Albrecht, K. (1994). *The northbound train.* New York: American Management Association.

Assael, H. (1984). *Consumer behavior and marketing action* (2nd ed.). Boston: Kent Publishing.

Bitran, G., & Pedrosa, L. (1998). A structured product development perspective for service operations. *European Management Journal,* 16(2), 169-189.

Crompton, J., & Lamb, C. (1986). *Marketing government and social services.* New York: John Wiley & Sons.

Edgett, S. (1994). The traits of successful new service development. *Journal of Services Marketing,* 8(3), 40-49.

Edvardsson, B., & Olsson, J. (1996). Key concepts for new service development. *The Service Industries Journal,* 16(2), 140-164.

Edvardsson, B., Thomasson, B., & Ovretveit, J. (1994). *Quality of service: Making it really work.* London: McGraw-Hill.

Ermer, D.S., & Kniper, M.K. (1998). Delighting the customer: Quality function development for quality service design. *Total Quality Management,* 9(4-5), S86-S91.

Gronroos, C. (1990). *Service management and marketing.* Lexington: Lexington Books.

Jacoby, J., Szybillo, G., & Busata-Schach, J. (1977). Information acquisition in brand choice situations. *Journal of Consumer Research,* 2, 209-216.

Johnson-Tew, C.P., Havitz, M.E., & McCarville R.E. (1999). The role of marketing in municipal recreation programming decisions: A challenge to conventional wisdom. *Journal of Park and Recreation Administration,* 17(1), 1-20.

Juran, J. (1992). *Juran on quality by design.* Don Mills: Maxwell Macmillan Canada.

Kindel, S. (1996, September). A brush with success: Colgate-Palmolive company. *Hemispheres,* 27-30.

Kotler, P., Armstrong, G., & Cunningham, P.H. (1999). *Principles of marketing.* Scarborough, ON: Prentice-Hall Canada Inc.

Lipsky, M. (1980*). Street-level bureaucracy: Dilemmas of the individual in public services.* New York: Russell Sage Foundation.

Lovelock, C.H. (1991). Creating and delivering services. In C.H. Lovelock (Ed.), *Services marketing* (2nd ed.) (pp. 223-235). Toronto: Prentice-Hall.

McCarville, R.E., & Garrow, G.W. (1993). Name selection and response to a hypothetical recreation program. *Journal of Park and Recreation Administration,* 11(3), 15-27.

Murdick, R.G., Render, B., & Russell, R.S. (1990). *Service operations management.* Boston: Allyn and Bacon.

O'Toole, J. (1996). *Leading change: The argument for values-based leadership.* New York: Ballentine Books.

Reichheld, F. (1996). *The loyalty effect: The hidden force behind growth, profits, and lasting value.* Boston: Harvard Business School Press.

Sandhusen, R.L. (1993). *Marketing.* (2nd ed.). Hauppauge, New York: Barron's Educational Series, Inc.

Schneider, B. (1988). Notes on climate and culture. In C. H. Lovelock (Ed.), *Managing services: Marketing, operations, and human resources* (pp. 352-358). Toronto: Prentice- Hall.

Sewell, C., & Brown, P. (1998). *Customers for life.* Toronto: Pocket Books.

Treacy, M., & Wiersema, F. (1995). *The discipline of market leaders.* Reading, MA: Addison-Wesley Publishing Company.

Zeithmal, V.A., Parasuraman, A., & Berry, L. (1990). Communication and control processes in the delivery of service quality. *Journal of Marketing,* 52, 35-48.

R. McCarville

CHAPTER

7

Communication Basics

Communication is the exchange of meaning. It is a process of sharing. Providers share their solutions with clients, while clients share compliments and complaints with providers. Marketers are preoccupied with communication. They seek communication from clients to discover problems and preferences while creating and disseminating their own messages regarding programs and services. The success with which communication is undertaken can mean the difference between prosperity and failure for the leisure provider.

Every contact between people or between people and an organization represents some type of communication. This communication helps the client understand the service offering. As Berry & Parasuraman (1991) suggest, "communications come from the company itself and from other interested parties; they are delivered in a variety of media and convey much about the service—for better or worse. From billing statements to advertising, from customer word-of-mouth communications to company signage . . . these various communications send clues about the service . . . [to] reinforce the firm's marketing strategy or scramble it in hopeless confusion" (p. 98).

The importance of communications may become exaggerated because the client is faced

with remarkably little else when judging service quality. Recall that all services are inherently intangible. As a result, clients must look for clues other than the service itself to judge its quality. Any tidbit of information offered by the provider, friends, or even strangers may be used to evaluate service offerings. Consequently, many service providers now view communication planning as a process of *evidence creation*.

There are many categories of communication clues that marketers might offer as evidence of quality. These clues may be sent intentionally or unintentionally, but all receive attention within the marketplace. Marketers know, for example, that price sends a variety of symbolic signals to prospective clients (Schiffman & Kanuk, 1997). High price often indicates quality and exclusivity, whereas low price may suggest affordability but also poor quality.

Service marketers have learned that some of the most powerful clues are visual in nature. In particular, clues arising from a physical setting may send compelling messages about service quality and provider reliability. Well-kept facilities may suggest provider care and attention to detail, whereas poorly maintained facilities may suggest provider indifference and apathy.

The focus of the next two chapters is on a particular kind of communication, that of promotion. Promotion is communication between the provider and potential participant designed to influence attitude or behavior. No marketing enterprise can succeed without promotion. It represents the lifeblood of any programming effort. Given its importance, marketers must understand the process of promotion and of communication basics. Once these are understood, marketers can begin to plan and execute promotional strategies. This chapter focuses on understanding client reaction to communication efforts. A basic communication process is offered and fundamental challenges for the communicator are discussed. The next chapter focuses on the creation of promotional strategy.

The Process of Communication

Communication is a rather straightforward process. It involves a *communicator* who sends a *message* through one or more *channels* to an *audience* (Figure 7.1). In this case, the communicator is the leisure provider. The provider sends a variety of messages to target groups. Messages involve any set of symbols the communicator sends to the client. These messages may be intended to inform, persuade, remind, or educate target group members (Crompton & Lamb, 1986).

Channels are the means through which these symbols are sent. Media such as brochures, flyers, and radio receive most of the leisure providers' attention. They are used almost exclusively in providers' efforts to notify and encourage clients to participate in leisure programs.

The audience is comprised of message recipients. Message recipients bring considerable personal baggage to any communication setting. They interpret any message in terms of their own memories, biases, and motives. This is known as *encoding*. Encoding is a process of organizing, interpreting, and deriving meaning from a message (Helgeson & Beatty, 1985). In order to facilitate accurate encoding, leisure marketers must ensure that their messages are both easily understood and relevant to prospective clients.

Many types of *noise* may also distort or confuse the original message. Noise is any external interference that serves to detract from the effectiveness of the intended message. For example, any stimuli that distract the participant might be classified as noise. A driver may ignore radio messages while negotiating through rush hour traffic. A reader may be distracted by family members while scanning a brochure. In both cases, the potential participant encodes a message that is less than or different from the intended message. The intended meaning is not shared and communication is compromised.

Feedback is any process through which the audience is able to communicate back to the sender. It is a very useful process that offers

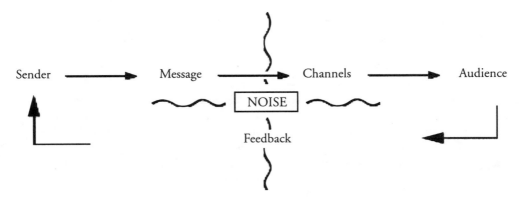

Figure 7.1: The Communication Process

the opportunity for clarification and evalua-tion. Marketers seek feedback in order to establish audience reaction to their promo-tional efforts. They relentlessly survey audience members to gather client impressions of different message mediums and formats. Such information guides future promotional decisions.

The Role of Marketing Communication

Communication efforts are typically designed to both encourage and direct behavior. Promotion is intended to assist and direct this progression. It is intended to convey individuals along a continuum, ranging from problem recognition and goal setting to decision making and action. As a result, marketing communication is largely an exercise in *persuasion*. As Bogart (1996) reminds us:

In advertising we are, in effect, trickling drops, spoonfuls, or buckets of persuasion into the reservoir of product information and opinion from which consumer actions are drawn. (p. 91)

Persuasion may occur through one of two routes. The central or deliberative route "emphasizes the information that a person has about the . . . object or issue under consider-ation [and is] based on a thoughtful consider-ation of the object" (Petty & Cacioppo, 1981, p.p. 255-256). Elaboration takes place as the individual reflects on the arguments presented in the message encouraging the development of new belief structures (Ajzen & Fishbein, 1980). This is considered the more logical and rational of the two routes and requires higher levels of motivation and cognitive energy.

The second route to persuasion is referred to as the peripheral (Petty & Cacioppo, 1981) or nondeliberative route. This represents a less thoughtful process than its elaborative counterpart and is characterized by low levels of motivation and cognitive energy. The peripheral route relies upon easily accessible rules of thumb or obvious cues when being persuasive. The individual may not elaborate upon the message, so existing cognitive clusters or biases may dominate this process. For example, a message may be persuasive because it is offered by a trusted provider rather than because of the quality of the message. In the same way, a program may be attractive because it is promoted by a trusted friend.

In order to be persuasive, marketers must understand how and when to rely on each of these routes. In particular, they must know how to design meaningful clues so that clients can understand and appreciate the message being presented. As a result, the following sections discuss how clients actually process these clues.

A Glimpse into Audience Limitations

Efforts to be persuasive are complicated by the ways in which clients use information. Most marketers subscribe to what is known as an *information processing perspective* (Bettman, 1979). This perspective describes how consum-ers gather, interpret, and store information while making purchase decisions (Jacoby & Olson, 1977). An information-processing perspective assumes that potential clients are confronted with countless choices on a daily basis, yet they possess limited capacity to deal with them (Bettman). They face being in a state of continual cognitive overload, so they look for shortcuts to assist them in understand-ing the world around them.

One means of dealing with these cognitive demands is the application of *heuristics* or simple rules of thumb to help make choices. These heuristics offer much needed cognitive shortcuts. These shortcuts help participants manipulate and assess information in the absence of critical thought. They help separate and categorize different products without undertaking complex comparisons. For example, a participant may group fitness facilities according to cost, location, or size. Reliance on these variables reduces the need to seek detailed information regarding any given program or facility. Clubs that charge higher fees, are located within fashionable hotels, or offer generous floor space may be grouped together in a high quality category. Competitors that lack these characteristics may be grouped with clubs considered to be of "lesser" quality. This offers a quick and easy solution for the prospective participant.

When a leisure service is assigned to a cognitive grouping, it is also assigned the characteristics associated with that grouping (Jacoby & Olson, 1977). Thus, a form of stereotyping occurs. Through this process, consumers need not assess each new leisure program on an individual basis. Rather, they need only to classify the activity in terms of a grouping that has already been evaluated. In this way, cues provide a link to a large amount of information stored in long-term memory (Jacoby & Olson).

Once they discover that a program is offered by the public sector, they may apply all the things they have learned about other public sector offerings to this program. If the same program is offered by the private sector, they may apply all the beliefs they hold regarding that sector. Havitz (1988) discovered, for example, that subjects tended to believe that private sector leisure programs were superior to public sector programs. Clients believed that private sector operations were more efficient and more ably administered. This was the case even when *the same program was being described* and only its private/public label was being altered.

The notion of information processing is important for anyone planning to communicate with potential leisure participants. Communication efforts must recognize inherent limitations in the processing capacity of those who receive promotional messages. It is rare that clients will devote all their cognitive resources to any given message. Instead they will browse over the message and if it is appealing, they may allocate more and more cognitive resources. If the message fails to attract attention, it will be ignored or soon forgotten. Information processing also suggests that clients may bend, fold, and manipulate

information to fit their own preconceived notions. The message a client receives may not be the message the provider intended.

Those who develop marketing strategy understand the limitations described by information processing theory and design strategy accordingly. For example, they know that one popular rule of thumb relates to familiarity. Statements or agencies that seem familiar are given more credibility. One study found that "familiarity emerged as a key mediator of the truth effect. When subjects experienced an 'it rings a bell' reaction, they judged the information to be even more true" (Hawkins & Hoch, 1992, p. 212). Promoters understand this tendency and often repeat corporate slogans hoping to increase consumer belief of the "truth" of that slogan. They also promote their products endlessly hoping to render these products more familiar (Kardes, Kalyanaram, Chandrashekaran, & Dornoff, 1993). Repeated exposure to even passing information about a provider may build support for that provider's services.

Audience Willingness to Accept Messages

A leisure marketer's audience may receive virtually thousands of messages each day. Audience members may be inundated with advertising about dishwashing detergent, political parties, automobiles, new homes, law firms, and soft drinks. The sheer volume of these messages may virtually derail the communication process. Leisure participants may have no energy left to process the leisure provider's message. In an effort of self-preservation, they may actively ignore all such messages. Breaking through this self-imposed barrier may be one of the most vexing ongoing challenges for any leisure marketer.

Encoding may be influenced by motivation and values, expectations and even the credibility of the information source. Information that is similar to one's own expectations will be *assimilated* (considered as more similar than it actually is), while information inconsistent with existing expectations will be *contrasted* (rejected as being irrelevant or unrealistic). As a result, participants whose views match those being promoted may be an "easy sell." They already believe and support the message that is being shared. However, when they disagree with a message or are unhappy with program elements, they represent a marketer's greatest challenge. They may reject or contrast a message, amplifying the discrepancy between the information that is being offered and the message they hoped to receive. For example, potential participants who hoped to receive a program free of charge may exaggerate the size of any fee that is charged, because the fee is inconsistent with their own expectations. In other words, they focus not on the actual price level, but on the gaps between what is being asked and what they expected. They typically react by rejecting message content (Petty & Cacioppo, 1981).

Involvement levels of those who listen to promotions will undoubtedly affect the way in which messages are encoded. High involvement is characterized by increased program relevance, client motivation, and product knowledge (Sherif & Hovland, 1961). As involvement increases, so too will participants' propensity for perceptual distortion. In particular, highly involved participants are more likely to assimilate or contrast messages depending upon how well they agree with their own expectations. "Highly involved persons have larger latitudes of rejection than less involved individuals. Both of these effects are presumably due to the fact that a person's own attitude acts as a stronger anchor under high-involvement conditions. Thus, assimilation and contrast effects are greater for highly involved individuals" (Petty & Cacioppo, 1981, p. 107).

For their part, low-involved participants are more likely to ignore promotional messages. They view these messages as irrelevant clutter that is best forgotten. They may hear or see advertisements several times without committing any of the ads' content to memory. You have no doubt experienced this phenomenon. A series of television advertisements have just concluded and you have no recollection of what or who they promoted. You may have watched a television show, but when asked about it the next day, you realize you have forgotten the premise, the punch lines, and the

names of the major players. Our minds are very efficient at removing unwanted clutter. Unfortunately, low involved participants may view much of your promotional material as clutter. They may ignore or forget it as a result.

There are many windows of opportunity during which clients are willing to accept messages, however. We know that many clients browse recreation literature hoping to learn of opportunities for themselves and their families. They may have nothing particular in mind but are simply scanning for ideas. In these cases, "the advertisement is not really evaluated. It is just seen, and a few bits and pieces of information are stored in the consumer's mind without active cognitive processes . . . Lastovicka refers to this process as information catching rather than information seeking" (Assael, 1984, p. 82).

Others have particular problems they wish to address. They hope to learn a new skill or try a new activity. Their search is often focussed and direct. They look for answers to specific questions and seek specific responses. Still others look to leisure sources for inspiration. Theirs is an almost emotional search. They are hoping to find powerful images or even humor that might serve to motivate and direct them. In all these cases, the client is willing to attend to promotional messages. The marketer's task is to gain the client's attention then help direct behavior.

Directing Behavior through Communication

Behavior and communication are linked through decision making. Decision making leads to behavior, but both are initiated by information. Marketing communication is intended to provide that information. It is intended to guide and direct the participants' actions by providing compelling information in a timely fashion. The communicator must understand that behavior occurs only after the participant has progressed through a series of cognitive steps. Movement through these steps requires that information be collected and assessed. Marketing communication efforts should facilitate this process.

The first stage, that of *problem recognition* and *goal setting*, is necessary to initiate action. The individual must recognize that a problem or at least a desire exists before any action is likely. An individual must feel hunger before seeking food. That individual then sets a basic goal, that of finding food. It is important to recognize the difference between needs and wants at this point. Clients may need food, but they marketer is most concerned with what they want in order to fulfill this need. A marketer can influence wants but not needs. For the leisure marketer, it is important to realize that a client may need exercise but can fulfill this need in many different ways. Marketers typically use communication to help direct how this selection occurs. A private sector marketer might encourage clients to choose his or her programs. A public sector marketer might simply encourage the selection of safe, healthy programs. Both are interested in directing behavior. Both hope to be persuasive. Both will use communication in doing so.

Problem recognition and goal setting are influenced by the individual participant's *psychological set*. This set is comprised of the background the individual brings to any given problem. This background may include memories of past events, idiosyncratic preferences and expectations, and experience with past programs and instructors. For example, two individuals may decide to lose weight. The first has a preference for physical activity, so she might decide to lose weight through participation in fitness classes. The second individual may identify the same problem (weight), but set very different goals in addressing that problem. This individual may have had great success in the past with dieting and may choose that option over exercise classes.

Once individuals are aware of a problem and preliminary goals have been established, they typically begin to seek alternative solutions. The solutions they hold in memory are known as an *evoked set*. Much of the advertis-ing that dominates current media outlets is intended to keep products and providers within the target markets' evoked set. Fitness clubs want clients to think of them once the decision has been made to improve fitness levels. Recreation departments want families to think of them when they decide to participate in leisure programs. They use communication to keep their offerings on, as they put it, the "top of their clients' minds."

Let's return to our client who hopes to lose weight through exercise. She may recall hearing advertisements about a local fitness club. If this club is considered an appropriate and appealing option, the search for solutions will cease. The communication that placed the club into the individual's evoked set of solutions has done its job. If, however, the club seems unacceptable, then others in the evoked set may be explored. She may look to clubs and programs with which she is aware. If none of these meet her requirements, more research may be required. She will look outside her evoked set, perhaps asking friends or calling a local leisure agency. Once adequate information is gathered, a decision can be made.

This *decision* may be to participate, to delay participation, or even to begin the process anew. This last option is often exercised when readily available alternatives seem unacceptable. In the fitness example, the individual may discover that available classes are too demanding or expensive or are offered at inconvenient times. The individual may begin the process again but seek related options (e.g., locations of walking trails, swim classes, hiking clubs) that seem to offer a more acceptable solution.

Types of Decisions and the Persuasive Challenge

Decisions can be of two types. The multi-staged process described here represents *complex* decision making. Complex decisions demand that the decision maker allocate cognitive resources in order to make them. As a result, participants typically engage in complex decision making only when they believe that some *risk* is involved. Risk exists when the purchase decision is characterized by uncertainty combined with elevated consequences. Uncertainty is a product of perception. If the individual believes that there is a likelihood of making an error or mispurchase (Assael, 1984), then uncertainty exists.

Perceptions of uncertainty vary widely from one individual to the next. One participant may believe that it is easy to make a poor choice, while the next may believe that it's difficult to go amiss. As a result, the same decision may be complex for one person but not for the next.

Uncertainty is much reduced in the case of highly standardized programs, because one is perceived as being the same as the next. For example, parents may not be concerned which open swim their child attends simply because they perceive all such swims as offering the same benefits.

The level and nature of consequences associated with a purchase may also influence decision making. Higher level consequences inevitably result in complex decision making. These consequences are typically psychological (pride, embarrassment) or monetary in nature. For example, a service that is consumed publicly, like a fitness class, generates higher psychological costs than does one consumed privately, such as an exercise regime undertaken at home. A public class is more likely to generate feelings of self-doubt, while exercise in the privacy of one's own home has less potential for embarrassment.

In addition, items that demand greater discretionary income elevate risk for the user. A high-cost item like an adventure tour is likely to generate more complex decision making than does purchasing a soft drink at a local festival. The tour presents more uncertainty, greater cost, and a variety of challenges that demand the attention of the hopeful participant. Participants deal with these challenges by shopping around, asking friends, and evaluating alternative offerings. The individual may be open to communication efforts during all of these activities. The goal of the communicator at this stage is to tell clients how a solution fits into and improves their everyday lives. This is done by reducing uncertainty and revealing the benefits to be gained by consuming the service.

A second type of decision making is less involving in terms of cognitive resources. It is called *low-involved* decision making. Low-involved decisions avoid the many steps that characterize high-involvement processes. In cases of low involvement, the goal is one of saving rather than using cognitive resources. In this, the "simplest case of choice among alternatives, the consumer has formed some goals, acquired and evaluated some information, and must ultimately choose some alternative" (Bettman, 1979, p. 174). This choice rarely results from in-depth reflection or thought. It is not a process of finding the best option, it is a process of deciding a satisfactory option.

Low-involved shopping often results from habit. Habit, as defined by Assael (1984), is "a limitation or absence of (1) information seeking, and (2) evaluation of alternative choices" (p. 56). Habitual purchase decisions take place with the virtual absence of thought. Consumers neither question nor reflect upon habitual purchases. They simply look to familiar programs and activities each time they recognize that a desire must be fulfilled. Families purchase the same toothpaste when supplies run low; they frequent the same hotel chains when they travel; they return to the same leisure providers when they desire to learn new skills.

Habitual decisions are most pervasive in the case of frequently purchased services. For example, consumers are likely unwilling to evaluate every service provider each time they needed a haircut. This would simply consume too much energy. Instead they find an adequate provider and return to that provider each time they need that service. They will abandon this provider only as a last resort. This creates a cycle of purchase and repurchase. Brand loyalty results because with each repurchase, the consumer spends less time on searching for information and consideration of other programs (Assael, 1984).

The desire to minimize cognitive effort typically emerges in two types of settings (Hoyer, 1984). The leisure provider is advised to provide clear and appropriate messages when these conditions are present. First, low-involvement decisions may be a result of the actual purchase conditions. If the purchase does not involve sufficient risk to warrant significant cognitive processes (i.e., fees are low, one program alternative seems to be the same as the next, etc.), then a low-involvement decision is more likely. In these cases, the client may simply choose the program that meets very basic criteria. The cheapest program may be chosen, or perhaps the most convenient program will be selected. This is a type of decision making that tends to ignore rather than collect information. As a result, communications for low-involving issues should be direct and to the point. The value the program or service offers the target group should be obvious.

Second, the experience the participant brings to the purchase setting may also encourage making low-involvement assessments (Hoyer, 1984). As suggested above, low-involvement decisions often occur when the participant has made the purchase repeatedly over time. The service has already been evaluated and unless obvious changes necessitate a reevaluation, this first assessment will be used as a guide. This is the reason that many promotional efforts are directed to existing clients (Levitt, 1983). Marketers design communications to support the individual's decision to make the original purchase. In this way, the individual is more likely to repeat that same purchase next time the need arises.

The Importance of Communication at the Point of Purchase (POP)

Most shoppers approach the shopping experience with what might best be described as an open mind. Once they have decided that a leisure-related problem exists and that they are willing to address this problem, they begin searching for enticing leisure opportunities. They conduct this search while attending special events, recreational programs, or

virtually any leisure setting. While taking their children to ballet at the Y, they may be assessing opportunities for themselves in the same setting. When driving past a golf course, they may assess the quality of the course for their own use. It seems that these potential participants are always "shopping" for familiar and compelling cues to aid them in selecting their next leisure adventure.

This tendency is well understood in the retail world. Retailers know that many purchases can be classified as "impulse" events. Tonken (1997) found that four out of five purchase decisions are made, not at home, but instead while the shopper is in the store. Apparently, many purchases are unplanned and result from interest generated by promotional displays. Assael (1984) reports that 27 percent of consumers bought more unplanned items because of in-store displays, 35 percent of consumers bought more unplanned items as a result of free samples and demonstrations, and finally, 56 percent of consumers bought more unplanned items as a result of price promotions.

The retail world has responded to this tendency with aggressive, point-of-purchase (POP) advertising. Such advertising efforts encourage either trial (an introduction function) or repurchase (a remind function). They do so by drawing attention to the product. This very act may be enough to generate purchase behavior. POP advertising also serves to remind loyal shoppers that their favorite service is available. This, too, may be sufficient to prompt action. For example, signs posted at a gymnasium might remind members to renew their lockers for the upcoming year. Sandwich boards outside a recreation facility might encourage passers-by to drop in for a complimentary tour of the facility. These simple techniques are wildly successful in encouraging and directing behavior. Indeed, the simple sandwich board, placed in high-traffic locations, has been identified by retailers as one of the single, most effective advertising techniques (Point-Of-Purchase Advertising Institute, 1997).

Communication and Group Decision Making

Not all decisions are made by individuals. Many decisions that affect the leisure marketer are made by small groups. Any effort to work with other providers, for example, will involve working with groups. Perhaps a leisure provider hopes to recruit sponsors for a major initiative. Sponsorship initiatives almost always involve the input of many individuals. Perhaps a festival organizer requires the assistance of service clubs in order to hold a special event. This, too, will involve the participation of several individuals and groups. As a result, leisure marketers now study how organizational decisions are made. Of greatest interest to this chapter is the impact of group dynamics on decision-making processes. Once these processes are understood, communication efforts can be planned accordingly.

Marketers assume that decisions made within the organizational or group context do not result from the actions or initiatives of one individual. Efforts to undertake, select, or negotiate cooperative initiatives will be made by groups called "buying centers" (Webster & Wind, 1972a. 1972b) or decision-making units (DMU) (Corey, 1983). Buying centers are comprised of several individuals, each fulfilling separate roles and functions. One individual may review initial applications to ensure that they comply with internal organizational policies. Another may compare various applications to establish their relative merits. At each stage of this process, communications must ensure that applications comply with the target group's policies and priorities.

The actions of all buying centers represent the coordinated behaviors of many interdependent subunits (Johnston & McQuiston, 1985). Though its members share a common purpose, each may pursue their own goals and priorities (Helgeson & Beatty, 1985). This suggests that communication efforts have to be designed for several key decision makers simultaneously.

The involvement of a buying center may vary with the complexity and risk associated with a given initiative. Robinson, Faris, and Wind (1967) offered the notion of "buy classes" to explain this phenomenon. Though this model is somewhat dated, decades of research continue to support its basic assumptions (Anderson, Chu, & Weitz, 1987). Buy classes represent a continuum of situations depending upon the relative novelty of the decision setting. A *straight rebuy* is characterized as a routine decision. Like the habitual purchase described above, it requires minimal levels of deliberation and limited involvement is required by members of a buying center. A single individual may be responsible for making this type of decision.

A *modified rebuy* may involve a routine decision, but additional information is deemed necessary before the decision can be made. For example, a local service club may make an annual donation to assist the local park and recreation department in holding a softball tournament. Each time the request is received, it is treated as a straight rebuy. The board of directors simply authorizes their treasurer to forward a cheque to the leisure agency. This year, however, a change has been introduced to the request so the decision-making dynamic will also change. This year, the leisure provider hopes to expand the tournament. The agency asks the service group for the traditional financial donation, but also asks for several volunteers to help with the event. This latest request might be considered as a modified rebuy because the traditional request has been altered to include the provision of volunteers. This change will necessitate the involvement of more decision makers. Their involvement will likely slow the decision-making process and may introduce greater uncertainty regarding the outcome of the deliberations. As a result, the leisure agency will have to provide much more specific and detailed communications to help with this new decision.

The final buy class, the *new task* setting, is characterized by the greatest degree of uncertainty, and an increased probability of error (Robinson et al., 1967). Consequently, the introduction of controversial information or a request for increased involvement might encourage a service organization to consider the request as a "new buy." Generally, as complexity and novelty grow, so too should the size and character of the buying center. While routine decisions may be dominated by small numbers of lower level staff members, costly new buys may involve higher levels of decision, makers (Pingry, 1976). Unfortunately, larger groups require more time to reach decisions, and progress toward final decisions may be erratic as a result (McCall & Kaplan, 1990). The communication challenge grows as uncertainty grows. Again, the communicator must show each member of the group how the service fits into the organization's own priorities.

Players in the Buying Center

Four player types or role patterns are common to the buying center. They are the (1) gatekeeper, (2) the influencer, (3) the decider, and (4) the buyer. *Gatekeepers* are those who control the types and amounts of information available to other members in the buying center. If they believe the program or initiative is a worthwhile endeavor, they ensure the rest of the group is exposed to relevant information on the topic. If they are unsure of the quality of the initiative or the provider, communication efforts will be ignored, and no one else in the group will learn of them.

Influencers are those who may have direct experience with the initiative or program being discussed. Individuals outside the buying center commonly act as influencers. They provide members of a buying center with advice or information on the quality of the initiative. Groups members may draw upon a surprisingly diverse cast of characters to help influence their decision. They may ask friends or even contact other participants rather than rely on formal communications with the leisure marketer. The views of these outsiders are taken into account as decisions are being made. Negative reports are likely to result in the decision not to cooperate with the leisure provider. This suggests the power of word-of-mouth communication in these instances.

Deciders possess the power to make final decisions. They occupy a variety of positions in any organization. Generally the more compli-

cated or costly the initiative, the more elevated the positions of the eventual deciders. Small, local projects may be referred to lower level members of the center whereas larger initiatives are directed to senior staff. Indeed, if a decision involves a great many organizational resources, it may even be sent to a group of senior managers (e.g., a board, task force, working committee, etc.) for final disposition. This complicates the communication process, because it simultaneously involves so many decision makers. Each may bring a unique perspective to the deliberations, and all these perspectives will have to be addressed through communication efforts.

Buyers undertake negotiations with the leisure provider. Buyers tend to consider the buying process as an exercise in negotiation. They expect and even prefer that ongoing negotiations take place while the actual purchase is being organized. Such negotiation might clarify misunderstandings, rectify problems, or simply help both partners respond as each project evolves. This suggests the eventual importance of two-way communication that can only be handled through personal means. This negotiation ensures that the corporation's interests are being preserved, so the leisure marketer must ensure that communications focus on benefits to the partner.

Family Decision Making

These industry-based insights also apply to family decision making. Consider the case in which a family is deciding upon leisure programs for the children in the household. It seems they, too, rely on gatekeepers to filter the many communications that enter the household. Howard and Madrigal (1990) found that mothers typically played this crucial role in determining what leisure programs were eventually considered by family members. In this way, mothers exert considerable influence over the number and types of options considered by the rest of the family. Mothers seem more influential than fathers (or children for that matter) during the search for recreation activities for their children. Children are more likely to play the ultimate role of decision maker, however. They tend to be given final authority when the actual purchase decisions are being made. In this study, fathers played only a limited role in making recreation activity decisions for the children.

Industry and family-based research on decision making suggest that communications must be designed for several different players when a group is involved in a purchase decision. No one communication effort will fulfill the criteria set by all group members. Industry responds to this demand through the judicious application of the promotional mix. For example, providers may create detailed brochures to help draw attention to their products, but they complement these written efforts with face-to-face contact by trained sales staff. They know that the gatekeeper may appreciate a glossy brochure, but the eventual decision maker will require more detailed information before a decision is possible.

The Importance of Program Name Selection

It seems that clients allocate only seconds when scanning brochures and other programming literature. They look for obvious *items of interest*. If these items are present, they may allocate additional cognitive resources to the publication. If these items are not present, they will ignore the rest of the publication. This is perhaps discouraging to those who spend months preparing these publications, but it reflects the often ruthless standards clients place on written publications.

One of the best ways to communicate, with low-involved participants in particular, is with judicious program name selection. The very human limitations discussed in this chapter render names as one of the single most important pieces of information a provider can offer. Names represent dominant cues to those seeking to make sense of leisure programs (Jacoby, Szybillo, & Busata-Schach, 1977). It seems that clients allocate only seconds when scanning brochures and other programming literature. They look for obvious *items of*

interest. If these items are present, they may allocate additional cognitive resources to the publication. If the items are not present, they will ignore the rest of the publication. This is perhaps discouraging to those who spend months preparing these publications, but it reflects the often ruthless standards clients place on written publications.

There is both anecdotal and empirical evidence suggesting that names represent "the hook that hangs the brand on the product ladder in the prospect's mind" (Ries & Trout, 1986, p. 71). Ries and Trout suggest that name selection is the most important marketing decision for any product. By way of example, they note that "Hog Island in the Caribbean was going nowhere until they changed its name to Paradise Island" (Ries & Trout, p. 71).

Names represent compelling links to existing cognitive groupings. They suggest where a product can be stored in memory (Helgeson & Beatty, 1985) and provide a means through which objects, people, and issues can be identified and classified (Jacoby, Olson, & Haddock, 1971). Consider the name assigned to a fitness center. The name "Exercise Center" might suggest that participation there demands exertion, thus leading to classification under the cognitive heading of physical activity. The same facility given the name "Weight and Stress Control Center" may generate a less physical classification.

In one study, subjects tended to seek less information once a brand name was provided (Jacoby et al., 1977). This was the case even when additional information was readily available. In other words, names helped clients categorize the product offering and discouraged the application of additional cognitive resources. Elaboration of further information seemed unnecessary once the name had been processed. As a result, clues like names should be chosen with care then used extensively to help clients understand product offerings.

Berry and Parasuraman (1991) offer very specific advice on name selection. Although they refer specifically to brand names, their insights are useful to anyone contemplating names for programs, services or facilities. They advise that, in order to be effective communication tools, names should pass four basic tests.

The first is *distinctiveness*. The name must clearly distinguish the program or provider from competitors. The term "swimming" classes, for example, is descriptive but fails to differentiate one swim program from another. The second test is one of *relevance*. Does the name generate an image that is meaningful to the target market? Further, does the name offer a fair representation of the service itself? The third test is that of *memorability*. Memorability refers to the ease with which the name can be understood, used, and remembered. Finally, the name must be *flexible* enough to accommodate changes in strategy over time.

One leisure agency took this advice to heart by renaming a swim program for novice adults called "Adult Swim." They decided upon the new name "Swim for Absolutely Terrified Adults." This new choice was more descriptive and certainly more memorable than its predecessor. The program increased in popularity, and the department has expanded the "absolutely terrified" theme to include programs on skiing, use of the Internet and computers, and even high school completion diploma programs. This name choice fulfilled all the criteria for a great name. It was memorable, it spoke to the concerns of the target client group, it was certainly distinctive, and flexible enough to be used in many related programs.

Communication and Message Design

The actual message represents the single most important element of the communication process. Each message must appeal to the target market in a way that encourages appropriate action. Messages are often divided into two basic sections. These sections offer background and foreground information. *Background* information provides essential but not very compelling information about the service. For example, material on the time and location of a swim program offers necessary background information, but it is unlikely to convince a potential participant to register for the program. This is why background information must be supplemented with foreground information.

Foreground information is intended to draw the attention of the user. This material must make clear how the service improves the life of the client. It must reveal how the service fits into clients' lives. Foreground components are typically used in a process of either *subverting* or *forcing*. Subverting "means presenting something that is disconcerting or charming, something unexpected enough that it slips past the guard of indifference"(Kover, 1995, p. 599). Subverting relies on messages that are cute, seductive, or compelling in ways that encourage the client to pay attention. This is often accomplished by using interesting photographs or appealing program names. The process of forcing is more straightforward in its approach. It "means jolting the viewer into paying attention" (Kover, p. 599) through surprise or amusement.

Message *content* may be based on one of three basic types of appeals. The first is that of the *rational* appeal. This appeal follows the *central* or *deliberative* route to persuasion discussed earlier. Deliberation takes place as the individual reflects on the arguments presented in the message.

As the individual considers the merits of the argument, new belief structures are encouraged (Ajzen & Fishbein, 1980). This is considered a logical and rational means of persuasion requiring high levels of cognitive energy. As was made clear earlier in this chapter, however, there is a growing body of research that suggests that consumers may ignore or resist messages that encourage deliberation. Distraction, existing biases, lack of relevance, and lack of motivation may all mediate the degree to which the individual accepts communication (Petty, Unnava, & Strathman, 1991).

A second type of appeal is less rational in its approach. It is the *emotional* appeal. It relies not on reflection, but instead on the creation of positive feelings. Persuasive effects enjoyed by emotional appeals may result more from cues generated by the message (i.e., mood) than from any elaboration of the actual message content (Batra, 1986).

Finally, a *moral* appeal relies upon audience members' sense of what is right or "appropriate." Leisure providers often use this approach while building support for their initiatives. They build upon existing notions of what is best for the participant, for important units like families, and for the community. Brochures asking citizens to volunteer for the good of the community, requesting donors to contribute much-needed funding, or encouraging campers to avoid littering all rely largely on moral appeals.

Both the emotional and moral approaches are similar in that they are often effective without requiring deliberation or reflection on the part of the audience. These approaches are effective simply because they avoid the pitfalls of the rational appeal. They follow the peripheral or nondeliberative route to persuasion discussed earlier.

Nondeliberative processes rely on existing biases and cue utilization (van Raaj, 1991). As a result, these approaches facilitate acceptance or rejection "in the absence of a diligent consideration of the true merits of the object or issue" (Petty et al., 1991, p. 245). Appeals to the peripheral route may be particularly effective for intangible or symbol-laden services (Holbrook & O'Shaughnessy, 1984). They may also be useful for complicated services, because they can "slip past the guard of indifference" set up to avoid dealing with such complexity. Nondeliberative messages can also help develop a positive mood toward the communicator. Once this is accomplished, the target population is more likely to listen and respond in a positive manner to subsequent messages from that source.

In a sense, positive mood helps avoid both distortion or disinterest. It encourages participants to open their minds to the message. As a result, many promotional campaigns now include emotion-based messages. They are intended to form a positive emotional link with potential participants. Once a link has been established, promotions then adopt a more detailed and personal format. At that point, the client may be more ready and willing to listen to complex message formats.

Nike has used this general approach to considerable advantage. For years their corporate advertisements exhorted consumers with the single phrase "Just Do It." This emotional appeal was devoid of any detail, so it discouraged counterargument. It did, however, encourage action. Nike's logic was straightforward. Once consumers obeyed their emotional appeal for action, they were more likely to visit sporting goods stores to equip themselves for activity. When in the stores, sales staff could offer more content-based messages. Typically, these staff would attempt to engage and enlighten consumers with additional information on the relative merits of their products.

Most automobile advertisements use the same approach. Television and print advertisements focus on the beauty and performance of the automobiles but offer little in the way of details. These ads are designed to encourage consumers to visit dealerships where trained salespeople are ready to use more personal and effective communication techniques. The promotional goal is one of appealing to the prospective consumer. Copywriters create appeal with something called "the Hook."

The Importance of the "Hook"

Marketers assume that their clients are bombarded daily with thousands of messages promoting one product over another. These clients are simply unable to process the thousands of messages they receive, so they begin to ignore many such messages. In effect, they cultivate personal disinterest as a means of self-preservation. Copywriters know this and assume that their target audience is profoundly uninterested in their efforts to communicate.

One copywriter, referring to a typical television viewer, paints a rather bleak picture of that individual's life:

This guy works hard all day. Nobody says anything good to him. He comes home to a family that pays no attention to him. He is tired. He has stuff to do around the house. It's too much. So he sits in front of the tube. He just sits and watches. He doesn't want to be challenged. It could be a woman, too. (Kover, 1995, p. 599)

Copywriters plan and execute their promotional efforts accordingly. They assume that clients wait for information rather than seek it out. They may accept an interesting message, but only after the message has penetrated the indifference they have erected as defence against information overload. Copywriters refer to the mechanism used to penetrate these defences as the *hook*. The hook must break through "clutter, dullness and resistance" (Kover, 1995, p. 599). It is intended to gain attention so that the marketer may begin a dialogue with the client.

Most hooks focus on benefits. The communicator discovers what the client wants, then assures the client that the service fulfills this desire. The communication must be direct and it must be believable. The best communications do this by:

1. Naming the benefit (and being specific while doing so).

2. Telling what the service will do.

3. Making it easy for consumers to visualize the benefit (Burton & Purvis, 1996).

The hook has been designed around a variety of themes. These themes have relied upon virtually any appeal that marketers have believed would be persuasive. Appeals have focused on negative emotions like fear, peer pressure, and guilt, as well as positive forces like excitement, self-improvement, and fun. Sex is a common theme, as is success, fame, and "the good life." All these themes are thought to gain and hold the attention of the

casual observer. Once attention is obtained, the marketer can then spread a more detailed message about the value to be gained through participation.

Main Points

· Communication conveys meaning.

· Every interaction between a provider and a client represents some type of communication.

· Clients use communication as evidence of the quality provided by a leisure provider.

· The process of communication is complicated by noise within the communication setting and by the cognitive limitations of the audience.

· Communication efforts all hope eventually to influence behavior.

· Communication efforts must recognize that individual decisions to participate in leisure programs are often made by groups.

· Decisions to participate in leisure programs may be influenced by seemingly irrelevant variables like program names or the appearance of a brochure.

· Persuasive messages can focus on emotion and/or the intellect when making their appeal.

References

Ajzen, I., & Fishbein, M. (1980). *Understanding attitudes and predicting human behavior.* Englewood Cliffs, NJ: Prentice-Hall.

Ajzen, I., & Peterson, G. (1988). Contingent value measurement: The price of everything and the value of nothing? In G.L. Peterson, B.L. Driver, & R. Gregory (Eds.), *Amenity resource valuation* (pp. 65-76). State College, PA: Venture.

Anderson, E., Chu, W., & Weitz, B. (1987). Industrial purchasing: An empirical exploration of the buy class framework. *Journal of Marketing, 51,* 71-86.

Assael, H. (1984). *Consumer behavior and marketing action* (2nd ed.). Boston: Kent Publishing.

Batra, R. (1986). Affective advertising: Role, processes, and measurement. In R. Peterson, W. Hoyer, & W. Wilson (Eds.), *The role of affect in consumer behavior* (pp. 53-118). Toronto: Lexington Books.

Berry, L., & Parasuraman, A. (1991). *Marketing services: Competing through quality.* New York: The Free Press.

Bettman, J. (1979). *An information processing theory of consumer choice.* Don Mills, ON: Addison Wesley.

Bogart, L. (1996). *Strategy in advertising: Matching media and messages to markets and motivations* (3rd ed.). Chicago: NTC Business Books.

Burton, P.W., & Purvis, S.C. (1996). *Which ad pulled best?* Lincolnwood, IL: NTC Business Books.

Corey, E.R. (1983). *Industrial marketing: Cases and concepts.* Englewood Cliffs, NJ: Prentice-Hall.

Crompton, J., & Lamb, C. (1986). *Marketing government and social services.* New York: John Wiley & Sons.

Havitz, M. E. (1988). Marketing is not synonymous with commercialism. *Parks and Recreation, 23(5),* 34-36.

Hawkins, S.A., & Hoch, S.J. (1992). Low-involvement learning: Memory without evaluation. *Journal of Consumer Research, 19,* 212-225.

Helgeson, J., & Beatty, S. (1985). An information processing perspective in the internalization of price stimuli. In E. Henselmann & M. Holbrook (Eds.), *Advances in consumer research* (pp. 91-96). Provo, UT: Association for Consumer Behavior.

Holbrook, M.B., & O'Shaughnessy, J. (1984). The role of emotion in advertising. *Psychology and Marketing, 1,* 45-64.

Howard, D.R., & Madrigal, R. (1990). Who makes the decision: The parent or the child? The perceived influence of parents and children on the purchase of recreation services. *Journal of Leisure Research, 22(3),* 244-258.

Hoyer, W. (1984). An examination of consumer decision making for a common repeat purchase product. *Journal of Marketing Research, 11* 822-829.

Jacoby, J., & Olson, J. (1977). Consumer response to price: An attitudinal, information processing perspective. In Y. Wind & M. Greenberg (Eds.), *Moving ahead with attitude research* (pp.73-86). Chicago: American Marketing Association.

Jacoby, J., Olson, J., & Haddock, R. (1971). Price, brand name, and product composition characteristics as determinants of perceived quality. *Journal of Applied Psychology, 2,* 570-579.

Jacoby, J., Szybillo, G., & Busata-Schach, J. (1977). Information acquisition in brand choice situations. *Journal of Consumer Research, 2,* 209-216.

Johnston, W.J., & McQuiston, D.H. (1985). Managing interorganizational marketing. In R.E. Spekman & D.T. Wilson (Eds.), *A strategic approach to business marketing* (pp. 30-39). Chicago: American Marketing Association.

Kardes, F.R., Kalyanaram, G., Chandrashekaran, M., & Dornoff, R.J. (1993). Brand retrieval, consideration set composition, consumer choice, and the pioneering advantage. *Journal of Consumer Research, 20,* 62-75.

Kotler, P., McDougall, G., & Armstrong, G. (1988). *Marketing: Canadian edition.* Englewood Cliffs, NJ: Prentice-Hall.

Kover, A.J. (1995). Copywriters' implicit theories of communication: An exploration. *Journal of Consumer Research, 21*(3), 596-611.

Levitt, T. (1983). *The marketing imagination.* New York: The Free Press.

McCall, M., & Kaplan, R. (1990). *Whatever it takes: The realities of managerial decision making.* Englewood Cliffs, NJ: Prentice-Hall.

Petty, R., & Cacioppo, J. (1981). *Attitudes and persuasion: Classic and contemporary approaches.* Dubuque, IA: Wm. C. Brown Company.

Petty, R., Unnava, R., & Strathman, A. (1991). Theories of attitude change. In T. Robertson & H. Kassarjian (Eds.), *Handbook of consumer behavior* (pp. 241-280). Englewood Cliffs, NJ: Prentice-Hall.

Pingry, J.R. (1976). The engineer and the purchasing agent compared. *Journal of Purchasing, 10,* 33-45.

Point-Of-Purchase Advertising Institute. (1997). *The Canadian Point-Of-Purchase Advertising Institute: Standards of practice.* Washington, D.C.: Point-Of-Purchase Advertising Institute.

Ries, A., & Trout, J. (1986). *Positioning: The battle for your mind.* New York: Warner Books.

Robinson, P.J., Faris, C.W., & Wind, Y. (1967). *Industrial buying behavior and creative marketing.* Boston: Allyn and Bacon.

Schiffman, L.G., & Kanuk, L.L. (1997). *Consumer behavior* (6th ed.). Englewood Cliffs, NJ: Prentice-Hall.

Sherif, M., & Hovland, C. (1961). *Social judgement: Assimilation and contrast effects in communication and attitude change.* New Haven, CT: Yale University Press.

Tonken, E. (1997). Appearances count. *Discount Merchandiser, 37,* 104.

van Raaj, W. (1991). The formation and use of expectations in consumer decision making. In T. Robertson & H. Kassarjian (Eds.), *Handbook of consumer behavior* (pp. 401-418). Englewood Cliffs, NJ: Prentice-Hall.

Webster, F.E., & Wind, Y. (1972a). A general model for understanding industrial buying behavior. *Journal of Marketing, 36,* 12-19.

Webster, F.E., & Wind, Y. (1972b). *Organizational buying behavior.* Englewood Cliffs, NJ: Prentice-Hall.

City of Waterloo

CHAPTER

8

Communicate Value

Leisure providers develop communication strategies hoping to influence behavior among target group members. Many of their communications offer clues about the value of their program offering. These clues are intended to provide a consistent and desirable image (Schneider & Bowen, 1995). This image must suggest both the desirability of the program offering and the suitability of the provider. Given the importance of this image, it is not surprising that promotional activities often dominate discussion of marketing activity. Unfortunately, casual observers and even many marketers often consider promotion as synonymous with marketing. They believe that marketing is largely an exercise in promotion. As this text attests, however, promotion is only one small part of marketing effort. It represents the marketer's formal efforts to communicate with client groups. It is an important component of the marketing mix, but only one component, nevertheless.

Promotion and the Marketing Mix

The primary promotional challenge is often characterized as one of communicating

benefit. The importance of benefit "is characterized by Leo McGinneva's famous clarification about why people buy quarter-inch drill bits: 'they don't want quarter-inch bits. They want quarter-inch holes'" (Levitt, 1983, p. 128). In other words, clients do not seek programs or services. Rather they seek the benefits these programs offer. The marketer is challenged, therefore, to make benefits clear.

The very intangibility of services increases the difficulty of this task. This intangibility can render services difficult to envision or appreciate. How then can benefits be made obvious when the service itself is not at all easy to understand? How does the marketer convey the happiness created by a recreation service, the contentment experienced as a result of a leisure program, or the satisfaction gained from a leisure task well done?

Promotion addresses these challenges by *tangibilizing* the service (Levitt, 1983; Berry & Parasuraman, 1991). Ads are used, for example, to emphasize tangible cues associated with leisure services. This has become a very popular technique. Pictures of facilities, happy participants, and park scenes adorn virtually all leisure agency publications. These efforts are intended to make benefits clear. If the promotional material can't highlight these types of tangible cues, the marketer might create tangible representations of the service. Mascots, logos, and program names are often used for this purpose. They are chosen for the image they convey (e.g., strength, speed, or even reliability) and the benefits they represent.

Though enhancing tangibility and perceptions of benefit is an important role for promotion, many now believe these efforts address only half the promotional challenge. Clients seek benefits but they also seek to reduce risk (Levitt, 1983). As suggested in the previous chapter, risk exists when the purchase decision is characterized by uncertainty combined with elevated consequences. Marketers know that participants' leisure choices often represent an exercise in risk reduction as much as they represent a search for benefit. Indeed, fear of mispurchase may act as a primary motivator in many consumption decisions (Assael, 1984). Clients are as worried about avoiding the wrong service as they are about finding the right one. As a result, communication efforts should not only offer benefits but also suggest how costs and risks might be reduced.

This suggests that communications must reduce clients' perceptions of risk as well as provide clues about benefits. Consider how a program brochure might focus on both enhanced benefit and reduced cost. While many leisure brochures begin with a message from an elected official or an advertisement, it may be better to open with a full-page advertisement offering "10 ways to get the most from this brochure." These tips can make suggestions on how and when to register, how to search for favorite programs, and how to navigate through the publication. These tips all suggest how benefits may be enhanced while reducing risk of errors and subsequent unhappiness.

Combining benefit enhancement and risk reduction is actually a process of communicating *value*. Value is that ephemeral quality that clients seek with each and every decision to participate. They hope that the action they take offers the greatest possible benefit while generating the fewest costs. Value draws the client to the provider. The importance of value permeates virtually all marketing discussions. Earlier in this text, the notion of the value

proposition suggested that the provider create a bundle of services that fulfill the requirements of the client. This is a process of value creation. Once created, the existence of this value bundle must be conveyed to the client. This is the process of value communication and no program can succeed without an effective communication strategy. The provider cannot succeed unless the client is made aware of the value that provider offers.

Creating a Promotional Strategy

Effective promotions begin with planning promotional strategy. Such strategy involves the judicious allocation of resources. Promotional strategy varies within different industries and with provider priorities. For example, the health club industry approach is often one of heavy promotion. New health clubs must typically adopt aggressive promotional strategies if they hope to compete with industry leaders. Conversely, public leisure agencies seem almost hesitant to promote their programs. They tend to rely on a few rather passive promotional techniques and rarely expand their efforts beyond seasonal brochures. Those who promote within the public context will likely promote in a way that is consistent with other public providers. Consequently, for better or worse, industry standards often shape general promotional strategy.

Promotional strategy is also determined by the provider's own marketing plan. The plan dictates who will be served. It outlines how best to reach key client groups and identifies their concerns, their hopes, and their constraints. Promotional strategy must then reflect these concerns. It must be consistent with overall marketing strategy.

Promotional strategy represents an exercise in fine-tuning the larger-scale marketing strategy. If marketing objectives focus on a particular target market that has been unresponsive in the past, then the promotional strategy must focus on that group with a compelling message, one that will encourage action. If the strategy is one of encouraging higher participation rates among active clients, then the focus will be on greater involvement for these group members.

Two basic promotional strategies are possible. A *push* strategy is designed to reach final consumers by pushing the programs through a provider's distribution channels. As shall be discussed later in chapter 11, leisure providers may distribute their programs through public agencies, not-for-profit organizations, or even sport governing bodies. A push strategy typically offers incentives, promotions, and personal selling to encourage these channel members' cooperation. It encourages participants to seek out and participate with these channel members. For example, a municipal leisure provider hoping to build support for community groups may offer discounts on community swim programs to all those who volunteer with those groups. This type of incentive can benefit everyone from the client to the channel member to the original provider.

The nature and extent of push communication efforts are typically based upon the size of the distribution network, the power of the channel members, and the nature of the provider-channel member relationship. For example, providers who rely on several small channel members will often use nonpersonal communication efforts, simply because these efforts are relatively inexpensive to carry out. This technique reduces the cost of each individual contact with many members. A municipal agency may send out regular communiques to neighborhood associations notifying them of upcoming programs and events. Conversely, they may devote more time and effort to large or powerful channel members. For example, they may schedule regular meetings with large sponsors or philanthropic donors who participate in their delivery system. They tend to be more careful and direct with powerful channel members because they cannot afford to lose these members. In these cases, personal communication is often the technique of choice.

A *pull* strategy is directed toward the ultimate consumer of a service. It is intended to create demand for the service among end users. Pull strategies comprise most of what is called marketing promotions. They, too, use time-intensive techniques like personal communication but by necessity, they are often large-scale efforts to reach hundreds, thousands, or even millions of potential consumers. The tools of the pull strategist are the same as those of the push strategist. They rely on techniques designed to create interest and action among potential client groups. These are described in more detail below. Whatever the strategy, communication efforts occur in stages. As always, the process begins with the client. The marketer must return to the opportunity assessment and ask, who is my audience?

Describing the Audience

The first step of communication is one of describing the client group for whom the message is intended. Strategies can then be developed that reflect the life conditions in which audience members find themselves. Obvious characteristics like age or place of residence are often used to describe end users. These descriptors have the advantage of simplicity. They are easy to measure and observe and typically offer considerable insight into audience habits and preferences.

Age

Age suggests the types of experiences client group members may have shared over the course of their collective lifetimes. Communication themes can be planned accordingly. For example, advertisers believe that clients are interested in images that are consistent with their own early years. They believe that baby boomers who grew up in the 1960s and 1970s will respond to images from that distinctive time in their own lives. Many advertisers rely on the sights and sounds of this period to generate positive appeal for the aging boomers.

Age is also indicative of client behavior patterns, and knowledge of these patterns may be of use to the communicator. Television is the single, most popular, leisure-time activity, and viewing increases with passing years. This suggests that many potential clients may be reached through television advertising. Marketers are also aware that teens tend to watch television late in the afternoon. Older adults tend to watch current affairs programming. This suggests when and how television-based efforts to reach these groups might be scheduled.

As an aside, many marketers are now exploiting the importance of television viewing without having to pay for expensive television advertising. Many advertisers now focus, not on television itself, but on written publications that are associated with television viewing. Media guides that grace most coffee tables are an ideal advertising venue. Clients move methodically though the guides each week to keep track of daily viewing opportunities. It is unlikely that any other weekly publication receives such scrutiny from potential clients. Providers know this and often highlight their own events throughout the week by placing them on the appropriate pages of the guide.

Place of Residence

Place of residence helps the communicator both locate and describe potential client groups. It's perhaps obvious how residence can help locate potential clients. Their residence is a location at which clients can be reached. Just as important are the patterns by which clients tend to locate their homes. Housing districts tend to attract people with similar interests and backgrounds. As a result, these districts each develop their own character and appeal. New neighborhoods often attract young families seeking other new families and open space for their young children. Downtown areas may attract upscale, unmarried residents seeking the convenience and status of the downtown core. Downtown areas may also attract the homeless because shelters and other resources are more available in core areas. The often unique character of these communities helps the leisure promoter plan targeted communications accordingly.

Values and Lifestyle

The most profound descriptors are those that focus on the client's own values and lifestyle. These values are typically expressed in terms of preferences, attitudes, and activity patterns. This insight is particularly relevant when creating communication strategy. Marketers must understand the client's perspective before meaningful communication efforts can be undertaken. The importance of preferences and attitudes is not lost on marketers. They often plan their communication efforts based upon their clients' desire or readiness to take part. They focus on what is known as the client groups' *stage of readiness* (Kotler, McDougall, & Armstrong, 1991). Stage of readiness refers to the group members' willingness to undertake the desired action. There are six readiness stages:

- *Awareness*. The clients are aware of the service but may express no interest in the service or the benefits it offers.

- *Knowledge*. The clients are not only aware of the service but understand how the service might meet their own particular wants and preferences; however, they place no emotional attachment to that service.

- *Liking*. The clients have begun to reveal some attachment toward some aspect of the service.

- *Preference*. The clients express a preference for one service over another.

- *Conviction*. Their preference for the service is crystallized and they decide to make a behavior choice.

- *Purchase/behavior*. Clients actually make the behavioral commitment to the chosen activity.

The notion of stage of readiness has tremendous implications for any communication strategy. Levitt (1983) suggests that much of the advertising undertaken by the private

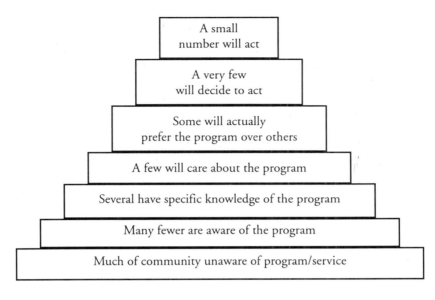

A small
number will act

A very few
will decide to act

Some will actually
prefer the program over others

A few will care about the program

Several have specific knowledge of the program

Many fewer are aware of the program

Much of community unaware of program/service

Figure 8.1: Profile of a Community Using Readiness Levels

sector is actually targeted to clients who have already taken part in an activity or made a purchase. This advertising is intended to congratulate these individuals for having made that decision and to encourage repeat participation. Levitt suggests that the private sector virtually ignores those furthest from the action readiness stage because the likelihood of their making a relevant purchase is relatively remote. Instead, they focus on pleasing and encouraging existing clients.

In terms of Figure 8.1, private sector marketers begin at the top of the readiness pyramid and work their way toward the bottom (resources permitting). Public sector advertisers tend to take a very different approach. They focus on communicating with the entire community, hoping to generate interest among the disinterested and activity among the inactive. They hope that by providing information on leisure programs to all of their citizens they will encourage these citizens to progress along the readiness continuum. This suggests that much of their promotional effort is directed to unresponsive or uninterested groups.

Whatever the approach, the marketer must begin by understanding potential target groups so that efforts can then be devoted to reach and appeal to group members. The next step in the communication process is that of deciding how each group is to be treated. This is a process of setting objectives.

Establishing Promotional Objectives

Any promotional exercise should be guided by agency objectives for that initiative. Objective setting often begins by establishing the type of *client response* the marketer hopes to encourage. What is the provider trying to achieve with this communication strategy? Specifically, what behaviors are the clients intended to change or undertake? Target behaviors might include making a purchase, taking part in an activity, or even of reducing another behavior that has become problematic (e.g., littering in parks, etc.).

Promotional objectives are often discussed in terms of the *hierarchy of effects*. The hierarchy focuses on the intended effect of the communication effort. Building on the notion of client readiness, the stages of the hierarchy are often expressed as Awareness, Interest, Decision, and Assessment (AIDA). Promotional objectives are typically intended to move clients through the hierarchy.

The most basic level within the hierarchy is that of awareness. Marketers know that action begins with basic awareness of a program or provider. Awareness may be necessary but it is certainly not sufficient to ensure behavior. It is simply a stepping stone to the more favorable stage of interest. Interest is a critical stage in the hierarchy, because it suggests that the client is now willing to entertain the thought of participation. While interest is a desirable state, it too stops short of success. The hierarchy dictates that those who are interested must now be encouraged to decide, then to participate, and finally to assess the quality of that participation.

Communications encourage potential participants to progress through the hierarchy by informing, educating, persuading, and/or reminding (Crompton & Lamb, 1986).

Informing refers to basic information such as program dates, locations, and times. This background material appeals to potential clients only once their interest in a program has been piqued.

Educating develops or improves potential participants' levels of understanding so that they recognize the value of participation (e.g., that cardiovascular fitness is desirable or attainable). It may also be intended to help clients make the most of leisure opportunities. Research devoted to service quality suggests that education may also be necessary to help clients consume and enjoy leisure opportunities. These educational efforts should help the client gain the greatest value from any given participation.

Persuading refers specifically to highlighting benefits of a particular program (e.g., convenience, atmosphere, or quality) in a way that encourages action on the part of the client. The persuasive component of any given message generally revolves around the notion of value. Benefits of participation are made clear, and costs of taking part are de-emphasized.

Reminding is used to reassure existing participants or supporters that the program is of value. Typically reminders fulfill two separate but related roles. The first is to remind satisfied users that they should repurchase or reregister. The second role is to remind these customers of the reasons they made this participation decision. Both increase the likelihood that clients will return to a given program, facility, or site.

Communication may pursue all four goals as marketers attempt to move clients along the hierarchy. They try to ensure that those who are unaware will be made aware, those who are aware will become interested, those interested few will make a positive decision to participate, and those who participate will remember that participation fondly. This final stage, that of assessment, is of critical importance to the leisure marketer. When evaluation of an event or a service is positive, the client is likely to seek out that event or service a second time.

A survey asked recreation professionals about communication goals for new or innovative programs (Johnson-Tew, Havitz, & McCarville, 1999). Over half (55.4%) of the respondents reported pursuing all four goals with their communication efforts. Two-thirds (66.1%) of their messages contained an element of persuasion, over half (55.4%) contained an element of education, and under one-third (28.8%) contained an element of informing. Very few (7.1%) considered reminding to be the most important message conveyed. This last finding suggests that many leisure professionals assume that current participants are already aware of the benefits of participation and that participation alone will convince them to return. This may represent a leap of faith on their part.

Planning the Promotional Mix

The *promotional mix* represents the way in which promotional resources are allocated (Nylen, 1990). The mix has four basic components, those of advertising, personal selling, publicity, and sales promotions. Each option varies in terms of its relative *efficiency* and *effectiveness*. For example, mass advertising can be very efficient, because it reaches large numbers of potential participants for minimal cost per contact. However, such efforts may be relatively ineffective for "closing" the sale, that is, convincing hesitant individuals to take part. Conversely, personal selling is ideal for closing a sale but can be costly and relatively inefficient.

Marketers recognize the inherent strengths and weaknesses of each component. They typically apply them in unison in order to achieve a variety of promotional objectives. The degree to which each of these components are applied makes up the character of the mix. The components of the mix are provided in Figure 8.2.

Advertising

Advertising is a relatively inflexible, impersonal communication tool able to reach large numbers of people at minimal cost per contact. It is comprised of mass media (print, electronic), displays (special events, posters, signs), and settings or atmospheres (office or building design, staff appearance). Advertising excels at building awareness or spreading knowledge and can build positive emotional ties to a service offering or provider. Any marketer hoping to make effective use of advertising must (1) establish advertising objectives, (2) develop the creative strategy, (3) develop the media plan, and (4) generate an advertising budget. Each is described here.

1. Establishing Objectives

Advertising efforts should be guided by both short- and long-term objectives. These objectives arise directly from promotional goals and the larger marketing strategy. Strategy may, for example, dictate that the provider adopt a "low-cost/high-volume" position in the marketplace. General strategic goals are then developed that help the provider occupy that position. For example, these goals might focus on program distribution (as wide as possible), cost (low-cost opportunities), and even staff training.

	Non-personal	Blend	Personal
Paid	advertising		personal selling
		sales promotion public relations	
Unpaid	publicity		Word-of-mouth PSA

Figure 8.2: The Promotional Mix

Source: Sandhusen, 1993, p. 399

Promotional goals are also developed to support these other efforts. Such goals offer a general direction for communication decisions. As discussed earlier, they typically do so by focusing on informing, educating, persuading, and/or reminding. Communication goals for new programs might dictate that promotions both inform and educate. Goals for non-responsive client groups might focus on persuasion, and so on.

Promotional objectives then establish how these goals are to be carried out. Recall that objectives are both specific and measurable. There may be several objectives arising from one communication goal. The object of this exercise is to outline the what, where, how, who, and why of each communication effort. Objectives can dictate for whom the communication is intended (e.g., 25 % of older adults living in their own homes will learn of program X by year end), deal with the way in which advertisements are distributed (e.g., advertisements will be placed in all three local newspapers prior to seasonal program registration), or they may focus on the details of each individual message (e.g., all messages will now provide the agency phone number).

2. Developing the Creative Strategy

Creative strategy determines the content and structure of the message being directed to the target audience. It is a statement of what the advertising effort is intended to achieve. It offers a focal point around which the creative process revolves and a benchmark against which ideas can be evaluated. The strategy must make clear the (1) target audience, (2) objectives of the effort, (3) the benefit package being promoted (why the participant should take part in this program), and (4) the tone of the advertising material. This final element, that of tone, is of particular importance to the effectiveness of any message. The tone of the message must be consistent with the position the provider hopes to occupy. Will the tone be child-like with great enthusiasm and warmth or mysterious with exotic images and colors?

Creative strategy often relies upon a few guiding principles. The first is one of *simplicity*.

As discussed in the last chapter, the advertising audience is often unable or unwilling to allocate significant amounts of cognitive resources to interpret and understand advertisements. Messages must be compelling and self-evident if they are to draw the attention of the casual observer. Further, complex messages are also prone to encoding errors. Audience members who are asked to recall long or complex messages may make errors in committing this information to long-term memory. Again, simplicity in advertising seems to enhance the communication process.

The second principle is one of *repetition*. Advertising asks the audience, in effect, to learn the message being offered, and learning often requires repetition. This is because "much of the information we acquire in daily life has no value to us beyond its immediate purpose—e.g., dialing a telephone number . . . Immediate forgetting is a great blessing, since most of the information we acquire is only of momentary value" (Bogart, 1996, p. 215). Repetition overcomes this limitation. Repeated brief messages are more likely to be stored in long-term memory. As a result, most advertising strategies demand repeated exposures of important messages.

The third creative principle is that of *convenience*. Once participants have decided to take part, the advertised message should make the next step obvious. Phone numbers should be readily available. A well-known mail order retailer lists its phone number on every page of its many catalogues. Once the client selects an item for purchase, the relevant telephone number is easy to locate. Critical information like deadlines or program times and locations should be equally obvious.

The final creative principle is that of *appeal*. Messages must appeal to the intended audience if they are to be noticed. In the last chapter, this was referred to as the "hook" that brought the message to the attention of the observer. This hook is often based upon the notion of value. A value-based hook offers benefit while reducing cost. Though the notion of value has universal appeal, what is actually valued will change from group to group, from individual to individual. Promises of fitness may appeal to one group, but leave another group bored or even repelled. References to skill development may excite some but alienate others. No one hook will appeal to all target groups. Neither will one hook appeal to every member of a family. The advertiser must constantly return to the client groups to determine what they find compelling, what they consider important.

3. Developing the Media Plan

The media plan outlines how resources will be allocated to achieve the creative strategy. It is concerned with *reach* (who is to receive the message), *frequency* (how often the message is to be sent out), *timing* (when the message is to be sent out), and *means* (the media and outlets used to distribute the message).

Reach—Reach is the "extent of coverage, the percentage of people brought within exposure range of the advertising over the stated period of time" (Bogart, 1996, p. 153). Reach may be considered in terms of breadth or intensity. If the marketer believes that the target group is large, then the reach strategy may focus on breadth of contact. The objective may be one of reaching a large group of potential clients. For example, most leisure agencies send brochures to virtually every household in their respective communities. In these cases, reach is intended to be virtually universal. Conversely, if the client group is small, the marketer might select a more intense campaign designed for that group alone. In this case, brochures might be circulated in single neighborhoods, or mailings may be targeted only to club members.

Reach and frequency typically compete for the same resources. A marketer who chooses a very broad advertising campaign may not have adequate resources to repeat the campaign on a regular basis. As a result, marketers in both sectors often rely on partners to help them extend their own advertising budget. This approach requires considerable coordination and cooperation. For example, a product manufacturer may advertise a product on a very broad scale hoping to build aware-

ness for that product. The manufacturer then provides background material to retailers so that they can offer more persuasive messages to local target groups. In the same way, a leisure provider may use advertising to draw attention to leisure pursuits then rely on neighborhood associations and sport groups to promote particular activities to the specific groups they serve.

Frequency and Timing—Marketers hoping to sell a product on a given day at a given price must advertise constantly. Retailers, for example, must advertise in local newspapers or on the radio on a daily basis. They must highlight their latest sale or their recent acquisitions, and the frequency of their advertising reflects this condition. However, most leisure providers are simply advertising to create an image for themselves and an awareness of their many offerings. As a result, most of their advertising is done on a relatively irregular basis. They may send out their messages in bursts, flights, or pulses.

Bursts represent the ongoing repetition of a message. The message might be sent out in the local newspaper once a week. The provider might even mail out a brochure once a month. This tactic has the advantage of keeping the message in the public eye. Some research suggests that once-monthly bursts can be more effective than weekly or biweekly efforts (Strong, 1977).

Flights simply repeat the message in clusters of repetition. For example, a leisure provider might advertise an upcoming program by making repeated announcements during a local sporting event. This concentrated repetition seems to make messages more memorable (Bogart, 1996).

Pulses refer to the occasional distribution of an advertising message. This is a tactic favored by many leisure agencies. They send out brochures on a seasonal basis to highlight the programs being offered during the upcoming months.

4. Means

In order for communication to occur, a message must be transmitted to an audience. The way in which this message is conveyed is referred to as the *means* of communication. There is an increasing array of means through which messages can be distributed. Word of mouth, media, seasonal brochures, the Internet, and even CD-ROMS are all used to pass along information to client groups. Marketers know that each means of communication possesses its own unique character, and this character will influence the meaning offered by the message. This is called the *source* effect. The printed word carries with it a sense of stability and permanence while television-based messages seem vibrant but transitory. The nature of the means selected may affect the power of the message just as much as does the message itself. As Marshall McLuhan once observed, "the medium is the message."

There is no one best choice when selecting means of communication. All have their own strengths and weaknesses. "In evaluating a medium, the advertiser must think of what can be obtained from it in terms of position, timing, scheduling, and public attention, rather than of the medium in abstract" (Bogart, 1996, p. 105). A simple brochure produced on the office photocopier may be more effective than a television advertising campaign costing thousands of dollars. An effective web page may be more meaningful than a full page in a local newspaper. The best choice is one that matches means and messages to target markets and their motives (Bogart).

Marketers typically begin with the current interests of the client group then attempt to plan advertising efforts accordingly. For example, they know that children can be influenced through television ads. Children watch television before school in the early morning, and after school in the late afternoons, so marketers who can afford television advertising focus on these time periods. Marketers' efforts must also be tempered by economic realities, however. Television ads can be expensive, so leisure marketers often target adults in the household through their most

trusted news source, the local newspaper. Older adults typically look to the printed word for information, and it provides a relatively cheap means of communication. By using newspapers, leisure marketers may be able to eventually reach the children in the home.

In other cases, television advertising may prove a low-cost and very useful option. Television viewing increases with age, and older adults look constantly to local television to stay informed. Local cable channels offer a very economical means through which they might be reached. These channels are constantly looking for new material to broadcast to the community, and they are open to suggestions from leisure providers. These channels have the dual advantage of having a very local focus and of being flexible in their broadcasting schedule. They can highlight local events with very little lead time, and will often rebroadcast the events upon request.

Teens look to what might be best described as high-tech information sources ranging from television to the Internet. The appeal of the Internet in particular seems limitless for teens. They can literally search the world for information and ideas, unfettered by the limitations of distance. Well-designed web pages may offer considerable appeal to this target market. In order to keep the interest of this group, the page will have to be continually updated. No one wants to return to a static site, especially youth.

The sheer volume of programming information that public leisure providers hope to circulate within the community lends itself to the seasonal brochure. The brochure format enables the provider to offer virtually thousands of pieces of information regarding everything from class times and locations to facility hours of operation and notice of special events. Though anecdotal evidence in many communities suggests that many households ignore these brochures, they do offer a valuable resource for community members interested in taking part in leisure programs. Whatever the means through which the message is transmitted, it is critical that the medium be consistent with the intended message and of interest to the intended client group.

5. Generating the Advertising Budget

The advertising budget is typically a function of the message to be conveyed and the media selected. Advertising choices vary in terms of their costs. Economic priorities are always critical to advertising decisions. Cost is a sensitive topic in communications-related deliberations, because advertising can be incredibly expensive, and the economic returns for this expense can be uncertain. For example, how does a marketer measure the effectiveness of an advertisement viewed by 100,000 prospective clients? Many of these clients may see an advertisement today but not require the service for months or even years. When the choice is finally made and participation takes place, how much of that participation can be attributed to that initial exposure to an advertisement? No one is certain of the direct connection between advertising and action. A relationship seems to exist between advertising and awareness as well as between advertising and attitude, but the link is less clear between advertising and action. As one advertiser lamented, "We know we're wasting half of our advertising budget . . . we just don't know which half."

There is no rule of thumb that determines how much budget will be allocated to communication. However, a few observations are possible. It seems, for example, that spending levels are sometimes a function of *brand differentiation*. Brand differentiation refers to client perceptions of differences across brands. Providers who are perceived as unique may not need to advertise as aggressively as those who are considered "run of the mill." Until recently, Disney theme parks did not advertise, because there was little need. Positive word of mouth conveyed the message of their appeal very nicely for them. If clients perceive that there are no real differences from one brand to the next, then providers may promote heavily to establish in their clients' minds the unique nature of their service offerings. In this way they hope to develop competitive advantage over competitors. Though this strategy is expensive and elevates communication costs, it

is used by many of the most successful service providers.

Spending levels may also be a function of service *complexity*. Marketers of services that are complex and/or expensive (e.g., personal fitness training programs) may have to devote additional communications dollars to help potential clients both understand and appreciate the offerings. They may develop a complicated system of teaser advertisements and promotional displays to draw clients into their facilities, then rely upon personal sales representatives to make the subsequent sale. This type of integrated effort is expensive because it includes a variety of potentially expensive communication techniques and requires highly trained staff to complete the sales process.

Public sector advertising efforts represent only a very small portion of their annual budgets. A regional survey undertaken in Canada suggested that public sector providers typically spend less than five percent of their operating budgets on promotions (Johnson-Tew, Havitz, & McCarville, 1999). This rather low expenditure level no doubt reflects the limited promotional choices that characterize many public sector promotional efforts. It may also reflect the amount of money agency administrators feel they should assign to promotional efforts.

Personal Selling

Personal selling is a form of direct promotion. Personal sales are the most flexible of communication techniques because they create the opportunity for face-to-face communication. Whereas advertising and publicity offer indirect contact between the provider and the client, personal selling brings together staff and potential clients. There are many instances in which personal selling can be used by leisure providers. Efforts to recruit partners, sponsors, or program participants may all best be accomplished through personal sales. Efforts to lobby, fundraise or atone for agency errors also enter the realm of personal sales (Crompton & Lamb, 1986). Popular with expensive and complicated products and services, personal selling can be very persuasive. However, it is also expensive and demanding of staff resources. As a result, marketers must ensure that sales staff are well trained so that their efforts are both effective and efficient. There are three categories of sales staff (Sandhusen, 1993). They are the order getter, the order taker, and sales support.

The Order Getter

We are all familiar with the stereotypical sales staff with limited fashion sense and the burning desire to sell products. They are the stuff that inspires television comedies and cartoon strips. Though this may be an unfair characterization of the typical order getter, it rings true with many of us because of the creative techniques these people use to sell products. Their job is to cajole, persuade, and remind in ways that create customers.

Order getters are at the heart of most complicated relationships between leisure providers and other influential parties. For the most complicated or high-stake initiatives, the order getters can be the most senior people in an organization. Heads of state spend an inordinate amount of time developing good relations with other heads of state. University presidents spend much of their time grooming influential friends and donors for their respective schools. Park and recreation directors spend time with board members, city councilors, and influential citizens. These are order getters at the highest levels. The success with which they attract orders may determine the success of their organizations.

The Order Taker

The order taker responds to clients who have already decided to become a customer. These are the receptionists, the registration clerks, the instructors, and the customer service representatives who process the thousands of orders for service each week. Their skill set is much different, but no less important, than that of the order getter. They are bound by process. Their world is deeply embedded in organizational procedures, yet they must

respond to the idiosyncratic needs and wants of the marketplace.

The order taker is often the first one called when errors have occurred. Perhaps a check has been misplaced, a child's name has been dropped from a list, or a program has been cancelled. These are issues that irritate the client and must be solved by the order taker. While order takers typically occupy the lowest level of the organization's hierarchy, their actions speak for the entire organization. For many clients, discussions with a receptionist may be the only personal contact they have with the leisure provider.

Sales Support

Sales support staff are all those who offer specialized assistance to staff members who either create or take orders from clients. They may specialize in accounts, computers, equipment rental, or scheduling. These individuals typically operate behind the scenes but may appear occasionally to assist with problem resolution. Their world is often a very ordered place. They have profound knowledge of specific policies and procedures, so much so that policy can take precedence over client needs. They can become insensitive to the needs of the client because their day-to-day efforts are divorced from those of the client.

There is a natural tension between the three levels of sales staff. Order getters and, to a lesser extent order takers, operate in a complex, dynamic environment. They often have mere seconds to plan an encounter, to evaluate the client's requirements, and to respond accordingly. Their world is often characterized by an endless series of encounters, each demanding a gentle hand and an attentive ear.

The world of the sales support staff is often very different from that of front-line counterparts. Those who act behind the scenes are, by necessity, removed from actual service encounters. Consequently, they may fail to appreciate the needs of front-line staff during those encounters. They may create or support policies and procedures that focus on internal efficiencies rather than the original value proposition. This is an ongoing concern because service gaps emerge when support staff fail to respond to client desires (Zeithaml, Parasuraman, & Berry, 1990).

Creating a Sale

A *sale* is loosely defined as any encounter that ends in the client agreeing to work more closely with the leisure provider (Sandhusen, 1993). It is an agreement to undertake an exchange. A sale may conclude with a participant registering for an event, a corporation agreeing to sponsor an event, or a philanthropist deciding to make a cash donation to the agency. Whatever the nature of the exchange, personal sales can be used to initiate and maintain the relationship. There are four stages in creating a sale.

Prospecting/Finding Leads

Sales begin with the search for exchange partners. This is called *prospecting*. The name is borrowed from those who search the earth for rare gems and minerals. Like traditional prospectors, marketers are constantly searching. Rather than search for ore, however, they search for individuals and organizations. Their goal is to find others who seek the mutual benefit of an exchange relationship.

This search is always guided by the goals and objectives of corporate and marketing plans. They are interested only in exchange partners who fit their own marketing criteria. For example, a public leisure agency may be seeking sponsors for a youth sporting event but policy forbids them from working with the tobacco or alcohol industries. Marketing objectives may also dictate the number of prospects to be contacted each year. Providers who have adopted aggressive growth strategies must constantly find new clients and partners. They may develop very specific growth projections, and personal selling will likely play a role in that growth.

Qualifying Leads

Prospects are typically broken down into categories that reflect their sales potential. This is the process of *qualification*. Qualification is intended to discover if the prospect (1) wants

to undertake an exchange, (2) is able to undertake that exchange, (3) has the authority to do so, and (4). is eligible to take part in the exchange (Sandhusen, 1993). The most important of these issues is the first one, that of willingness. If the prospect is unwilling, the rest of the issues become unimportant. Sales staff are anxious to establish willingness levels before making initial contact with the prospect. By doing so, they may save themselves considerable time and energy.

There are a few rules of thumb to assess the willingness of a prospect before formal contact is made. For example, those who have been clients in the past are often considered to be excellent prospects for future exchanges. Further, those who have expressed interest in a provider's services are also considered prime prospects. They may have contacted the provider for information or sampled a program on a previous occasion. These are the types of prospects who receive the greatest amount of attention from those hoping to generate sales.

A lesser category of prospects are those who have been referred by knowledgeable third parties. A current participant may suggest a friend, or an organization may suggest its own members. Such referrals are often very useful in helping identify interested parties. It is so useful that many organizations now reward the party who has made the referral by offering a variety of incentives.

The least likely prospect is identified by what is called the "cold call." Cold calls are unsolicited contacts made by sales staff hoping to identify a willing prospect. These are the least efficient of all contacts because their likelihood of success is quite limited. The average individual is understandably hesitant to drop everything and listen to a sales pitch from some unknown salesperson. The salesperson is hoping that the individual or organization being contacted will view this call as an opportunity to have a problem solved but this is a rare occurrence. For this reason, sales staff often avoid cold calling except as a last resort.

The Presentation

Once the prospect has been identified, a presentation must be offered. The *presentation* represents the sales staff member's attempt to explain the value to be gained through the proposed exchange. It may take the form of a demonstration, a verbal introduction, or a visual display. Sales staff are trained to offer the necessary material, then to listen for objections or questions. These objections are then dealt with through a quick restatement (to ensure the objection is understood) then a response that clearly and honestly deals with the pertinent issue. If the sales people are unsure of how to respond to the objections, they are instructed to ask questions of clarification. Typically, answers to these questions offer insight into the reason for and solution to the objections.

The presentation ends with what is called *the close*. The close is the last act in the presentation. It asks the prospect to formally undertake the desired exchange. The sales person might ask the prospect to enroll in a program or complete an order form, a donor may be asked to make a pledge, or a corporation may be asked to complete a sponsorship agreement. Part of the close is the simple process called *the thank*. The thank is a simple and honest thank you offered to the client. It reflects the organization and sales person's appreciation for the client's willingness to complete the exchange.

Many clients, and particularly those undertaking large investments, often hope to delay the sale so that they can think it over. When this is the case, the sales person is encouraged to ensure that any nagging questions are answered and that the client makes at least a nominal commitment to the exchange. They might agree to use the services free for a week so that they can sample the program without cost to themselves. In this way, their own experience can answer their many questions.

Whatever the level of the sales staff, whatever the nature of their respective jobs, they must be briefed on the ingredients of a successful sales encounter. As they apply the insights offered here, they must do so with:

— a thorough knowledge of the service under discussion,

— an equally thorough knowledge of the client's wishes,

— the willingness and ability to take the client's point of view, and

— the capacity to fulfill the client's wishes.

The Follow-Up

The last stage in creating the sale is that of the *follow-up*. The follow-up is a second contact after an agreement has been reached. This contact often takes place before the terms of the sale have been completed. For example, salespersons will likely contact a sponsor long before the sponsored event is held. They will wish to discuss the sponsor's own priorities and concerns so that they might all be addressed as the event is planned.

Follow-up efforts also take place after the terms of the sale have been completed. To continue the sponsorship example, event organizers typically contact sponsors after the event has been held. They do this to ensure the sponsor is made aware of the value gained from that sponsorship. Several other worthwhile goals are pursued through these follow-up sessions. They are used, for example, to monitor the client's satisfaction with the exchange. This satisfaction is, after all, the reason for the exchange. They might also be used to solicit additional exchanges, to gather referrals, or simply to gather feedback on the delivery process.

Publicity

Publicity represents press coverage that is not paid for by the provider. Though it represents a form of free advertising, it has a very distinct disadvantage. The provider has little control over what is actually released to the public. A public agency may ask a local newspaper to promote an upcoming event but they have no control over the amount of space devoted to the event, the number or type of words used to describe it, and so on. As a result, marketers are typically ambivalent toward publicity. Though they are drawn by the appeal of free press coverage, they worry about the nature and extent of this coverage. They often hope for positive publicity but plan as if no such coverage was forthcoming. In this way, they are never disappointed when hoped-for publicity fails to materialize, and are pleasantly surprised when it does.

Many marketers rely on a blend of advertising and publicity in order to spread the word of their programs. It is common, for example, that they rely on advertising by purchasing posters that promote their events. However, they also rely on publicity because they ask partners to display these posters at no cost. They ask partners like neighborhood associations, sporting goods stores, and even doctors' offices to display their materials hoping to reach the clients who visit these locations.

Even those merchants who do not sell leisure-related products are routinely co-opted to provide publicity. For example, private sector companies frequently offer rewards (e.g., entry to contests, etc.) to seemingly unrelated merchants if they post selected posters in and around their premises. They may target golf courses or any variety of settings that attract the attention of their target groups. The merchant benefits because he is given the chance to win a valued prize at no personal cost, and the advertiser gains virtually free advertising space in a desirable setting.

The Advocacy Approach

An emerging media *advocacy* literature makes it clear that publicity generated through cooperation with the media can amplify the effect of any communications campaign. This effect arises from the profound relationship which exists between media, the public, and policy makers. Groundbreaking work by Rogers, Dearing, and Chang (1991) offers a case in point. They were interested in the process through which social issues gathered support in the community. They wanted to learn the stages through which a nonresponsive public became responsive. They did so by interpreting the evolution of the AIDS crisis through the interplay between the media, the public, and policy makers.

They found that the process of encouraging participation among uninterested clients involved three stages. The first is that of "setting the media agenda." Media attention and publicity, the first elements in the process, were fuelled by information that was readily available and deemed newsworthy by media gatekeepers. Information that aided in "personalizing and humanizing" the issue seemed most effective at gaining and sustaining media interest.

Parenthetically, the researchers concluded that the simple reporting of research statistics proved insufficient to maintain public interest. It seems that issues must be "framed" in a way that is of interest to the public (Wallack, 1994). Uninteresting message formats were either rejected by media gatekeepers or ignored by the public. Several well-known techniques are now commonplace in making messages more newsworthy. All messages should be developed with these techniques in mind. They are

1. localizing (adapting a general story to appeal to local interests),

2. social math (using statistics to generate interest), and

3. event creation (creating newsworthy incidents like competitions).

Members of the media require clear statements of relevance before they pick up an issue, yet they often lack the resources to send their own staff out to establish the importance of every issue. Leisure marketers hoping to work with the media must provide those statements. They might well borrow a page from the advocacy community and prepare extensive information kits for media outlets, then invite media representatives to related photo opportunities. If a media outlet is unable to send a representative to the photo shoot, then the marketer can send along a set of complimentary photographs or a video.

Many leisure providers are now working hard to use publicity in extending their promotional potential. In an effort to "reinvent municipal recreation programming," the Waco Texas Leisure Services Department recruited the media community as a key partner in program delivery. They "began to foster a close relationship with the media . . . incorporat[ing] media representatives on all program boards" (Gavlik, 1995, p. 115).

The Waco group may be on to something. Rogers and his colleagues (1991) found that sustained media interest was able to influence public response. They called this the process of "setting the public agenda." In their analysis of decades of national survey data, they found that media attention/publicity reduced public confusion while increasing public awareness, sense of public urgency, and support for government spending on related issues. This attention also seemed to have resulted in important changes in lifestyle among community members.

Sustained public interest then helped set the "policy agenda." In this case, the term "policy" refers to any level of the political or bureaucratic structure able to plan appropriate interventions at the community level. The authors concluded that increased public attention was subsequently responsible for sweeping policy changes. Federal allocations for relevant research approximately doubled annually during the study period. Policymakers then instituted a series of regulations designed to encourage positive behavior at the community level. In the end, the effective use of publicity may help create widespread change within a community. It can "change the ecology of that community" (Stokols, 1996) by identifying problems, while offering solutions to that community.

The challenge for public sector marketers is to influence policy without being perceived as interfering in the political process. While it is true that public officials may welcome community and media support for their own favorite projects, they may bristle at staff efforts to create support for unwelcome initiatives. The answer seems to be one of alignment. Public sector marketers are likely to enjoy greater success when they pursue objectives that have the widest possible support base. In doing so, they are simply galvanizing

opinion that is already forming and encouraging action that is already getting under way. Working in conjunction with key members of the media community, leisure marketers can highlight important issues and offer solutions to ongoing problems. Such efforts will not only help influence community members' own actions, but may also create political support for leisure-related initiatives.

Sales Promotions

Elements of the promotional mix are typically used in unison to effect behavioral change among target groups. Each is used to supplement or leverage other elements of the mix. Leveraging is the process of using existing resources to better effect. It amplifies the effects of a given strategy. This trend is perhaps most true with the use of sales promotions. *Sales promotions* consist of short-term incentives intended to encourage purchase of a service. Techniques include samples, coupons, price packages, sales promotions, and point-of-purchase displays. All such efforts are typically designed to support other communication strategies. Each is described here.

Samples and Trials

Marketers often promote their services through samples or trials (Copeland, 1991). Trials are often favored because they encourage sampling by consumers who are unfamiliar with a given service. Trials are free of risk in that consumers may sample and evaluate a service without making a financial commitment. They can avoid "mispurchase" or the acquisition of a product that does not satisfy (Laurent & Kapferer, 1985), thereby reducing possible dissatisfaction and inconvenience. Also, samples help reduce the time clients use to search for and assess new products. If a trial suggests that a product meets their own personal criteria, then subsequent shopping effort is reduced. They need only identify and purchase the new product (Assael, 1984) as required.

Coupons

The coupon provides basic product information and may also offer a cash or other incentive to purchase the product. Coupons have enjoyed considerable success in the retail industry in North America. Consumers in the United States redeem over $7 billion in coupons annually, while Canadians redeem just over 200 million coupons each year (Why do people clip coupons?, 1991). The immense popularity of discount coupons seems to result from four effects (Larson, 1994). These effects are

1. the monetary or discount effect,

2. the advertising effect (coupons provide the consumer with product information),

3. a reminding effect (they enhance awareness through repeated exposure to the coupon), and

4. a utility effect (satisfaction is gained through the redemption process).

Though the monetary appeal of discount coupons seems self-evident, the utility effect seems to account for much of the appeal enjoyed by the discount coupon (Jain, cited in Why do people clip coupons?, 1991). Using coupons helps boost consumers' sense of pride as competent shoppers. Indeed, coupon users may even be motivated less by savings and more by psychological rewards like satisfaction and perceived competence. Further, coupons also reduce psychological costs or risks associated with trying new services (Jain, cited in Why do people clip coupons?, 1991). Though shoppers seek variety in their own consumption patterns, they may be unwilling to pay full price for unfamiliar products. The monetary incentive offered by coupons helps reduce this risk, thereby encouraging the trial purchase of new services. This benefit is particularly relevant to those hoping to increase sales among new target groups.

Coupons offer one additional benefit that marketers appreciate. They can monitor sales arising from a promotion by tracking the redemption of coupons. Consequently, coupons assist marketers in estimating return on investment. Finally, coupons are portable. Their format lends itself to distribution through traditional printed media like seasonal mailings and brochures. They can be included with monthly bills, included with gifts, or placed in fruit baskets. Virtually any space available to the marketer can accommodate a coupon or two.

Price Incentives

Price packages offer a welcome incentive for most shoppers. No one likes to pay a fee, and efforts to reduce price levels are always appreciated by leisure participants. As suggested in chapter 10, there are several types of packages, often called "Price Adjustment Techniques," that can be used to attract the attention of potential participants (Finch, Becherer, & Casavant, 1998). The first is that of *packaging* or *bundling* in which various program elements are offered at a reduced price. Bundling has the added advantage of convenience. It brings together two program components that normally would have to be purchased separately. Members at a health facility might receive free towel service with a basic membership, while participants in an art class might receive a set of complimentary paint brushes with their registration. Any package the provider offers must recognize participants' preferences, priorities, and use patterns.

A second technique, called *differential pricing*, offers price discounts based upon a variable that is important to both the client and the provider. Typically, this variable is time. For example, leisure facilities all experience periods of low demand during the day. They may also experience periods of overcrowding during which participants must wait in line. Differential pricing is used to alter demand patterns or to redistribute demand. It does so by rendering unpopular time periods more desirable. Typically, discounted prices are offered during slow periods in hopes of diverting demand from peak periods. Price is used to modify demand so that crowding is reduced but business (during slow periods) is also increased. It is the type of technique that helps everyone win.

Point-of-Purchase Displays and Demonstrations

The facility or recreation site (also called point-of-purchase or point-of-sale environment) has a significant impact on consumer choice (Assael, 1984; Lucas & Prensky, 1997). Introduced in the last chapter, the point-of-purchase or POP can be defined as "any merchandising device, sign, or advertisement used inside or outside a retail store to provide information about products or services available there, with the purpose of influencing and motivating favorable buying decisions among shoppers or passersby" (Gorrie, 1993, p. 28).

POP aids in generating awareness, communicating information and understanding, stimulating trial, and encouraging repeat purchases. POP is unique in that it is able to reach potential consumers who, because they are in a facility setting, are beyond the reach of traditional promotions (Berger, 1992). In this way it is typically viewed as the producer's "last chance" to reach consumers. POP does not act alone, however. It is typically used in conjunction with larger promotional efforts. For example, external advertising is used to build general awareness of and support for a brand, a product, or even a corporate logo. However, these efforts are typically unable to reach into the facility where many purchase decisions are made. It is at this point that POP reminds the consumer of this larger effort. It reminds the consumer that the product highlighted elsewhere is available. External advertising cannot reach its full potential without a presence at the point of purchase.

The point of purchase environment consists of several component parts used either in isolation or in combination. Each is used to provide positive reinforcement for current customers and to alter the normal buying habits among potential customers through the provision of timely and compelling cues. These cues call attention to the program or provider (often through displays) then highlight their

appeal by noting new features, benefits of purchase, price specials and premiums (Kotler et al., 1991). There are a variety of POP displays and demonstrations that are likely to attract the interest of participants.

Store displays and signs, both inside and outside stores, play an important and influential role in encouraging purchase behavior. Consumers seem to desire clear, legible signs that help direct attention to purchase opportunities or values (Budish, 1994). They may even interpret the location of a display as an indication of value. For example, many shoppers believe that end-of-aisle sales indicate that the item highlighted there is on sale.

Although services cannot be displayed in this manner, relevant signage may be placed elsewhere in the retail setting to gain the attention of the shopper. Janofsky (1994) states, for example, that one of the single most effective displays yet devised has been the sidewalk sign. It tends to draw the attention of passers by, thereby creating interest and encouraging action.

Promotional items such as T-shirts and hats are often made available as POP initiatives. Paralusz (1998) notes that these promotional items help advertisers gain visibility for their products. They may be placed on products that are associated with healthful lifestyles (golf shirts or hats), on items that facilitate the use of their own services (exercise water bottles), or on items that are of inherent interest to the particular group they wish to target (flying disks, mouse pads). In each case, the promotional item builds awareness of and support for the service or provider being promoted.

Unfortunately, leisure providers seem hesitant to utilize all these promotional tools. In particular, they avoid promotional techniques that might appear ostentatious to the general public or to policymakers. Without exception, agencies in one study utilized only one primary means of communication, that of seasonal program brochures (Johnson-Tew, Havtiz, & McCarville, 1999). In the study region, this single media choice represented, by far, the most widely used means of promoting programs and services.

Word-of-Mouth Communications

A fifth element of the promotional (advertising, personal selling, publicity, and sales promotion) mix is *word-of-mouth communication.* Word of mouth is often considered an informal member of the mix or is ignored completely because it is so difficult to control. It is exceedingly difficult to arrange for friends and relatives to provide useful bits of information about a given leisure program in a way that is completely satisfactory to the provider. While it may be difficult to control word-of-mouth communication, its importance is undeniable. As a result, it should not escape the attention of the marketer.

The power of word of mouth arises from two of its very basic characteristics. It is both *available* and *credible.* In terms of availability, word-of-mouth communications originate with friends, family, acquaintances, or even strangers. These reports are readily available, often at critical points, in the decision-making process. Participants may seek advice as they are about to choose a program or they may ask for help as they select a provider. At such decision points, the potential participant is very much open to suggestion. This suggestion often arrives in the form of word-of-mouth communication, and its importance can be dramatic.

Credibility represents the degree to which the source of a message is considered believable or worthy of attention. If the audience believes the source to be credible, the message is more likely to be accepted. Source credibility is most powerful under the condition of *unfamiliarity* (Assael, 1984). In other words, clients are more likely to focus on credibility issues if they are unfamiliar with the program or service. Credibility is itself a product of the following three variables (Kotler, McDougall & Armstrong, 1988):

1. *Expertise* —the degree of knowledge possessed by the communicator regarding the discussion point.

2. *Trustworthiness* —the honesty and objectivity of the communicator.

3. *Likability* —the appeal of the communicator.

Unfortunately, advertising is generally thought to be the least credible among communication efforts. Because advertising is viewed as an attempt to sell a service, many clients feel unable to separate truth from exaggeration (Assael, 1984). Conversely, word-of-mouth communication is often perceived as a rational, unbiased report of quality and performance. Prospective shoppers trust information provided by friends because their input is considered both relevant and credible. As a result, clients often ignore advertising and rely instead on word of mouth. Such is the case even when such sources lack any expertise in the subject area.

Potential participants will ask friends about automobiles, even when they know little of mechanical details; they will ask family members about leisure agencies, when they may not even have participated in an agency program. For this reason, the agency must ensure that word-of-mouth communications about their programs and services are uniformly positive. This is often achieved by the judicious use of the other elements in the promotional mix. Samples and sales are offered to increase trials, promotions and contests are created to attract interest, and advertising is designed to generate word-of-mouth communications.

Main Points

· Marketers' formal efforts to communicate are typically called promotion.

· Promotional strategies may focus on the ultimate clients (a pull strategy) or on the provider's distribution channels (a push strategy).

· All promotional strategies must be based on a clear understanding of the intended audience, including knowledge of audience members' current life conditions.

· Promotional strategies are guided by objectives that relate to both the client (emotional and behavioral outcomes) and the provider (cost and reach).

· The promotional mix is comprised of advertising, sales promotions, personal selling, and publicity. Further, word-of-mouth communication often acts as an informal but powerful member of the mix. Each alternative possesses its own unique strengths and weaknesses.

· Advertising efforts often comprise the bulk of leisure providers' promotional activity. These efforts require a media plan that describes how promotional efforts will be pursued. The plan is generally concerned with reach, frequency, timing, and means of communication.

Case Study

A recreation director in a city of 75,000 people has a dilemma. He has always relied almost entirely on seasonal brochures to promote his programs and his agency. He's kept a column in the weekly local paper over the years in which he highlights upcoming events, but he has always considered the brochures to be his primary means of communicating with his community. Four times a year, the 100-page brochures are mailed to every household. This effort used up virtually all of his promotional budget (and his marketing director's time), but he considered it money well spent. He had always believed that each household used the brochure as a sort of leisure planner. He had assumed that members of the household walked through the brochure, selecting their favorite activities then planned their season accordingly.

He hired you to confirm his long-held beliefs, but you have just reported that the brochure may be a colossal failure. After surveying the community you found that fully 60 percent of the brochures were thrown away without being opened, and clients who did open them spent, on average, less that 10 minutes browsing through them. They tended to read the brochure while doing something else (watching television, chatting with family members), and only three percent of those surveyed could recall more than five pieces of information contained in the publication.

· What are the strengths of the director's current approach to communication with the community?

· Is the brochure program a failure?

· Develop a communications strategy that better disseminates information to target groups in the community.

References

Assael, H. (1984). *Consumer behavior and marketing action* (2nd ed.). Boston: Kent Publishing.

Berger, K.A. (1992). *The rising importance of point-of-purchase advertising marketing mix.* Washington, D.C.: Point-of-Purchase Advertising Institute.

Berry, L., & Parasuraman, A. (1991). *Marketing services: Competing through quality.* New York: The Free Press.

Bogart, L. (1996). *Strategy in advertising: Matching media and messages to markets and motivations* (3rd ed.). Chicago: NTC Business Books.

Budish, R. (1994). Designing for the 90s: Making the pack look nice just isn't enough anymore. *Marketing, 99*(4), 12.

Copeland, R.P. (1991). *Sport sponsorship in Canada: A study of exchange between corporate sponsors and sport groups.* Unpublished master's thesis, University of Waterloo, Waterloo, Ontario, Canada.

Crompton, J., & Lamb, C. (1986*). Marketing government and social services.* New York: John Wiley & Sons.

Finch, J.H., Becherer, R.C., & Casavant, R. (1998). An option-based approach for pricing perishable services assets. *Journal of Services Marketing, 12*(6), 473-483.

Gavlik, S. (1995). Reinventing recreation programming: Waco Leisure Services Department. In M. E. Havitz (Ed.), *Models of change* (pp. 109-120). State College, PA: Venture Publishing Inc.

Gorrie, R.G. (1993). The power of point-of-purchase advertising. *Canadian Packaging, 46,* 28-29.

Janofsky, M. (1994, March 21). Advertising. *The New York Times,* pp.D9.

Johnson-Tew, C.P., Havitz, M., & McCarville R.E. (1999). The role of marketing in municipal recreation programming decisions: A challenge to conventional wisdom. *Journal of Park and Recreation Administration, 17*(1), 1-20.

Kotler, P., McDougall, G., & Armstrong, G. (1988). *Marketing: Canadian edition.* Englewood Cliffs, NJ: Prentice-Hall.

Larson, C. (1994). Discount coupons: Beyond the price discount effect. In E.W. Goddard & D.S. Taylor (Eds.), *Proceedings of the NEC-63 Conference on promotion in the marketing mix: What works, where and why* (pp.42-52). Guelph, Ontario: University of Guelph.

Laurent, G., & Kapferer, J. (1985). Measuring consumer involvement profiles. *Journal of Marketing Research, 22,* 41-53.

Levitt, T. (1983). *The marketing imagination.* New York: The Free Press.

Lucas, J., & Prensky, D. (1997). Evaluating the effectiveness of place-based media. In W.D. Wells (Ed.), *Measuring advertising effectiveness* (pp. 371-383). Mahwah, NJ: Erlbaum Associates.

Murphy, J., & Cunningham, I. (1993). *Advertising and marketing communication.* Toronto: The Dryden Press.

Nylen, D. (1990). *Marketing decision-making handbook.* Toronto: Prentice-Hall.

Rogers, E.M., Dearing, J.W., & Chang, S. (1991). AIDS in the 1980s: The agenda-setting process for a public issue. *Journalism Monographs, 126,* 1-47.

Sandhusen, R.L. (1993). *Marketing* (2nd ed.). Hauppauge, NY: Barron's Educational Series, Inc.

Schneider, B., & Bowen, D.E. (1995). *Winning the service game.* Boston: Harvard Business School Press.

Sherman, J.S., & Havitz, M.E. (1991). Introducing an innovative recreational facility: Lessons from a success. *Journal of Park and Recreation Administration, 9*(3), 29-40.

Stokols, D. (1996). Translating social ecological theory into guidelines for community health promotion. *American Journal of Health Promotion, 10*(4), 282-298.

Strong, E. (1977). The spacing and timing of advertising. *Journal of Advertising Research, 17*(6), 25-31.

Wallack, L. (1990). Media Advocacy: Promoting health through mass communication. In K. Glaniz, F.M. Lewis, & B.K. Rimer (Eds.), *Health behavior and health education: Theory, research, and practice.* San Francisco, CA: Jossey-Bass.

Why do people clip coupons? (1991, May 29). *Toronto Star,* p. 1.

Zeithmal, V.A., Parasuraman, A., & Berry, L. (1990). Communication and control processes in the delivery of service quality. *Journal of Marketing,* 52, 35-48.

CHAPTER

9

Pricing Basics

Price is one of the most talked about elements of the marketing plan. It is a popular topic because it has profound implications for the participant and the provider alike. For the participant, price represents a critical element in all purchase or participation decisions. It has been estimated that up to 40 percent of all information participants seek prior to purchase relates to price and that price information is likely to be the first, rather than the last, piece of information sought before purchase (Jacoby, Chestnut, Weigl, & Fisher, 1976). In these cases, price may serve a type of accept/reject function. If the price is within a given range, participation is likely. If it is either above or below this level, then participation is unlikely.

For the marketer, price is important because it represents the only element of the marketing mix that actually generates revenue. Each of the other elements necessitates short-term expenditures. Marketers who hope to promote, deliver, or develop services are faced with an array of related costs. The pricing element is most closely tied to income generation, so marketers often concentrate on pricing issues as they develop marketing strategy.

The Many Costs of Leisure Participation

There is a often confusion surrounding the issue of pricing. Though the notion of price is often considered to be a monetary issue, a price can be virtually any cost a participant must incur in order to enjoy a service. Costs may be related to *time, effort, psychological*, or *monetary* issues (Walsh, 1987). Time costs relate primarily to interaction time. Interaction time is the time required to take part in a program. Longer programs require more extended commitment and effort. This may be too high a price to pay for those patrons who prefer short-term participation. Many providers are now reducing such costs by offering innovative programs in which people can come and go as they wish. For example, they enable participants to sign up by the hour, week, month, season, or year. Participants pay more for the convenience of the shorter registration periods, but seem not to mind, because they do not feel pressured into allocating more time than they wish.

Time and effort both relate to "running around." A simple example is that of access to phone numbers. Clients' emotional costs are driven skyward when they cannot find relevant phone numbers in brochures. As suggested in chapter 8, to reduce such costs, many providers now place their phone numbers on every page of their seasonal brochures. When clients see a program they like, they need only to glance down the page and begin to dial that number. In this way, time and effort costs are reduced and convenience levels are increased.

These convenience-based costs pale in comparison to more psychological costs. Psychological costs represent a formidable barrier to participation because they attack the very motivation of the potential participant. Perhaps the greatest psychological cost for leisure programs is *fear of ridicule*. Almost all programs require special skills or knowledge. Consider golf or tennis. The beginner faces a bewildering array of birdies, eagles, lets, and loves. Everyone hates to look stupid, so we not they may ignore very useful programs rather than face these costs. Marketers must be ever vigilant to reduce all such costs.

Another psychological cost relates to *uncertainty*. Uncertainty arises when consumers are unsure if a program offers the benefits they seek. Uncertainty also exists because patrons are unsure whether a program will be fun or entertaining. Finally, clients may be uncertain if they themselves have "what it takes" to enjoy the program. Given the importance and power of these many costs, it is perhaps surprising that monetary costs receive much of the attention devoted to the price of leisure participation. Much of this text is devoted to understanding and removing the many ancillary costs that plague participation in leisure programs. Diminishing costs related to time, effort, convenience and even psychological costs are all considered as the marketing process is discussed.

This chapter now turns to issues arising from monetary costs for leisure services. The topic of monetary price has proven particularly problematic and divisive for public leisure providers and has been the topic of much debate. Concerns over monetary costs have dominated and guided this debate with battle lines being drawn between those opposed to and in favor of fees. The debate has been so polarized that many of the key issues are being lost in the rhetoric surrounding the discussion.

This chapter seeks to navigate through much of this rhetoric and to offer some clear and useful guidelines to anyone hoping to develop pricing strategy.

The Emergence of Fees

The pricing of leisure services has received considerable attention over the past decade. Indeed, user fees are now being used extensively to supplement existing resource levels while diversifying public agencies' traditional funding bases. An emerging pricing literature offers some support for pricing public and not-for-profit sector services on both ethical and pragmatic grounds. In ethical terms, Crompton and Lamb (1986) reported that "in some cases, failure to price will effectively penalize poor people" (p. 323). They argued that young, well-educated, and high-income residents were more likely than their low-income counterparts to enjoy the benefits of public leisure programming. They reported that, "providing [tax] subsidized services as opposed to charging direct user prices may not achieve the anticipated redistributional results" (Crompton & Lamb, p. 322) because people from disadvantaged groups participate at lower rates. An early nationwide study conducted in the United States suggested that disadvantaged segments of the population shared this assessment (Economic Research Associates, 1976). The authors reported that lower-income and older segments of the population were most in favor of fees and charges for public sector leisure opportunities.

However, the case for pricing is typically justified on more pragmatic grounds. Administrative concerns regarding funding diversification, scarcity, resource deterioration, and crowding may all be addressed through pricing initiatives (McCarville, Driver, & Crompton, 1993). Consequently, user fees now account for at least 20 percent of park and recreation agencies' budgets (Crompton & McGregor, 1994; McCarville & Crompton, 1988).

In spite of growing support for pricing, there still exists considerable opposition to the pricing of public and not-for-profit leisure services. This opposition is based primarily on the exclusionary nature of pricing. When a price is charged, potential participants may be excluded from participating. Such exclusion seems contradictory to the mandate of public and not-for-profit leisure service providers who typically operate under explicit social service mandates (Kraus & Curtis, 1990). Leisure is considered an essential component of a happy, productive lifestyle, and exclusion for monetary reasons is viewed as inappropriate. Goodale (1985) argued that "service delivery and distribution is a matter of policy . . . and not simply a matter of finance. Services for those without resources must be assured somehow, and that is a collective responsibility" (p. 23). Fee initiatives that exclude potential participants may therefore be considered as a societal abrogation of this responsibility.

The potentially negative consequences of even seemingly trivial fee levels can be staggering. For example, a local school board decided to charge nonprofit groups like Girl Guides a fee of $10.00 per hour for the use of meeting space. This may, at first seem a very fair-minded and even inconsequential charge for such facilities. No doubt it cost the school board much more than that to provide those same facilities. However, this single initiative cost the local nonprofit group an additional $10,000 in rental fees annually. This "fair-minded and inconsequential" initiative may bankrupt a nonprofit group that serves thousands of young women in the area. Clearly, even small fees can be destructive.

How might the financial needs of leisure providers be fulfilled without displacing the very people the providers hope to serve? Few studies have attempted to reconcile the pragmatic demand for pricing public and not-for-profit leisure services and possible displacement caused by the imposition of fees and charges. It is unlikely that leisure providers will be able to resist the pressure to introduce or raise fees. The question becomes then, "How might fees be introduced so that they minimize the effect of their own inherently exclusionary properties?"

This chapter explores this topic from a marketing perspective. It reflects on the role

and impact of fees for leisure services. Once marketers understand what pricing means for service providers, they can begin to develop effective pricing strategies.

Common Pricing Concerns

The pricing debate has been characterized by misunderstanding and confusion (Ellerbrock, 1982). Some of this confusion arises from the emotional nature of the topic. Prices are, after all, exclusionary, and their imposition seems to guarantee that members of the community will be denied leisure opportunities. At least this is the assumption. This section focuses on the moral and practical consequences of fees. Once these issues have been outlined, the discussion can then focus on the pragmatic issue of pricing technique.

The Role of Pricing in the Public Sector

Jacobs (1994) suggests that two moral systems guide the public and private sectors. The private sector is guided by the moral system of the *merchant*. The merchant's focus is on profit and the competitive nature of the marketplace. The merchant has experienced little angst over the issue of pricing over the years. A price is simply a tool through which profits can be generated. The challenge is simply one of balance. Prices must be set at a level that generates profit while ensuring that valued users are not displaced. The focus is on expediency and profit.

The second moral system is that of the *guardian*. The guardian's focus is on community well-being. Public sector goals are based on the role of guardianship rather than profit. The public sector has tended, therefore, to rely on nonfinancial objectives when allocating resources. Its goal is one of improving conditions in the community through the *redistribution* of resources (Lineberry, 1977). In other words, the public sector gathers resources from the community at large and redistributes them

---

in a way that is considered fair or just. In the context of public leisure services, resources are gathered through taxation then used to support leisure programs. By doing so, public leisure providers are using tax dollars to benefit the community.

Conventional wisdom suggests, therefore, that the pricing mechanism should play only a limited role in the public sector. Prices, by definition, limit access based upon financial ability. Fees dictate that those who cannot or will not pay these fees will be denied service. The negative consequences of this selective refusal to offer services is compounded by their symbolic importance. Lineberry (1977) suggests that those denied service not only fail to receive their perceived "fair" share but also suffer from the stigma that arises from this condition. "Service inadequacies not only diminish real income, but symbolically emblazon subordinate status" (Lineberry, p. 14).

The cumulative effect of these problems can be devastating. Lineberry (1977) continues, "People relate to municipal governments in small, seemingly insignificant, but cumulative ways. Citizens perform mental factor analysis, but with extremely sparse data" (p. 14). Repeated exclusion based on inability to pay may create profound perceptions of marginalization, discrimination, and unethical treatment.

This discussion reflects conventional wisdom, which suggests that pricing is inappropriate in the public sector. The role of this sector is one of guardianship, and guardianship cannot, on ethical grounds, be denied to members of the community based on their ability to pay. For this reason, pricing has proven problematic for public sector leisure professionals.

Pricing and Equity

The notion of equity lies at the heart of "ethical" pricing in the public sector. *Equity* refers to who gets what (Crompton & Lamb, 1986). Equity decisions are those that allocate or distribute public resources. Decision makers may allocate resources according to three equity models. Each is considered to be

"equitable," but all create very different outcomes (Crompton & Lamb). Public perceptions of any equity decision are typically based upon community standards of what is fair or just (Rawls, 1971).

The *compensatory model* promotes the allocation of more resources to residents with the greatest perceived need. The *equal opportunity model* suggests that equal opportunity be provided to all residents. It is important to note that this model may not ensure equal treatment to all. Everyone is given an equal opportunity to participate, but it is unlikely that all will do so. Equality, in this sense, refers to opportunity (and, in some cases, agency input) but not to actual benefits received from a given program (Wicks & Crompton, 1986). Finally, the *market equity model* advocates that resources should be allocated to those who are willing and able to pay for those resources. This approach traditionally has been associated more with the private sector than with public sector agencies.

Both the compensatory and market equity models reflect traditional marketing strategy. Each is based upon the selection of market segments and the development of strategies that are responsive to these segments' needs and resources. However, the equal opportunity model has dominated in public leisure services. In pricing terms, prices have traditionally been maintained at artificially low levels through subsidization, and these low prices are available to everyone. In effect, everyone's real income is increased, because they are being subsidized by tax dollars.

Pricing per se is not inconsistent with any of the dominant equity models. Equity refers to the allocation of resources. Pricing simply offers one more means of gathering resources to be allocated. As such, pricing policies can be designed to accommodate virtually any allocation scheme. In terms of the compensatory model, for example, prices can be charged for programs and these resources can then be redistributed to those community members who express the greatest need. In this way, the compensatory model is being used and fees are also being charged. The often repeated argument that fees are "inequitable" seems to stem more from a misunderstanding of equity than it does from an ethical position.

Within the three equity models, public resources may be reallocated in two ways. One school of thought, advocated by Rawls (1971), suggests that it is preferable to distribute resources directly to the citizen. Public providers might distribute vouchers, coupons, or credits to be allocated as participants see fit. This system creates a unique relationship between the guardian, the merchant, and the participant. The guardian offers resources to participants so that they might better take advantage of merchants' services.

A second approach involves providing resources to the provider who then redistributes these resources to the client. Public sector leisure providers have typically taken the latter approach. They are given resources which they then use to supply programs free of charge or at a subsidized price. This represents an equal opportunity model in that it treats everyone the same. While there are many proponents to this approach, it is not perfect. It ignores the particular needs of subgroups located within the community. Further, it treats all programs as if they are equally deserving of tax support. As a result, programs of limited benefit compete for resources with those programs that contribute more profoundly to community well-being. As will be noted later, such blanket approaches may wreak havoc if and when prices are eventually instituted.

When Pricing Is Appropriate for the Public Sector

Public sector pricing strategy is often developed around a very simple classification system (Crompton & Lamb, 1986). Services are placed along a continuum, bound by public programs on one end and private programs on the other. Merit programs exist along the middle of the continuum. Services that benefit the entire community are designated as *public goods,* and they are not priced. They either cannot or should not be priced because of their peculiar nature. As a result, costs associated with their provision is borne by the entire community via tax dollars.

Conversely, *private goods* are thought to benefit only those who take part. As a result, only those who take part are expected to pay for those services. *Merit services* fall somewhere between purely private and public classifications. They benefit most the consumers who participate in them, but they are perceived to benefit all community members to some degree. In such cases, equity norms suggest that it is appropriate for individual users to pay prices that reflect some but not all of the costs associated with that activity.

This rather simple public-merit-private classification suggests that fees may be appropriate for some services offered by public leisure providers. Not all services provided by the public sector are public in nature. A program of tennis instruction for adults seems more private than public in character. Access to squash courts, too, seems more a private than a public service. In these terms, it seems that pricing may be appropriate for many leisure services.

The view that fees are inconsistent with equitable delivery of leisure services is based on two assumptions. First, this view assumes that programs offered through public leisure services are deserving of support (either public or merit in character). Second, this view also assumes that even if the programs are not worthy of support, the participants are worthy of assistance.

More leisure providers are beginning to argue that neither of these assumptions withstands careful scrutiny. Decades ago, Ellerbrock (1982) noted the flaw in the logic which demanded that all public leisure services be provided free to all; free regardless of the relative importance of the program or the personal means of the participant. At that time he warned, "If we have a goal of providing free recreation to all citizens, then we will be destined for failure and frustrat[ion]" (Ellerbrock, p. 59). By way of explanation he suggested that, "Striving to subsidize everyone hinders the opportunities for people who are poor. Charging those who can afford recreation allows subsidization of a greater number of people who cannot" (Ellerbrock, p. 59).

Ellerbrock (1982) was suggesting that the compensatory and market equity models can be used in tandem. Consistent with the "Robin Hood" principle, resources gathered through market equity policies can be used to gather resources to help those who require additional financial assistance. In other words, tools employed by the merchant, like market segmentation and pricing, can be used to great advantage by the guardian (Havitz, 1988). Ellerbrock suggested that to ignore the opportunity offered by pricing is to invite even greater scarcity and to compound the problems faced by those most in need of assistance. He concluded that fees are not at all inconsistent with the service ethic, which dominates the public sector. Indeed, under conditions of scarcity, fees can help provide resources needed to aid socioeconomically disadvantaged participants. The challenge becomes one of maintaining a service ethic while operating on the boundaries of the moral system dominated by the merchant (Jacobs, 1994).

Unfortunately, research suggests that current public sector practices often fall short of standards established by either the guardian or the merchant. For example, Havitz and Spigner (1993) reported that few public agencies segmented their communities according to relevant criteria like income. Neither did these agencies offer price discounts to low-income residents or coordinate efforts with official unemployment agencies. As a result, the widespread imposition of fees may be regressive for those who lack the discretionary income needed to take part.

Further, though many public agencies believe they are using marketing techniques in their day-to-day operation, few adapt programs or fee initiatives in order to respond to the needs of different user groups. It seems that many agencies may be introducing fees for programs without due regard to the compensatory or market equity models. In the tradition of the equal opportunity model, their pricing policies continue to treat everyone the same. This undifferentiated strategy may have been adequate when fees were nonexistent, but it may create considerable hardship once fees have been instituted.

If prices are sometimes "appropriate," then the question becomes one of client response. How will the client react to a fee initiative? Will clients be displaced by fees? If pricing occurs, will it discriminate or exclude in a way inconsistent with the guardian role of the public sector?

Public Reaction to Fees

Client response to fees for leisure services is not well understood. The traditional economic perspective suggests a generally negative correlation between price and participation. As price increases, demand should fall accordingly. The reasons for such a decline are straightforward. Fees force users to allocate finite resources in order to enjoy a service. The relative cost of this trade-off is referred to as *opportunity cost*. Users relinquish the opportunity to acquire one product or service when they allocate their resources to acquire another.

Manning and Baker (1981) reported a case in point. They found that users overwhelmingly favored the use of city taxes to support public parks and recreation programming. These users generally opposed the introduction of fees, presumably because they hoped to minimize the personal costs they might incur. There is also some evidence that fee subsidies can encourage participation. Emmett, Havitz, and McCarville (1995) found that the promotion of a fee subsidy program encouraged low-income participants to enroll as club members at a fitness facility in unprecedented numbers.

Unfortunately, the consumer behavior literature suggests that response to fees is often less certain than the economic perspective suggests. Reasons for this uncertainty arise from the idiosyncratic ways in which individual participants assess price information. Fees affect behavior only after they have been perceived, processed, and interpreted by the participant. Subsequent responses to pricing may, therefore, surprise the casual observer.

Recall the results from a United States national probability sample survey cited earlier, which indicated that groups like the elderly, poor, and rural residents offered the greatest support for user fees for public outdoor recreation services (Economic Research Associates, 1976). Perhaps these potentially marginalized groups were least likely to take advantage of public recreation programs, so they supported fee structures that placed the financial burden on user groups. Conversely, those who might benefit most from these programs seem unwilling to pay fees to support them. The same study found that active participants like young, well-educated adults did not favor the introduction of fees. Perhaps they feared, with some justification, that new fees would weigh most heavily on them. They participated most often, so their costs could increase dramatically with the introduction of fees.

Several other studies further suggest the complexity of public response to pricing in the public sector. Wilderness users, for example, supported prices for services that had previously been available free of charge, if the prices limited use and reduced crowding (Shelby, Danley, & Peterson, 1982). Driver (1984) found that there was little opposition to entrance fees at a public recreation area if that fee was perceived as enhancing the quality of service. Public park visitors were also willing to pay higher prices when the fees were directed back into the facility at which they were collected (Miles & Fedler, 1986). Consumers seem more willing to pay higher fees when they know that such fees will be used to develop and maintain valued service offerings.

Whatever user reaction to fees, pricing in the public sector is bound inexorably with public perceptions of equity. The concept of price connotes exclusion based upon monetary criteria. Residents unwilling or unable to allocate required funds may be denied access to services provided through the public sector. Such measures suggest that "all do not share equally in the bounties of public policy" (Lineberry, 1977, p. 11). Equal treatment cannot be assured when some potential consumers are excluded from participating, while others are not. The next section is therefore devoted to recommendations that minimize possible discriminatory effects for pricing of leisure programs.

The Role of the Safety Net in the Public Sector

However creative the pricing strategy, regardless of the measures taken, prices will, in the final analysis, discourage some potential participants. In the private sector, this result may be considered an inevitable consequence of doing business, but in the public sector this outcome is often considered unacceptable. The service ethic demands that those who seek public services should receive those services. In particular, meaningful leisure opportunities should not be denied on the basis of ability to pay. Most public providers now recommend that a *safety net* be extended each time fees are introduced. This safety net ensures that those who desire services will be able to gain access to them, regardless of their financial resources.

The challenge has become one of balancing agency needs for self-generated funds and the needs of selected client groups for funding assistance. One popular technique has been one of simply subsidizing the entire program. For example, public leisure agencies may offer selected programs free of charge believing they attract members of specific disadvantaged target groups. Park departments often subsidize selected tennis courts for this reason. They hope to encourage economically disadvantaged youth to play tennis. This approach has proven somewhat problematic in its application, however. Target populations may not participate in those activities regardless of fee levels. Even if they do participate, they risk being marginalized in "their" own subsidized programs (Thompson, 1968).

A second approach has been to partially subsidize programs. Havitz and Spigner's (1993) survey of park and recreation departments serving major U.S. cities suggested that many agencies' safety net policies typically revolved around price discount policies. However, the benefits of these programs seem to be unevenly distributed among needy participant groups. For example, only 17 percent of agencies charging fees offered discounts for unemployed participants, as compared with 86 percent each for children and senior citizens. Other studies have suggested that leisure service agencies' pricing policies are seldom based on the financial needs of individual clients. Pricing policies are more often based primarily on agencies' revenue needs (Brademas & Readnour, 1989; McCarville & Smale, 1991).

While the technique is a good one, it has a few practical limitations. Problems sometimes arise because discounted services may be of lesser quality than their full-priced counterparts. They are offered during less convenient periods, tend to be highly standardized, and may lack the options available through other programs (Lovelock, 1992). Consequently, users who opt for discounted programs may also be opting for lesser quality programs. This issue will be discussed in more detail in the next chapter.

Differential pricing is a variant on the discount theme, so it is often used to extend the safety net. This approach has the dual advantage of offering lower costs to some, while generating resources for the provider. In these cases, prices are set so that programs scheduled during prime time cost more than those scheduled during less popular time periods and so on. As suggested earlier, the logic behind such strategies assumes that potential consumers will, given such choices, select the level of price most acceptable to their personal circumstances.

Another approach involves altering fees according to the financial means of individual clients. This client-centered approach assumes that clients differ in their ability to pay for leisure opportunities, so measures should be designed around the needs of the client. The most prevalent of these measures is typically the assistance program. These assistance efforts offer help to those who can establish that they need additional help from the providing agency. For the safety net to work, the assistance program must be sensitive to the desires and perceptions of potential clients. Many programs require clients to submit paperwork that establishes their income level and their respective needs. This may be problematic for those who are unwilling to declare their income levels in a document that may be circulated to several staff members.

One agency, operating a fitness center, developed a policy that permitted clients to personally negotiate with select staff members an acceptable price level for the basic membership. The policy focused on those who wished to become members but were unable to pay the full fee. The policy dictated that no one would be denied access to programs and services for financial reasons. Members seeking assistance are asked to follow these steps when applying for membership:

1. Tour the facility to ensure their needs can be met by the center's programs and services.

2. Arrange an appointment with staff to discuss their particular requirements for subsidy.

3. Complete a 20-30 minute interview with a membership representative who will discuss a conducive monthly payment plan.

4. Arrange payment through a preauthorized payment plan unless extenuating circumstances exist.

The organization has aggressively promoted this policy in all formal communications with the community and it seems to be exceeding all their original expectations (Emmett et al., 1995).

Further, program names may have much to do with their success or failure. For example, the term *assistance* carries with it considerable negative baggage. It has a ring of charity that is often distasteful to those who might benefit most from the program. In order to remove this potential constraint, many agencies have begun to call their efforts *welcome* or *scholarship programs*. This may seem a small step, but it provides a useful starting point in creating any safety net.

Developing a Safety Net

Recall that three equity models can be used to guide pricing decisions. Together they seem well suited to act as an ethical guide as price policies are imposed and safety nets are established. Wicks and Crompton (1986) suggest that:

> Determination of the appropriate model of equity should evolve through evaluation of three basic principles: (1) equal opportunity should be recognized as the point of departure; (2) deviations from this point of departure should be encouraged if they benefit the least advantaged; (3) there should, in all cases, be a stated minimum level or floor below which quantity or quality should not fall. (p. 344)

A resulting pricing policy might first dictate that fees only be used under conditions of scarcity or financial exigency. Second, the policy might adopt the tenet that equal access is the basis of the public leisure delivery system. It might then include a variety of checks and balances ensuring that potential users are not excluded. For example, several "principles of implementation" might be adopted. These principles could be especially helpful in reducing disruption caused by the application of new or increased fee levels. They might include: (a) reasonable limits will be set on annual fee increases, (b) increases will be phased in over predetermined periods, (c) increases will be accompanied by heavily promoted discount opportunities, and (d) welcome policies will be developed and promoted aggressively.

Assistance programs have gained great popularity over the years and many versions have emerged. Some assistance programs offer a set number of opportunities to those thought to be in need (e.g., participants might be able to register for three programs free of charge, but have unlimited access to drop-in programs). Other versions dictate that the participant pay a small amount of the registration fee ($10 to $20 is common), while the rest of the fee is paid by the agency. In all cases, the best programs ensure that the participants' subsidized status remains confidential. They are issued passes that are identical to those of participants who pay full fare. In this way, embarrassment costs are kept to a minimum.

Administrators are constantly looking for new and better ways to extend access to all members of their community. One ongoing challenge has been to establish who is "deserving" of fee subsidy. In many cases, staff members interview applicants to establish their level of need. This process can be both embarrassing for the applicant and time consuming for staff. One agency estimated that over $100,000 in staff hours were allocated annually to such interviews. A few leisure providers are now joining with other public sector agencies to simplify this task for all concerned. They tell their clients that if they qualify for some form of social assistance, they also qualify for leisure subsidy. No questions are asked and no interview is required. Participants need only apply to one public agency. Confidential information is not shared between agencies. The clients simply indicate that they are part of a recognized assistance program and subsidies are made available automatically. Marketers must be ever re-sourceful in discovering ways to ease access to their programs. In this case, the answer may lie in coordination and cooperation between public agencies.

In conclusion, it seems that the danger of fees lies not in their application but in their misapplication. Fees provide an increasingly popular solution to scarcity, yet they can displace the very clients the provider hopes to serve. Several reports indicate that pricing activity in the leisure community is often undertaken in a rather haphazard manner. Little effort is undertaken to ameliorate the debilitating effects price may have on needy members of the community. Years ago, Tom Goodale (1985) warned of the pitfalls of adopting the merchant's methods. Like Jacobs (1994), he wondered if the drive to gather funds might bend the service mandate and subvert the worthwhile goals pursued by the public sector. He ends his admonition with an excerpt from T. S. Eliot's *Choruses from the Rock* which asks, "When the Stranger says: What is the meaning of this city . . . what will you answer? . . . To make money from each other or 'This is community?'" (Goodale, p. 206). We might well remember these words as we ponder pricing strategies in the public sector.

Main Points

- Leisure participants face many costs, both monetary and nonmonetary, when considering taking part in leisure programs.

- Increasingly, leisure providers have been turning to fees and charges to support programming efforts.

- While private sector merchants are relatively untroubled by the introduction of fees, public sector providers worry about their exclusionary nature.

- Though notions of equity or fairness are often used to condemn fees for public sector leisure programs, fees are consistent with all models of equity.

- Not all public sector programs seem equally deserving of tax support, so fees may be more appropriate for some programs than for others.

- While no one wants to pay a fee, client reaction when fees are actually charged is uncertain. Fees seem to both attract and repel prospective participants.

- Providers may use several approaches to fees in order to provide needed revenue for themselves but also meaningful choices to participants.

- Fees tend to displace people who lack financial resources so, in the public sector at least, fee initiatives must be supported by an extensive safety net.

References

Brademas, D., & Readnour, J. (1989). Status of fees and charges in public leisure service agencies. *Journal of Park and Recreation Administration, 7*(4), 42-55.

Crompton, J.L., & Lamb, C. (1986). *Marketing government and social services.* New York: John Wiley & Sons.

Crompton, J.L., & McGregor, B.P. (1994). Trends in the financing and staffing of local government park and recreation services 1964/65-1990/91. *Journal of Park and Recreation Administration, 12*(3), 19-37.

Driver, B. (1984). Public responses to user fees at public recreation areas. *Proceedings: Fees for outdoor recreation on lands open to the public conference* (pp. 45-52). Research Department, Appalachian Mountain Club.

Economic Research Associates. (1976). *Evaluation of public willingness to pay user charges for use of outdoor recreation areas and facilities.* Washington, D.C.: Heritage Conservation and Recreation Service.

Ellerbrock, M. (1982). Some straight talk on user fees. *Parks and Recreation, 17*(1), 59-62.

Emmett, J., Havitz, M.E., & McCarville, R.E. (1996). A price subsidy policy for socioeconomically disadvantaged recreation participants. *Journal of Park and Recreation Administration, 14*(1), 63-80.

Goodale, T. (1985). Prevailing winds and bending mandates. In T. Goodale & P. Witt (Eds.), *Recreation and leisure: Issues in an era of change* (pp. 195-207). State College, PA: Venture.

Havitz, M.E. (1988). Marketing is not synonymous with commercialism. *Parks and Recreation, 23*(5), 34-36.

Havitz, M.E., & Spigner, C. (1993). Unemployment, health and leisure: The role of park and recreation services. *Trends, 30*(4), 31-36.

Jacobs, J. (1994). *Systems of survival.* New York: Vintage Books.

Jacoby, J., Chestnut, R., Weigl, K., & Fisher, W. (1976). Pre-purchase information acquisition: Description of a process methodology. In B. Anderson (Ed.), *Advances in consumer research* (pp. 306-314). Cincinnati, OH: Association for Consumer Research.

Kraus, R., & Curtis, J. (1990). *Creative management* (5th ed.). Toronto: Times Mirror/Mosby.

Lineberry, R. (1977). *Equality and urban policy.* Beverly Hills, CA: Sage Publications.

Lovelock, C.H. (1992). *Managing services: Marketing, operations, and human resources* (2nd ed.). Toronto: Prentice-Hall.

Manning, R., & Baker, S. (1981). Discrimination through user fees: Fact or fiction? *Parks and Recreation, 16*(9), 70-74.

McCarville, R., & Crompton, J.L. (1988). A review of selected local park and recreation financial indicators in the first half of the 1980s: A challenge to conventional wisdom. *Journal of Park and Recreation Administration, 6*(3), 43-54.

McCarville, R., Driver, B., & Crompton, J.L. (1992). Persuasive communication and the pricing of public leisure services. In M.J. Manfredo (Ed.), *Influencing human behavior: Theory and applications in recreation, tourism, and natural resources management* (pp. 263-291). Champaign, IL: Sagamore.

McCarville, R.E. & Smale, B.J.A. (1991). Involvement in pricing by municipal recreation agencies. *Journal of Applied Recreation Research, 16*, 200-219.

Miles, A., & Fedler, T. (1986). *Paying for backcountry recreation experiences: Understanding the acceptability of user fees.* Presentation at First National Symposium on Social Science in Resource Management, Oregon State University, Corvallis, OR.

Ostrom, V., & Ostrom, E. (1977). Public goods and public choices. In E. Savas (Ed.), *Alternatives for delivering public services* (pp. 7-49). Boulder, CO: Westview Press.

Rawls, J. (1971). *A theory of justice.* Cambridge, MA: The Belknap Press.

Shelby, B., Danley, K., & Peterson, M. (1982). Preferences of backpackers and river runners for allocation techniques. *Journal of Forestry*, 80(7), 416-419.

Thompson, W. (1968). The city as a distorted price system. *Psychology Today*, 2(3), 30.

Walsh, R. (1986). *Recreation economic decisions*. State College, PA: Venture.

Wicks, B., & Crompton, J.L. (1986). Citizen and administrator perspectives of equity in the delivery of park services. *Leisure Sciences*, 8, 341-366.

City of Waterloo

10

Create Pricing Strategy

The potential participant views price with a mixture of longing and regret. Longing exists because participants often confuse price with quality. As discussed later in this chapter, higher prices are often considered synonymous with improved quality. Participants seek this improved quality, yet no one really wants to pay premium prices. As a result, high prices can attract and repel potential clients simultaneously. Conversely, lower price services are often suspect because they suggest lower quality services. In this way, even low prices may attract and repel at the same time. What is the leisure marketer to do? How can prices be set so that their attractive properties are maximized and their potential to displace minimized? Happily, the pricing literature suggests that these goals are best pursued through strategic price setting.

Pricing Policy vs. Pricing Strategy

Currently the typical public sector leisure provider manages pricing through statements of policy. Policy, it seems, is the public sector's way of dealing with most contentious issues. Pricing policies tend to make sweeping statements about how groups will be priced or how prices will be set. They may dictate, for example, that preferential fees will be offered to older adults and children or that public services will not be priced. Often these policies are established through third parties like city councils or park commissions. Recreation providers must then set prices according to these guidelines.

Such policies offer a mixed blessing. In positive terms, they invariably emerge from well-intentioned efforts to serve the community. As a result, they delineate how members of the community should be treated by those setting price levels. They often dictate that elements of the population thought to be particularly vulnerable or deserving of assistance should receive preferential treatment. They also indicate which services are essential to the well-being of the community and suggest that they should be priced accordingly. For the provider, these policies provide unequivocal guidelines and represent a clear call to action.

In less positive terms, policies have a rather dramatic shortcoming. They represent a rather blunt instrument. They are necessarily sweeping in their scope and can be unwieldy as a result. They typically focus on one or two variables (like age or program type) then tie the hands of the provider who is trying to serve that age group or deliver that program. For example, local politicians in one city decided that recreation opportunities were essential to the well-being of the city's children. They therefore determined that no child would be denied access on the basis of price and set their pricing policy accordingly. Parks and recreation staff were told that they could no longer charge fees for children's programming.

Problems arose within weeks of the policy taking effect. Staff members were inundated with requests for new programs and their resources were quickly used up. Thousands of children were placed on waiting lists because the agency lacked the resources to accommodate so many requests. Parents even offered to pay fees so that the agency could organize additional programs, but policy dictated that they were not permitted to do so. Anything offered to children must be offered free of charge. In the end, the agency was millions of dollars below their revenue targets, programs were being cancelled as a result, and thousands of children waited for places in overcrowded programs.

In this case, a pricing policy designed to facilitate participation by children actually ensured that many thousands of children would not be able to take part. Clearly, policy must be supplemented with a more flexible pricing strategy. Pricing strategy determines the role that price will play within the larger marketing effort. What segment is being targeted by the service that is being priced? What image is the provider hoping to project with this service? What is the role to be played by this price? Is price being used to attract large numbers of clients or to restrict numbers of clientele (Nagle, 1987)? Which equity model is being used to price this service? Is this to be a price based on the market equity model or is it more compensatory in its approach? Answers to these questions should establish pricing strategy and guide subsequent pricing decisions.

Guiding Principles for Pricing Activity

Pricing strategy should be based upon four basic principles. The marketer ignores them at her peril. They relate to fairness, choice, balance, and communication.

The Importance of Fairness

The first pricing principle is that of fairness. Fairness refers to what is right or appropriate. Prices that are thought of as appropriate will receive little comment from users, while inappropriate prices will generate considerable outrage. The leisure marketer is advised to ensure that all prices are considered fair.

The assessment of fairness is actually a complicated process. Any client uses several criteria or standards in making a fairness assessment. The first standard is that of rationale. Clients want to know why a fee is being charged and more particularly, why are they being asked to pay. This is the classic "why me?" question. They are often uncertain why they are being asked to pay a fee at all. Why does a participant pay to use a trail or a sport field? Aren't the rocks, grass, and trees provided by nature? Why should they pay to enjoy them? Why should they pay to register their child in programs that use volunteer coaches and leaders? Isn't this leadership provided free of charge? This problem is particularly acute for public sector programs. Participants may believe that they have already paid for the program through their taxes. This is a very common assumption. Why should they be asked to pay "a second time?" When asked to do so it seems unfair.

The second standard of fairness relates to "how much." It relates to the actual levels at which fees are set. Leisure participants evaluate prices in terms of prices they have paid before, prices they have seen advertised, and prices they think "should" be charged. These expectations establish a *reference point* that helps participants evaluate prices they see advertised. Prices that exceed these expectations are often thought to be "unfair," and outrage results.

This problem typically rears its head when fees are introduced for the first time or when fees are increased dramatically. For example, a large city recently increased its fees for facility rental. In one case, fees charged for a meeting room rented to an older adult club jumped from $12 per night to about $100 per hour. Group members, who had been accustomed to paying pennies an hour were now being asked to pay a fee that violated their reference point. With considerable outrage, group members descended on a city council meeting and forced a reversal of the policy.

The heaviest users of a program or facility are most likely to notice changes in fee levels. Because of their ongoing attendance, they have been exposed repeatedly to existing prices, programs, and policies. They have internalized these standards, and these standards have become powerful expectations. Findings reported by Kerr and Manfredo (1991) seem to confirm this assumption. In a study of New Zealand back country hut users, they found that past experiences influenced reaction to new fee initiatives. Those who had paid for similar services elsewhere seemed untroubled by the prospect of paying fees at the test sites. Those who had not paid in the past were very troubled by those same fees. Payment experience was sometimes even more influential, in terms of intent to pay future fees than was the actual price to be charged. Those unaccustomed to paying fees may most resent new fee initiatives because any fee, regardless of its magnitude, violates the existing status quo. Such violations suggest unfair treatment to these users.

The Desire for Choice

Once the fairness of a price has been established, the client is then concerned with *choices* or *options*. Choice is the second pricing principle that leisure marketers ignore at their peril. The concept of choice is an absolutely integral part of any pricing strategy. Everyone seeks choice when making participation decisions. As a result providers must make

options available. Options offer two great advantages.

First, they make customization possible. Options help clients customize their own leisure programs. A new golfer may hope to join a country club. During the first year of membership the golfer may seek instruction and club rental, but will not require caddies or golf carts. The golfer will welcome choices from among these augmentations. She will be happy to pay for services she has chosen to use, but be pleased to avoid the costs of services she does not require. In this way she can customize both her golfing experience and her payment total.

Second, options enable participants to pay in terms that are least important to them. Someone with monetary resources but little time will likely pay more for a program that offers convenience. Someone who lacks monetary resources but has an abundance of time might seek low-cost alternatives regardless of the time at which they are offered. Choices enable clients to choose the price that is least important to them. This latter benefit is particularly important for public sector providers. Given their mandate of service to the community, they are particularly hesitant to charge fees because such fees may displace clients. With the introduction of meaningful options, such displacement becomes less likely. Clients can choose options that are most appropriate to their circumstances.

Choices can be made available in both the level and type of charges for leisure programs. Recall that the participant must pay many costs to participate in a leisure program. Fees represent the client's contribution to the operating costs of a given program. This contribution helps with the cost of service provision. Are there different ways, other than through fees, that the client can assist with the provision of the program? If so, can fees be reduced accordingly? For example, an aerobics program required staff to attend its many classes to register participants. This became quite an expense, so they asked for volunteers to assist them with the task. A volunteer was asked to arrive early prior to each class, then punch the attendance cards of all who attended class that day. In return for rendering this service, the volunteer was permitted to participate free of charge. This procedure cost the program planners very little and offered volunteers the option to avoid monetary fees in return for a bit of time and energy.

Programmers can be very creative in finding ways to have clients "help" them provide programs and thereby enjoy discounts. List the costs of any given program and find ways that clients can help reduce those costs. Then offer discounts to those willing to help out. For example, one of the great challenges of facility operation is smoothing demand. Everyone wants a facility for a few hours after dinner or during the weekend, but demand drops off dramatically during early morning or late evening hours. The challenge is one of encouraging at least a few clients to participate during traditionally slow periods. Discounts are typically used for this purpose. Selective discounts not only reduce crowding during peak periods but also generate additional funds.

The Search for Balance

The third pricing principle is that of *balance.* Any delivery system must be sustainable if it is to serve the leisure participant over the long term. *Sustainability* results from a balance between revenues and expenditures. For many years, public sector providers looked to tax allocations to ensure this balance. Unfortunately, the tax dollar has proven an uncertain source of funds over the years, so fees are being used increasingly to supplement delivery efforts. This brings up the touchy point of the bottom line. Many leisure providers are now being told to at least "break even" by generating as many funds as they are expending. Others are being told to generate a portion of the funds they expend. Recently, a volunteer board was instructed to generate half its budget through fees and charges. They took this directive literally and began to cut all programs that did not achieve "50 percent break even". In the process, the board discontinued several excellent programs because they failed to meet the new guideline.

Such sweeping measures seem a needless waste and a dreadful mistake because they

focus on the wrong "bottom line." They expect each program to stand on its own, to be judged on the basis of its own bottom line. Instead, marketers might consider a more balanced view. For revenue purposes, each individual program might well be considered as part of a larger package. Individual programs that lose money can always be subsidized by other programs that generate a profit. This Robin Hood approach is the key to saving those many worthwhile programs that will never, and perhaps should never, operate at a profit. The only bottom line that counts is the grand total of all operations.

The Need for Communication

The final principle for developing pricing strategy is that of *communication.* Active and ongoing communication is an essential component of any pricing strategy. Participants should be informed "why" they are being asked to pay fees, what choices are available, and what paying those fees means to them (i.e., what benefits are being purchased). For example, tell clients if fees are being used to improve service levels. Research tells us that participants are more likely to support fees intended to make improvements. Tell participants where and how the revenues are being used. Again, research suggests that campers, for example, are in general agreement that fees should be allocated back to the site at which they were collected. They prefer that their favorite sites benefit from their fees. In other words, they are more likely to support fees that will help make their next visit even better.

These results offer insight regarding possible communication strategies designed to support first-time fee initiatives. Such strategies should inform users of the need for fee-based revenues as well as the personal advantages accruing from payment. Communication strategies focusing on these principles may help users judge fees in a more positive context. For example, a parks agency was considering increasing fees dramatically over a three-year period. In order to prepare their client group for the increases, they developed a strategy to

- communicate reasons for price increases long before those increases were instituted, and

- change price expectations with new information so that expectations might rise with the new prices.

This strategy, developed by a private communications firm, was comprised of several elements including a documentary series, a multi-use "flagship" brochure, and radio blitzes prior to long weekends throughout the summer months.

Specifically, measures were taken to establish the agency's increased need for revenue. This was done through a documentary series developed through a regional cable television operator. This series, comprised primarily of interviews with park service staff, highlighted two points. First, a case was made for the decline in tax-based appropriations. Messages indicated the relatively small proportion of operational funds that now originated with the tax dollar. They made it clear that program quality would suffer if fees were not increased. Second, the consequences of fee payment (or failure to pay) were outlined. Users were reassured that fees were not being wasted or allocated at the whim of bureaucrats. They were told how their fees would make a difference by either maintaining or improving valued resources. For more information on this strategy, refer to Appendix 1 at the end of the text.

Strategic Options

Three basic pricing options exist. Although each pursues very different goals and produces very different consequences, each can be used simultaneously by any leisure provider. The first option is that of penetration pricing.

Penetration Pricing

Penetration prices are kept low in order to encourage participation. Marketers charging low fees are typically attempting to entice potential participants to begin to take part or to continue or increase existing participation patterns. In the private sector, low prices are also intended to draw footloose participants away from other, more expensive service providers. The goal is one of appealing to, then holding, these participants.

Penetration pricing is the traditional strategy of the public leisure provider. Many leisure programs are heavily subsidized ensuring that fees are kept to a minimum. The advantage of this strategy is obvious. It offers added value to clients, thereby encouraging participation. This additional value is particularly appealing to those who either lack financial resources or are unsure whether the program is of interest to them. For both these groups, high fees generate a hardship that they are typically unwilling or unable to bear. As a result, they are repelled by high fees, but may be attracted by low fee levels.

Penetration pricing is not without its challenges. First, penetration pricing annoys competitors and partners alike. To them it seems an obvious effort to distract and lure their own clients to your programs. Consequently, penetration pricing invites often negative countermeasures like negative advertising and complaints. Penetration prices are also easily copied and may generate what is best described as "price wars." In these battles for customers, providers repeatedly drop prices to match those of competitors. Clients become opportunistic, hopping from one provider to the next, searching for the lowest price. Inevitably, program quality suffers and instability is introduced to the marketplace. In the end, both the client and the provider may suffer under these conditions.

Penetration prices represent a particularly sticky issue when private and public sector agencies offer similar programs. Access to tax dollars enables the public provider to subsidize programs, to reduce fees, and to penetrate the marketplace. As a result, private-sector providers often complain that the public provider creates unfair competition through artificially low price levels.

The success of penetration pricing is based on the assumption that clients are automatically motivated by saving money.

Such is not always the case. For example, the low prices of penetration pricing rarely succeed for low-cost or trivial items. Most shoppers are simply unwilling to search for the lowest price, when the saving is likely to be marginal at best. Occasional bathers who pay $1.00 for a swim at a public pool are unlikely to be lured by lower fees at facilities across town. The saving of a few pennies simply offers an insignificant reward structure to justify the added inconvenience. To put this discussion in perspective, recall that the price a client pays for a leisure service is measured in terms of monetary, convenience, time, and even psychological costs. Reducing one cost while ignoring, and perhaps even increasing, other costs does little to encourage participation in a leisure program.

There are other reasons why clients may be unmoved by low prices. Habitual shoppers who have found a "favorite" location or provider are unlikely to be lured by the savings offered by lower prices at another location. They are happy with the current location and risk being disappointed when moving to alternative sites or trying alternative program offerings. Most shoppers are unwilling to accept this risk. Called *fear of mispurchase*, this fear acts to reduce participants' willingness to shop around for lower prices. Such fear is a function of the participants' assessment of the marketplace. If, for example, the participant believes that programs vary dramatically in quality, this fear may discourage movement between providers. Conversely, movement is encouraged if the participant believes that all programs are essentially the same in their capacity to serve. This is why so many providers' advertising attempts to convince potential clients that their services are somehow unique. Participants are less likely to abandon unique providers, regardless of the savings to be gained by shopping elsewhere.

Neither will reduced prices appeal to those who seek prestige items. Although the search for prestige may seem a rather shallow motive, it is surprisingly pervasive. We may all, at one time or another, desire a product or service because of the prestige it offers. We have hoped to attend major sporting events, to visit well known tourist sites and theme parks,

or to try new or demanding sports that offer prestige because of their unique qualities. Price is rarely the issue when it comes to purchasing prestige. Indeed, low price may actually reduce prestige potential. High cost carries with it a certain level of prestige, and low-cost alternatives diminish this prestige potential. Clearly, those who seek the prestige of expensive country clubs may not be enticed by low-cost facilities provided by public leisure agencies.

Participants' ongoing concern for program quality also limits the effectiveness of penetration pricing efforts. Participants often infer quality from price. Remember the adage, "You get what you pay for"? This old rule of thumb arises directly from the assumption that quality is a function of price. This is a very powerful cognitive rule, and it is made more powerful if participants know little of the product or the marketplace. If participants know nothing of a service, they are more likely to use price as a cue to its quality. They reason that a better program costs more. The program of lesser quality is the one with the lower price. As a result, many clients may doubt the quality of programs that cost too little. For many of these individuals, penetration pricing efforts may actually discourage participation.

Another problem is one of commitment. Many leisure providers contend that participants who invest little to participate are more willing to drop out of any given activity. Participants in free programs, for example, may believe that there is little harm done by dropping out because they invested almost nothing to attend. They may be distracted by competing opportunities and miss classes as a result. Those who invest larger sums to take part may be more willing to hang in to the very end of the program. By doing so, they hope to increase the value they received from their investment.

Third, penetration pricing is problematic because it is a rather passive technique. It assumes that participation is tied directly to fee level. As fee levels drop, participation rates should rise accordingly. Although this may be true for the interested few who base participation decisions on fee levels, it falls short when applied to the general population. A quick review of current participation patterns suggests why this is the case. Much of what we call participation in a given activity is undertaken by a relatively few individuals. For example, Barber (1998) reports that about 8 percent of adults generated almost 85 percent of all adult running activity. Four percent of adults generate 81 percent of all adult tennis activity. This general pattern seems to extend to most "popular" recreation activities. Lower prices are not likely to encourage avid users to participate more often. Regular participants lack the time and energy for more participation. For them price is simply not the issue.

Finally, even if penetration prices could encourage avid users to become more avid, in many cases it is still unlikely that the general population will be lured into trying an activity. If sky diving was offered free of charge, would the general population rush to take part? If bungee jumping were free, would most grandparents or small children rush in their efforts to jump headlong from the nearest bridge with elastic cords tied around their ankles? Though these may seem to be extreme cases, the point must be made that there is limited interest in any given activity. Low prices are only effective if unfulfilled demand exists among client groups that are discouraged by current price levels. Penetration pricing cannot generate demand where demand does not currently exist. As a result, lower prices may serve more to reduce revenues than to increase demand.

Neutral Pricing

The second pricing option is to adopt a *neutral price* strategy. Neutral pricing avoids high prices, so that fewer potential clients are likely to be displaced. It also avoids artificially low prices, so those using price level as a cue to quality are reassured by the price level. This strategy intentionally minimizes the importance of price (Nagle, 1987). The provider simply sets a price level that seems to be neither high nor a "bargain" then relies on other tools, like customer service to encourage purchase and participation. There are many reasons for adopting a neutral price strategy.

First among these reasons is client reaction. Higher prices might discourage participation, while low prices may create suspicion as to program quality. Neutral prices avoid both these issues.

Neutral prices also respond to the organization's need for revenue. Neutral prices are often preferable to penetration prices because of tight profit margins. Neutral prices are rarely established at less than break even levels. As a result, neutral prices are generally able to maintain the programs they support.

Next, neutral pricing represents strategic freedom for the provider. Penetration prices focus attention on price. This is inherently limiting for the marketer. Participants desire more from providers than low prices. They seek, among other things, great customer service, reliability, and easy-to-use services (Treacy & Wiersema, 1995). Neutral pricing encourages the marketer to focus on more than simple price. The success of this option relies on the total program package, the "solution" provided for the client.

The final reason for neutral pricing relates to the reaction of competitors and partners. Neutral pricing is less likely than penetration pricing to generate countermeasures from competitors. Other providers tend to be more complacent when fee levels seem consistent across the marketplace. It is little wonder that this strategy is also called the stability option.

The neutral pricing option is not without its own unique problems, however. Its primary problem is its basic assumption that price can be rendered "unimportant." This assumption is as simplistic as it is misleading. The point has been made repeatedly in this text that the public is anything but a homogeneous mass. There are actually many publics, many groups in the community. A price that is not an issue for one group of users may be a great problem for another group. It may be easy for a single working adult to register for a $50.00 program, but this same cost may create an insurmountable barrier for a single, underemployed parent of two. The price may be neutral in one instance but not the next.

Skim Pricing

The final pricing option is that of *skimming*. A skimming strategy focuses on revenue generation. Prices are not based on cost of service provision but on "what the traffic will bear." The marketer offers a service that is very much in demand and charges prices that far exceed cost of service provision. It is a process of profit maximization. Generally, skimming is a strategic option "only when the firm faces a large enough segment of buyers whose decision to purchase the product is relatively price insensitive" (Nagle, 1987, p. 114). When clients are *price insensitive*, their demand for a service varies little with price increases. Clients who do not react to reduced or increased fees are thought to be price insensitive. Such individuals are the preferred targets of most skimming efforts.

It is perhaps ironic that price insensitivity arises from caring combined with indifference. The client must value the product but remain relatively indifferent to the price being charged for it. Figure 10.1 lists many of the conditions that lead to insensitivity toward price. Generally speaking, "yes" responses are consistent with price insensitivity and "no" responses generate considerable price sensitivity. Use this simple checklist to determine if a client group is likely to be price sensitive or insensitive.

Most of these conditions are internal to the client and difficult for the marketer to address. However, one of the most important variables in creating price insensitivity is within the control of the marketer. That condition is scarcity. *Scarcity* artificially increases demand, because it creates a certain urgency around a sale. When one does not purchase a scarce item, a unique opportunity may be lost. It is for this reason that vendors will try to create crowds at their point of sale. One wily individual, hoping to sell his own car, advertised in a local newspaper and received three calls from potential buyers. Rather than schedule the buyers at regular intervals spaced an hour apart, he scheduled them all to arrive at his home at the same time. Their coming together created a sense of scarcity, because only one of the three could purchase the one auto. A bidding process ensued as the hopeful

	Yes	No
Few substitutes thought to be available.	✓	
Item perceived to be a necessity.	✓	
Comparison with similar products is difficult.	✓	
Purchase price represents insignificant amount of client's resources.	✓	
Client pays only portion of total price.	✓	
High switching costs exist. (Has client already invested considerable resources and time into this activity?)	✓	
Price is used by client to infer quality.	✓	

Table: 10.1: Establishing Price Sensitivity Among Client Groups
Source: Morris & Morris, 1995.
* Yes responses reduce the perceived importance of price.

buyers suddenly became willing to pay prices they had considered unacceptable even hours before.

This story is offered here not to suggest how to "sell" products, but rather to point out the importance of perceived scarcity. Scarcity is created by several conditions. The "most common" is simply limited production capacity. Small operations can serve only a limited number of participants. Highly customized programs require considerable time and energy to deliver. As a result, they can be offered only in limited numbers. Second, scarcity exists for programs that offer unique benefit structures to their clients. In related terms, scarcity often exists when new programs are first introduced to the marketplace. New programs are inherently unique until they can be copied by other providers. Their unique nature renders them a scarce commodity. In all these cases, limited supply often drives demand higher. With higher demand comes increasing price insensitivity and the possibility for charging higher prices.

There are advantages to the skimming option. The most obvious is that of its capacity to generate revenue. Skimmed prices increase revenues far in excess of program costs. This is good news for leisure providers in any sector. For the private sector, this revenue increases profit potential. For the public sector, it helps providers gather resources to subsidize other efforts. Like Robin Hood, skimmed prices gather resources from one group so that they can be distributed to another.

The second advantage of skimming is one of high prices' ability to curtail demand. The traditional economic model suggests that as prices rise, demand generally falls. High prices are often able to reduce stress on natural areas, facilities, and any number of programs that are unable to satisfy demand. This fact is appreciated by managers and users alike. In a study of river users, researchers found that the most ardent recreational users of the river actually favored the introduction of fees in order to reduce use levels on the water system. These users knew that higher fees would discourage many of their counterparts on the river and, hopefully, reduce use levels.

The third advantage of this option is the positive signal it sends to uncertain clients. Clients tend to use price as a cue to quality. As suggested earlier, the less clients know about a program or service, the more they will infer quality from price. Participants will be inclined to infer quality from price level to the extent that "(1) they believe qualities differ within the product class; (2) they perceive that low quality imposes a risk of a large loss; and (3) they lack other information enabling them to evaluate quality before purchase" (Nagle, 1987, p. 67). Those who are uncertain of the quality of a product may use price to ease that uncertainty. Although they may be repelled by the notion of high prices, they may also be comforted because of the quality these prices suggest.

Marketers are reminded, however, that fees represent only one cue to potential users. As users try the service, as friends begin to compare notes on the quality of that service, the importance of price will wane. Consequently, the connection between quality and cost is tenuous at best. Clients will not be satisfied by high prices and poor quality. As they judge the program, they must perceive that program characteristics are consistent with price levels.

Like all pricing options, a skimming strategy is not without its flaws. Three problems are particularly noteworthy. First and most obvious among them is the problem of displacement. High prices are likely to displace users who would otherwise hope to use the service. Groups that lack economic resources are usually the first to be displaced by high fees. The demands of skimming strategies fall most heavily upon lower income groups. To rely on skimming strategies is perhaps to deny services to these groups. This may be an acceptable strategy for some private sector providers, but it is problematic for the public and not-for-profit sector providers.

Second, skimmed prices may be viewed as unfair. There is a growing literature that tells us that clients view prices as being "right" or "wrong" as much as being "high" or "low." Artificially high prices will likely be viewed as unfair, and clients may respond with considerable outrage as a result. In hypothetical exercises, Kahneman, Knetsch, and Thaler

(1986) found that subjects were typically willing to boycott unfair service providers even when it was against their own individual interests to do so. Stevenson (1989) may have observed this same phenomenon when he found that senior citizens were displaced by increased prices for camping opportunities at a Colorado State park. Those displaced were both aware of and very much against the price increases that displaced them. Rather than continue doing business with the agency that increased those prices, many preferred to do business elsewhere even when they were forced to use *more expensive* sites. It's clear that many unhappy clients will go to considerable lengths to abandon providers with whom they have become disenchanted. Skimming strategies have the distinct potential to cause just such disenchantment.

Finally, skimming strategies require price insensitivity, yet price sensitivity is a dynamic creation that ebbs and flows with time. It is likely, for example, that price insensitivity may grow with experience. Participants may become less price sensitive as they come to know and trust a favored fitness instructor. As they purchase more activity-related equipment, they may be less willing to try other activities. Once they come to value product attributes, they may be unwilling to allocate the time, effort, and risk associated with finding another program as prices rise. As a result, their price insensitivity may grow.

It is just as likely, however, that price insensitivity will erode with experience. As suggested above, knowledge gained through experience may serve to increase price sensitivity. The more easily price comparisons can be made and the more readily other relevant information is available, the more price sensitive a leisure participant is likely to become. When such information is available, the relative merits of purchase alternatives can be judged. If alternatives are found to be equally effective and reliable, the participant may choose them as prices rise (Nagle, 1987).

For all these reasons, participants may oscillate between acceptance and rejection of fees for similar program offerings. It is perhaps little wonder that Howard and Selin (1987) found price tolerances for public leisure services could differ wildly from one individual to the next. They seemed even to differ within the same individual from one program to the next. As price sensitivity varies, so too, will the success of a skimming strategy.

Single pricing strategies like the penetration, neutral or skimming options should not be considered in isolation. Each has its own respective strengths and weaknesses. Each will succeed and each will fail over time. The question to ask, is not "Which strategy should I use?" but rather, "How can I use all three strategies simultaneously to best advantage?" A single agency could pursue all three strategies depending upon its objectives for a given service, a specific target group, or even for a point in time. The way in which each option is introduced and coordinated is a question of pricing strategy.

Setting Price Levels

Pricing strategy in general and price levels in particular are established using three criteria. These criteria relate to priorities, the program, and the marketplace. Each set the boundaries within which strategy might be pursued and price levels set. Each helps the marketer ask the right questions so that optimal decisions might be made. Together they represent what is often called *the pricing triangle.* (Figure 10.2)

Agency Priorities

Priorities are reflected in goals, pricing objectives, and internal price limits. First consider the issue of *goals*. Goals arise from the mission of the provider. Private sector goals tend to focus on market share and growth. Not-for-profit providers are motivated to serve specific user groups. In the public sector, goals arise from questions of equity, and service to the community.

Priorities are pursued through *pricing objectives*. What are the specific objectives being pursued of this pricing strategy? Do they relate to altering or smoothing demand, monitoring interest, positioning the agency or

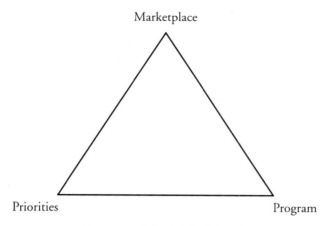

Figure 10.2: The Pricing Triangle

program in the mind of the user, or raising revenue? The answers to these questions should aid in deciding price level. They will help determine whether or not the program should operate on a loss, break even, or profit basis. For example, higher fees often produce greater profit but reduce demand. If the goal is to generate demand in a program, lower fee levels should be considered.

The marketer must then move beyond organizational priorities. These priorities represent only one set of concerns in any price setting initiative. The next factor, that of the program itself, must receive the attention of the marketer.

The Program

Program characteristics also help establish price levels and general pricing strategy. Consider first the issue of the *public good*. Public sector users expect prices to vary according to who benefits from that program. Programs that serve the entire community are typically offered at the greatest loss. Those that benefit only the user are generally operated at a profit. *Level of service* can also determine whether or not a program might make a profit. As a rule of thumb, basic programs offered during inconvenient time periods, or those scheduled when demand is low, are typically offered at reduced price levels. Customized programs are usually priced higher than

standard programs. The client is receiving an improved level of service and generally expects to pay higher fees as a result.

The second issue arising from the program itself is one of *program cost*. How much does it cost to deliver the program? Most providers use a cost-based approach in setting their fee levels. They begin with their own costs, then determine how much loss or profit to build into the subsequent price level. Providers' costs are determined by staff salaries, facility rentals, and equipment costs. All too often, however, these costs of service provision seem out of the control of the service provider. As a result, those who rely on this technique often believe that price levels are also out of their control.

Those who subscribe to this notion might take a lesson from the genius of Henry Ford as he produced his Model T automobile. Ford was famous for setting prices at levels he knew his customers could afford, *then* establishing production practices that would make profit possible at those price levels. As Ford recalled, "We have never considered any costs as fixed costs, therefore we first reduce the price to the point where we believe more sales will result. Then we go ahead and try to make the prices. We do not bother about the costs. The new price forces the costs down . . . We make more discoveries concerning manufacturing and selling under this forced method than by any method of leisurely investigation"

(Ford, 1923, p. 147). This was no idle boast on Ford's part. He wanted to build an automobile that the common farmer could afford. Assembly costs of the day made this seem an impossible goal. Impossible, that is, until he abandoned the traditional ways of thinking about assembly. He developed a process to dramatically reduce costs. This process is now known as the assembly line.

There is a double lesson here for all those who set prices based upon cost of provision. The first lesson is one of *control*. There is always a way to reduce costs if the provider is determined to do so. The assembly line Ford developed offered a complete departure from the way assembly had been undertaken up to that time. Before Ford's innovations, the shop floor of an assembly operation was typically a chaotic jumble of craftsmen going about their respective tasks at their own pace. In order to reduce the chaos and related costs, Ford began to control the order in which tasks were undertaken, the equipment used to undertake them, and the speed at which they were performed. He was able to offer his automobile at costs thought impossible at the time. Like Ford, leisure providers must be ever creative in reducing and controlling the costs of provision.

The second, and more profound, lesson to be gained from Ford's story is that of *focus*. Ford's focus was on the client rather than on internal concerns like costs. Ford viewed internal operations and even the larger marketplace from the perspective of the client. It is for this reason that Levitt (1983) called Henry Ford the most innovative marketer of our time. Yes, cost plays an important part in price setting, but it must be secondary to the requirements of the client.

The Marketplace

The last of the three price setting criteria, that of the marketplace, is perhaps the most important of all. While the first two factors have largely been inward looking, this factor looks outward. It brings together all those forces that are outside the control of the provider. These are the forces with which the provider must negotiate. These are the forces the provider must satisfy. These are the forces

that make up the environment in which the provider operates.

The marketplace is a complex array of partners, competitors, and, of course, clients. Each must be considered in any price-setting exercise. Partners, for example, are those other providers who assist you in your marketing efforts. They might be sponsors, community groups, sport governing bodies, or even private sector providers. All have an interest in the way in which you set your fees. For example, private and not-for-profit sport groups look to municipal leisure agencies for help in generating interest in their respective sports. The groups expect municipal providers to provide low-cost opportunities for prospective participants to learn the basics of their respective sporting activities. As the players become more skilled, other providers hope that they will graduate to the programs they offer. As a result, partners often hope that leisure providers will keep fees low to maximize interest among prospective participants.

The prices charged by partners and competitors alike will also influence client expectations for fees. Leisure participants internalize the fee levels charged by other providers for similar services. As noted, these internalized prices will become the price anchor against which your own fees are evaluated. If fees are comparable to this price anchor, a price is generally thought to be acceptable. If it is either well below or above the anchor, suspicion or even outrage may result. No pricing strategy can afford to ignore existing price standards. Remember, too, that a marketer's own prices may have helped provide that standard. Existing fee levels will suggest to clients what they should pay "next time." This is the power of *price last paid*. As a result, pricing strategy should ensure that prices not be permitted to jump dramatically. Such jumps violate the price anchors that currently exist and create considerable anger among client groups.

Clients differ in more than price expectations. They vary in terms of their interests, activity patterns (volume of use, level of expertise or experience), and socioeconomic characteristics (age, income, level of employment). They all bring their own requirements

	Penetration	Neutral	Skimming
Priorities			
Program Characteristics			
The Marketplace			

Figure 10.3: A Pricing Matrix

to the pricing context. This variability must be accommodated as prices are set.

A Price Strategy Matrix

Establishing effective pricing strategy often begins with the creation of a pricing matrix (Figure 10.3). The matrix is a rather simple representation of the three pricing options open the marketer. The options penetration, neutral, and skimming represent the columns, while priorities, program characteristics, and the characteristics of the marketplace represent the rows. These variables are all critical in establishing any pricing strategy.

The marketer first assesses programs in terms of their strategic potential. Simply place the name of each program to be priced in the appropriate box or cell. Do not worry about vertical placement at this stage, because the categories are not mutually exclusive. For example, a profitable program designed for upscale participants may offer a variety of customized services. The planner would be justified in plotting that program anywhere in the right hand column. Place it wherever it best fits. It is most important at this point to simply determine the balance of current offerings.

Marketers can tell, from even a cursory glance, whether the number of programs

offered at penetration levels prices (perhaps even at a loss) are counterbalanced by those operating at a profit. In this way, the matrix can be used as a planning tool. As new programs are planned and new prices set, the goal should be one of "filling" the cells in the matrix with program names. For every program that loses money, plan another that operates at a profit. For every basic program, offer a more advanced alternative. This helps create balance in the program schedule. Once programs are designated as candidates for the most appropriate strategic option, the marketer can then begin to establish price levels.

This matrix might also be used to conduct a quick assessment of existing pricing strategy. Such an assessment requires that the marketer (1) identify relevant programs, (2) profile the programs, then (3) place them in the matrix according to the profile characteristics. Do fee levels reflect the goals the agency is trying to pursue? Are the fees appropriate for the varied user groups? Do they reflect a range of program characteristics? The marketer can also evaluate the "balance" within a program offering by plotting existing programs on the matrix.

Once programs have been plotted on the matrix, the actual price level can be established. The key is to find prices that please the client then serve the agency. The actual price setting is done in three basic steps (Tung, Capella, & Tat, 1997). Note that the steps bring together many of the topics discussed in this chapter.

1. Establish Your Own Price Limits

Each provider must set limits within which prices can be set. These limits establish the general pricing level within which the provider is willing to operate. Final price is often a negotiated construct. It is negotiated by the client and the provider, as one attempts to push price up and the other works to hold price down. It is helpful to know one's limits before such negotiation begins.

When establishing your own price limits, first ask yourself three questions:

1. What is my price objective for this program? Do I plan to break even, make a profit, or lose money on the program?

2. How much flexibility do I have? For example, can I afford to "lose" money on this program to help attract more clients?

3. How much does it cost to offer the program?

Now simply pick a limit below which you are unwilling to go and a high-end price that would meet all your costs and objectives. This is the range within which you can operate comfortably.

2. Establish Your Clients' Price Limits

To establish your clients' price limits, ask yourself two questions:

1. Do clients feel the program is unique? Though this may be the case, it is probably best to assume that no program or facility is truly unique.

2. What price are clients accustomed to paying? Leisure managers operate within the competitive marketplace. When potential visitors consider taking part in a leisure program, they compare what they think the program offers to what they think other

providers offer. If they believe the program offers a valuable experience *compared to other available options*, they are more likely to take part in that program. If they think that equally valuable options exist for comparable or lesser costs, they will be displaced to those other options. This is the reason leisure marketers must price programs in a way that is competitive with other providers.

Consider both direct and indirect competitors in your calculation. *Direct competitors* compete directly with your own program offerings. They offer the same basic programs that you offer. They may be friends or even partners.

Indirect competitors offer an alternative to your programs, but do not offer the same benefit package. They simply offer an alternative to the potential client. They compete for the discretionary dollar of potential clients.

Recall that participants will internalize the fee levels charged by other providers for similar services. These internalized prices establish your clients' price limitations. Recall, too, that your own prices may have helped establish these limitations. As a result, pricing strategy should ensure that prices not be permitted to jump dramatically. Such jumps violate the price anchors that currently exist and create considerable anger among client groups.

Then establish an average price paid (at your own and competitors' sites) and establish a price range around that average. This will establish clients' price limits. If your prices are generally consistent with this average, then clients are likely to be accepting of your price level. Remember, too, that different clients will possess different price expectations, so options should be made available.

3. Estimate Demand Levels to Discover Your Best Price

You should now have a general price range in mind. It is comprised of a range of prices currently being charged, the cost of operation, and the range of prices that you yourself are willing to entertain. You can then estimate client demand for each price in that range. If demand is too high, then a higher price might be contemplated. If anticipated demand is too low, then a price at the lower end of the range might be considered. If the service is truly unique, demand may be somewhat insensitive to price changes. Higher prices may not result in displacement. However, if clients are aware of other comparable services that are offered at cheaper rates, they will be displaced toward the lowest price level.

Main Points

· Though many providers seek to establish pricing *policy*, they and their clients may be better served by creating a more flexible pricing *strategy*.

· Participants often react emotionally to fees, especially when fees are first introduced or when they are increased dramatically.

· Participants seek choices in both the type and level of price they pay.

· Active and ongoing communication is essential to any pricing strategy.

· Pricing can pursue penetration (low prices intended to increase market share), neutral (prices that promote the status quo), or skimming (profit taking) strategies.

· When setting price levels, consider your own goals for that particular program, characteristics of the program itself, and conditions within the general market place, including the requirements of the clients who will take part in the program.

Case Study

Three adjacent communities have recently amalgamated into one larger entity. The new city was created to reduce administrative costs and to avoid redundancy in local government. The new parks and recreation director is faced with quite a dilemma. She has to combine three very different pricing schemes into one coherent pricing strategy. (The largest of the three) communities offered virtually all programs free of charge, another heavily subsidized its programs, while the third offered programs at a wide variety of price levels.

The director has been told that she cannot offer all programs free of charge, and neither is heavy subsidization an option in all cases. She must generate fees to support her programming. She is afraid that whatever option she chooses will alienate members of the community. Those who traditionally received programs free of charge will be outraged by any new fees, whereas those who are accustomed to paying higher fees may become suspicious of program quality if fee levels drop.

The director knows that this will be a very public process. The new city council has given her specific instructions to establish fees that are both fair and appropriate. She isn't certain what this means, except that the council may blame her if complaints are made. The mayor, in particular, has made it clear that the new prices had better be well conceived. He has stated publicly that no one would be refused leisure opportunities because of the new fees and has told her privately that he will be "unhappy" if public outcry results from the new fees.

· What rules of thumb might the director adopt when establishing a pricing policy?

· How can the director convince those who have never paid to begin paying for programs?

· How can she charge fees without displacing low-income members of the community?

References

Barber, N. (1998). *Canadian participation rates in selected leisure activities.* Unpublished honours thesis. University of Waterloo, Waterloo, Ontario, Canada.

Ford, H. (1923). *My life and work.* New York: Doubleday, Page & Company.

Howard, D., & Selin, S. (1987). A method for establishing consumer price tolerance levels for public recreation services. *Journal of Park and Recreation Administration,* 5(3), 48-59.

Kahneman, D., Knetsch, J.L., & Thaler, R. (1986). Fairness as a constraint on profit seeking: Entitlements in the market. *The American Economic Review,* 76(4), 728-741.

Kerr, G., & Manfredo, M. (1991). An attitudinal based model of pricing for recreation services. *Journal of Leisure Research,* 23(1), 37-50.

Morris, M.H., & Morris, G. (1995). *Market-oriented pricing.* Lincolnwood, IL: NTC Business Books.

Nagle, T. (1987). *The strategy and tactics of pricing.* Englewood Cliffs, NJ: Prentice-Hall.

Stevenson, S. (1989). A test of peak load pricing on senior citizen recreationists: A case study of Steamboat Lake State Park. *Journal of Park and Recreation Administration,* 7(1), 58-68.

Treacy, M., & Wiersema, F. (1995). *The discipline of market leaders.* Reading, MA: Addison-Wesley Publishing Company.

Tung, W., Capella, L.M., & Tat, P.K. (1997). Service pricing: A multi-step synthetic approach. *Journal of Services Marketing,* 11(1), 53-65.

City of Waterloo

C H A P T E R

11

Program Delivery Basics

The Role of Delivery

Service delivery is the process of presenting products to clients. It is "concerned with where, when, and how the service product is delivered to the customer" (Lovelock, 1992, p. 23). Delivery has two distinct stages. The first stage is that of distribution. *Distribution* is the process through which resources are brought to the client. The distribution process has received the lion's share of attention from goods marketers. The traditional marketing literature views distribution like a spider's web that emanates from the producer's shop floor. This web provides the means and routes through which resources are carried from one source to many outlets and from these outlets to eventual consumers.

The success of the web, or distribution system, arises from its structural integrity. Weaknesses in the overall design or in key points along the structure's length and breadth can cause failure to the entire delivery system. As a result, the concerns of traditional distribution efforts typically focus on the logistics of moving the finished good from the producer through intermediaries to final consumers (Nylen, 1990). Issues of warehousing, transportation, and the particular demands of the retail community often dominate this discus-

sion. Though a few of these issues are of concern to the leisure service marketer, they address only half the challenge of service delivery.

Recall that services cannot be warehoused. Instead they must be produced as they are consumed. As a result, the client and the provider often come together in order to co-produce the service. This issue, called *inseparability*, is a wrinkle not faced by the marketers who deal in manufactured goods. Marketers who deal in cans of beans, for example, need not be concerned if those who process those cans are bad tempered, unimaginative, or dressed in outrageous clothing. They are hidden from the ultimate consumer. This is not the case with leisure services. Those who provide the programs do so in the presence of the consumer. They must deliver a performance with each new interaction (Grove & Fisk, 1991). The ultimate success of program delivery depends almost entirely on the ability of front-line staff to deliver this performance during each and every encounter.

Unfortunately, service encounters are dynamic. Like all interactions, they evolve from one instant to the next, from one encounter to the next. This characteristic, called *heterogeneity*, introduces an almost infinite variability to the service encounter. Each encounter is unique. The challenge for the service provider is that of ensuring services are consistent enough to ensure unfailing quality but flexible enough to adjust for ongoing change. Consequently, service providers spend considerable time thinking about how best to control client-provider interactions.

The importance of the service encounter highlights the second stage of program delivery, that of *presentation*. Presentation is the process through which services are offered to the participant. Those who plan the distribution of services are now, more than ever, focusing directly on the act of presenting the service to the client. This act, often called the "moment of truth," extends the traditional role of distribution to include staff, facilities, and other participants in the delivery process. It demands that service providers "manage the evidence" to ensure that the encounter is both positive and efficient. This topic will be considered in detail in the next chapter.

Together, the complementary notions of distribution and presentation comprise the delivery process. Together, they suggest the complexity of program delivery. This chapter focuses directly on the issue of distribution. It describes the challenges common to any distribution process. Topics include direct and indirect provision, recruiting and selecting channel members, channel organization, and channel cooperation. The next chapter then deals with the process of presentation. In that chapter, presentation is compared to organizing a stage play. Like any good play, the stage is set, the actors have their lines prepared, and the goal is to please the audience. The next chapter outlines how this is done.

Coordination and Communication: Themes in All Delivery Efforts

First and foremost, the delivery of leisure services demands *coordination*. When dealing with resources ranging from facilities to stacking chairs and with groups ranging from unions to children, coordination becomes that most precious of commodities. Coordination requires that efforts be timely. In many cases, the instructors, facilities, equipment, and clients must all come together at precisely the same time. A delay of even minutes can be disastrous. Asking 100 fitness class participants to wait in the cold until a door can be opened or until a tardy instructor arrives can create immediate and long-term dissatisfaction.

Multiply these complexities by hundreds of programs, and one begins to appreciate the complexity of delivery and the challenge of coordination. Precise execution is required if program delivery is to succeed. Coordination requires that efforts be directed toward the same purpose. Sometimes referred to as "uniformity of purpose," this is one of the most basic elements of any successful delivery.

The best way to achieve coordination is through *communication*. Communication, the process of creating shared meaning, it is surprisingly difficult to achieve. This difficulty arises from the number of parties involved in typical delivery systems. For example, program delivery often relies upon a variety of intermediaries, partners, and suppliers. Consider the challenge faced by a recreation department hoping to offer programs in a local school. Perhaps the agency has contracted a franchised fitness group to conduct the class on its behalf. This same department has decided to augment the basic program by offering water bottles and energy drinks to its participants. This provider must rely on several other groups to ensure the program is a success. It must communicate with school authorities (including a unionized maintenance staff), the franchised instructors (who in turn rely upon the assistance of the franchising group), and the companies who manufacture and supply the bottles and energy drink. Communication and coordination are indeed essential if this type of effort is to succeed. They represent one of the great challenges of program delivery.

The Delivery Process

Delivery begins with the leisure provider's own service strategy. Recall that the service strategy outlines the way in which the provider plans to offer solutions to the client. It blends the wants of the client with the capacity of the provider and the demands of the marketplace. Every action must be measured against the intent of this strategy, and delivery efforts are certainly no exception. Indeed, delivery efforts are perhaps most tightly bound to the dictates of the service strategy, because they are so very visible to the client. Delivery unites the client and the provider, so it brings life to the entire marketing effort. It represents the tip of the marketing iceberg that is visible and obvious to the client. It is the embodiment of the entire service strategy, so it must be tightly integrated with that strategy.

Recall, too, that a good service strategy can be expressed in a very few themes or guidelines. This simplicity helps to generate both support for and understanding of the overall strategy. These themes typically focus on the need to build relationships with clients while providing superior services reliably (Treacy & Wiersema, 1995). Resulting delivery efforts should attempt to breathe life into these guiding principles. For example, a leisure provider might decide that the best strategy is one of providing safe and easily accessible skill-based programs to children. The delivery process should then be created or built around

the basic themes of safety, accessibility, and skill development for children. Actions that support these themes build value for participants and become part of the delivery process.

The eventual delivery process is created in stages. At each stage, basic questions are asked, and the resulting answers help to shape and organize delivery efforts. These questions are typically organized around two basic issues, those of intensity and of distribution channels (Lovelock & Wright, 1999). Intensity is concerned with the degree to which a service will be made available. Will the service be made widely available or will it be delivered selectively?

Distribution channels are the routes through which services flow, or are delivered to, the leisure participant. What is the role of the leisure provider? Will the provider offer the service directly, or will partners assist in the delivery process? What role will these partners assume? The answers to these questions bring form and structure to the delivery system.

Distribution Intensity

Intensity is a critical component of any distribution strategy. It refers to "the relative availability of a service to the consumer" (Crompton & Lamb, 1986, p. 193). Intensity decisions involve both facilities and services. "The intensity of distribution of *facilities* refers to the relative number of physical facilities that an agency operates. The intensity of distribution of *services* refers to the relative number of outlets at which a person can receive the service" (Crompton & Lamb, p. 193). Intensity issues may be addressed through two layers of facilities and services.

The first layer is comprised of the actual physical facilities that are made available to the target markets. Though traditional leisure providers often build and maintain their own facilities, many providers now operate from within facilities that are controlled by others (e.g., malls, schools, and park authorities). The nature and location of these facilities often represent a foundation from which services are delivered.

Leisure programs represent a second layer through which distribution takes place. Programs represent various services offered to the community. They may be activity-based but are increasingly becoming information-based. Though programs may be offered independent of facilities, they are often provided in conjunction with physical facilities like schools and community centers. The way in which facilities and programs are offered to the target groups establishes the intensity with which they are offered.

There are several intensity options available, ranging along a continuum bound at one end by intensive distribution and at the other by exclusive distribution. (Figure 11.1) *Intensive* distribution, as the name suggests, creates maximum numbers of opportunities to enjoy a program. The program is readily and widely available to the target population. There are many examples of intensive distribution in any community. Sanitation engineers come to each home to collect garbage. Water is also sent to each and every home to ensure access. Municipal park and recreation programs typically locate park spaces intensively throughout their communities. The goal is to ensure that children are all assured of open-space play areas within a short distance of their homes. With such an intensive distribution strategy, no household is far from a park space.

The other end of the continuum is occupied by an exclusive distribution strategy. *Exclusive* strategies limit access to the product. Exclusive programs are often offered through a single outlet. Further, they may be offered to only a very select clientele. For example, elite sport programs are, by nature, exclusive. Whereas intensive sport programs are used to generate a broad base of support for a particular sport, exclusive programs train athletes with notable talent or skill in that sport. Only the very best athletes qualify for the opportunity to train and compete at the elite level. They receive coaching, access to facilities, and competition that are reserved for only the fastest, strongest, and most agile. Exclusive programs may also be used to serve very limited target markets. A leisure department offering "how-to" classes on writing plays for radio likely does not intend to offer the program on an intensive basis. Interest would be limited to a literary few who are interested in this rather unique craft.

Exclusive distribution tends to elevate the value many participants place on a product. This strategy is often followed in the retail world to control supply. Controlling supply helps providers focus on each client by limiting the number of transactions. Controlling supply also maintains higher demand levels, thereby increasing potential for skimming price strategies. It is perhaps little wonder that this strategy is popular among high-quality products and services in the private sector.

Selective distribution lies between the extremes of intensive and exclusive distribution. *Selective* distribution possesses characteristics of both its counterparts. A selective strategy might offer a wide range of programs but only to a selected group or geographic area. Staff at an older adult recreation center might make programs readily and widely available to the target population, but only at a single location (that center). A selective distribution strategy might also focus on a number of geographic areas, but provide only a limited selection in each area. For example, in the retail world, a brand may be distributed through many outlets across the country (intensive strategy), but only the very best outlets are chosen (exclusive strategy).

In a leisure context, a municipal recreation department may make programs available around its metropolitan area but place them only in their own facilities. This strategy is inherently selective in character, because it ignores the variety of other venues (e.g., malls, religious centers/facilities, and schools) where the program might be offered.

Intensive	Selective	Exclusive
I	I	I

Figure 11.1: Levels of Distribution Intensity

Making Distribution Decisions

Distribution intensity decisions are typically a function of strategic priorities and marketplace realities. Strategic priorities are established early in the marketing process and offer guidelines as to who is served and how this service might best be arranged. They suggest how problems will be overcome and priorities will be pursued (Nylen, 1990). Distribution intensity decisions must always acknowledge these guidelines. For example, if the provider's strategic vision was one of serving the poor, then distribution strategies would be required to reach out to that segment of the population.

Intensity decisions also reflect more immediate realities that surround any programming initiative. For example, costs may influence the nature and extent of any distribution network. Leisure providers may not be able to afford offering programs single-handedly and may look to partners to assist with distribution efforts. While these partners will likely extend a distribution network, they also complicate the distribution process.

Unfortunately, financial and other programming realities often demand that any distribution scheme be the result of considerable negotiation and compromise. Providers must negotiate with funding agencies, sponsors, partners, and even the clients themselves in order to ensure delivery. They must compromise in the number and types of programs that are offered and the ways in which they are provided. These demands may sometimes override the strategic goals the distribution scheme was originally intended to accomplish. In order to ensure that any distribution scheme continues to fulfill the provider's own goals, marketers look to four variables to guide them in their deliberations (Nylen, 1990). They are product design, price, consumer requirements, and market requirements.

Product Design

The programs themselves often guide the marketer as to how they might best be distributed. Programs must be distributed in ways that meet the peculiar needs of each program type. There are programs, for example, that seem to demand exclusive distribution so that staff are able to devote the time needed to help each client. These are the complicated programs that tend to confuse and discourage prospective clients: new programs that are difficult to understand and long-term programs that require ongoing staff monitoring and tracking. Though popular, many fitness and physical activity programs can be very complicated to the neophyte. Beginners who hope to undertake a fitness program may need the support of trained staff to get started. Exceptional athletes may seek individualized advice from coaches in order to reach their full potential. Whatever the context, those undertaking physical activities often require additional assistance from staff if they are to enjoy the offering. Program characteristics like these must be considered as distribution schemes are being developed.

Price

Price has two related, although seemingly contradictory, effects on distribution intensity planning. Price brings with it its own set of expectations. It is expected, for example, that high-priced services will be of better quality than lower-priced services. This is typically a fair expectation. Higher prices make lower volume possible, and lower volume creates lower numbers of distribution points. Both serve to improve service quality. Fewer distribution points reduce the opportunity for errors in coordination. Lower volume also helps providers focus on each individual encounter. It seems natural then, that high-priced services are likely candidates for exclusive distribution patterns.

Further, with high cost comes prestige. This prestige is often heightened if distribution is undertaken on an exclusive basis. Providers have long known this and often control supply in order to generate prestige and increase profit margins. The exclusionary policies of expensive clubs, shops, and organizations reflect this inevitable connection between price and exclusive distribution. High-priced items simply encourage the application of exclusive or selective strategies.

Conversely, on some occasions, high price may also encourage more intensive distribution. High price often results in enhanced expectations for convenience. Clients who pay more may often expect easy access to leisure programs. This may only be possible through intensive distribution. As taxes rise, citizens may no longer be happy with a single, centralized swimming pool for example, and may lobby instead for a series of small neighborhood swimming pools. This trend would create pressure for more intensive distribution.

Consumer Requirements

Consumer requirements will also influence distribution decisions. Consider first the issue of client demographics. Where are potential clients located? Are they widely dispersed or located within a small geographic region? Widespread distribution suggests intensive distribution, whereas small, identifiable pockets of clients might favor a selective or exclusive strategy. The marketer might also consider the client groups' demographic characteristics (Nylen, 1990). Children and older adults tend not to be as mobile as young adults. As a result, green spaces frequented by both the very young and the not-so-young are typically distributed intensively in most communities.

Distribution intensity can be influenced by shopping needs. Providers must ask, what is the frequency of purchase/consumption? Programs that are consumed with great regularity are typically offered on an intensive or selective basis. For this reason, product marketers always distribute convenience goods intensively. The most obvious leisure equivalent is that of drop-in programs like swimming. Participants typically attend repeatedly during hot summer months, for example. As a result, these programs are best offered in locations convenient to the participant. This need extends even to program registrations.

Where registrations once were handled only at the main leisure facilities, they are now handled off-site, over the telephone, through special kiosks, fax machines, on the World Wide Web, and the like. These various registration venues are simply efforts to broaden distribution intensity; they represent efforts acknowledging clients' wishes to register in a quick, convenient manner.

Market Requirements

Conditions found in the greater marketplace may also determine distribution intensity. If many potential channel members exist, then intensive distribution is possible. If the number is limited, another option may have to be pursued. The marketer's distribution system may also be limited by the capacity of channel members. Must channel members possess great skill or high levels of resources? For example, leisure providers who contract out their travel programs must ensure that contractors and their partners around the world are safe, reputable, and financially sound. Travel involves great planning and often requires both skill and luck to ensure happy clients. Failure can result in vacations that are both unhappy and hazardous to participants. Are potential partners willing and able to work with the leisure provider?

The more that is expected from channel members, the greater the reward they will expect in return. What does the provider have to offer potential channel partners? Can the leisure provider guarantee a minimal volume level? Will the channel member receive exclusive rights to that program? In the case of the travel contractor, the contractor may insist on first rights to all travel initiatives over a given time. Can the leisure provider make such a promise? Does that member represent a "good fit" with the leisure agency and its value system?

Clearly, distribution decisions require planning. As is suggested here, this planning begins with the organization's own goals and strategies. These strategies must be modified to accommodate competing demands and priorities. As a result, distribution decisions are rarely easy decisions. Compromise is often the order of the day. Remember to use these few guides—product design, price, consumer requirements, and market requirements—when planning any distribution system.

Making Location Decisions

The importance of location has been affirmed and reaffirmed throughout recorded history. The earliest peoples to inhabit the earth knew that survival depended on location. Favorable locations provided water, shelter, and access to food. History books tell the story of migrations from one location to the next as our ancestors searched for better lives by finding better locations. History is filled with stories of seemingly continual conflict over location. Over the centuries, location has determined either the success or failure of most ventures.

The very best locations become virtual hubs of activity, while lesser locations fail to attract interest. There is nothing so important as a good location. Understandably, location has traditionally been considered one of the most fundamental distribution decisions. It is important because it links production and consumption (Jones & Simmons, 1987). A good location brings the service to the client, and as such it plays an important role in eventual participation.

Though this section deals exclusively with the location of facilities, recent trends in technology may be reducing the importance of physical location. The Internet, for example, has revolutionized the retail industry. Small retail operators may gain access to clients worldwide through the magic of the World Wide Web. They are able to open virtual rather than physical shop doors to the world. This trend may also apply to many leisure programs. Leisure researchers have long discussed the freedom necessary for true leisure. Unfortunately, clients are often bound to the schedules and demands of the leisure provider when they attempt to participate in many leisure programs. They must visit the sites and facilities of the provider if they hope to take part. In the future, providers may begin to offer virtual programs that are not constrained by time and place. They may simply provide information that tells prospective clients how to prepare and enjoy activities that they themselves plan and control. Consequently, location may eventually lose much of its traditional importance, but for now location remains paramount.

Social Goals

Social goals influence distribution decisions (Claus & Hardwick, 1972). Social goals relate to the larger community. They focus on the health and well-being of that community. These goals often dominate the deliberations of public sector providers. A leisure agency's social goals may dictate that under-serviced areas receive priority when location decisions are being made. Areas in which residents are under-employed or somehow disenfranchised may become priority locations for facilities or programs. The City of Toronto, Canada, did just that by creating "priority centers" based upon socioeconomic indicators in many of their neighborhoods. These centers were intended to serve areas in which residents were thought to be particularly deserving of community resources.

There are less abstract categories of social goals. One of the most prominent among the social goals is that of *safety*. Locations for recreation sites must be chosen with safety in mind. Playgrounds should not be located beside busy highways, unsupervised bodies of water, or any number of hazards. They should be placed in locations that permit adequate lighting for those traveling to and from the site, as well as for those participating on site. Leisure facilities should not be located so that they increase motor vehicle congestion and the potential for accidents. Hundreds of players and spectators may depart a sport facility at the conclusion of a children's soccer game. Will they be able to do so quickly and safely?

Another priority, sometimes considered as a lesser social goal, is that of *political acceptability*. Political acceptability is a goal that must be pursued by all sectors. All sectors must ensure that their location decisions meet with political approval. Without this approval, permits may not be issued, and plans may not proceed. The political process is most prominent for public-sector providers. Political decision makers may seek to use program and facility locations to pursue their own unique goals. These goals may refer to the greater good or to their own survival within the political process. In either case, political figures may seek to control location decisions as part of their own agenda. It is unlikely that major location decisions will be free of political influence.

Aesthetics

The second strategic element to influence location is that of *aesthetics*. Aesthetics refers to the appeal of a facility. Is it appropriate to its surroundings? Is it pleasing to the eye? Though there is ongoing and impassioned debate over what is or isn't beautiful, location can both enhance or detract from the appearance of a facility and the area surrounding it. For example, how far will facilities be set back from the road? A facility that is located out of sight of passers by may fail to generate sufficient interest. Conversely, a building located close to the highway may attract attention but be considered an eyesore as a result of its prominence. Aesthetics also involve the other senses when applied to facility location. Those facilities located close to major roads tend to suffer from traffic noise. This noise can detract dramatically from the aesthetics of an outdoor facility. Those located near industrial sites may be subjected to the many noises, smells, and dust that emanate from those sites. Again, aesthetics may suffer. While this point may seem self-evident, many leisure facilities are located near such sites because of costs. Lower-quality sites cost less and are easier to acquire. Again, this suggests the ongoing need for negotiation and compromise in all location decisions.

Practicality

The third strategic element is that of *practicality*. Is the location practical for both the provider and the client? Consider first practicality from the user's point of view. The marketer must become familiar with how clients will use the facility. What is the pattern of daily traffic? Will clients tend to drop in on their way home from work? This is the case for many fitness facilities, so they tend to locate in downtown areas near large office complexes or on major highways leading from downtown areas to the suburbs. Will the facility be considered a destination facility? Destination facilities tend to draw visitors from wider catchment areas so they can be located close to major traffic arteries.

The location must also be practical for the provider. There are many practical issues from the provider's point of view. Two seem to receive much of the attention of decision makers.

· The first is *cost*. Can the location be acquired at reasonable cost?

· The second refers to *ongoing maintenance*. Is the facility located in a way that eases ongoing maintenance? Can supplies be brought in without difficulty.

A park district decided to place picnic and camping areas on a series of islands. These islands offered natural and pristine settings and were considered ideal locations. Planners soon discovered, however, that these locations were difficult to maintain and monitor. They actually had to reorganize their workforce to meet the new demands these locations placed on their staff. Staff had traditionally been responsible for one or two primary tasks. One staff member might be in charge of garbage collection, another in charge of fee collection, and still another in charge of client services. Given the difficulty in traveling to these new sites, however, managers found it too expensive to send several staff members to any one island. Instead, they decided to retrain each staff member to handle virtually any task that might be encountered while on-site. In this case, a location decision created severe and costly problems for staff and managers. It took years of effort to overcome this one location decision.

Consumer Location

The fourth strategic issue is that of *consumer location*. Facilities and programs must be placed where clients can gain access. This suggests that ideal locations are closest to the greatest number of clients. This is perhaps the greatest single rule that guides location decisions. Proximity and access to clients are the keys to location success. Generally speaking, reduced distance increases contact between a client and a provider. Economists tell us that reduced distances also lower unwelcome travel costs, thereby encouraging participation. This point is obvious to anyone who has witnessed the popularity of fast food franchises when they locate near high schools. They tend to be inundated with clientele who attend the nearby school.

However, proximity alone does not guarantee success. Location planners note that access is also critical to this success. Though often used interchangeably, proximity and access are very different concepts. *Proximity* refers to geographic distance. It refers to the spatial separation of the client and the program/facility location. *Access* refers not to distance but to ease of entry. A playground separated from a high-rise complex by a busy highway may be close to that complex, but it is certainly not accessible. The highway serves as an insurmountable obstacle to the children from the high-rise hoping to use that playground. There are many less dramatic cases that may reduce accessibility. Traffic congestion, left-hand turns, and poor access roads all tend to reduce location accessibility. Each of these examples diminishes interest levels and eventual participation in leisure programs, because they limit perceived access among potential users. As a result, location decisions for most facilities are preceded by detailed studies that monitor traffic patterns and other access issues.

There is a certain irony in the location process. Many of these elements may seem contradictory, in that pursuing one seems to violate another. The location that is the most aesthetically pleasing may also be impractical because it is the most expensive one available. The least expensive site is also the one closest to an existing industrial site. Location planning is rarely a "neat" process with clear answers and easy solutions (Jones & Simmons, 1987). It is not a process of finding absolute answers. Rather it is a process of juggling, of finding balance among conflicting priorities. The best location decisions are able to simultaneously address the needs of the site, the client, and the provider. They are able to satisfy the politician, the maintenance worker, and even the curious passerby.

Channels of Distribution

Once intensity and related location decisions are resolved, channel-based issues must be addressed. Distribution channels are comprised of "the set of organizations, agencies, and outlets that share the responsibilities for making a service available and accessible to target populations" (Crompton & Lamb, 1986, p. 188). The first question of any channel discussion must be "who does what?" Who delivers the program or portions thereof? Should the provider offer the program or should someone else be given that opportunity? If the leisure provider decides to offer the program, will partners be required to ensure success? There are several issues that must be addressed when arranging channels of distribution. They relate to finding, selecting, recruiting, and enlisting the channel members.

Types of Channel Memberships

Understandably, there has been growing interest in exploring various delivery models that might best serve leisure providers' target groups. Most of these models rely, to some extent, upon finding partners in the community to assist with some aspect of program delivery. The move toward finding channel partners has gained such popularity that special issues of popular journals and professional magazines are regularly devoted solely to partnership issues (Vaske, Donnelly, & LaPage, 1995).

The private-sector marketer has long dealt with a variety of partnerships. Most marketing texts have full sections devoted to the organization and maintenance of channel relationships. They have found that channel development is fraught with challenges and corresponding rewards. Samples of each are provided throughout this chapter.

The appeal of finding other players to assist with program delivery is perhaps obvious. When other providers take responsibility, share resources, and make decisions, it reduces the demands placed on a single provider. The involvement of other players is not without its limitations, however. Channel decisions always involve a trade-off between capacity and control (Nylen, 1990). While involvement by other providers lightens one set of demands, it carries with it a corresponding burden. That burden is the loss of control. Reliance on others reduces control for the original provider. The sole provider is best able to control the delivery process. That provider makes all the relevant decisions, uses trusted internal resources, and retains the power to adjust the delivery process on an ongoing basis. Involvement of other parties reduces the control available to any one player.

There are several approaches to delivery available to the leisure provider. They exist along a continuum. On one end, the provider assumes complete responsibility for the program with all the costs and proceeds that accompany it. At the opposite end of the continuum, an independent provider assumes complete control of the delivery process. Note that personal control is greatest at the left of the continuum. With control comes sole possession of both costs and profits, ease of coordination, and with coordination, enhanced levels of predictability. Moving to the right brings fewer direct costs and increasing freedom. This freedom comes from less involvement in direct program delivery. Coordination becomes more complex but losses can be shared.

There are five options found within the bounds of this continuum (see Figure 11.2). Employing a *partner* continues to offer considerable opportunity for control to the original provider. A partner is another party that relies on the provider for at least part of its own success. Both members of a partnership hope to achieve results that would not be possible with either group working in isolation. For example, a corporation may sponsor events organized by a leisure provider in order to direct attention to its own products. For her part, the leisure provider needs the corporation's funding for the special event she hopes to hold. Though each party seeks different rewards from the relationship, each is willing to cooperate to ensure the success of the venture. As a result, the relationship between the provider and the sponsor is often characterized by ongoing communication and cooperation. In this way, mutual control is assured.

Reliance on a *contractor* provides a bit less control for the provider but is even less demanding of resources. A contractor carries

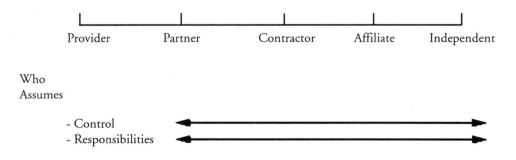

Figure 11.2: Program Delivery Options

out the duties assigned by the provider and does so according to a pre-arranged agreement. The provider has complete control over this agreement and its many terms of reference. However, once the contract is signed, the contractor need only live up to the terms of that contract. Ongoing negotiation may not be possible. If the contractor fulfills the original terms of the contract, the provider has little opportunity to make changes. The quality of the original contract often determines the quality of the eventual program. For example, a leisure agency may contract a private-sector company to provide leaders for an instructional program. This approach frees the agency from having to train and supervise its own instructors. Unfortunately, the agency will be blamed if the instructors are of questionable quality and, worse still, agency staff may be unable to change the situation until the contract concludes.

The next relationship one might pursue is with the *affiliate*. An affiliate has an almost passing relationship with the leisure provider. The provider may have a bit of control over the affiliate, but this control is minimal. For example, a community organization may apply to a municipal provider for an operating grant. This grant may represent only a small portion of this organization's budget, but they are willing to meet some basic demands in order to receive it. In order to qualify for the grant, they may be willing to make several spots available to low-income children, agree to help maintain sports fields, and so on. This group represents a classic affiliate. They help the agency pursue its agenda but in an almost informal way.

The last type of player is called the *independent*. This is the party that has no formal contact with the agency but pursues a similar or at least complementary agenda to that of the provider. The provider has no control over this relationship but may benefit from its existence. For example, a public agency might discover that a private-sector provider offers an excellent instructional class of some sort. The public agency may be so impressed with the program that staff members may decide not to compete with that program. They may even recommend it to interested patrons. The public agency may go so far as to provide subsidies so that needy participants may take part. The independent provider will continue with the program, oblivious to the public agency's involvement, but both are aided by the other's actions.

Leisure providers typically use more than one channel or partner at any given time. The agency might operate a craft program independently in one community center but through contractors in another. The approach used will depend upon availability of channel partners, the expertise and resources available to staff, and even the preferences of user groups. Organization complexity tends to vary dramatically from one setting to the next. A network created by a small community recreation department will likely differ from another created within a highly competitive urban environment. The small agency may be able to develop informal and short-term relationships, while the more volatile environment may demand a more structured approach.

Finding Channel Members

Members of a channel organization can become an integral part of the provider's success formula. Leisure agencies are already adept at finding channel members. Few leisure providers work in isolation from other providers in the community. The informed reader is likely familiar with traditional channel members like the YM/YWCAs, other social service agencies, and private sector sponsors. Mutual interests often bring these providers together in a variety of contexts. Given their common objectives, all stand to benefit by pooling their respective expertise and experience.

The search for the best possible channel members begins with the opportunity assessment described in chapter 2. The goal is to recall your own strengths and weaknesses identified during that stage so that you can then find others able to help build on your strengths and diminish the importance of your weaknesses. What does the client want and who can best help provide it? For example, a municipal park and recreation department may lack facilities needed for evening programming, such as classrooms, and gymnasiums. This is an apparent weakness if demand exists for such facilities. However, the local school board likely has many such facilities, and these facilities may be available to the community after regular school hours. A partnership between the school board and the park and recreation agency would certainly extend the capacity of the leisure provider's distribution network.

The marketer must then determine what type of relationship is desired with this channel member. How much cooperation from other providers is needed to provide quality leisure programming? Agency staff may discover that they lack the expertise or finances to offer a proposed program. They may discover that their programs are not well known among target community members. They may find that potential partners are simply better at providing this service. In all these cases, the nature of the problem determines the channel relationship. The provider must either remedy these problems internally or find others who can help solve them.

Once the potential partner has been identified, the leisure provider can determine whether or not this other agency represents a likely channel prospect. How can these decision makers be (a) induced to participate, and (b) retained as active contributors? What can the leisure marketer offer partners that helps them offer greater value to their own clients (Fifield, 1998)? This is one of the most important questions the marketer can ask before establishing a channel relationship. All such relationships are based upon the promise of mutual advantage. Each must understand the advantage she can offer the prospective channel member before making contact.

No discussion of channel partners is complete without reference to *power* and *status* (Nylen, 1990). All channel arrangements are first and foremost exchange relationships. As such, they are affected by power and status. The channel member with the most power can dominate the relationship to the detriment of the lesser members. The best relationships are those that offer a balance in power. Members or groups of members in balanced relationships are able to ensure that all benefit from the exchange.

The status of a single member may change from one channel organization to another. A city recreation department may be at the top of one structure but at the bottom of another. For example, a municipal recreation department may establish a complicated channel organization involving partners, affiliates, and even independent operators. This department may have virtually complete control over the shape and size of the channel structure. Simultaneously, this same department may be at the very bottom of a national sport governing body's delivery structure. This governing body may use the department to reach its own clients. However, in this instance, the city has little power to influence the overall channel structure.

Selecting Channel Members

Selection of a channel member is a critical step in any channel organization. Selection requires that several important issues be resolved (Nylen, 1990). The first is one of *value*. What does the potential member offer other members of the channel organization? Does the potential member fulfill a need that is not currently being addressed? Leisure providers often seek out other providers who can provide in-kind support such as computing services or volunteers to hold a special event. They also recruit channel members who reach their intended client group. Candidates who cannot provide value are dropped from further consideration, for this project at least. An affirmative response does not suggest that the candidate is automatically acceptable as a channel member, however. Several more criteria must be fulfilled.

The second question is one of *perceived consistency*. Is there an adequate fit between public perception and the task being assigned to this candidate? For example, a leisure provider may consider admitting a voluntary neighborhood association into its channel organization. They may discover, however, that while members of that neighborhood look to that association for basic leisure programs, they look elsewhere for highly specialized or risk-related programs like rock climbing or hang gliding. What is the nature of the program the candidate will be asked to offer? Is it consistent with the image of that candidate? If so, they represent an adequate fit. If not, other members may have to be recruited.

The third question is one of *procedural consistency*. Does the candidate offer the level and type of service that is consistent with that of the leisure provider? Return to the notion of service strategy. The candidate must share the provider's own vision of value. Are the candidate's policies consistent with those of the leisure provider? There are many aspects to this question. Is the image projected by the candidate consistent with that of the provider? If not, the candidate may not fit as a member of the provider's own channel organization.

Further, does the candidate share the leisure provider's own strategic vision? Marketers must establish their channel members' own mandates and strategic priorities. Do they seek the same goals that the leisure provider seeks? If so, the relationship is likely to flourish. If they share radically different views of success, then the relationship may suffer over the long term. For example, many school boards have operational priorities that are very different from those of leisure agencies. They see their prime responsibility as that of educating children during the school day. Efforts to make school facilities available during evenings and weekends may be regarded as detracting from the educational process. Janitorial staff may complain of increased workload, evening programs may increase depreciation or even cause damage to school property, and so on. In such instances, school authorities may resist community programs, considering them to be troublesome and inconsistent their own particular mandates. They may represent a poor choice as a result. They simply do not share the same vision and mandate as that of the leisure provider. Clearly, selecting channel members requires thoughtful and careful consideration.

Finally, is the candidate *available*? Are suitable channel members available to take part? There are many components to the availability question. The first relates to willingness. Any channel organization must be built around cooperation, consistency, and common purpose. When seeking available channel members, the marketer must consider not only resources and expertise, but also their willingness to coordinate their efforts. Are they willing to accept the role assigned to them or the terms of the channel agreement? Will they agree to the overall marketing strategy? Will they deliver their portion of the agreement? Channel members may wish to be compensated in order to take part in your channel organization. They may wish to negotiate agreements that ensure preferential treatment well into the future. This preferential treatment may take the form of special access to client groups or even operating grants.

A second availability question is that of readiness. The candidate must be ready and able to take part in the delivery process. It is often surprising how few are able to do so. They may already be fully involved in their own program delivery or they may be uncertain of the success of the cooperative venture. As a result, building a channel organization often takes years of careful planning.

Initiating a Channel Relationship

When approaching a potential channel member, remember that managers, on average, engage in a different activity every few minutes (Mintzberg, 1973). Consequently, they may be unprepared to reflect on the relative merits of proposals prepared by leisure marketers. "In making decisions, managers tend to avoid analytical data" (Bazerman, 1994, p. 6). Instead, they tend to rely on a variety of simplifying or heuristic strategies when assessing sponsorship applications. As a result, obvious details, like the length or appearance of an application may be used to guide judgments of that message. Such details may be more influential than the content of that same application, because they are more readily available.

Those hoping to initiate channel relationships should ensure that applications are both informative and easy to understand. This is not to suggest that they be simplistic, but rather their value should be self-evident. The prospect should not be compelled to search for the value in the application. This value should be obvious from the appearance of the report itself as well as the content within. It will also help to highlight past successes when initiating new relationships. In one study, researchers found that prospects were more open to new partnerships when provided with success stories about the applicant. They subscribed to the maxim, "Nothing succeeds like success" (Weppler & McCarville, 1995). As a result, ensure that prospects are made aware of successful efforts from the past as well as plans for the future.

Those seeking channel cooperation must understand potential members' own corporate objectives. Marketers must discover these priorities if they are to succeed in the business-to-business sales milieu. As a result, person-to-person contact is the centerpiece of channel development. There is no better way to gather information than through personal contact. Marketers are encouraged to develop proposals customized to meet the needs of fellow channel members. They may then ensure success for their own programs and those of their partners for years to come.

Main Points

· Program delivery involves distribution (bringing resources to the client) and delivery (presenting those resources to the client).

· Delivery requires coordination and communication.

· Intensity of distribution must reflect the provider's strategic direction, as well as more specific concerns like the product's own characteristics, price, the requirements of the participant, and the general marketplace.

· Location decisions reflect a variety of distribution intensity, social, aesthetic, practical, and accessibility-based priorities.

· Distribution channels help make services available and accessible to target populations.

· Leisure providers may adopt many different types of relationships with channel members. The key is to recruit members who are best able to assist in achieving your own goals.

· Channel relationships are best developed around mutual benefit, natural fit (in terms of public perceptions and procedural consistency), and availability.

References

Bazerman, M. (1994). *Judgement in managerial decision making.* Toronto: Wiley & Sons.

Claus, R.J., & Hardwick, W.G. (1972). *The mobile consumer.* Don Mills, ON: Collier-Macmillan Canada Ltd.

Crompton, J.L., & Lamb, C. (1986). *Marketing government and social services.* New York: John Wiley & Sons.

Fifield, P. (1998). *Marketing strategy* (2nd ed.). Oxford: Butterworth Heinemann.

Grove, S., & Fisk, R. (1996). The dramaturgy of services exchange. In C.H. Lovelock (Ed.), *Services marketing* (3rd ed.) (pp. 97-105). Toronto: Prentice-Hall.

Jones, K., & Simmons, J. (1987). *Location, location, location.* Toronto: Methuen Books.

Lovelock, C.H. (1992). *Managing services: Marketing, operations, and human resources* (2nd ed.). Toronto: Prentice-Hall.

Lovelock, C.H., & Wright L. (1999). *Principles of service marketing and management.* Upper Saddle River, NJ: Prentice-Hall.

Mintzberg, H. (1973). *The nature of managerial work.* New York: Harper & Row.

Nylen, D. (1990). *Marketing decision-making handbook.* Toronto: Prentice-Hall.

Treacy, M., & Wiersema, F. (1995). *The discipline of market leaders.* Reading, MA: Addison-Wesley Publishing Company.

Vaske, J.J., Donnelly, M.P., & LaPage, W.F. (1995). Partnership for the 21st century: A return to democracy. *Journal of Park and Recreation Administration,* 13(4), x-xi.

Weppler, K.A., & McCarville, R.E. (1995). Understanding organizational buying behavior to secure sponsorship. *Journal of Festival Management & Event Tourism,* 2(3/4), 139-148.

S. Czekus

12

Present the Service to the Client

In the last chapter, I suggested that delivery had two distinct phases. The first is that of distribution. Distribution is concerned with issues like intensity and channel organization. The second phase, the topic of this chapter, is one of presenting the service to the client. This stage brings together the client and the provider. The point of contact may be a face-to-face encounter, a telephone conversation, or even an Internet connection. Whatever the nature of this contact, its impact on service quality can be profound.

The Moment of Truth

The act of presentation takes place during what has been termed the "moment of truth." This is the moment during which the service is delivered by the provider and consumed by the client (Carlzon, 1989). The moment of truth is an apt phrase. It is that instant during which the client and the provider come together. The provider has only seconds to determine the client's requirements and to serve that client. It is indeed a moment of truth. Only skillful and determined application of key resources will ensure that the moment concludes successfully.

The importance of the moment of truth cannot be overstated. Given the *intangibility* of services, it is sometimes impossible to separate the service from the delivery of the service. In many instances, the delivery process *is* the program. Imagine that friends have decided to join a fitness club. The club offers new members a complimentary fitness assessment. The friends arrive to be tested with some trepidation. They are unsure what a fitness assessment entails, but have a pretty good idea that they will be asked to take off at least some of their clothes. Further, they are certain that they will be told something they already know—that they are less than ideal specimens of humanity. They imagine their worst fears being confirmed when they will be asked to undress and to complete a variety of embarrassing and often difficult tests. This scenario would create considerable potential for a very unhappy encounter.

To their relief, these friends are greeted warmly by a obviously caring and attentive staff member. This individual seems genuinely concerned with their well-being and makes every effort to treat them with a level of respect and kindness that exceeds their expectations. Though their fears about their physical condition may be confirmed, they are likely to be delighted with the quality of the treatment they received. The outcome of the encounter was not unexpected, but the reception they received far exceeded their expectations. As a result, despite the rigors of the assessment, the visit might seem a raging success. Clearly, the quality of that visit was determined, not by the series of tests these friends experienced, but by the way the tests were administered.

The friends will likely have searched for tangible cues to help guide their assessment of the encounter. The many gadgets and charts they observed being used or even the cleanliness of the room in which the assessment took place may well have influenced their evaluation. While the service itself (the assessment) was perhaps difficult to grasp, the elements that made up the program delivery were not. It is these interpersonal and physical elements that clients typically use to evaluate leisure programs. It is the presentation of service that will draw their attention.

There are three basic tenets that guide efforts to present a service to the client. These tenets suggest that service presentation is akin to a play. Like any play, the presentation demands coordination of front and backstage effort, of people, and of supporting systems. Effective presentation also demands that the audience adopt a role in the successful delivery of the play.

Tenet 1: Separate Front and Backstage Activities

Delivery is first and foremost a set of procedures. These procedures convert inputs like money, people, and equipment into outputs that are desired by clients. Together these procedures comprise a system of components that are both visible and invisible to the client. Service marketers typically label the visible components as *frontstage* activities. This terminology reflects the belief that service acts visible to the client are analogous to theater. They represent a carefully choreographed interaction between clients and the agency.

Thanks to technology, the frontstage component of service delivery may actually be shrinking (Lovelock, 1991). Registrations that used to take place over the phone or in person are now being conducted via the Internet. Clients who once stopped by the office to

collect information on new programs now do so by checking in at information kiosks provided at local malls and at special event sites. There are two interpretations of this trend. The first is that face-to-face encounters are losing their importance and will soon be replaced by technology. The second interpretation, and perhaps the more accurate of the two, is that such measures actually inflate the importance of personal contact once it finally occurs. Machines, regardless of how efficient and helpful they have become, are simply less capable than are staff of providing caring, individualized attention.

Backstage efforts are those that support frontstage delivery. Backstage operations are those systems or infrastructures that sustain the production of customer service (Davidow & Uttal, 1989). Though backstage efforts may involve hundreds of staff members and require complex networks of resources, they are typically invisible to the ultimate consumer. Backstage operations can be physical (facility design, equipment, materials, and supplies), human (scheduling or training), or informational (quality control processes) in nature.

Though both front and backstage efforts are complementary, they are best separated. Specifically, backstage activities are generally hidden from the watchful eyes of the client. This trend first began in the retail industry a century ago.

> By 1900 department store retailers tried to conceal from customers the bleaker parts of the stores, not only with mirrors but also by segregating the bookkeeping floors . . . clearly from the merchandising ones. As late as Word War I, Macy's in New York was still struggling to complete the isolation of its 'nonselling employees on the undecorated high floors.' (Leach, 1993, p. 75)

There are many reasons for this separation. For retailers, the primary reason has been one of *mood*. Retailers of a century ago, and even today, want to portray their stores as places of refuge where dreams could be pursued and troubles forgotten. As a result, they intended to get "rid of every indication that the store was really a business enterprise where people sweated and worked" (Leach, 1993, p. 75). This sentiment also holds true for many leisure providers. The goal of the leisure provider is to place the client in a "container" in which leisure is more likely to occur (Henderson, Bialeshki, Shaw, & Freysinger, 1989). Leisure episodes are, by definition, "non-serious," with reality being suspended for the duration of the activity. Backstage activities can be messy and even chaotic and may bring too much realism to the setting. Messy desks, unused equipment, and unfinished projects are all reminders of work not yet completed. They are inherently unpleasant as a result, and are best left out of sight.

There are other more compelling reasons for separating front and backstage activity. Primary among these is the issue of *responsiveness*. Clients expect staff to be responsive and helpful. Unfortunately, backstage staff may not be willing or able to assist clients. The training offered to a janitor may leave her unprepared to help with registration questions. A staff member trained to reconcile bank records may not be able to answer questions posed by passing patrons. Given this inability to assist clients, backstage staff may seem to needy clients to be indifferent or incompetent. This suggests that staff not serving participants should not be visible to those who might seek assistance. For example, staff responsible for answering phones, maintaining accounts, or any number of office-related tasks should not be visible to patrons if they are not available to serve them.

However hard these employees work, however dedicated their efforts, if they do not help those in need of assistance, they may be labeled as unresponsive and idle. This, as you might expect, can be a very great problem. Research conducted by the author with students Christina Colenutt and Jen Coleman (Coleman, McCarville, & Colenutt, 2000) found that staff who seemed unresponsive were particularly likely to elicit a negative emotional response from clients. They were also more likely to be blamed for a variety of problems, and their lack of action diminished client' mood and satisfaction levels. This is the case

even when staff are well meaning in their efforts to help the client. Perceptions of the service provider suffered as a result. Thus, only staff who are ready and willing to assist clients should be placed in view of clients who are waiting for service.

There are a few instances, however, in which backstage activities might well be brought to frontstage. In some cases, backstage activities are now being brought front stage to draw the client more deeply into the leisure or tourism experience. For example, amateur paleontologists can now participate in "digs" for prehistoric fossils. They can witness and take part in all the dust and labor that comprise such a dig. A few retailers have for years recognized the appeal of some backstage activities and highlight them for all to see. Fudge makers will surround their kitchens with glass walls enabling passing shoppers to watch the fudge being created. This show adds to the appeal of the fudge itself. As passers-by see what happens behind the scenes, the experience is somehow enhanced. One city opens the doors of its park maintenance garage once a year so children can visit with staff and see the equipment, ranging from mowers to plows. The children are able to sit in the drivers' seats and generally get up close to these huge machines. It is a hit with the kids each and every year. Once backstage is brought frontstage, it too becomes part of the theater called service delivery. It is no longer backstage, and must be viewed as a front stage activity.

Tenet 2: Staff Members Are Critical to the Success of the Encounter

For much of the past decade, service providers have been reducing staff levels. As a result, clients are being asked increasingly to fend for themselves in many service situations. In some cases, this trend has been welcomed by consumers. Easy-to-use technology has evolved to an extent that clients are now able to serve themselves through devices like automated teller machines (ATMs). By using such devices, clients can avoid queues and enjoy expanded service availability. For example, ATMs are more widely available than are bank branches (and they are never closed). Clients now use scanners conveniently provided by retailers to check prices on merchandise. Travelers may even plan their own trips, purchase their own tickets, and reserve their own hotel rooms on the Internet.

Even though technology seems to be reducing the need for client-staff interaction, front-line staff members continue to provide a critical link between the provider and the client. It is the staff member who puts a human face on the agency and its programs. On the whole, agencies tend to be cold and formal. They communicate using one-way tools such as brochures and posters. They administer through policy and decree. They act largely behind the scenes as they plan, cancel, and otherwise manipulate programs. Even the most devoted client will find it difficult to warm to an agency. It is simply too amorphous and too distant.

Instead, clients develop relationships with staff members. Where the agency is amorphous, the staff member is tangible. Where the agency is cold, the staff member can be attentive, responsive, and friendly. Where the agency is distant, the staff member is present. It is the staff member who helps the client make sense of the offering and the procedures that go with it. It is the staff member who can customize the program to meet the individual's specific requirements or preferences. It is the staff member who creates value for the client.

Clients often experience a truly profound sense of loss when separated from favorite staff members. Bob Tasca, top salesman with Ford Motor Company tells the story of how clients often feel like "orphans" when staff members leave an organization. These orphans can become a pretty unhappy lot. Mr. Tasca explains,

> A number of years ago, we at Tasca [Auto Sales] met with a disturbing number of complaints about customer satisfaction. Each time a complaint arose, we'd assign someone in either sales or service to deal with the unhappy customer. . . . There didn't seem to be any pattern to the complaints . . . we were confused . . . Eventually, one of us figured it out: *All the complaints originated from customers whose salesperson had recently left us . . . they'd become orphans.* They felt abandoned, and because they couldn't put into words their feelings, they acted them out; they found fault with our routine dealings with them. (Tasca & Caldwell, 1996, p. 112)

There are two important lessons to emerge from this story. The first is the importance of staff. At the risk of becoming repetitive, this point should be made time and time again. Staff members are key to all marketing effort. They are absolutely critical to the value proposition offered to clients. Without the ongoing assistance of staff, like any "orphan," clients may feel lost and alone.

The second lesson is that of the cascading nature of dissatisfaction. If clients are unhappy with one aspect of service, they will find other reasons to be unhappy with you. Much of the next chapter is devoted to dealing with such errors, but one point is noteworthy within this discussion of staff members. Staff members represent a critical resource in correcting the errors created by the orphaning process. This, too, points to the profoundly important role staff play in the marketing effort.

The marketer must constantly look for ways to improve interactions between clients and staff members. One perhaps obvious tool is the humble name tag. All staff members can wear a name tag. Most agencies prefer first names, rather than first and last names on these tags. They do this for both human and security reasons. In human terms, clients prefer to address staff on a first-name basis. It just seems more friendly and more personable. In terms of security, the first-name-only tags deny clients access to staff members' full identity. Clients are unaware of last names, thereby offering a certain anonymity to staff members. Such anonymity is often reassuring to staff as they deal with an increasingly uncertain and complex workplace.

Name tags represent a wonderful means of communication. Clients tend to glance at name tags as they approach staff so they offer all the advantages of a walking billboard, albeit a small one. Some organizations place stickers on name tags that highlight the daily schedule or upcoming events. Many organizations now award staff members with service pins that can be placed on these tags. The pins can be based on years of service, on positive evaluations, or commendable performance of any kind. They tell clients that this staff member is both worthy of recognition and a valued member of the staff team. They are then more likely to trust and value the assistance of this staff member.

Tenet 3: Clients Participate in Service Production and Delivery

Clients often become part of their own service provision. Their role typically revolves around information and/or effort (Mills & Moberg, 1982). Both are necessary for effective service delivery. In terms of information, providers often ask clients to indicate their own preferences, skill levels, or even financial histories so that programs can be planned accordingly. In this way, clients actually help plan their own services.

Further, clients typically take an active part in service delivery. They travel to the site at which they participate; they stand in line and wait their turn; they pick up their towels at a designated location; and they return them to the laundry bin upon completing their workout. These are only a few examples of clients' involvement in leisure provision. Given their important role, clients of services are often called *partial employees* (Kelley, Donnelly, & Skinner, 1990). They are partial in that they are temporary participants in the delivery process. Their role concludes once participation is ended.

The challenge for the provider is to manage the service encounter so that clients are both aware of and able to fulfill their respective roles. Clients must know how to register for programs, rent locks in locker rooms, or use the self-serve snack bar. They must be aware of policies regarding dress requirements, willing to take a number and wait for service during busy periods, and familiar with the location of nearby recreation centers.

Partial employees pose a considerable challenge for service providers because "marketing managers generally are not able to reward and/or reprimand partial employees as they do traditional employees" (Kelley et al., 1990, p. 316). Partial employees may continually violate rules and regulations. They may let their dogs run free in parks where dogs should be leashed. They may continually "waste" resources by asking the same questions time and time again. After all, they are not interested in efficiency; if they want an answer, they need only call the leisure provider. The training of this group is one of the great ongoing tasks that occupy the marketing professional. An entire section of this chapter is devoted to the training of partial employees.

Tenet 4: Support the Encounter with Appropriate Systems

Edward Deming, one of the fathers of quality management, was absolutely firm on the need for precise execution in all aspects of delivery. In his view, unless individual *processes* and overall *systems* were correct, no good could come from efforts to offer services (Dobyns & Crawford-Mason, 1994). A process is the way in which two or more resources are brought together, and a system is the plan or blueprint used to organize various processes in order to serve the client. Deming's premise seems particularly relevant for delivery efforts. Deming stressed that it was not enough for individual processes in the system to be effective. Each process had to be managed so that the entire system was maximized. It is insufficient that leisure providers ensure that the facility is ready, or that promotion is undertaken, or that the instructors are contracted. All these processes and more must be coordinated if the system is to succeed.

To make this point, Deming liked to introduce a game in his seminars called the "red bead experiment" (Dobyns & Crawford-Mason, 1994). This game involved the movement of beads from one container to another. There were both red and white beads, and the task was to move only white beads to a second container. Though it seemed a relatively simple task (there were only 800 red beads and 3,200 white beads), volunteers who tried to carry out Deming's task were always doomed to failure. The system was set up in a way that ensured this failure. The only implements available to move the beads were large scoops. Regardless of how hard the seminar participants tried to separate the white and red beads, the implements were simply inappropriate to the task, and they failed. The scoops were symbolic of a flawed system.

As a part of the exercise, Deming always introduced a series of typical management strategies to encourage the workers to do a better job. He established complicated and precise instruction manuals. He congratulated those who were able to at least reduce the number of red beads and chastised those who were unable to do so. With each successive failure, he introduced new procedures. He established detailed reporting procedures and clear lines of authority. He promised bonuses, threatened dismissals, and even fired those with the most red beads in their scoop.

Deming repeated this exercise many times over the years, and the volunteers failed each and every time. There was no perceptible change, whatever staff-related measures he adopted. Overall results were always discouragingly inadequate, and that was exactly Dr. Deming's point. If the system is wrong, then failure is inevitable. There is nothing workers can do to improve results if the system is inadequate. To blame the worker is to miss the point entirely. The system has to be right if the provider hopes to succeed. The question now becomes, "What does it take to get it right?"

There are many programs now promoted as the best method of mobilizing resources, of getting it right. Though all may take slightly different approaches, all are common in their purpose. All attempt to avoid errors and to minimize the negative impact of errors should they occur. Berry and Pasuraman (1991) call this the process of "getting it right the first time" and "getting it very right the second time." One of the best methods of ensuring success is that of planning the service encounter.

Planning the Service Encounter

Any visit to a leisure facility or any participation in a leisure activity is actually made up of long a series of encounters. Exposure to an advertisement promoting a program or service is often the initial encounter between a client and a provider. This encounter may be followed up with a phone call seeking information on that program. This represents a second encounter. The participant may then visit a facility to take part in that program. The view that greets clients as they approach a facility represents another encounter. The way in which they are greeted by staff upon entry represents another encounter, and so it goes. The goal for the leisure marketer is to separate each of these encounters and plan them accordingly.

Discover Clients' Expectations and Requirements

The first step in planning any encounter is one of establishing the client's requirements and expectations. One of the great challenges in this regard is to understand when the client wants to *coproduce* the service and when the client wishes only to be served. This may be difficult, if not impossible, to determine every time, so it is best to offer meaningful options to clients. As is the case in many banks, the client can choose to stand in line for service or can self-serve at an ATM. Each option has its own advantages and disadvantages, and only the individual clients know which option is best for their particular situation. When clients feel rushed, they may prefer to use automated kiosks. However, at times when they feel uncertain on how to proceed with their request, they may prefer to wait for staff assistance. Let clients self-select the level of service that best suits their needs.

The client's particular requirements may be influenced by the focus of the service. Services like skate sharpening or racquet stringing focus on an object, while fitness classes or swim classes focus on an individual. Those services focusing on inanimate objects often require a less intimate client/provider relationship than do those that focus on the individual client. Indeed, clients may be miles away while the service is being performed on their sports equipment. They may be in another city while their tennis racquets are being restrung or their bicycles are being repaired. Their equipment may even be returned by mail.

For the most part, these owners are unlikely to seek the reassurance of relations with staff members. They may deal with a company for years without ever meeting the individual who performed the actual service on their belongings. However, if errors occur, if the quality of the work falters, or if deadlines are not met, clients may become very interested in dealing directly with these staff members. When problems arise, they will likely seek the comfort of a helpful responsive staff member. Delivery systems must allow for these types of demands.

Finally, client expectations and requirements change with the nature of the product being exchanged. A food concession at a recreation facility serves the client through the provision of goods, while leisure counseling is likely free of goods of any kind. As a result, pure services tend to be more intimate than their goods-bound counterparts. When assessing food services, for example, clients look for clean and efficient operations. These are relatively easy to assess. With pure services, however, they are more likely to use more personal indicators. Is the staff member affable, available and able? Relationships are more likely to set the tone for the encounter where pure services are concerned. The marketer must plan accordingly.

Decide How the Client Will Be Served

The marketer must now ask, "During each encounter, how will the client be served?"

(Lovelock & Wright, 1999). To what extent will clients be asked to coproduce the service they eventually consume? Will the client come to the provider, or will the provider bring the service to the client? Will clients be served in groups, or individually? These questions are at the heart of the *delivery process*. Three strategies are possible (Murdick, Render, & Russell, 1990):

Fixed position strategy—The client remains at one station and everything—the provider and necessary equipment—is brought to the client. This station might be the client's own home, a hotel room, or even a room in a leisure facility. Think of room service in a hotel and you get the idea. Everything from the phone and menu to the actual food is brought to the client.

The reason for choosing the fixed position strategy is typically that of client immobility. How willing or able is the client to come to the provider? Sometimes the provider has little choice but to bring the service to the client. Interior decorators, plumbers, and landscapers must all come to the client's home. The client is not able to take these items to the providers' shops. One of my students understood this issue very well and created a business around teaching swimming in backyard pools. She coordinated a highly portable home instructional program for families hoping to have their children learn to swim in their own backyard.

On other occasions, the client may simply prefer to stay in one place and be served at that location. The fitness industry has realized this and has begun to serve clients in their homes and at their workplaces. One fitness consultant realized that famous individuals were often hesitant to travel to public leisure facilities. They valued their privacy and visits to public places could attract unwanted attention. He gathered together a virtual gymnasium of equipment into a van and brought the gymnasium to his clients. They were able to enjoy a workout with a private trainer without having to leave their own home. This approach can be demanding in terms of staff costs. It demands portability of both staff and equipment. This can become very expensive, so this approach is often used in customized, high-end personal services.

Process-based strategy—This strategy groups together equipment or services of similar capabilities. For example, fitness equipment might be placed together in a single room within a larger leisure complex. Even within that fitness room, equipment might be grouped around the types of exercise they offer. Rowing machines might all be placed in one corner, while treadmills might be located in another. Further, the lockers are located in a nearby room and showers in another. Clients move in batches from one location to the next (e.g., from locker room to gym, to pool, etc.), so service is intermittent and full of stops and starts. The equipment used in this process is typically low capacity and intended for general purpose. The locker room would soon be overwhelmed if all clients gathered there at the same time. This system works because everyone gravitates to different service groupings.

Service-based strategy—Service based strategies send the client through a prescribed sequence of steps. Cafeterias are perhaps the best working example of this principle, but many leisure providers also base program registration on this approach. Clients are placed in a sequence of single-purpose stations, and each quickly moves the client to the next station. This strategy offers an assembly-line approach and is ideal for handling large numbers of clients over short periods of time. For example, in many communities, youth sport groups often come together for one day registration-a-thons. They may gather at a central location, such as a local mall or a community center and ask interested participants to register at some point during the day. Thousands of hopeful participants may arrive within hours, and systems are established to process them quickly and accurately. Information is taken, money is exchanged, and selections are made during virtually thousands of encounters.

It is likely that all group registrations are based on some form of the service-based strategy. First, queues are created to ensure that clients begin the process at the correct location. Stations are then established to ensure that documents are signed by caregivers, participants' fees are paid, times and locations of competitions are exchanged, and so on. Each station is intended to fulfill one function, then to send the client along to the next step in the sequence. Delays at one station can create enormous problems further down the line.

This is a marvelous system when client volumes are high, but the strategy lacks flexibility. Single-purpose stations are effective only when the client requires the single service offered at that station. What happens when a client at station #3 discovers that she has incorrectly completed the forms from station #1? Typically, she must begin the process again. There is no room for error. Neither can clients change their minds halfway through the process. They cannot jump to the middle of another queue. They are committed to the chosen courses of action. As a result, instructions to clients become very important to ensure smooth transitions from one station to the next. The demands placed upon the client at each step must be transparent and obvious.

Blueprint the Encounter

The next step is one of blueprinting the actual encounter. *Blueprinting,* also called *flow charting* or *process charting*, helps organize resources effectively and efficiently. It establishes the sequence in which steps are taken to serve the client. The process "considers every activity needed to create and deliver a service, as well as specifying the linkages between these activities" (Lovelock, 1991, p. 230). These efforts outline: (1) actions performed on people, information, and materials, and (2) the relationship among processes.

> A basic service blueprint identifies (1) all the tasks and activities necessary to the performance of the service, (2) the means by which these tasks and activities are rendered, (3) the "evidence" of the service that is presented to the customer and the "encounter points" through which the customer experiences the service . . . ,[and] (4)

the facilitating goods and services that support the service system. (Shostack, 1995)

It does this by following a few basic steps. As the term "blueprinting" suggests, this is an exercise in graphically charting the service encounter. There may be many blueprints, each supporting a different type of encounter. For example, a blueprint might be created to plan registrations, another to support on-site participation, one to handle refunds, and another to assist with emergency encounters like accidents. The key is to begin with a client encounter, the moment of truth then, mobilize resources around that encounter.

The ultimate goal of service blueprinting is improved service. It does this by focusing on *responsibility*, *coordination*, and *timing*. Responsibility issues establish who must support the client; coordination issues establish how resources are to be mobilized; timing issues establish when they are to be mobilized. Blueprints deal with these issues by making processes and relationships explicit. They tend to include specific time dimensions, means of identifying and addressing errors or fail points, and the extent to which standardized procedures can vary in order to address these errors (Lovelock, 1991).

Time lines are an important component of any blueprint. They typically state how long providers have to complete an assigned task. They can be very specific and tend to lend a certain urgency to staff members' actions. Times lines might dictate that phone calls be answered within three rings or that return calls be made within three hours, or that refunds be mailed out within 24 hours. Time-based standards might also specify clients' maximum waiting periods while in registration queues or the amount of time it takes to process a single application. Errors or problems might be flagged if time targets are violated or when complaints about the process are registered. Staff might then be empowered to break with standard operating procedure to resolve these potential failures.

The blueprinting process simply assigns roles and responsibilities for supporting the client and the encounter. These responsibilities typically exist both within and between departments. The actual blueprint typically takes the form of a very basic planning grid. The intent of the grid is to mobilize resources in order to support the wishes and actions of the client. Consequently, the process begins with a statement of client requirements. These are typically placed at the top of the chart. The rest of the chart then outlines how the provider plans to fulfill these wishes and support these actions. The "process is depicted from left to right on the horizontal axis as a series of actions (rectangles) plotted chronologically along the horizontal axis of the . . . blueprint. A flow line marks the service path by connecting discrete action chronologically" (Kingman-Brundage, 1989, p. 98).

The vertical axis is comprised of both front and backstage activities undertaken to support the encounter. Recall that frontstage activities are those that are witnessed by the client. Backstage activities are those that support frontstage efforts. Frontstage activities might include telephone contact, face-to-face encounters, and encounters arranged through automated means like automated kiosks. Backstage activities might relate to staff training, coordination efforts, or planning exercises.

A sample blueprint is provided in Diagram 12.1. This sample offers a skeleton plan in that it provides only the basic steps in a very straightforward process. Many blueprints include standards and guidelines to help direct efforts as they progress through the plan.

Walking through the Blueprint

Assume that a participant hopes to register for a class provided by the leisure agency. This individual has likely been exposed to various advertising and promotional efforts. These efforts will have helped establish expectations regarding the program and the agency. Let's assume that the client has decided to register. The first step is to contact the agency. This blueprint applies to any registration effort but, for the purposes of this exercise, assume that the client has decided to drop by the provider's offices to register in person. Upon entering the office the client interacts

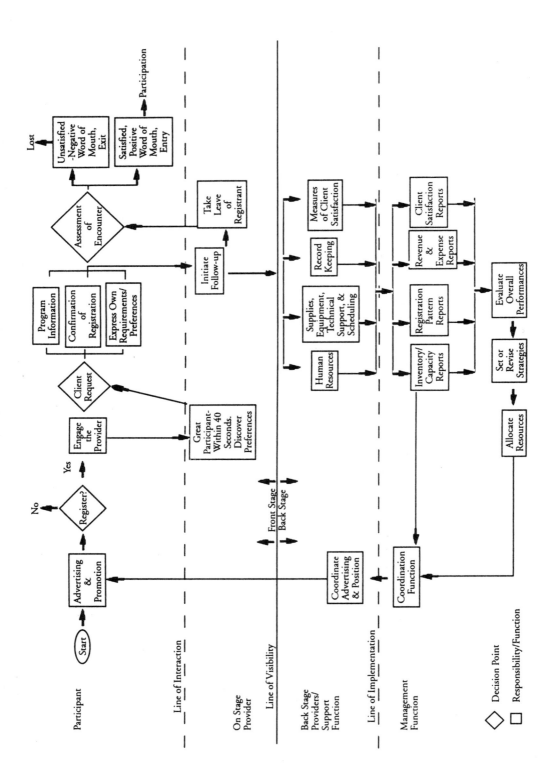

* adapted from the "service system management model" developed by Kingman-Brundage, 1989.

directly with the provider. The client and staff interact across the *line of interaction*.

The blueprint now requires that the client be greeted. Standards can be established regarding the nature and timing of this greeting. Perhaps standards dictate that the client be greeted with a smile and a verbal exchange within 40 seconds of entering the office. This exchange should be scripted so that the staff member, in addition to offering a greeting, offers assistance to the participant. Several options can be made available to the participant. Anything from simple program information to directions on how to find a community center could be readily available at this time. Clients may want to learn of program benefits and costs, the identity of instructors, or even the time and location of classes around the community. This information should be easily retrieved by any staff member who undertakes the registration task.

If the decision to take part is made, the staff member should be able to process the request immediately and provide confirmation of the time and location of the relevant program. This may not be possible for some programs. When demand is high, providers often take names and preferences first, then later attempt to schedule programs to accommodate these requests. Whatever the system being used, the provider should offer as much information as is possible at this stage. Care should be taken not to over promise. Such efforts only inflate expectations and invite disappointment later.

Also, the staff member should be able to provide information regarding the requirements of participation. Those registering for a fitness class might be informed of clothing requirements, those in an art class might be told of necessary supplies to bring along. The standards might direct the staff member to ask if there is anything else that might be done for the client. If not, the client ends the encounter.

Upon completing the encounter, the client will undoubtedly evaluate the experience. Did the surroundings create a positive impression? Was the staff member helpful and well informed? Was the available selection consistent with expectations created by the provider's own advertising and promotions? If

the responses to these questions are positive, the prospective participant is more likely to repeat the encounter. Service providers are aware of the importance of such positive evaluations, so they often build an evaluation component into this encounter. Standards often require that staff ask clients to evaluate the encounter before leaving or that clients be asked to complete evaluation forms upon their arrival home.

Staff and systems then ensure that the organization begins to mobilize resources to fulfill the client's requirements. These efforts take place above the *line of implementation* and are classified as support functions. These support functions ensure that the human resources, such as instructors are available, that required supplies and facilities are available, that records are kept regarding client preferences and payment status, and that any measures of client satisfaction have been recorded and tracked. Much of the activity and most of the staff in a leisure agency are devoted to these support functions.

Management functions exist below the line of implementation. Managers do not implement programs, but rather, they monitor and coordinate the various phases of implementation. They rely on regular reports involving capacity and registration, revenue and expense, and especially client satisfaction, in order to assess and alter strategy. They allocate resources in order to fulfill demand, while recommending policy and strategic changes based upon the information offered by front and backstage providers.

As management makes these recommendations, two issues seem to dominate their discussions. First, the thorny issue of *responsibility* arises. Who is ultimately responsible for client satisfaction when many departments are involved? Unfortunately, gaps tend to emerge when no one takes ultimate responsibility and clients may "fall through" the resulting cracks. Service suffers as a result. The blueprint must seal shut these cracks.

The second issue is that of *coordination*. This can be quite a challenge because different departments are often physically isolated from each other. Different departments may also share different priority systems. Finance department personnel likely have very different priorities and procedures than do their colleagues in programming. They may insist that certain controls be exercised over the handling of money. While these controls are necessary, they may complicate the procedures for the programmers. Add to this the priorities of front-line instructors. The instructors may simply wish to offer quality programs and maximum flexibility to their clients, but both record keeping and finance departments insist on establishing controls and limiting this same flexibility. The blueprint must make sense of all these procedures and priorities. It must reconcile the often competing demands of the client, the frontstage employee, and the backstage worker.

Once the blueprint is developed, staff can then compare the proposed process to the original service plan. Does the blueprint fulfill the promise of the original plan? Are resources being mobilized in ways that maximize the encounter both for the client and the provider? Are there *failure points*? In other words, are there spots in the plan where the process can be delayed or derailed? For example, does a front-line worker need approval from a third party (a manager or supervisor) before issuing a refund? This hierarchical type of policy could delay the refund process. Does the plan provide alternative options when clients' first choice for programs are unavailable? If not, the system may fail the client and an opportunity may be lost.

The blueprint should also be checked for obvious redundancies and internal economies (Brown, 1995). One way to evaluate the plan for weakness is to ask, "Does this step add value to the encounter, either for the client or the provider?" If it does, then it is a probably a necessary component of the plan. If not, it should receive a second look. Perhaps it can be dropped from the blueprint.

The service blueprint is a wonderfully robust tool. Blueprinting requires that the service provider outline time expectations to complete various operations, standardize the order of operations, and identify failure points. This process not only helps in planning the many facets of a service encounter, but also forces the marketer to consider the many

responsibilities, relationships, and requirements that comprise effective service delivery. Blueprints can even be used in training and evaluation because they make clear to employees how successful encounters are carried out.

Train Clients to Coproduce Services

As suggested earlier, clients act as partial employees by helping to produce the services they consume. They travel to recreation centers to enjoy programs, they find their way through various policies and procedures, they learn rules, and they develop the skills necessary to participate in many leisure activities. Providers may want to help clients maximize their use of agency resources and do so by helping train them as service *co-producers*. The process used to train clients is called *organizational socialization*. Like any socialization, it is a process by which participants learn what is expected of them as well as the skills necessary to complete their appointed tasks. Some socialization processes are profoundly negative experiences. For example, some providers socialize their clients by teaching them the amount of deference that is due the providers (Lipsky, 1980). In these settings, clients who fail to complete forms correctly or who fail to meet preset criteria soon learn that the system will not serve them. These are not socialization efforts to inspire confidence in prospective clients.

More enlightened socialization efforts enlist the aid of the client in making the leisure encounter more enjoyable, the process more efficient, and a positive outcome more predictable. The goals of such socialization efforts can be *cognitive, behavioral,* or *affective* (Feldman, 1981). All three goals should be pursued to ensure that clients are both ready and able to assist in their own program delivery.

Cognitive goals typically relate to expectation formation. Recall that expectations form internal standards against which actual experiences are compared. Cases in which positive expectations are fulfilled result in satisfaction and perceptions of quality. Encounters that fail to meet positive expectations are likely to result in dissatisfaction. This suggests that encounters are more likely to be positive if expectations are realistic, or at least, consistent with current operating procedures. Efforts to communicate realistic expectations to clients prior to participation may reduce possible disappointment and dissatisfaction. For example, health clubs often warn participants that they may have to wait for access to popular pieces of equipment if they visit during peak hours. Clients can then make informed decisions about when to visit and when not to visit the facility. If they must attend during peak periods, they have at least been warned what to expect. This warning may help reduce any subsequent disappointment.

Socialization can also focus on behavioral goals. Behavioral goals relate to teaching clients how and when to act in order to complete the encounter. It is a process of helping clients learn their organizational roles. This process is an absolute necessity for effective leisure delivery. Clients may be required to travel to the site of an activity, to use complicated or dangerous equipment (sports using sticks or bats come to mind), and to understand complicated rules and procedures in order to enjoy the activity. These clients must act in a very prescribed manner if they are to take part. To do otherwise may result in mayhem or even injury.

There are a variety of procedures used to socialize clients in terms of their behavior. Many providers send a handout to all those who register, indicating what should be worn, when programs will be offered, and who should be contacted if problems arise. Others begin classes with instructional sessions designed to teach group members the requisite skills and responsibilities. These sessions may be conducted informally through videos or manuals or more formally through staff or leaders. Whatever the means used, the goal is twofold. The first is that of helping clients understand how best to contribute to their own satisfaction. The second goal is one of reducing potentially unpleasant elements in

any encounter. Socialization can reduce the potential for confusion, injury, embarrassment, or disappointment.

Finally, socialization addresses the issue of affect or emotion. As clients learn more of their role in service provision, they will inevitably begin to assess organizational norms, values, and procedures (Kelley et al., 1990). They will assess the climate that these conditions create, and the value they receive in return for their effort. Socialization efforts should be undertaken to establish an appropriate context in which these assessments can be made.

This process is also called "internal marketing," because it is directed inward to employees and clients rather than the community at large. For example, clients may wonder at the need to follow a given procedure. Perhaps they are being asked to wear a bathing cap in a swimming pool or to wear a piece of protective clothing during a sporting event. Without any background information, these clients may chafe at the restrictions posed by these policies and ignore or resist these directives.

Internal marketing efforts could be used to provide additional, helpful information which would place these policies in perspective. Directives regarding the protective clothing might indicate that this single piece of equipment has been found to reduce the most common injury in that sport by 95 percent. Signs asking that bathing caps be worn might give the health-related reason for this request. In other words, clients are offered a compelling reason for the requested behavior, which in turn builds commitment for both the policy and the provider.

Generally, clients can be trained in terms of the *process* and in terms of the *product*.

Process-related training might include:

· how to participate (e.g., maps to find the way, activity suggestions, phone numbers, payment options);

· what to expect (e.g., provider's philosophy, guarantees, warranties, obligations, what to wear);

· how to complain (e.g., what to expect, who to contact); and

· how to ask for help (e.g., what to do, where to go, who to contact).

Product-related training might include:

· what to expect (e.g., benefits of purchase, availability, quality of work team, quality of program);

· how to evaluate/select from among options (e.g., desirable characteristics, key variables when making comparisons);

· intended use of service (e.g., for whom it is intended, level of skill/fitness required); and

· how to use the product safely, and to one's full advantage.

Set the Stage by Controlling Sights and Sounds

Years ago, Phillip Kotler (1983) used the phrase *atmosphere* to capture the importance of the setting in any service encounter. He suggested that atmospheres were comprised of designed environments intended to create or reinforce clients' tendencies to consume. In a leisure context, the goal of the setting is to encourage participation or other meaningful types of involvement. The importance of the service environment is not new. A visitor to Paris back in 1886 noted in his diary the many elements that rendered Paris the "best store-keeping city in the world" (Leach, 1993). He commented repeatedly upon the interiors of the stores and even the Louvre, noting in particular their use of glass and mirrors. He marvelled at how Parisians increased the allure of the merchandise while hiding the less attractive parts of the facilities.

Much has been written about atmosphere since these early days. Its importance to leisure delivery arises from all services' inherent intangibility. Services themselves offer few clues as to their quality. As a result, customers become "detectives" attempting to determine the value of the service (Berry & Parasuraman, 1991). They typically begin doing so by using tangible cues to establish the nature and worth of the service. The task of the marketer is to "tangiblize the intangible," to give substance to the service setting (Levitt, 1983).

The marketer has three basic tools with which to create a service environment (Baker, 1987). The first category of tools is ambient in nature.

Ambient Conditions

Ambient conditions exist below the client's own awareness levels. They include air quality, noise, and even smells. If these conditions are neutral, they are likely to remain below participants' levels of awareness. As such, they may not affect the quality of the encounter. If they are pleasing, they may actually enhance the experience. This is why many department stores place cosmetics counters at their entrances. These counters ensure that shoppers are greeted with bold displays and perhaps even a pleasing fragrance as they enter the stores. Shoppers' moods may be enhanced without their even being aware of the reason for the change. Conversely, if ambient factors are less than satisfactory, the experience can be ruined. Think of the effect an unpleasant smell can have on virtually any activity, and you get the idea.

Sounds also represent very potent ambient cues. Music, for example, is thought to improve facility image and staff mood, reduce employee turnover, and stimulate customer purchasing. The tempo of music played in the background may even affect sales volume (Milliman, 1982). Higher volumes seem to be associated with slower tempos. Consequently, marketers assume that consumers purchase more in stores with background music playing while they shop. One reason for this increased purchase behavior is that of elapsed time. Consumers may spend more time in a store with background music than they would in a store without it. As a result, they are more likely to be exposed to the store's products and more likely to purchase those products.

Design Features

The next category of tools used to develop atmosphere are those related to design. *Design features* virtually grab the attention of the participant. They may be either *aesthetic* or *functional* in nature (Baker, 1987). Aesthetic features relate to architectural shapes, patterns, materials, and colors. Together these features can create what is often referred to as the wow effect. The "wow" effect is achieved when users are both pleased and, hopefully, entranced when they enter a facility. In Bollingbrook, Illinois, for example, the park district erected a recreation facility intended to make everyone feel welcome and at home. They achieved this largely through design features. They paid particular attention to the reception area because it was so central to the first impression created for each and every user. The design was described as "light, open, airy and welcoming" (Stimac, 2000).

Functional features, as their name implies, relate to convenience and comfort. At another Bollingbrook recreation facility, staff worked very hard at increasing convenience through design. They knew, for example, that parents hated to travel from one end of the facility to another, yet they were continually asked to do so while escorting their various children to different programs. They tried to change all this through design features. Program areas were located in a more central fashion so that access was improved.

Functional issues may refer to layout, comfort levels, and even signage. Carl Sewell, a car dealer in Texas, knows the importance of these features for both the client and the provider. He searched for leaders in various service fields to help him design his own facilities. He has adopted the type of tile flooring used in McDonald's Restaurants, reasoning that they should also be able to handle the foot traffic at his dealerships. He hired the individual who designed the signs for a local airport to design signs for his facilities, because he believed that signs that worked in the hectic airport environment would also work in his dealerships. His insights regarding signage are particularly revealing. "In our dealership you won't see huge signs . . . we are trying to create an atmosphere where you feel at home, and most people don't have banners in their homes" (Sewell & Brown, 1998, p. 125). As Mr. Sewell points out, design features must be consistent both with your own service strategy and with the wishes of your clientele.

Retailers seem to excel at using design features to create positive environments within their stores. Perhaps leisure providers can learn from their colleagues in retail. Several lessons might be learned, for example, from the retailer who placed a juice bar in his store. The logic behind the juice bar is noteworthy. He knew that clients often drove for an hour or more to arrive at his location. He reasoned that if friends dropped by after having made the same long drive, he would certainly offer them a drink of some kind. Why not do the same for his customers? He offers free coffee, mineral water, or chilled juice to all his customers.

The same retailer looked to his service strategy for additional insight. The strategy was straightforward, that shopping should be fun (Stackhouse, 1991), so he developed a variety of service features accordingly. Believing that "there are all kinds of little things you can do to let [the customers] know they're understood, appreciated and valued" (Stackhouse, p. 22) he offered anyone who came in on his or her birthday a split of champagne, a silk rose, and a $5 coupon. In a stroke of brilliance, he also realized that shopping must be comfortable, not only for the shopper but also for the reluctant entourage that often accompanied his clientele. "Since most [customers] are women, he furnished the store with massage chairs and piles of magazines for bored husbands and a large color TV, basketball hoop, coloring books and Legos for children" (Stackhouse, p. 23).

There are many examples of little features that help build a positive atmosphere in any facility. A well-known hotel chain places child-size platforms at their front desks so children can climb them to see above the level of the desktop. The children can then feel as if they are participating while their adult companions go through the process of checking in. This relieves boredom for the children and ensures that they do not wander off. This simple little platform is a wonderful innovation for all concerned. Another chain often provides a small, school desk, complete with crayons and paper (highlighting the hotel chain's logo) beside the front desk. This enables the child to emulate the adults and have a bit of fun while check-in is being completed. Anyone who conducts program registration could use and adapt these simple ideas.

Social Factors

The next set of tools that shape the physical environment are social in nature. *Social factors* relate to other people in the environment. These others may be fellow participants or staff members. Consider the effect of fellow participants on a leisure experience. The effect of these groups may be determined by their number, appearance, or behavior (Baker, 1987). Consider the issue of numbers. There is extensive literature on crowding that explores the effect of other participants on an individual's own leisure experience. There are times (e.g., backcountry hiking trips) when seeing even one more individual will detract from the experience. Many hikers seek solitude in the backcountry, and the presence of other hikers represents a very unwelcome intrusion into that solitude. There are other times when the lack of other participants (e.g., a mass sporting event) will actually ruin the experience. When fans attend a sporting event, they hope that the stands will be filled with like-minded spectators. Such examples suggest the profound effect other users can have on a leisure experience. The number of staff members also affects the quality of a leisure encounter. Are staff readily available to assist the client? Are they present in sufficient numbers to both greet and aid clients when necessary?

Like it or not, clients may apply a higher standard when evaluating staff actions than when evaluating their own actions or those of other participants. They themselves may not always smile and greet others as they pass by

but may expect staff members to do so. They may not maintain a neat appearance at all times, but will expect staff to do so. This is why many retailers attempt to choreograph or *script* encounters between clients and staff. These retailers know that the mood created by staff behavior is important to the overall experience within their stores. These encounters must not be left to chance.

Allocating Limited Resources

Recall that services are perishable. Unsold services cannot be stockpiled, inventoried or reclaimed. The opportunity to sell an empty seat in a theater is gone forever once the show has begun. It cannot be set aside and sold later as can a manufactured product. Uneven demand may prove a considerable challenge to the service provider. When supply exceeds demand, facilities sit idle and resources are wasted. When demand exceeds supply, clients must wait for service or be turned away. Neither condition is desirable. Unfortunately, both supply and demand may vary dramatically throughout the day, week or season. The provider may have to take extraordinary steps in order to ensure that supply always matches demand.

The goal is one of maintaining a balance. In doing so, providers are faced with two alternative solutions (1) alter capacity (supply) or (2) alter demand. (Lovelock, 1992):

Capacity (supply) can be altered through the following:

- Physical facilities (e.g., add more chairs, lockers, larger facility, remain open more hours).

- Equipment (e.g., rent or purchase more phones, towels, etc.)

- Labor (e.g., add more people during peak periods).

· More frequent delivery (e.g., offer classes more often).

· Increased speed of transaction/stay (e.g., fast food restaurants often use uncomfortable chairs to discourage clients from lingering).

· Alternative time and place of transaction (e.g., registration kiosks or off-site ATMs).

Before responding to demand issues, ask these key questions (Lovelock ,1992, p. 157):

· Does the level of demand follow a regular and predictable cycle, such as varying by the time of day or week?

· What are the underlying causes of demand variations? Employment schedules, school hours and vacations, time of year?

· Can demand be altered? Will different user groups respond in systematic ways so that demand might be smoothed over time?

· What random occurrences (e.g., weather, crime, etc.) might alter demand?

Once these questions have been addressed, appropriate measures might be taken to alter demand:

· Let it work itself out. Clients may learn not to visit facilities during times of peak demand. The problem with this option is the attendant irritation among clients, which discourages future participation.

· Shape demand by decreasing interest during peak hours while increasing interest during periods of low demand. This is typically done through:

— differential pricing (pricing the same product at different levels depending upon demand for the product), and

— communication (reminding users of the benefits of using the service during nonpeak hours). For example, at a YMCA in Calgary, they have placed a chart on the wall indicating the projected peaks and valleys in demand for the week. This enables clients to plan their own schedule around existing demand.

· Inventory demand through:

— reservations, which help balance demand with service availability, and

— priority queuing (first-come/first-served).

The Challenge of Priority Queuing

This final option, that of priority queuing, is an intuitively obvious solution to crowding. It is perhaps the single, most widely used technique to handle an imbalance between supply and demand. Waiting has become an almost inevitable part of many leisure experiences. Leisure providers ask participants to wait in line in any number of leisure settings ranging from ski lifts and theaters to special events and concessions. They wait for pieces of equipment in fitness clubs, for service at front desks, for space on tennis courts. Indeed, waiting for leisure is almost as common as leisure itself.

Unfortunately, those in a queue are faced with a rather bleak choice. If they decide not to stand in line, they lose the opportunity to take part on that occasion. There is little choice but to wait in line or lose access to the program or event. Though participants know that they may enjoy leisure programs at the conclusion of a wait in line, the act of waiting can prove to be a profoundly negative experience. It even has been compared to being held captive. While queue experiences may be troubling for anyone, they can be especially problematic for older or younger participants. Children, in particular, may be unprepared for the demands of queues.

Waiting and the Leisure Experience

The queuing experience is a problem for the leisure marketer, because it flies in the face of all that the marketer is trying to achieve (Colenutt, 1997). Leisure marketers hope to provide experiences characterized by choice and freedom, yet queues seem to rob both, at least temporarily, from the participant. One way to combat the boredom and other negative emotions that might be generated through queues is to focus on clients' assessments of their time in queue.

When queues seem inevitable, many providers now attempt to alter participants' assessment of the experience by altering expectations. They hope that by making expectations consistent with "reality" dissatisfaction with unexpected queues will be reduced. The process of altering expectations is now used widely in leisure settings like theme parks. Many successful theme parks actually post waiting times outside each attraction that are generously overestimated. In other words, participants would be asked to expect a 25-minute wait when a 15–20 minute wait was more likely. Theme park administrators' belief that such measures alter expectations (and subsequent satisfaction levels) seems justified. "One comes away mysteriously grateful for having hung around 20 minutes for a 58-second twirl" (Katz, Larson, & Larson, 1991, p. 45). This suggests that participants' assessments of a queue-type wait are susceptible to cues provided by leisure programmers.

Information, regarding the cause and duration of the delay may also alter perceptions of a queue-type wait (Larson, 1987). Known and explained delays may seem shorter than unknown and unexplained delays (Maister, 1988). Although the provision of relevant information regarding a delay does nothing to reduce the actual waiting time, such information is appreciated by those in the queue and might increase their tolerance for the wait

(East, 1997). These views have received some support in the airline industry, where "timely announcements of reasons for . . . delays, clear signs explaining waiting rules, and the frequent estimates of progress all . . . reduce anxiety and enhance waiting experiences" (Heskett, Sasser, & Hart, 1990, p. 145). Again, the role of such messages seems largely one of altering and directing expectations. The provider is offering new reference points from which participants might adjust expectation levels. All these techniques could be used while leisure participants are queued.

The leisure provider might also go beyond simple explanations in reducing dissatisfaction over delays. Maister (1988) contends that queues are problematic both for the delay they represent and for the boredom they engender. Queues typically require that participants stand while waiting with little to observe but the back of individuals who stand ahead of them in the line. Under such conditions, time may actually seem to pass more slowly than usual, thus accentuating the length of the delay. As William James (in Maister, p. 178) observed, "Boredom results from being attentive to the passage of time itself." The drudgery of a queue-type delay may be alleviated if those in line are entertained, or at least engaged, while in the queue. The purpose of such engagement is that of drawing participants' attention away from the more static conditions within the queue.

The many examples of such engagement offer anecdotal support for its utility. Music offered while callers wait on hold, or the magazines provided to patients waiting in a physician's office and to shoppers waiting in line at grocery stores, all speak to the popularity of engagement during delays. Katz et al. (1991) studied the effect of an electronic news board displayed to those in queue. They concluded that more positive waiting experiences were likely when participants' attention was focused away from the wait. While the news board offered engagement for those in line, it offered an additional bonus of physically altering their position. Their perspective was no longer of standing back to front, but of side to side. Apparently this repositioning and the engagement provided by the news board improved the quality of the queue experience for those who took part.

Finally, dissatisfaction with delays might be reduced by symbolic acts on the part of agency staff. Such acts offer tangible indicators of staff remorse for the delay they are imposing on participants. They represent an act of contrition. Goodwin and Ross (1992) studied the influence of symbolic acts on customers' responses to service delays. The four services examined were auto repair, vacation air travel, dental service, and restaurant meal service (Goodwin & Ross). The scenarios presented to respondents included problems such as an "overnight delay due to over booking by the airline" or a "15-minute delay while waiters serve others" (Goodwin & Ross, p. 162). Participants were exposed to messages suggesting either inaction (e.g., "There is nothing we can do at this time") or a positive response by staff members (e.g., 10 percent discounts, free meals, and complimentary hotel stays) (Goodwin & Ross). The authors concluded that even small compensations, such as a free drink or 10 percent discount supplemented by an apology, could reduce dissatisfaction with service delays (Goodwin & Ross).

Main Points

· Services are presented to clients during encounters called moments of truth.

· Activities not intended to enhance the actual encounter should be kept backstage and out of view.

· Staff are critical to the success of the moment of truth.

· Clients help deliver or coproduce the services they consume. Like staff, they too must be trained and rewarded for doing so.

· Service encounters should be supported by backstage systems and processes that offer staff easy and immediate access to needed resources.

· Service encounters must be planned and choreographed, and this process begins with discovering clients' expectations and requirements.

· Each encounter evolves in a sequence. Clients are first greeted, then served, then supporting paperwork is processed, and so on. Blueprinting, also called flow charting and process charting, is often used to plan how resources will be allocated to support each type of encounter.

· The encounter setting is like a stage in a play because it helps establish an atmosphere that is appropriate to the encounter.

· The encounter may be adversely effected by crowding and queues. The provider must maintain a balance between supply and demand.

Case Study

The manager of a local indoor swimming pool has been called into the director of recreation's office. It seems that not all is well. The pool has been losing money for years, but recently its losses have been reaching levels that are unacceptable to the city council. Something has to change. Upon receiving the bad news, the pool manager's first act was to call his staff together and brainstorm over what is wrong and what they might do about it.

One of the office staff has been reviewing attendance levels and thinks she has identified one major problem. The issue seems to be one of uneven demand for their services. She indicated that the pool is virtually full during after-school hours but almost empty during week days from 9:00 a.m. until 3:30 p.m. In effect, though they are paying bills to heat and maintain the pool all day long, they are relying on only a few hours to generate needed revenue. Why not try to fill the pool during the entire day, she suggested. This would extend the revenue-generating capacity of the facility.

Another staff member, who has been with the facility longer than anyone else in the group, stated flatly that this idea simply will not work. It requires the increased attendance of adults, and in his words, "They will never ever become loyal to this swimming pool. It's embarrassing for them to parade about in bathing suits, it's cold, and we have too many rules. Years ago we tried to get adults into this pool, and while they might come out for a week or two, they never come back. It won't work, I tell you!"

The pool manager feels that there might be something to both staff members' views. It was true that getting more adults to come out during weekdays would help revenues, but it was equally true that adults seemed generally to avoid the pool. The front entrance is cold and uninviting, staff members act as guards looking to discover errors made by patrons, and the change rooms are damp and often smelly. The pool deck is often cluttered with swim-team paraphernalia, and signs are posted throughout the facility, that state only "DO NOT..." then

offer a list of infractions that would result in ejection from the pool. Children may be accustomed to this kind of treatment, he reasoned, but adults are not. They seem to abandon us when we treat them in this manner.

The pool manager has decided that if pool staff are to encourage adults to come out more regularly, they must begin to treat them in a more friendly manner. They must change the way in which clients are greeted and treated in the facility. The staff must now come up with a plan to improve the service encounters between the pool facility and its adult clientele.

· What kinds of "solutions" might adults (and their families) seek when they visit a pool facility?

· How might the different parts of the facility—entrance, change rooms, and pool deck— be arranged to render the facility more adult friendly?

· How might staff be trained to better serve the requirements of this client group, while continuing to offer a safe aquatic facility?

References

Baker, J. (1987). The role of the environment in marketing services: The consumer perspective. In J.A. Czepiel, C. Congram, & J. Shanaha (Eds.), *The service challenge: Integrating for competitive advantage* (p.80). Chicago: American Marketing Association.

Berry, L., & Parasuraman, A. (1991). *Marketing services: Competing through quality*. New York: The Free Press.

Brown, S.A. (1995). *What customers value most*. Toronto: John Wiley & Sons.

Carlzon, J. (1989). *Moments of truth*. New York: Perennial Library, Harper & Row.

Coleman, J., McCarville, R. E., Colenutt, C. (2000). Queues and the leisure experience: The consequences of waiting for leisure. *Leisure/Loisir*, 24(3/4), 207-231.

Colenutt, C. (1997). *Selected emotional consequences of various queuing experiences*. Unpublished master's thesis, University of Waterloo, Waterloo, Ontario, Canada.

Davidow, W., & Uttal, B. (1989). *Total customer service*. New York: Harper & Row.

Dobyns, L., & Crawford-Mason, C. (1994). *Thinking about quality*. New York: Times Books.

East, R. (1997). *Advances and applications in marketing*. Toronto: Prentice-Hall.

Feldman, D.C. (1981). The multiple socialization of organization members. *Academy of Management Review*, 6(2), 309-318.

Goodwin, C., & Ross, I. (1992). Consumer responses to service failures: Influence of procedural and interactional fairness perceptions. *Journal of Business Research*, 25, 149-163.

Henderson, K.A., Bialeschki, M.D., Shaw, S.M., & Freysinger, V.J. (1989). *A leisure of one's own: A feminist perspective on women's leisure*. State College, PA: Venture Publishing Inc.

Heskett, J.L., Sasser, W.E., Jr., & Hart, C.W.L. (1990). *Service breakthroughs: Changing the rules of the game*. New York: The Free Press.

Katz, K.L., Larson, B.M., & Larson, R.C. (1991, Winter). Prescriptions for the waiting-in-line blues: Entertain, enlighten, and engage. *Sloan Management Review*, 44-53.

Kelley, S.W., Donnelly, J.H. Jr., & Skinner, S. J. (1990). Customer participation in service production and delivery. *Journal of Retailing*, 66(Fall), 315-335.

Kingman-Brundage, J. (1989). The ABCs of service system blue printing. In M.J. Bitner & L.A. Crosby (Eds.), *Designing a winning service strategy* (pp. 96-102). Chicago: American Marketing Association.

Kotler, P. (1983). *Principles of marketing* (2nd ed.). Englewood Cliffs, NJ: Prentice-Hall.

Larson, R.C. (1987). Perspectives on queues: Social justice and the psychology of queuing. *Operations Research*, 35(6), 895-905.

Leach, W. (1993). *Land of desire: Merchants, power, and the rise of a new American culture*. New York: Pantheon Books.

Levitt, T. (1983). *The marketing imagination*. New York: The Free Press.

Lipsky, M. (1980). *Street-level bureaucracy: Dilemmas of the individual in public services*. New York: Russell Sage Foundation.

Lovelock, C.H. (1991). Creating and delivering services. In C.H. Lovelock (Ed.), *Services marketing* (2nd ed.) (pp. 223-235). Toronto: Prentice-Hall.

Lovelock, C.H. (1992). *Managing services: Marketing, operations, and human resources* (2nd ed.). Toronto: Prentice-Hall.

Lovelock, C.H., & Wright, L. (1999). *Principles of service marketing and management*. Upper Saddle River, NJ: Prentice-Hall.

Maister, D.H. (1988). The psychology of waiting in lines. In C.H. Lovelock, *Managing services: Marketing, operations, and human resources* (2nd e.d.) (pp. 176-183). Toronto: Prentice-Hall.

Milliman, R.E. (1982). Using background music to affect the behavior of supermarket shoppers. *Journal of Marketing*, 13(Summer), 86-91.

Murdick, R.G., Render, B., & Russell, R.S. (1990). *Service operations management.* Boston: Allyn and Bacon.

Sewell, C., & Brown, P. (1998). *Customers for life.* Toronto: Pocket Books.

Shostack, G.L. (1995). Service blueprinting. In J. Heilbrunn (Ed.), *Marketing encyclopedia: Issues and trends shaping the future* (pp. 107-114). Chicago: American Marketing Association.

Stackhouse, J. (1991, June). Sit back, relax and buy something. *Report on Business Magazine*, 20-23.

Stimac, J. (2000). Put "awe appeal" into your community center. *Parks and Recreation*, 35(8), 96-102.

Tasca, B., & Caldwell, P. (1996). *You will be satisfied.* New York: Harper Business.

S. Czekus

C H A P T E R

13

Recover from Errors

Levitt's (1983) observation that for providers "the object is to get and keep a customer" has been repeated several times in this text. It conveys the importance of loyalty to successful leisure delivery. Loyalty is a much desired commodity, because it reduces costs and increases benefits for participants and providers alike. For participants, loyalty reduces psychological costs. By returning to trusted providers, participants can minimize the stress associated with making new purchases. They seek a program or service that they can rely upon. In this way, psychological costs are reduced and loyalty develops. Such loyalty brings with it the comfort of certainty and predictability. These qualities are much desired by many leisure participants.

From the providers' perspective, loyal clients reduce acquisition costs because fewer clients need to be enticed into programs. Loyal clients also reduce operating costs, because experienced clients cost less to service. They are already familiar with operating procedures and with the requirements of participation. They require less direct supervision and are less likely to ask for assistance with basic operating requirements. Further, loyalty boosts base profits because loyal clients tend to increase involvement over time. Positive word-of-mouth communications also seem to increase with loyalty. Consequently, loyal clients are more likely to attract fledgling program participants to the benefit of all (Reichheld, 1996).

Conversely, lost clients represent lost profit. Lost clients are those individuals who once chose to participate in program offerings but have since discontinued that participation (Backman & Crompton, 1991). Reichheld (1996) estimates that such loss, which he calls disloyalty, stunts corporate performance by 25 percent to 50 percent. As a result, private sector providers are typically distressed over "lost" clients. This issue is equally problematic for both the not-for-profit and public sectors. Though they are not as concerned with profit as are their private sector counterparts, they too benefit from loyal clients (Backman & Crompton). For all sectors, client loss or displacement represents failure, failure to provide for the wants expressed by user groups. Leisure providers all seek retention, because it ensures that participants will continue to benefit from their involvement in leisure activities.

Understanding Loyalty

In an early paper on loyalty, Buchanan (1985) suggested that loyalty is bound up in notions of commitment, dedication, devotion, and attachment. Each of these notions implies a consistent willingness to embrace one activity and/or provider over alternative options. Though traditional indicators relied solely on behavioral evidence when defining loyalty, Buchanan conceptualized commitment as a function of

· consistent behavior,

· affective attachment, and

· involvement in related interests or side bets.

The first two characteristics are self-evident. Those committed to a given activity will tend to repeat that activity and feel positive about that participation. Side bets involve additional and related investments in the activity. A photography enthusiast may invest in cameras and lenses. A triathlete may purchase a specialized multisport bicycle. A hiker may purchase lightweight camping equipment, and so on. These side bets tend to increase loyalty because they add financial as well as emotional commitment to the activity.

Subsequent research efforts have largely supported Buchanan's assumptions. We know, for example, that participation alone represents an insufficient indicator of interest in or support for a program or provider. Backman and Crompton (1991) report that program participants may frequent a given program without attaching any emotional commitment to that program. They termed this as "spurious loyalty," suggesting that these participants are easily dislodged from that program if acceptable alternatives can be found. For this reason, marketers are encouraged not to confuse participation with loyalty. Mere participation is simply not enough to ensure loyalty. The attachment must be deeper, more emotional than simple behavior. Clients must feel an emotional attachment, as well as take part, in order to exhibit true loyalty.

The Evolution of the Customer

Kotler (1999) suggests that as loyalty develops, clients evolve or progress through a type of career with that provider. It is the provider's goal to nurture this evolution. The first stage in the evolution is that of *repeat customer*. The repeat customer displays a behavioral commitment to the provider but has not yet developed the desired emotional commitment.

The second stage is that of the *client*. In Kotler's terms, the client is created as the provider begins to collect more personal information on the customer. The marketer can then begin to develop a more personal relationship with that individual. The client might be greeted by name, might receive a birthday card from the provider, or might have his or her program preferences listed in a personal file. These preferences can be consulted when new programs are offered or when schedules are set. In this way, programs and schedules can be customized to the preferences of the individual. These efforts help develop commitment on the part of both the provider and the participant.

The next level, that of *advocate*, suggests that the client has adopted the role of apostle of the provider. The advocate actively promotes the provider's programs through positive word-of-mouth communication. This suggests considerable emotional commitment to the organization. Current participants are ideally suited to promote programs. As suggested earlier in this text, their views are perceived as being unbiased, and therefore more trustworthy, by listeners. As well, they possess detailed information of the provider's own programs and services. The actions of the advocate can promote considerable goodwill for the leisure provider and all his programs.

Kotler (1999) suggests that the advocate might then evolve into the *member*. Members are typically offered special privileges such as discounts and preferred access to popular programs, and additional services like towels and lockers. While many providers, ranging from clubs to athletic facilities, offer membership privileges, they are not without their shortcomings. They require considerable commitment from both the members and providers. Both must be willing to allocate their own resources to ensure that the relationship offers adequate benefits to their partners. Further, offering special privileges to members can alienate nonmembers. They may feel, with justification, that they are not gaining access to all the benefits that their member friends are enjoying.

The final stage in the evolution of the customer is that of *partner*. A partner represents, in Kotler's view, the most advanced stage of the evolutionary process. Partners help the provider design, develop, and improve programs and services. Kotler notes that many providers already seek their customers' input through focus groups, customer complaint cards, and client surveys. While he applauds these efforts to discover client expectations, requirements, and observations, Kotler's notion of partner extends far beyond such simple data collection.

Kotler (1999) suggests that the role of client be expanded so that clients are brought more directly into the planning process. Partners become an integral component of the planning and delivery process. They are brought into the backstage process where programs are planned and implemented. This level of involvement is certainly not for everyone. Many customers, clients, advocates, and members may wish simply to be served. They may not wish to become engaged in the business of service provision. Also, many providers may not wish to become so deeply involved in partnerships with their own clients. Such partnerships require considerable commitment and organizational resources, if they are to be effective.

Service Failures and Client Loyalty

There are times when service errors will test the loyalty of even the most devoted participant (Berry & Parasuraman, 1991). Service errors occur when the provider fails to meet clients' expectations. They may be associated with increased complaint behavior,

lost goodwill, and lost clients (Bearden and Oliver, 1985). Unfortunately, it seems that such errors are an inevitable part of service delivery (Hart, Heskett, & Sasser, 1990). No provider can make delivery error free on all occasions. The key seems to be one of avoiding problems, while simultaneously preparing for when they will inevitably occur.

How can loyalty be maintained and perhaps improved even as errors occur? There are two schools of thought on this issue. The first suggests that errors are intrinsically damaging to the client-provider relationship. Loyalty may be irreparably damaged once failures have occurred. Researchers operating in a leisure center report, for example, that service recovery efforts were unable to erase all the negative feelings generated by service failures (Howat, Murray, & Crilley, 1999). In this case, failures lead inevitably to lost clients and disloyalty.

Other researchers contend that service failures need not destroy loyalty. They suggest that timely and effective resolution of problems can cancel the sting of dissatisfaction, replacing it with client satisfaction, increased loyalty, and positive word-of-mouth communication (Goodwin & Ross, 1992). Indeed, these researchers suggest that the "secondary satisfaction arising from complaint handling may build even stronger loyalties than satisfaction with the initial service" (Goodwin & Ross, p. 150).

Both points of view may be correct, depending upon the nature of the failure and the quality of the recovery effort. For example, the scope of the failure may affect response to that failure. Minor problems may be forgotten more quickly than major inconveniences. The quality of the resolution may also affect client response. Well-conceived recovery efforts may, for example, be better received than clumsy attempts at compensation. The remainder of this chapter deals with the many elements of effective recovery efforts.

The Importance of Complaints

Dissatisfied clients tend not to complain. Rather, they simply abandon the offending provider (Goodwin & Ross, 1992). Marketers generally believe that this unhappy client tells, on average, nine others of her dissatisfaction. This suggests that an unhappy client represents a triple loss. First, the individual is unlikely to complain, so the provider remains unaware of the problem. Second, the individual is likely to abandon the provider, so their relationship is severed, perhaps forever. Finally, through negative word-of-mouth communication, others learn of the service failure, and they, too, avoid the same provider.

The tendency not to complain is increased when staff members are unresponsive to complaints made by clients. It must be acknowledged that in many cases, client complaints are simply ignored by service providers. There are three seemingly good reasons for this. First, complaints are unpleasant for symbolic reasons. They suggest that the provider has failed, and that programs and staff are somehow lacking. No one wants to be reminded of personal failure, so complaints are often ignored. Second, complaints can be professionally damaging. They suggest that the provider is somehow incompetent. As a result, they are often hidden from others to avoid unwanted questions about capabilities. Third, complaints tend to demand resources. Clients may ask that fees be returned, that programs be repeated, or that staff provide greater assistance. All these requests require resources, and these resources may not be available.

It is best, however, if unhappy clients complain. A complaint represents a double opportunity. First, it notifies the provider of a service failure. Those who complain speak for themselves and the many others who may have experienced the same problem but chose not to speak out. This leads to the second benefit, that of resolution. A complaint represents a necessary first step in problem resolution. Once providers have been notified of a service failure, they can begin to remedy the situation. As a result, complaints play a very positive and essential role in any delivery system. Many providers now view them not as a curse, but as a gift bestowed upon them by clients.

Understanding Service Failure

This discussion highlights the importance of resolving service failures to the satisfaction of clients. In order to create satisfaction in spite of failures, the marketer must have a basic understanding of client satisfaction and of its unpleasant counterpart, that of service failure. Psychologists tell us that expectations are central to the notion of client satisfaction (Zeithaml, Parasuraman, & Berry, 1990; Oliver, 1980). If expectations are fulfilled or exceeded, clients are likely to respond with satisfaction or even delight. Failures typically result when experiences fail to meet clients' own positive expectations (Berry & Parasuraman, 1991).

Expectations are formed not only in terms of goal fulfillment, but also in terms of the perceived fairness of the exchange (Hegtvedt, 1990). The notion of goal fulfillment is perhaps obvious. Clients will reflect on an experience to determine if it has fulfilled the goals that motivated the activity in the first place. A participant interested in learning a new skill will reflect on whether or not participation in a workshop actually helped develop the desired skill level. If initial goals were achieved, then satisfaction is likely. If the goals were not achieved, then a service failure may have occurred.

Whereas goal fulfillment refers to *end results*, the client may also reflect on the *process* through which the program was delivered. For example, clients often assess whether or not they were treated fairly in their exchange with the service provider. Fairness is judged in terms of (1) the level of the actual service *compared* to the expected level of service (Markovsky, 1988) and (2) the level of benefit *compared* to that received by the exchange partner (Martin & Martin, 1986). Clients' basic goals may have been fulfilled, but they if believe that they were shortchanged in some way, they may become angry. If this occurs, a service failure will have occurred.

Failures fall into two basic types or categories. The first arises from *system failures*.

System failures occur when the core service promised by the provider somehow fails to meet expectations. Perhaps promised services are unavailable, service seems unreasonably slow, food is cold, or the facility is dirty. These are common problems that demand constant vigilance on the part of providers. Sometimes providers even create their own system failures as a matter of policy. For example, public providers routinely offer programs only tentatively until demand levels can be determined. Many even insist that registrants pay in advance for these programs. Once demand levels have been established, programs are offered or cancelled accordingly. Popular programs survive, while less popular programs do not. Programs for which clients registered and paid are sometimes cancelled. Undoubtedly, those whose programs have been cancelled will experience a sense of failure at this turn of events.

The second failure type is that of *response failure*. Response failures are those that fail to react to particular client demands. These demands may or may not be overtly expressed by the clients themselves. For example, clients standing in queue may be bored, anxious, or even angry about the need to wait in this way. They may expect staff to recognize their plight without their having to complain. Staff who fail to do so may create considerable animosity among those in line.

Other response failures may occur when staff fail to respond adequately to explicit requests from staff. Staff who refuse to take complaints seriously or who fail to respond to requests may generate bad feelings among their clients. Requests for action include special requests (e.g., asking providers to customize programs to suit participant's own preferences), solving problems that arise from participant errors, and dealing with others in the service environment that have become disruptive (Hoffman & Bateson, 1997). All represent considerable challenges for unprepared staff members.

When Failures Occur

Service failures are likely to generate *attributional assessments*. Attribution is a process through which individuals attempt to explain their own behavior, the behaviors of others, or the events they observe (Bitner, 1990). Unexpected and negative events, such as service failures are more likely to generate attributional activity than expected or positive events (Folkes, 1988). After experiencing a service failure, participants typically strive to discover the reason for the problem. A model of attribution, developed by Weiner (1979), suggests that, in doing so, they ask three types of questions. They might attempt to establish

1. locus of causality ("Who is responsible for the failure?");

2. stability ("Is my experience typical of this type of setting?"); and

3. controllability ("Could this problem have been avoided?") (Chebat, Filiatrault, & Gelinas-Chebat, 1995).

Participants' conclusions regarding these questions influence the client's ultimate to the service failure, be it anger, complaint behavior, or a lack of intent to return (Bitner, 1990). Consider the importance of each question in turn. In terms of locus of causality, the cause of the failure may be internal (attributed to the individual) or external (attributed to something in the environment) (Taylor, 1994). The alternative that the participant chooses has important implications for the service provider. If those in line decide that the failure is a result of their own actions (e.g., their own inexperience), then dissatisfaction with the provider is likely to be reduced. However, if the attributional assessment suggests that the provider's actions have led to the failure (e.g., not having sufficient staff on hand to assist new participants), then dissatisfaction is likely to be elevated (Folkes, 1984).

The locus of causality also influences beliefs about who should solve problems. If the failure is believed to be the fault of the service provider, the provider is typically considered responsible for finding a solution (Folkes, 1988). Consequently, refunds and apologies are believed to be more deserved when the failure is considered to originate with the provider than with the participant.

Consider also the importance of event stability to participant response. There is a significant correlation between the stability of the reason behind the failure and client anger. Failures thought to originate from stable sources, such as a chronic lack of staff are troubling because of their perceived propensity to recur. The more common or stable the cause of delay is perceived to be, the more angry clients become. Conversely, failures resulting from unstable sources (e.g., unusually high demand) are less likely to irritate because they are less likely to threaten future encounters (Folkes, 1988).

The third dimension of attribution is controllability. When the cause of the failure is perceived to be within the provider's control, customers are more dissatisfied than when they perceived the provider as having no control (Bitner, 1990). The more control the provider is perceived to have over the failure, the more angry participants are likely to become. The degree of control also influences participant communication patterns. When a high degree of control is attributed to the provider, users are more likely to complain and warn others not to conduct business with that provider (Folkes, 1988). Not surprisingly, Folkes, Koletsky, and Graham, (1987) found that as perceptions of provider control over failures increase, the likelihood of repurchase decreases.

The Need for Service Recovery

In order to place the potentially devastating effects of service failures in perspective, many providers now discuss clients in terms of their lifetime spending potential. For example, a family that frequents a given leisure facility might spend tens of thousands of dollars in that facility over the years. They will buy memberships and register for classes while purchasing athletic equipment and food. Thinking of clients in terms of their total possible expenditure makes clear the impor-

tance of satisfying each client during each encounter. It may seem ridiculous to spend $125 to replace a racquet for an angry patron but very reasonable to do so to save a $10,000 long-term customer. Those uncomfortable with this profit-based appeal might draw a similar analogy with hours of participation. A typical family might participate in 5,000 hours of leisure activity at a given facility over the years. Is it worth jeopardizing this many hours over small issues like accessibility of lockers or lost towels? It always seems better to please the client so that participation continues.

Unfortunately, many providers are hesitant to spend resources on complaints because they fear that clients will try to take advantage of them. In some cases they are probably correct. We must accept that a few clients will cheat, lie, and steal given the opportunity. These are the clients that all service providers fear. Carl Sewell (Sewell & Brown, 1998) tells the story of a criminal who sent a fictitious letter of complaint to several Cadillac dealers across America. This letter complained that a shirt had been damaged by staff during a recent visit to the dealership and demanded restitution. Many of these dealers were fooled by this letter and sent money along as requested. They were more concerned with satisfying a client than with worrying about the intent of the person who wrote the letter.

Two insights can be gathered from Sewell's story. The first takes a negative spin, assuming that clients, and complainers in particular, are not to be trusted. Unfortunately, service providers often treat clients, and particularly those who complain, with suspicion. Like Sewell, they have heard stories of unscrupulous individuals who will drain the service providers' resources for personal gain. Consequently, they tend to discourage clients from reporting failures (complaining) and respond only hesitantly to the few who do complain.

Resulting policies designed to recover from failures tend to be very restrictive. A client can receive a refund, but not after the first week of a leisure class. A staff member may have to receive permission from a supervisor before refunds are possible. There might even be an administration fee or penalty for requesting this refund. The client may have to visit some central office to receive the refund. Unfortunately, these procedures rarely inspire any kind of loyalty. They seem more focused on stopping "complainers" from taking advantage of the provider than on satisfying the unhappy client. These types of policies add to dissatisfaction levels among unhappy clients. The client is already dissatisfied as a result of the service failure, and dissatisfaction increases

dramatically when the provider seems hesitant to help resolve the problem. These situations often lead to perceptions of victimization on the part of the client.

The second insight to be learned from Sewell's story is more positive than the first and carries with it more useful conclusions. Sewell's anecdote reveals that the Cadillac dealers who were involved in this story viewed this complaint as an opportunity to fix a problem, to

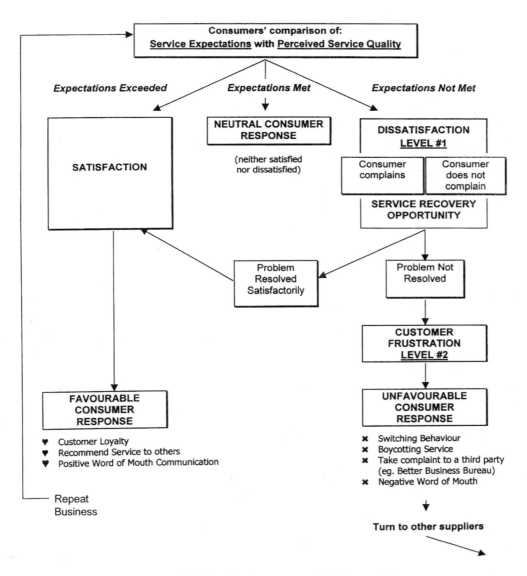

Figure 13.1: Model of Service Recovery and the Stages of Customer
Satisfaction and Dissatisfaction

Source: Colenutt (1997)

right a wrong. This is the more useful of the two insights. The dealers knew the letter may have been from an unreliable source, but their first reaction was to resolve a failure. As Sewell himself notes, this type of expense is just the cost of doing business. It is often futile to worry about separating clients who are dishonest from those who have legitimate concerns. It seems better to establish policies designed to aid in service recovery rather than to simply protect the provider from unscrupulous con artists.

A Model of Service Recovery

Service recovery is the process of resolving problems to the satisfaction of the client. It is only necessary when the client is dissatisfied with some aspect of the service encounter. This dissatisfaction leads to Level 1 frustration. Given this dissatisfaction, the client is faced with the choice to either complain or not to complain (Figure 13.1). Most choose not to and are often lost as a result.

If unhappy clients do complain, however, the provider is given a second chance, an opportunity to recover from the failure. If staff are able to remedy the problem to the satisfaction of the client, the client may then veer back to the satisfied column. The satisfaction they experience at this point is called *secondary satisfaction*. Secondary satisfaction is that most desirable of conditions in which the client has discovered that the provider is willing to help out when the chips are down. Clients who experience secondary satisfaction may be among the most loyal of clients. They know that mistakes will inevitably happen and that the provider is willing to respond in a fair, attentive manner.

If after a complaint has been made and the problem is still not resolved, the client will descend into Level 2 frustration. The client has complained, asked for help, or indicated some dissatisfaction, and the provider has failed to respond satisfactorily. The dissatisfaction that arises at this level can be profound and very personal. Clients at this stage are often termed *terrorists,* because they engage in behavior designed to damage the provider. They will complain to anyone who is willing to listen and spread negative word of mouth in addition to abandoning the provider.

The Dynamics of Service Recovery

Eighty percent of clients will support service providers who make mistakes *if* resulting problems are handled to the clients' satisfaction (Goodman, 1989). Unfortunately, as noted above, few unhappy clients will complain regardless of how disappointed they are with service. The reader has probably witnessed this phenomenon personally. Perhaps you visited a restaurant with friends only to discover that the food and service are terrible. Staff members are trained to ask how the group is enjoying the meal and when this occurs, no one is likely to complain. Instead, everyone at the table typically indicates that everything is fine. Complaint behavior carries so much negative emotional baggage that clients are unlikely to complain even when they face considerable personal loss by remaining silent. Complaining is embarrassing, and clients have been taught, from birth, that if they cannot say something nice, they shouldn't say anything at all. Instead, they simply abandon the provider and tell others of their dissatisfaction.

Effective complaint resolution, often called service recovery, has three distinct stages. It demands *problem identification*, requires *staff empowerment*, and relies upon specific *recovery procedures* (Berry & Parasuraman, 1991). Though this may seem a straightforward process, it can be exceedingly difficult to implement. Each of these stages is discussed below.

Identifying Problems

If failures do occur, the provider must discover and address them before they become problematic. The key is to monitor customer complaints, then discover the root cause and fix it so the problem does not recur. This process requires that clients complain when problems arise. If they fail to do so, problems cannot be isolated and solutions cannot be sought. Though it may seem strange, and even counterproductive, it is best that the provider encourages complaint behavior.

The best way to do this is to make it easy to complain and to respond positively when clients do so. Many providers actually reward clients for complaining. For example, one grocery chain provides its own corporate "dollars" to any client who returns an unsatisfactory item. The number of dollars the client receives is always twice the value of the original product. In this way, the client is actually rewarded for helping the provider identify problems in the store. The store is rewarded because the complaint helps with problem identification and may ensure that future business is not lost. Clients must redeem these dollars at the original store, so the store manager is certain they will return. This offers another opportunity to please the customer.

Empowering Staff

Once problems have been identified, providers must be prepared to *resolve failures* (Berry & Parasuraman, 1991). First, the provider must prepare employees for recovery efforts. The best way to do this is to assign responsibility for problem resolution to each and every employee. This is known as "owning the problem," and it is critical to problem resolution. All clients want action once they have complained. They are unimpressed when staff members must ask permission from a supervisor before they can help or when staff send them to another department for assistance. For the provider, the key is to ensure that all staff members are both authorized and encouraged to take the appropriate actions to please the client. Problem ownership is a powerful concept that guides and directs all staff members once a complaint has been received. It suggests that everyone is responsible for making the client happy. The individual who receives the complaint automatically becomes responsible for ensuring that complaint is addressed.

A friend recently visited Disney World in Florida with her young family. While riding on one of the small trains that transport guests within and between the parks, her daughter lost a new hat they had just purchased on site. The little girl was understandably upset, so after leaving the train they stopped at the first shop they encountered to inquire about the possibility of retrieving the hat. This was not the location at which they had purchased the hat, but they were desperately looking for solutions to comfort their now sobbing child. The staff member affirmed their worst fears, noting that it was unlikely that they would ever find the hat, but without hesitation pulled an identical hat from a shelf in the store, placed it on the little girl's head and said simply, "Have a Disney Day." It was in the staff member's power to solve the problem, and she did so without hesitation. This is a great example of owning the problem.

The true genius in this small but significant act was the slogan used when giving the hat to the little girl. The phrase "Have a Disney Day" combined an act of kindness with the name Disney. It used the name synonymously with superlatives like "great" (Have a great day) or positive affect (Have a happy day). This proved to be a powerful and positive combination that the whole family raved about upon their return. An unhappy situation was resolved by the staff member's willingness to own the problem.

In some situations, staff members may be asked to "own a problem" while they lack both the expertise or resources to remedy the situation. For example, if a client complains to a program leader about registration procedures, the leader may be tempted to send the complainant to the department that handles registration. That department may, in turn, be tempted to pass the individual along to the finance department, and so on. In each case, the staff member can legitimately claim no knowledge of or responsibility for the problem. While this is an understandable response from busy staff members, it tends to drive clients to distraction.

When staff members own the problem, this program leader becomes responsible for making the client happy. The leader might take the client to the correct office to have the problem rectified or may take the necessary information and promise to call the client later in the day with an update. The leader may also provide a coupon for a free drink at the facility's coffee shop, or even one operated next door by a private sector provider, and suggest that the client "have a coffee on us then come back in 20 minutes. The problem should be solved by then." Whatever the strategy used, clients are comforted knowing that the staff member they trusted with their original complaint will help them through the process of resolving the problem.

Staff preparation also requires a relevant reward structure. Providers must reduce the fear and drudgery associated with problem resolution. Staff will, with considerable justification, fear that problems will be blamed on them. As a result, they may be hesitant to acknowledge errors because they fear reprisal from managers. Nothing discourages open conversation quite like fear. If staff are to be involved, it must be made clear that problem resolution is actually a great service to the group and should be treated as such.

One way to increase willingness to resolve failures is to distribute corporate dollars to staff when they handle complaints satisfactorily. These rewards may also be distributed when managers receive positive comments about individual staff members. These dollars can be turned in for rewards like concert tickets, placed in drawings for monthly prizes, and so on. Any reward program, whether for employees or clients, must show genuine support for initiatives that improve service and problem resolution.

Staff must also have access to all the tools required to facilitate problem resolution. For example, staff members often require considerable flexibility to recover from errors. They may have to gain immediate access to information or change computerized records in order to solve the problem. Do policies, procedures, and existing systems make this possible? Must they gain the approval of some third party, such as a manager or supervisor, or are they empowered to solve the problem on their own? If they must look elsewhere for solutions, they cannot own the problem or create the necessary solutions.

Establish Recovery Procedures

The next step is that of establishing *recovery procedures* that will address the needs of both the client and the provider (Berry & Parasuraman, 1991). These procedures must provide (a) the opportunity for the client to express his views, and (b) the opportunity for the client to alter the outcome of the encounter. In other words, providers must be willing to respond to clients' concerns with meaningful action. This response begins with a simple acknowledgment.

An acknowledgment that the client is unhappy—When complaints are received, many providers' first impulse is to deny the problem. They might indicate that "this is the first complaint we've had" or "no one else has complained." This type of response suggests that the client is in error or the problem is an anomaly. While such suggestions are intended to minimize the provider's culpability, they simply fuel the dissatisfaction that already exists.

A far better response is to acknowledge that the participant is unhappy. An immediate acknowledgment of this dissatisfaction is an essential first step in service recovery (Bell & Zemke, 1987). Staff explanations may be necessary at his stage (Bitner, 1990), but what clients want most is for staff to listen. They desire *procedural fairness*. Procedural fairness exists when the unhappy client is given the opportunity to vent or give voice. Clients want the opportunity to express their concerns and feelings and present relevant information to a responsive decision maker.

Staff must be made aware that clients may wish to tell them about what happened. The clients hope to explain, to complain, and to give their side of the story. To ignore this need is to further victimize the client. They wish the provider to know that they are unhappy. Efforts to deny that this is the case or to minimize the situation will simply exacerbate the problem.

An apology—Like anyone who feels someone has failed them or that they have been wronged, unhappy clients often wish to hear a sincere apology. This apology need not admit wrongdoing. For example, providers need not admit that they have erred. They need not indicate that their policies are flawed, their personnel inattentive, or their facilities unsafe. This apology is not about accepting blame. Instead, it is an acknowledgment that the encounter has failed at some point, and that the provider is sorry for that failure. Staff need simply indicate they are sorry that the individual is unhappy. The individual came to the provider to be happy, to be satisfied, and this did not occur. For this the provider can apologize.

Prompt problem resolution—The client then seeks *interactional fairness*. This fairness is assessed according to the provider's response to clients' concerns. Does the provider take steps to remedy the situation? Immediate remedial action is considered another key to service recovery (Hart, Heskett, & Sasser, 1990). As Bell and Zemke (1987) suggest, "The customer must perceive that the provider is doing the absolute best possible job to get things back to the status quo" (p. 34). Zeithaml, Parasuraman, and Berry (1990) have termed such action as "responsiveness" and consider it a major determinant of service quality.

At this stage, the provider must be seen to want to help. Grudging assistance is not what is being called for in this situation. Efforts to quote policy or to agree to make an exception "just this once" are not helpful. They suggest a hesitation to respond. They suggest that policy seems more important than the concerns of the client. They suggest that on another day or with another staff member, this assistance may not be forthcoming. These are not the kinds of signals that providers send out when they hope to recover from service failures.

Clients hope that, by complaining, they will receive prompt problem resolution. Providers should ensure that staff are empowered to resolve problems presented to them. Many service providers provide their staff with resources they think might be needed to handle any eventuality. Private sector providers, primarily in the hospitality sector, now provide staff with a "virtual" petty cash account,

ranging from $300 to $1,500 to pay for incidental costs that might arise from their own problem resolution efforts. One hotel promotes the story of a client who called the hotel from the airport indicating that he had left his briefcase in his room. He reported that he would miss his flight if he returned to the hotel to retrieve it. Without hesitation, a staff member told the worried client that he would place the briefcase in a cab and send it to him at the airport. The staff member was comforted in knowing that the hotel would reimburse him for the full amount of the fare, so he did not hesitate to offer this option as a solution. He was encouraged to be responsive and given the resources to be just that.

Symbolic atonement—All these actions indicate to the client that the provider is empathetic to the problem. They indicate that the provider is anxious to resolve the failure to the benefit of the client. These actions are necessary but not sufficient to resolve a problem, however. Goodwin and Ross (1992) found, for example, that problem resolution without some type of token reward for the client may be considered as insincere. Bell and Zemke (1987) refer to this reward as "symbolic atonement."

Symbolic atonement represents a tangible sign of provider contrition; it is the organization's way of saying "We're sorry you're unhappy and would like to make it right." Remember that unhappy clients often feel victimized and may be seeking "reparation" (Goodwin & Ross, 1992). There are many ways to provide symbolic atonement, ranging from discounts and coupons to free upgrades. One popular means is the discount card distributed by staff members. Any staff member can provide an unhappy client with this simple card that offers a discount on their next purchase or registration. Many leisure providers now have staff members carry coupons that authorize a free swim or a free coffee that can be used as symbolic atonement.

Follow-up—One of the most obvious ways to deal with service failures is to avoid them. There is simply no substitute for reliable service delivery. Recall that reliability refers to providing the promised service consistently (Zeithaml, Parasuraman, & Berry, 1990). Reliable delivery reduces the need for service recovery, because it minimizes gaps between expected and actual service levels. It is best not to make errors. Fewer errors lead to fewer failures, and problems are thereby avoided.

Reliable delivery also requires that efforts be made to avoid mistakes the second time (Berry, 1995). This requires *follow-up* activity. Follow-up has two distinct stages. The first is the process of discovering why the failure occurred. Were staffing levels too low to serve the volume of participants at that point in time? Did staff members fail to pass along crucial information? Did the program fail to meet the expectations established by agency advertisements and promotions? Problem identification is critical to ensuring that failures do not recur. For this reason, many delivery systems track information suggesting that errors have occurred. They track how many participants have withdrawn from programs, how many products were returned, and how many complaints were made. Using this information, marketers can trace the source of errors or dissatisfaction and ensure the problem is dealt with before it recurs.

The second stage in the follow-up process is one of ensuring that the failure does not happen a second time. Once the reasons for the failure is identified, steps can be taken to ensure that it does not occur again. Failures teach valuable lessons, and these insights are lost if the provider ignores the lesson. It is perhaps forgivable that a mistake happens once, but not if the same error occurs repeatedly. This exercise is one that requires the involvement of all staff members. Front line staff members, in particular, can be very helpful in identifying problems as they occur.

Many leisure providers now monitor the types of solutions that staff members are developing on their own initiative. Weekly staff meetings might include agenda items on problems and solutions. They ask, "What problems have arisen, and what have we done both to solve them and to avoid them in future?" Tracking these patterns indicate the types of errors and the cost of addressing them, as well as the solutions that seem to work best.

Client Involvement in Service Recovery

Service recovery efforts can be labor intensive. Such efforts typically break the regular routine in the workplace and may draw considerable resources from that routine. For example, Heskett, Sasser, and Hart (1990) describe an admirable example of service recovery organized by Club Med personnel. It seems that a charter flight bringing guests to a Club Med resort had suffered from a long series of delays and considerable turbulence. Upon arrival, the irate and shaken guests were treated to "a special greeting." Half the resort staff arrived at the airport "where they personally greeted each person, helped with their bags, listened sympathetically to their tales, and drove them to the Club Med Village . . . the other half of the staff had prepared a lavish welcoming banquet, complete with a mariachi band and champagne" (Heskett et al., p. 101).

Though this story speaks highly of the resort's efforts to recover from that unfortunate flight, it also suggests the tremendous strain that service recovery may place on a provider's resources. When resources are already strained, service recovery efforts may suffer. Further, many service failures occur when staff are least able to devote the extra time needed to recover effectively. Indeed, it is often the lack of available staff that results in customer irritation (Lovelock, 1992). As a result, many providers now look to their clients to assist with service recovery efforts. Such a measure is intuitively appealing. It is likely that the client is motivated to resolve the problem and is best able to determine when her expectations have been fulfilled.

It is also likely, however, that many clients will be hesitant to take an active role in service recovery efforts. Role theory suggests that partners in an exchange are bound by the demands of the roles each believes he or she is playing (Czepiel, 1990). For example, clients able to resolve a problem may hesitate from doing so, because such an act would violate role expectations imposed on them in that service context (Solomon, Surprenant, Czepiel, & Gutman, 1985). They may be unwilling to adopt the problem-solving role traditionally assigned to the service provider. They might be willing to make their own bed at home but resist doing so while on vacation. Such *role expectations* may hamper service providers' attempts to involve the client in service recovery. Such involvement is a worthwhile goal, however. Active problem solving on the part of the client may reduce the disruption associated with recovery efforts while simultaneously diminishing client irritation.

Involving clients in recovery efforts should be undertaken with care and only once basic requirements are met. First and foremost, it should be an option of last resort. As noted above, clients expect to be served by staff, and this expectation is greatest after errors have occurred. There is no substitute for knowledgeable, responsive staff members. Second, the context of the failure must be considered. Once the provider has decided to involve the client in service recovery, there must exist a clear call for action. The problem must be clearly defined and the solution must be equally obvious. Subtle or complex issues may not lend themselves to self-help solutions. Third, the client must be provided with the knowledge needed to undertake recovery efforts. Important phone numbers, the location of on-duty staff, or even instruction on the use of basic equipment might be provided to aid clients in their efforts.

Clients should be offered considerable latitude when addressing their own problems. If towels are missing from their locker area in a leisure facility, they might be invited to visit the desk and "pick up as many towels as they require." Such open-ended instructions offer dual benefits. First, they suggest the provider's faith in the client as a competent and trusted partner during the recovery process. Second, they empower those most affected by the failure to determine when the failure has been resolved (Lashley, 1997).

An additional discount may be needed to encourage clients to accept the role of problem solver. Several years ago, Christina Colenutt and the author conducted an experiment to discover if clients could be encouraged to help solve service failures and to discover those conditions under which they were most willing to do so. In the experiment,

we monitored hotel guests' response to hypothetical scenarios. Each scenario suggested that a service failure had occurred—they had checked in to a hotel but found that towels had not yet been delivered to their room (Colenutt & McCarville, 1994). The scenarios asked subjects to resolve the resulting problem through their own actions.

Guests asked to undertake this self-help solution seemed willing to do so but only when they were offered a discount in return for their inconvenience. Subjects who received a 30 percent discount message—management would deduct 30 percent from their bill (an example of symbolic atonement) if they were willing to come to the front desk to pick up their own towels, reported the greatest satisfaction among the treatment groups. These clients were uniformly positive in their assessment of this hypothetical hotel stay even though they were asked to "solve" a problem created by hotel staff. Those who received the offer of the 30 percent discount were unlikely to avoid the hotel in future or to engage in negative word-of-mouth communication regarding their experience.

Main Points

· Service errors or failures occur when clients are unhappy with some aspect of service provision.

· Although service failures are best avoided, they are sometimes inevitable; staff in the front lines of service delivery must be empowered to solve problems as they occur.

· While unsuccessful encounters can result in lost clientele, successful resolution of failures can actually enhance clients' loyalty to the provider.

· Unhappy clients strive to understand why errors have occurred. They will feel victimized if their concerns are not dealt with quickly.

· The resolution of problems often begins with client complaints. The few who do complain aid the provider by (a) identifying problems, and (b) speaking for the vast majority of unhappy clients who do not complain. As a result, all complaints should be treated as gifts to the provider.

· The responsibility for solving problems, called "service recovery," is best assumed by staff members who first receive a complaint. This is called "owning the problem."

· Recovery efforts should (1) acknowledge the client is unhappy, (2) offer an apology, (3) provide prompt resolution,(4) offer a token of apology (called "symbolic atonement"), and (5) follow up on the problem to ensure that it is not repeated.

References

Backman, S., & Crompton, J.L. (1991). Differentiating between high, spurious, latent, and low loyalty participants in two leisure activities. *Journal of Park and Recreation Administration*, 9(2), 1-17.

Bearden, W.O., & Oliver, R.L. (1985). The role of public and private complaining in satisfaction with problem resolution. *The Journal of Consumer Affairs*, 19(2). 222-240.

Bell, C.R., & Zemke, R.E. (1987, October). Service breakdown: The road to recovery. *Management Review*, 32-35.

Berry, L. (1995). *On great service*. New York: The Free Press

Berry, L., & Parasuraman, A. (1991). *Marketing services: Competing through quality*. New York: The Free Press.

Bitner, M.J. (1990). Evaluating service encounters: The effects of physical surroundings and employee responses. *Journal of Marketing*, 54, 69-82.

Buchanan, T. (1985). Commitment and leisure behavior: A theoretical perspective. *Leisure Sciences*, 7(4), 401-420.

Chebat, J., Filiatrault, P., Gelinas-Chebat, C., & Vaninsky, A. (1995). Impact of waiting attribution and consumers' mood on perceived quality. *Journal of Business Research*, 34, 191-196.

Colenutt, C. (1997). *Selected emotional consequences of various queuing experiences*. Unpublished master's thesis, University of Waterloo, Waterloo, Ontario, Canada.

Colenutt, C., & McCarville, R. (1994). The client as problem solver: A new look at service recovery. *Journal of Hospitality and Leisure Marketing*, 2(3), 23-35.

Czepiel, J.A. (1990). Service encounters and service relationships: Implications for research. *Journal of Business Research*, 20(1), 13-22.

Folkes, V.S. (1984). Consumer reactions to product failure: An attributional approach. *Journal of Consumer Research*, 10, 398-409.

Folkes, V.S. (1988). Recent attribution research in consumer behavior: A review and new directions. *Journal of Consumer Research*, 14, 548-565.

Folkes, V.S., Koletsky, S., & Graham, J.L. (1987). A field study of causal inferences and consumer reaction: The view from the airport. *Journal of Consumer Research*, 13, 534-539.

Goodwin, C., & Ross, I. (1992). Consumer responses to service failures: Influence of procedural and interactional fairness perceptions. *Journal of Business Research*, 25, 149-163.

Hart, C., Heskett, J., & Sasser, E. (1990, July-August). The profitable art of service recovery. *Harvard Business Review*, 148-156.

Hegtvedt, K.A. (1990). The effects of relationship structure on emotional responses to inequity. *Social Psychology Quarterly*, 53(3), 214-228.

Heskett, J.L., Sasser, W.E., Jr., & Hart, C.W. (1990). *Service breakthroughs: Changing the rules of the game*. New York: The Free Press.

Hoffman, K.D., & Bateson, J.G. (1997). *Essentials of services marketing*. Forth Worth, TX: The Dryden Press.

Howat, G., Murray, D., & Crilley, G. (1999). The relationships between service problems and perceptions of service quality, satisfaction, and behavioral intentions of Australian public sports and leisure center customers. *Journal of Park and Recreation Administration*, 17(2), 42-64.

Kotler, P. (1999). *Kotler on marketing*. New York: The Free Press.

Lashley, C. (1997). *Empowering service excellence*. London: Cassell.

Levitt, T. (1983). The *marketing imagination*. New York: The Free Press.

Lovelock, C.H. (1992). *Managing services: Marketing, operations, and human resources* (2nd ed.). Toronto: Prentice-Hall.

Markovsky, B. (1988). Anchoring justice. *Social Psychology Quarterly*, 51(3), 223-235.

Oliver, R. (1980). A cognitive model of the antecedents and consequences of satisfaction decisions. *Journal of Marketing Research*, 17, 460-469.

Reichheld, F. (1996). *The loyalty effect: The hidden force behind growth, profits, and lasting value.* Boston: Harvard Business School Press.

Sewell, C., & Brown, P. (1998). *Customers for life.* Toronto: Pocket Books.

Solomon, M.R., Surprenant, C.F., Czepiel, J.A., & Gutman, E.G. (1985). A role theory perspective on dyadic interactions: The service encounter. *Journal of Marketing*, 49, 99-111.

Taylor, S. (1994). Waiting for service: The relationship between delays and evaluations of service. *Journal of Marketing*, 58, 56-69.

Weiner, B. (1979). A theory of motivation for some classroom experiences. *Journal of Educational Psychology*, 71, 3-25.

Zeithaml, V.A., Parasuraman, A., & Berry, L. (1990). *Delivering quality service: Balancing customer perceptions and expectations.* New York: The Free Press.

S. Czekus

CHAPTER

14

Understand the Client/ Marketplace through Research

The marketer cannot succeed without a profound grasp of the client's wants, needs, and preferences. The client exists at the center of the marketer's professional world. It is for the client that resources are mobilized, that solutions are sought. As a result, much of what we consider successful marketing arises from a firm understanding of the client. This understanding is typically gathered through marketing research.

The Role of Marketing Research

Relevant and timely information is a prerequisite for all marketing action. As in life, it is best to gather necessary information before making decisions. Market research is the process through which marketers collect and assemble the information needed to understand the marketplace. Specifically, marketing research:

links the customer and the public to the marketer through information— information used to identify and define marketing opportunities and problems; generate, refine, and evaluate marketing actions; monitor marketing performance; and improve understanding of marketing as a process. (Bennett, 1988, p. 114)

Although marketing research can be devoted to gathering information on everything, including economic and political trends and even competitors, the vast majority of marketing research is devoted to understanding client groups. Generally, this research is undertaken before or after the client consumes a service. Data collected beforehand helps the marketer plan programs, develop communications, and offer prices to suit the preferences of that client. Data collected after the fact helps judge the success of these programs, communications and prices. Whatever the timing of the data collection, it is considered an element of marketing research.

Marketing Research Basics

Research has three basic purposes (Babbie, 1982). The first is that of *exploration*. Exploration is the process of discovering new areas of study, gathering insights into emerging areas of interest. One perhaps obvious example of exploratory marketing research is that which investigates shopping on the World Wide Web. There are tremendous resources being devoted to creating organizational web sites and monitoring activity at those sites. Virtually all leisure providers now have their own Web sites, but they are unsure how to optimize their use. For example, site creators want some parts of the site to be "sticky," in that they want shoppers to linger in these areas. Sticky areas highlight programs and services. Conversely, they hope to render other parts of their sites "slippery." A help section on a Web page is an example of a slippery section. Site creators want users to spend as little time as possible in these sites and to move users into more sticky areas. Little research exists on what renders a section sticky or slippery, yet these are issues that are important to virtually all marketers. It is an area ready for exploration.

The second purpose of marketing research is that of *description*. Description is the process of providing snapshots of conditions or populations. A large proportion of marketing research undertaken by leisure providers might be classified as descriptive research. Surveys that attempt to establish community views, user preferences, or participation patterns are all descriptive in nature. These types of studies are the stock and trade of research firms, ranging from pollsters to focus group specialists. They help providers measure the pulse of their respective communities.

One example of descriptive research is the ongoing effort to gather community views on fees for public leisure services. Public leisure providers have been anxious to gather this type of information for the last three decades, and this trend is intensifying. They are introducing new fees at unprecedented rates, often where none had existed in the past. As a result, they have been concerned with negative public reaction to the initiatives. They conduct research to discover who is opposed or not opposed to fees. They hope to determine under what conditions fees are acceptable and when they are generally condemned. In order to answer these questions, virtually hundreds of surveys have been conducted over the years. All have been intended to discover the level

and degree of community support for fee programs.

The third purpose of research is that of *explanation*. Explanation moves beyond simple description by focusing on the reasons behind trends. While descriptive research attempts to determine what "is," explanatory research is more interested in establishing "why." This is considered a step beyond simple explanation, because it probes deeper into the phenomenon being studied. For example, a leisure provider may discover that a portion of the community supports fees for childrens' programs. This finding establishes the extent of the support but not the reasons for that support. Why do community members support, or fail to support, such fees? Are there conditions present that might influence response patterns? These are the types of questions that require explanatory research.

Explanatory research typically examines relationships between variables, the strength of these relationships, and even the direction of the relationships (Babbie, 1982). The strength of a relationship establishes the extent of the influence one variable has over another. In the fee example above, researchers might find that the presence of young children in the household may determine the degree of support for fee-based children's programs. In this case, the strength of the relationship is likely very strong. This suggests that marketing efforts are unlikely to shift the existing preference patterns. Marketers might be advised to simply plan with the relationship in mind. Research might also establish the direction of this influence. In this case, direction indicates whether this influence is positive or negative. Researchers may find that the presence of children reduces support for fees, while the absence of children increases this support. A household with children may tend to register for more public recreation programs than does a household with no children. As a result, it is in the best interests of the household with children to support free programs. They simply have more to lose if fees are instituted. This type of research establishes not only that a clear pattern exists, but also why and where it exists. Programs and strategies can be planned accordingly.

Research Applications

There are many marketing applications to which research might be devoted. All focus on understanding the marketplace. Any marketplace is made up of other providers, potential participants, and existing participants.

Competitive Intelligence: Research on Other Providers

Research is often used to collect competitive intelligence. This information is used by decision makers as they decide how to position their offerings in terms of their relative strengths within the larger marketplace. Providers are always interested in their ability to offer services relative to other providers in their area. It makes little sense to offer an inferior service to the same people who are currently enjoying a superior product from competitors. Not only is this a waste of resources (even the most devoted clients will abandon inferior programs), but it also deprives your own participants of the benefits offered by the competitor's superior program.

In the past, public leisure agencies have collected only the most rudimentary competitive intelligence. This intelligence was primarily focused on program ideas or successful administrative practices. For example, it is common for leisure providers to watch others develop programs and practices, then adopt the most successful among them. It is also common for providers to use competitive intelligence to determine the price levels charged by other providers and judge their own price levels accordingly. This information may be gathered by staff or brought to light by the complaints or comments of clients who have been making price comparisons. All these practices are often informal in nature. Few leisure providers undertake formal data-collection strategies that monitor and respond to competitive forces.

This trend is likely to change, because two emerging conditions are altering the traditional status quo. The first is the growth of private sector leisure providers. The private sector has recognized the profit potential of leisure delivery and is increasingly involved in areas that were once the exclusive domain of the public sector. Second, fee levels for public service leisure programs are rising. As public sector agencies begin to rely on fees for more and more income, it seems likely that many clients will soon begin to compare public providers to their private sector counterparts. When this occurs, it will be necessary for both sectors to collect more competitive intelligence from the other.

Market Surveys: Research on the General Population

A variety of market surveys are constantly being conducted to (1) determine a general product use patterns and (2) the extent and effectiveness of media exposure (Blankenship & Breen, 1993). As noted earlier, these surveys are typically conducted by private sector firms who are willing to sell the information they gather. These firms (e.g., Print Measurement Bureau in Canada or Simmons Market Research Bureau in the U.S.) ask sometimes thousands of members of the general public about how they spend their time, their money, and their resources. They gather information on a wide range of activities, from use of media and consumer products to general lifestyle and family participation/shopping patterns. This material, combined with demographic information, can offer surprisingly detailed insight into the lifestyle pursued by a state or province, a region, or even a nation.

These data sources are particularly useful for tracking patterns over time or comparing trends from one region to the next. They track everything from the number of new automobiles bought and sold in a given area to leisure trends among the general population. Barber and Havitz (2001) used data from the Simmons organization to monitor leisure participation trends over the past decade. They found that, within their study area (Canada), participation rates in active sports were gradually declining over time. In particular, the number of "avid" participants was declining in many sports. This type of information can be very useful to marketers in national sport-governing bodies, federal agencies or even local park and recreation departments hoping to gain insight regarding large scale trends.

Program Use/Participation Patterns: Research on Users

Leisure marketers devote a great deal of effort to determining participation levels within their communities. Unlike general surveys, these efforts are typically single purpose efforts. They are concerned with leisure activities of an isolated group or community. These numbers are used to judge progress, to separate success from failure, to justify continuation or cancellation. Trends and patterns are particularly important when evaluating program use. First and foremost, trends in participation patterns help gauge demand, thereby guiding ongoing programming decisions. Popular programs, for example, receive more resources because of their apparent success and often proliferate because of their appeal.

Second, the perceptive marketer will also use trend-based data to measure the success or failure of specific marketing efforts. For example, participation patterns may be monitored in terms of specific promotional measures. Typically these measures revolve around promotional initiatives like the distribution of value coupons or of advertising blitzes. In the context of coupons, research might be undertaken to establish if participation rates changed with the distribution of these coupons. If so, who used them? Did the intended user group take advantage of the coupons? Did more people take part as a result of the coupons or did the same users simply come out more often?

This general approach can be used to monitor the results of any basic marketing initiative. Are participation rates reduced with the introduction of fees? If so, is this pattern widespread or more pronounced among different user groups? Does interest in programs increase with the distribution of seasonal brochures? If yes, then what is the nature of the increased interest? Are staff receiving more calls of inquiry? Are these calls being converted into new clients?

Client Profiling: Describing Clients

One of the marketer's greatest ongoing challenges is that of understanding the client. One of the first steps to understanding clients is that of describing them. What do they value? What are their attitudes toward relevant ideas, people, or things? What kinds of activities characterize their lifestyle? Marketers often use marketing research to *profile* their consumers in terms of their responses to these very important questions. By doing so, market researchers hope to understand clients' hopes and dreams, preferences and priorities, intentions and ambitions. Once created, these profiles can be used to plan programs, to design communications strategies, and to establish organizational priorities.

A wide variety of descriptors are used to create client profiles. These profiles typically include basic sociodemographic data like age grouping, sex, income, and education. It is also likely that they will include more ambiguous variables like motives and values. Finally, client profiles often include lifestyle elements, like participation patterns or activity levels. Taken together, these elements can present compelling profiles of target group members. They may describe a client in terms that virtually bring the client to life for program planners. These planners can then offer programs and services with this profile type in mind.

Think for a moment of the ways a group profile could be used by a leisure marketer. Perhaps this marketer is interested in encouraging physical activity among a sedentary client group. The marketer may find that group members have positive attitudes toward physical activity, suggesting that communications need not be devoted to convincing group members of its value, but they seem unable to integrate regular activity into their daily patterns. Perhaps the group is comprised of busy young professionals who feel they lack the time necessary to take part in physical activities.

The details provided by this basic profile suggest both the problem and the solution. Group members are motivated to change their lifestyle, but feel they lack the time to do so.

Programmers could then focus on convenience when planning for this group. Early morning sessions could be scheduled, so that the truly motivated could take part before going to work in the morning. Lunch-hour running groups and swim programs could be created. The emphasis would be on creating opportunities within the traditional workday. Advertising copy, distributed through workplaces where group members are employed, could then focus on the convenience of these sessions.

Though these profiles typically describe groups, technology is now making possible the development of profiles, even at the level of the individual consumer. Many providers are now experimenting with "smart cards" that track their users' activity patterns. The card is swiped as clients enter and leave a facility so that marketers can track their use patterns. This information, tied to the individual's own sociodemographic information, helps the marketer understand an individual participant's participation patterns.

Facility managers may find that older adults tend to use facilities at one time of day, while young families attend at another. They may find that young males focus on one set of resources while females another. This informa-tion could assist with everything from staff scheduling to maintenance planning.

Many marketers now use this very personal information to develop and maintain long-term relationships with valued clients. Staff might monitor participation patterns and actually contact clients whose participation has dropped off to discover if anything is wrong. While some users consider such attention intrusive, others are pleased with this level of personal attention.

Program Evaluation: Describing Outcomes

Several types of failures or "service gaps" reduce client satisfaction with services (Zeithaml, Parasuraman, & Berry, 1990). These gaps result from differences between the clients' preferences and the agency's programs. They are created by management's misperceptions of client preferences, faulty performance standards, poor staff performance, or inaccurate communication with clients. Program evaluation research often tries to identify and fill these gaps by focusing on improving existing service levels.

Generally, five sources of data are available for evaluative purposes. (See Figure

	Clients	Staff	Confederates	Other Providers	Enternal System
Excellent Source for...	-Problem Identification -Evaluating Solutions	-Generating and Implementing Solutions	-Identification of Service Gaps	-Identification of Leaders' Standards and Procedures	-Problem Identification -Evaluating Trends -Evaluating Solutions
Appropriate Data-Collection Procedures	-Surveys -Focus Groups -Ongoing Contact	-Regular Meetings -Suggestion Procedures	-Formal Comparisons of Service to Standard	-Surveys -Formal and Informal Contact	-Budget -Reprints

Figure 14.1: Sources of Information

14.1) Each offers its own distinctive contribution to program evaluation and its own challenge in terms of data collection. Not surprisingly, the first source is the actual *client*. Clients are the best source for information on the success of programs or their component parts. Their ideas may be collected through a variety of surveys, focus groups, or any other vehicle that solicits their views on actual or potential product offerings. Whatever the means of data collection, the focus of these efforts is typically one of determining whether or not the provider's programs meet or exceed the clients' expectations (Chakrapani, 1998).

The second source for information is that of *staff* members, specifically those who interact directly with the client. These staff members gather insights both from their own experience and from the clients they serve. Some observers believe that employees are even more important to evaluation than clients. "Each employee has information from *hundreds* of consumers, while each consumer has only his or her experiences . . . employees are a potential *marvelous* source of critical information" (Schneider, 1988, p. 357). Further, staff are able to appreciate both the clients' desires and the organization's own capacity and mandate. They can help not only identify problems but also offer meaningful solutions to those problems.

The third source is that of the provider's own agents or *confederates*, like "phantom shoppers." Phantom shoppers aid in the evaluation process by identifying gaps in service delivery. Typically, these confederates are used to evaluate staff performance. They compare the actions of staff to existing service standards. They do so by anonymously consuming selected services while evaluating staff response to their requests. They might visit programs or facilities requesting assistance in one instance, taking part in another, and requesting a refund in another. During each encounter, they measure staff response against procedures established by the organization. They then report to managers on the success or failure of these encounters. This technique is used by hundreds of retail organizations, ranging from pizza shops to retail chains.

Staff might use *other providers* to help evaluate their own service offerings. As noted above, marketers are constantly gathering competitive intelligence in order to gain insight from other providers. Recently a process known as *benchmarking* has gained considerable popularity within the service industry. Benchmarking is the process of discovering other providers' procedures and applying these procedures to improve your own delivery system. Typically, industry leaders are identified, and others seek insight from these leaders.

Sewell and Brown (1998) remind us that benchmarking efforts need not rely on leaders in a single industry for insight. A leisure agency may learn more from a retail or fast food chain than from another leisure agency. Sewell, a car dealer, offers several examples of insights he gathered from the hospitality and fast-food industries. Indeed, many of the insights offered in this text have been gathered from outside the traditional leisure literature.

Fifth and finally, *internal systems* are an invaluable source of information for improving client services. Leisure providers collect information on registration and participation patterns, drop-out rates, program costs, and even instructor ratings. All this information can be used to evaluate and alter programming practices. Planners in one agency found, for example, that participants were dropping out of programs that continued for several weeks. It seemed that they were simply unable to commit regular blocks of time to the program over extended periods. In the end, clients were missing valuable program time and were paying for time they were unable to use. Programmers decided instead to shorten the length of the program and to charge less for the reduced offering. This improvement was only possible because internal systems collected and monitored this type of information.

Forecasting/Predicting the Future: Establishing Intentions

Marketers are always interested in how potential participants will react to future initiatives. They want to know if there is sufficient interest to offer a new program, how many sessions to schedule, and how many instructors to hire. Success at making such predictions will determine the long-term success of these very programs. Marketers typically make such predictions by measuring *intent* to participate, because intentions are the building blocks of behavior.

Marketers may use several techniques in order to establish intent. First, they often conduct general surveys in order to discover trends within the community. For example, they often provide clients with a series of activity categories (e.g., sports, playground, crafts, etc.), then asked respondents to check off those categories in which they were interested in taking part. They may even ask clients to indicate their interest in specific activities like running or yoga.

Unfortunately, results gathered through these surveys rarely translate into specific, predictable participation patterns. There are simply too many variables that might intervene between this basic interest and actual behavior. For example, a respondent may indicate a strong desire to join a running club. This individual has the skills, the cardiovascular capacity, the appropriate equipment, and especially the motivation to join that club. The marketer may then arrange for the individual to join such a club, only to discover that this hopeful runner is working during the club's weekly meeting times. As a result, she may intend to participate (in this case by joining the club), but this intention may never be realized. She is simply unavailable when the club meets. This is why specificity is the key when eliciting any kind of intention. It is not enough to ask if someone is interested in a sport or a program. It is best to also outline the consumption context.

When establishing a specific context, leisure marketers often look to the constraints literature for insight. Constraints may diminish the desire to participate, reduce the benefits enjoyed through participation, or diminish the perceived opportunity to do so. It is critical, therefore, that possible sources of constraints be considered whenever intent is measured. In a relatively early study, Romsa and Hoffman (1980) considered reasons for nonparticipation in 19 outdoor recreation activities. They

reported that price, time, and lack of facilities were offered as primary barriers to participation. It would seem prudent, therefore, to include reference to all three variables when measuring intent. It seems better to ask "Would you register for a noon adult learn-to-swim program offered at the recreation center pool for $5.00 a day?" than "Are you interested in a swim class?" The better question format offers a context for participation. It notes the nature of the class (instructional) and maturity of fellow participants (adult), as well as the time, location, and cost of the classes.

The extensive amount of detail required to measure intent discourages many marketers from using surveys for that purpose. Instead, they use more intimate settings like focus groups, because focus groups bring the researcher and the client together for several hours. In the focus group setting, researchers can outline a service or program, discuss what it means for the client, then ask small groups of clients for their reaction to that offering. In this way, specificity is possible. Remember, measuring intent is actually an exercise in predicting the future. This is never a venture that offers much certainty, and it is fraught with difficulty. As a rule of thumb, try to minimize error through specificity.

Conducting Research

Asking the Question

Whatever the application, research begins with clear and precise questions. For what purpose is the information being gathered; to what end is it dedicated? This is the classic "why" that dominates deliberations over marketing research. The precision with which questions are asked often determines the quality of the answers that research can provide. As a result, researchers must be absolutely clear on what they hope to learn from research effort. For example, there is increasing interest being devoted to measuring satisfaction and service quality in leisure programs. Though both terms are often used interchangeably, they represent very different constructs. Satisfaction is the rather transient positive sensation created when positive expectations are confirmed or exceeded. Service quality is the more long-term assessment of a service or provider. Although both arise from positive expectation confirmation, quality is a more intellectual assessment than is satisfaction. Satisfaction is an emotional assessment, whereas service quality represents an intellectual judgement.

Both measures are useful, but each are very different indicators of client response. This suggests that these concepts should be measured in different ways. The more transient notion of satisfaction is probably best measured on site because it will decay rapidly once the participant has left the setting or facility. The more stable notion of service quality is a more likely candidate for traditional surveys that can be completed at home and after the fact. These may seem small issues, but they are critical to the success of any data-collection strategy. They suggest the importance of establishing "why" before the research is undertaken.

Much of the time, the answer to "why" dictates the nature of the collection process as well as the type of data being collected. Questions focusing on competitors' strategies may demand the use of secondary data like annual reports and advertising copy. Questions regarding client preferences may necessitate the collection of first-hand data through focus groups. Once the purpose of the research is clear, the associated methodology also gains clarity.

Generally, marketing research is intended to establish customer wants and preferences in terms of the provider's own offerings and those of competitors in the marketplace. As a result, most research begins with what we now call "customer-first questions" (Zangwill, 1993). These questions focus on the products' and services' abilities to meet the clients' expectations and preferences. Three such questions dominate most consumer research. They are:

1. What major problems that the customer faces does this [service] solve that no competitor solves?

2. What major benefits does this [service] provide for the customer that no competitor provides?

3. What is the customer's motivation to purchase this [service]? (Zangwill, pp. 141-142)

If these represent the dominant questions in most marketing research, how then does the marketer go about answering them? The process begins with gathering information.

Gathering Information

The term research implies the collection of information. Market researchers must answer questions about how the information is to be created, where it is to be found, and how its quality is to be assured. These methodological questions are at the heart of data collection. They establish the quality of the data, the relevance of the data, and the credibility of the data. If the data is flawed in some way, then resulting decision making is also flawed.

Once the "why" of research has been established, the marketer must decide "who" will collect the information. Who should collect the information? Who is best able to collect information that is both relevant and credible? There are no easy answers to these questions. The answers will vary with the situation in which marketers find themselves. In some instances, the marketer may lack the requisite skill to conduct the research. In others, staff may be too busy with other responsibilities to undertake research in any meaningful way. Indeed, only a handful of leisure providers in North America have hired research staff who possess both the time and expertise to devote to research. As a result, leisure marketers often look outside their own staff for research expertise. Hundreds of consulting firms are available for this purpose. These firms often specialize in collecting *primary data*. Primary data is gathered directly from the client or source. Other firms can provide *secondary data*. Secondary data originates from a source other than the ultimate client. In other words, a third party has collected the information from the client, and the marketer gathers the information from the third party.

Reliance on outside expertise can be expensive. Research firms often charge a flat fee for undertaking any given research project, then add additional charges for each question asked. They may charge several thousand dollars for each such question, then apply additional fees for anything but the most basic of analyses. These costs can add up very quickly; however, they can be well worth it. Research firms understand the importance of good research design and of asking the right question in the best possible way. They can bring experience and knowledge to a difficult and demanding task.

All three levels of government collect information that might be used by the leisure provider. Census data, collected federally, can establish large-scale trends in the larger population, ranging from income levels to family size. Provinces and states regularly collect information on regional trends as diverse as industrial development and the sale of recreational equipment like boats. Communities collect their own information, including the numbers of building permits being issued and the number of dog licenses being sold. All this secondary information can be used to help marketers understand their respective communities.

Most leisure providers use a blend of approaches to address their research needs. While they may rely on outside expertise for large or complicated research problems, they generally try to avoid this added expense. They typically rely on internal resources for small data-collection efforts or use secondary data when it is available. Each option is useful for gathering insight that can assist the leisure marketer in making ongoing programming decisions. Whatever the technique, the marketer is advised to continually consult the public to monitor the pulse of the community. While doing so, however, the marketer must keep in mind that each consultation is a request for assistance. Such requests cannot be undertaken lightly or without purpose. They represent opportunities for honest exchange and for program renewal. Every data-collection effort should lead directly to program change

and improvement. If this is not the case, the marketer must question the utility of the exercise.

Although data collection is a critical part of marketing research, it is beyond the scope of this text. The discussion in this chapter is intended only to introduce the reader to the importance of marketing research. Although several related topics are discussed here, their coverage is necessarily brief, given the space limitations of this text. The reader is directed to any number of books devoted entirely to marketing research for more information on any of these topics.

Data Management

The reader is likely familiar with the seemingly obvious truth that information brings knowledge and with knowledge comes power. Unfortunately, neither knowledge or power are inevitable once information is gathered. The sheer volume of marketing information now being gathered is staggering. It is estimated, for example, that the amount of data now available (per brand) is 150 times that available 30 years ago (Blankenship & Breen, 1993). How can reams of data be made useful? One source compared the workplace to a swiftly flowing river clogged with the flotsam and jetsam called data. Relevant insights come to the marketer in a seemingly random way, swirling past while mixed with irrelevant half-truths and outright errors (McCall & Kaplan, 1990). The trick is separating the errors from the truth, the relevant from the irrelevant.

How does the marketer separate useful data from irrelevant clutter? How does one ensure that it is available where and when it is needed? Increasingly, marketers are turning to marketing information systems (MIS) to "assemble all pertinent marketing data about a product line (or a single product)—both from external and internal sources" (Blankenship & Breen, 1993, p. 64). The intent of MIS is to assemble many bits of information so that they can be used to solve a problem or monitor ongoing marketing activities, to coordinate information so that it may be reduced from a disorganized flood to a more coherent and manageable flow (Marshall, 1996).

Comprised primarily of computerized software packages, MIS may include a variety of *external* systems that focus on clients (e.g., tracking sales and customer support efforts) or on the marketplace (e.g., competitors, rate of technological change, economic/sociopolitical environment), as well as *internal* systems that monitor costs or employee activity patterns. Although decision makers review several sets of numbers each month, a few stand out from the rest. They first monitor revenues and expenditures by each department. These are the numbers that strike fear or hope in the hearts of many administrators. All administrators deal in finite financial resources, and revenue/expenditure totals are the dominant way of keeping track of these resources.

In terms of client behavior, leisure researchers typically monitor activity levels. As suggested earlier, they watch registration levels (primarily the number of classes offered each quarter) to get a sense of interest, volume, and general participation patterns. Registration levels tell only part of the tale however. Leisure providers offer many opportunities for leisure that do not involve registration of any kind, such as community parks and natural areas. Many now use traffic counters, located at park entrances, to track activity patterns in the park. They use these numbers to help schedule maintenance programs and staff as well as to justify expenditures at these sites.

Marketers also watch for reports of satisfaction and dissatisfaction. These reports help judge the ultimate success of their efforts. In particular, they monitor program cancellation rates. Cancellations occur when insufficient numbers register for a given class or program, and they represent a double loss. For the department, they waste resources. It is a waste of time and energy to organize and advertise programs in which no one wants to participate. Canceled programs also fail the community. Resources that could be used serving eager clients are wasted on programs that for some reason fail to appeal to users. MIS help bring these many pieces of information together both to make the information available and to help make sense of the information once it is collected.

Main Points

- Marketers conduct research in order to find links amongst the community, target groups, and the leisure provider.

- Marketing research may seek to explore, describe, or explain phenomena in the marketplace.

- Research may focus on other providers, the general public, or be confined to client groups. Research on client groups often considers their participation patterns, satisfaction levels, and future intentions.

- There are several sources of research information, ranging from those which are external (clients and other providers) to those which are internal (reports and staff) to the organization.

- Research begins with asking timely and relevant questions. Most marketing research focuses on customer first questions dealing with problems, benefits sought, and motives.

- Client information may be gathered directly from the client (primary data) or from others who have already collected the information (secondary data).

- Data management is becoming increasingly important as technology makes possible the collection of increasing amounts and types of research data.

References

Babbie, E.R. (1982). *Social research for consumers*. Belmont, CA: Wadsworth Publishing Company.

Barber, N., & Havitz, M.E. (2001). Canadian participation rates in ten sport and recreation activities. *Journal of Sport Management*, 15(1), 51-76.

Bennett, P. (1988). *Dictionary of marketing terms*. Chicago: American Marketing Association.

Blankenship, A.B., & Breen, G.E. (1993). *State of the art marketing research*. Lincolnwood: NTC Business Books.

Chakrapani, C. (1998*). How to measure service quality and customer satisfaction*. Chicago: American Marketing Association.

Marshall, K.P. (1996). *Marketing information systems*. Scarborough, ON: Nelson Canada.

McCall, M., & Kaplan, R. (1990). *Whatever it takes: The realities of managerial decision making*. Englewood Cliffs, NJ: Prentice-Hall.

Romsa, G., & Hoffman, W. (1980). An application of nonparticipation data in recreation research: Testing the opportunity theory. *Journal of Leisure Research*, 12(4), 321-328.

Schneider, B. (1988). Notes on climate and culture. In C.H. Lovelock (Ed.), *Managing services: Marketing, operations, and human resources* (2nd ed.) (pp. 352-358). Toronto: Prentice-Hall.

Sewell, C., & Brown, P. (1998). *Customers for life*. Toronto: Pocket Books.

Weiss, C.H. (1972). *Evaluation research: Methods of assessing program effectiveness*. Toronto: Prentice-Hall Inc.

Zangwill, W.I. (1993). *Lightening strategies for innovation: How the world's best firms create new products*. Toronto: Maxwell Macmillan Canada.

Zeithmal, V.A., Berry, L., & Parasuraman, A. (1988). Communication and control Processes in the delivery of service quality. *Journal of Marketing*, 52, 35-48.

S. Czekus

CHAPTER

15

Encourage Continuous Improvement

Leisure marketers are faced with a daunting task. They must constantly improve the services they offer or fall behind in the marketplace. This is due to the dynamic nature of expectations. In order to satisfy their clients, marketers must meet or exceed clients' own positive expectations. When clients' positive expectations are confirmed, these clients are thought to be satisfied. If their positive service expectations are exceeded, they move beyond satisfaction into the realm of delight. To delight the client is the goal of every marketer.

However, there is a certain perversity in the process of positive expectations confirmation. It seems that as expectations are exceeded, clients begin to elevate the expectations they bring to the service encounter. Service that once exceeded expectations will only meet expectations the next time the client is served. A service level that is perceived as superb during one encounter may be viewed as quite ordinary during the next. As a result, the marketer must continually improve service offerings. To remain the same is, in effect, to fall behind. Consequently, continuous improvement lies at the heart of all successful marketing effort.

Expectations may even be elevated by experiences with other seemingly unrelated service providers. Improved services at grocery stores may lead clients to expect improved services from leisure providers. As these stores remain open for longer periods, customers may come to expect leisure providers to increase the duration of their open hours. Improved services at banks, like automated teller machines, may lead clients to expect leisure providers to install 24-hour registration kiosks.

No leisure provider can avoid the challenge of elevated expectations. Advertising by a myriad of service providers assures consumers that they can gain instant access to the information they require and to the resources they demand. Expectations may rise exponentially as these promises are trumpeted from every television and radio. Given these conditions, no provider can plan to provide the same service year after year and hope to please clients. Maintaining client interest requires constant improvement. Mandatory change has become an organizational priority in virtually every organization.

The need for continuous improvement also arises from the complexity of service delivery. Services are intended to solve problems faced by clients. These problems are themselves becoming ever more complex. Clients must juggle their own personal schedules and those of friends, family members, and employers in order to enjoy leisure opportunities. The challenges posed by timetables, distance, and cost must all be negotiated before participation is possible. The challenge for the leisure provider is to render these negotiations effortless for the client. The provider must anticipate the desires of these many clients, must understand the circumstances in which clients find themselves each day, and must respond to the dynamic nature of these demands.

The challenge for the leisure provider is to create and maintain a delivery system that can respond to these demands. The key to a responsive system seems to be a responsive work force. Members of a responsive work force are willing and able to change ordinary, everyday procedures to accommodate client requests. Such flexibility is often called *organizational citizenship behavior* (OCB). Organizational citizenship behavior represents employees' willingness to deal with unexpected contingencies in their dealings with clients or fellow staff members (Podsakoff & MacKenzie, 1997). Staff are given (and accept) the latitude needed to make thousands of small daily changes to the status quo.

A responsive workforce means willingness to disrupt daily work patterns in order to improve service levels. This willingness is the stock and trade of successful marketing effort. Staff members must be willing and able to pursue the client's own particular agenda if they intend to please that client. Staff members may be asked to respond to varied and often demanding requests, so this pursuit often requires considerable flexibility.

Improvement Requires Change

Ongoing improvement requires organizational willingness to adapt or change. Change may be evolutionary or revolutionary. *Evolutionary* change is made up of many rather small but important changes in the ways things get done. No one evolutionary change is particularly important on its own. These changes tend to be nonthreatening, because they rarely challenge the status quo. However,

the cumulative effect of many such changes can be dramatic. For example, programmers are continually adjusting their registration procedures or program offerings in order to respond to client demand. Though the effect of each successive change is minimal, many years of continual tinkering can dramatically change a provider's offering.

Revolutionary changes are more profound, both in their intent and in their impact. Revolutionary changes are typically efforts of last resort. Often a result of desperation, they require dramatic changes in the way in which the organization does business. They are sweeping in their scope and often attack the very heart of a delivery system. For example, leisure providers occasionally find their traditional programming methods to be inadequate. While some believe that programs have become too expensive to operate and others contend that traditional programs may fail to reach deserving client groups, several have attempted to abandon traditional programming efforts. A few have begun to contract services to private sector operations. Others have assigned programming responsibilities to volunteer community groups. Both options may require revolutionary change within the organization. Old ways of accomplishing tasks are abandoned and new methods are sought. It can be a time of great angst for all concerned because of resulting uncertainty.

Whatever the nature of the change, whatever the extent of the change initiative, it is virtually certain that it will be resisted. Change is inherently difficult. It is rarely sought or welcomed. As Hutton (1995) indicates, "All people who are affected by change experience some emotional turmoil. Even changes that appear to be 'positive' or 'rational' involve loss and uncertainty" (p. 31). Centuries ago, Machiavelli warned that there is nothing so despised as change (Bechtell, 1993), and history seems to bear him out.

Resistance to Change

It is very difficult to accomplish change in any organization. Service providers constantly propose and even implement change initiatives, hoping to improve services, but such efforts are typically doomed from the outset. Improvement initiatives rarely succeed over time (Goodman & Dean, 1994; Tabak, 1996). Those undertaking such initiatives tend to stagger through their implementation (Grant, Shani, & Krishman, 1994) to such an extent that "most well-intended quality programs die a quiet death" (Steininger, 1994, p. 605). This seems to be the case, not because of laziness, inadequate motivation, or even poor planning. Proposed improvements fail because they represent change. "Change is neither sought after nor welcomed. It is disruptive and intrusive. It upsets the balance" (Strebel, 1996, p. 86).

Resistance to change seems one of the great barriers to service improvement and subsequent marketing success. It may result from

- resentment arising from previous change initiatives or from the belief that change indicts current methods of operation,

- perceived threat to current status,

- loss of control or routine, or

- fear about future competence and related uncertainties (Kanter, 1985).

Change initiatives typically upset the implied obligations and commitments that are reciprocated between employees and the organization. As a result, they are often doomed almost as soon as they are envisioned (Strebel, 1996).

Marketing managers hoping to institute and manage change are faced with a dilemma. How can a process that creates emotional and organizational turmoil be managed so that resistance is minimized? The key to the dilemma rests more with the manager than with staff. As O'Toole (1996) indicates, The question is not, "Why do followers resist?" but rather, "Why do leaders fail to do the things necessary to overcome their followers' natural resistance to change?" (p. xi).

Resistance to change is not only inevitable, it is also desirable. Resistance is a type of immune system that an organization develops to resist the introduction of potentially harmful forces. These forces are actively resisted until they are shown to be useful to the larger organism. Resistance is very useful because it keeps an organization "on track." For example, changes that are inconsistent with the organization's core values are most likely to fail. In keeping with the immune system analogy, rejection is most likely if the intruder does not match the organism's own priorities. Resistance also ensures that changes are not undertaken in a haphazard way. Change is a difficult process and must be planned accordingly. Potential resistance ensures that successful change initiatives receive the attention they deserve. Those who hope to create change know that "failing to plan means planning to fail."

Conditions Needed for Change

If resistance to change is inevitable, how can change ever be accomplished? The change process is enhanced by the existence of conditions within the workplace. These *antecedent conditions* help set the stage for any change initiative. If they are present, staff members are more likely to be accepting of efforts to improve service quality. If they are absent, change will be resisted. Three of the most fundamental antecedent conditions are those of (a) trust, (b) external pressure, and (c) individual readiness for change.

The Need for Trust

Change requires *trust*. In particular, staff members must trust colleagues with whom they develop and implement change initiatives. There are three organizational levels within and between which this trust must exist. First, there must be mutual trust within the work group. Work group members are those who work together on a daily basis toward the same basic goals and objectives. If group members believe that all are working toward the same group goals, then acceptance of change is more likely to exist (Mishra & Mishra, 1994). The positive work experience created by the work group seems to enhance group members' flexibility. They sense that fellow group members will help ease the hardship of change and their personal burden will be reduced as a result.

There must also be trust between staff members and their supervisors. Do the staff members believe that their supervisors will support them during the planning and implementation of any change initiative? Staff members who believe that supervisors are supportive are, in turn, more likely to support change. They know that with change, failure is always a possibility. These failures are less troublesome if direct supervisors are likely to help out rather than criticize, to compliment rather than condemn.

Finally, staff must trust upper-level decision makers and their commitment to the change initiative. Has upper-level management truly committed to this change, or is it simply the "flavor of the month" that will soon be abandoned in favor of another initiative? This seems to be a particularly pervasive concern for lower-level staff members. All too often they learn that upper-level managers have decided upon a course of action that will soon be superseded by another "great" idea. As one commentator complains,

> Quality circles, management by walking around, total quality management, and reengineering—they've succeeded one another in sometimes an overlapping and contradictory fashion. The chronically trend-battered [staff] are likely to grow apathetic, resisting the next round of change even more staunchly than the last. Says Barry Spiker, a consultant who specializes in helping companies create lasting change, "I sometimes wonder if people at the top . . . are afflicted with attention deficit disorder. They don't stay focused." (Fisher, 1995, p. 127)

Presence of External Pressure

The presence of *external pressure* may also encourage change. External pressure is a powerful source of motivation, because such pressure inevitably creates a sense of urgency, and this urgency spurs action (Kotter, 1998). Kotter relates the story of an executive who constantly engineers crises among his managers in order to minimize complacency and facilitate acceptance of change. Kotter concludes that without these crises, inertia would bring change to a halt. External pressures may result from sources as diverse as political processes, the media, or client groups dissatisfied with existing arrangements.

Readiness to Change

The issue of willingness or *readiness* to accept and manage change is at the heart of any change initiative. There are personality variables that influence staff members' readiness to accept change. As suggested in chapter 5, Rogers (1983) identified and described five adopter categories in terms of their readiness to adopt new programs or initiatives. Recall that the five categories are (1) innovators, (2) early adopters, (3) early majority, (4) late majority, and (5) laggards or late adopters. Innovators are the first to experiment with change. Their successes can encourage other groups to undertake the same change. This suggests that the key to organizational change is acceptance by an adventurous few who adopt the change when it is first proposed. This also suggests that their initial efforts must be seen as ending in success. Once others observe this success, acceptance of new initiatives is more likely. As a result, efforts to introduce new programs must be designed to create interest, acceptance, and positive word-of-mouth communication among potential adopters.

Who are the early adopters? Who are these individuals who seem willing and able to cope with the uncertainties that accompany change initiatives? Research tells us that these individuals tend to possess positive self-concepts. They feel that they will be able to handle whatever change brings. The second characteristic they share is that of risk tolerance. They are comfortable with ambiguity and are willing to change their own opinions when provided with new information (Judge, Thoresen, Pucik, & Welbourne, 1999). They tend to receive positive performance ratings from supervisors and seem very satisfied with their current jobs. These are the personality types to seek out when change is being contemplated.

Early adopters, regardless of how motivated they become or how positive their views, cannot carry a change initiative. They must be supported by the larger work force. Conditions must be created that encourage acceptance by ever increasing numbers of staff. These conditions can dramatically increase staff ability to cope with change. We now know virtually all staff members can be encouraged to undertake change if provided with adequate levels of information, rewards, and the opportunity to provide input (often called bargaining). Each of these issues will be discussed later in this chapter when the discussion turns to implementing change. At this point, it is important to note only that, though antecedent conditions set the stage for meaningful change, they are not sufficient to ensure that change will take place.

The Nature of Successful Change

The nature of the proposed change itself will enhance or impede acceptance by staff and clients alike. Innovation diffusion is a useful concept when trying to understand successful change. Diffusion of innovation was reviewed earlier in this text as it relates to acceptance of new program ideas. Recall that an innovation is an idea, behavior, or object that is perceived to be new by the adopting individual or organization (Rogers, 1983). Recall also that changes or innovations will be more acceptable if they possess a few basic characteristics.

In review, the first characteristic is that of *relative advantage*. This advantage refers to the perceived or actual superiority of an innovation compared to the status quo. Staff members must believe that the change is desirable, that it will improve conditions they face, and that it is both fair and appropriate (Welch, 2000). Participants in a change initiative ask them-

selves, "Does this change make my life easier?" If the response is positive, then acceptance of the change is more likely. If the response is negative, acceptance is unlikely. The change must be viewed as purposeful. It must move players in a direction that both helps them as individuals and the organization as a whole.

The second characteristic is that of *compatibility*. Compatibility refers to the fit between the innovation and the existing working environment. The working environment refers to organizational structure, corporate culture, and day-to-day working practices. Changes that fit nicely into existing structures are more likely to be accepted. Those that represent a departure from current operating procedures are likely to be rejected. Initiatives that alter existing systems like record-keeping and staffing policies or necessitate changes in general work patterns are particularly likely to be rejected. These activities often form the bedrock of day-to-day operations, and staff are often loath to change them.

The third characteristic is that of *complexity*. Complexity suggests the degree to which change initiatives can be readily understood by those involved in them. Complex initiatives are more difficult to understand and are, therefore, more likely to be rejected.

The issue of complexity leads directly to a fourth characteristic, that of trialability. *Trialability* represents the possibility of implementing the change on a limited basis without negative consequences. If ideas or programs are difficult to understand, if their ultimate consequences are difficult to understand, staff members may wish to adopt them gradually. In effect, they will want to "test drive" the concept before considering adoption. In this way, they can assess the program before making a long-term commitment to it, thus avoiding potentially negative, long-term consequences.

Observability refers to the visibility of the results of adoption. Are the consequences of adopting the innovation clear? Are they easy to communicate? Increased observability enhances acceptance. It makes the results, and perhaps the relative advantage of the innovation, more clear. Observability is often enhanced by the actions of role models. Staff members may wish to observe the actions of, and consequences for, those who are actively committing to the change initiative. For example, acceptance may be enhanced if staff are able to observe a test team that tries the new initiative on a limited basis. They will watch to see if participants in the test project are given adequate resources to undertake the required changes. They will note if staff members are punished when inevitable errors are made. They will monitor whether or not the consequences of the test group's actions are clear and positive. The results of these observations will help determine their acceptance or rejection of the initiative.

Overall, the ease with which change is introduced largely depends upon the nature of the suggested change and the interpersonal dynamics within and between groups asked to undertake the change. The interplay between these very basic variables will likely determine the fate of any change initiative. In terms of the change itself, any change must possess certain traits if it is to survive. The greater the relative advantage, compatibility, trialability, and observability and the less complexity an innovation offers, the faster and more extensive its adoption will be. Further, players must be willing to entertain the notion of change. This willingness is, to some extent, determined by conditions found within the organization and within the players themselves.

Implementing Change

Change is both a technical and an emotional process. It is technical in that it typically requires organizational resources, flexible systems, and extensive coordination if it is to succeed. Change is also emotional because of the natural resistance that engenders. Managers who focus on either process, but not both, may find that their efforts fail. Success is more likely if a prescribed set of steps is taken to support any change initiative (Kotter, 1998). These steps are remarkably robust in that they apply to virtually any

change effort. They are useful, whatever the size or intent of the change.

Create Need

Like most things in life, organizations tend to be ruled by *inertia*. Inertia is the tendency to repeat the same behaviors. We are all subject to inertia. We repeat behaviors that proved successful in the past. Change requires that inertia be overwhelmed. It requires that old ways be altered or abandoned. The best way to begin change is to create a reason for that change. This begins by *establishing a sense of urgency* (Kotter, 1998). Urgency generates a sense of need. It suggests that the status quo is no longer satisfactory, that a "business as usual" approach is simply inadequate and change is required.

Build a Team

The second step in creating change is that of *creating a guiding coalition* to lead the change effort. One of the best single steps managers can take seems to be the creation of a Transition Management Team (TMT) (Buck, 1998). The TMT should include members from any level of the organization affected by the proposed change. Its role is typically one of coordination. Although formal teams are usually created only for large-scale initiatives, informal teams are often created around any change initiative. Any worker who hopes to change a given procedure or improve a policy will first consult with others who might help bring the plan to fruition. An office worker who develops a more efficient way to process registration forms will likely bounce this idea off others who also handle registration. Teams, whether formal or informal, must be involved in any change initiative.

One of the TMT's first tasks is to generate organizational discussion around the change proposal. Such discussion will help identify sources of possible resistance, generate insight from a wide variety of perspectives, and provide a venue through which employees can express ideas and concerns. Buck (1998) emphasizes that it is critical that this process not be closed before these new ideas have been explored and evaluated. This process will not only create better solutions but also will generate employee support and understanding.

Encourage Communication Around the Initiative

The third step is that of creating *communication* about the initiative. Communication is a driving force behind any successful change initiative. Change requires an almost lavish use of communication. It helps the workers both understand and commit to the initiative (Buck, 1998). As reported here, change is almost inevitably unpleasant until participants have the opportunity to mold events or at least understand how upcoming changes will affect them. Open and frank communication is the only way to ensure that this takes place.

Any effort to encourage discussion around change will facilitate understanding and acceptance of that change. Communication should help focus attention and emotional energy, so it must be readily available and accurate (Berry, 1995). Unfortunately, efforts to communicate are often inadequate, and many change initiatives fail as a result. In a study of 43 organizations, Smeltzer (1991) found that the presence of inaccurate and negative rumors were the most commonly cited reason for change failures. Such rumors seem to proliferate because of "management's reliance on 'lean' channels of communications such as memos rather than using face-to-face techniques" (Richardson & Denton, 1996, p. 203).

The exchange of information is often coordinated by a *project champion*. Goodman and Dean (1994) suggest that such a champion is an essential element of any change initiative. The champion, sometimes called "sponsor" in the change literature, provides the ongoing catalyst needed to focus attention on the group vision, to communicate the need for and means of achieving change.

Enable Others

The fourth step is that of *enabling* or *empowering* others to create the change. Staff must be provided with resources they need to overcome inertia and make improvements (Buck, 1998). The TMT must have both the power and responsibility necessary to allocate resources as it sees fit. Consequently, it should be given responsibility for the change without having to constantly seek approval from upper-level managers. The TMT must also ensure that virtually all staff are given the flexibility and resources to pursue the change. Recall that marketing involves all staff members. This suggests that all must be brought into any efforts to improve services and programs.

The process of empowering has several distinct components (Goodman & Dean, 1994). Empowerment requires training, commitment, and appropriate reward structures.

Training ensures that staff are both aware of and able to complete the new work behaviors. Management should take a long-term view of training and continue to support change initiatives over the long term.

Commitment is enhanced when staff are given the opportunity to voluntarily support the new initiative. Staff members must feel that their participation is voluntary and based on their own individual workplace priorities.

Rewards must be distributed in a way that both recognizes and supports the change initiative.

Ensure Success

The fifth step in implementing change is very emotional in nature. Staff members are motivated by success, so change agents must *plan and create visible improvements*. In other words, managers must enable and publicize short-term accomplishments arising from the implementation of the change. Many leisure providers do this by circulating staff newsletters that highlight staff activities and success stories. They might focus on the work of individuals or groups, but the emphasis is always on helping the staff member understand the innovation and the positive results from implementing that innovation.

Consolidate

The sixth step is one of *consolidation*. Improvements must be consolidated by an ever-increasing improvement process. Old programs that fail to contribute to the change initiative must gradually be altered and improved. The TMT must coordinate effort around the change program. Policies, communications, and especially reward structures must be made consistent with the change initiative. Otherwise, the change becomes little more than the "solution of the month" that is quickly forgotten as the status quo grinds along unhindered.

One of the great challenges to consolidation is that of isolation. Small-scale efforts or those that are isolated within the larger organization often wither because they lack support from the larger group (Goodman & Dean, 1994). When initiatives are not part of a larger unified organizational effort, change agents may find that the larger organization is ambivalent to their efforts. Support for their initiatives may wane as a result.

The best antidote to isolation is that of change *congruence*. Changes that are clearly consistent with well-understood organizational values and structures are most likely to survive over time (Goodman & Dean, 1994). They succeed because their intent is consistent with the larger goals of the organization. Initiatives thought to contribute to the shared vision of the organization are most likely to gain acceptance over time. This is perhaps the single most important factor in the long-term survival of an innovation.

Main Points

· Continuous improvement lies at the heart of all successful marketing effort, because clients' expectations rise over time.

· Improvement requires ongoing change, yet change itself is inevitably resisted by service staff.

· Several measures ease acceptance of change in any organization.

· The antecedent conditions of (a) trust, (b) external pressure, and (c) staff members' readiness levels encourage acceptance of change initiatives.

· The nature of the change initiative will further influence acceptance of the initiative. Changes that are easy to understand, consistent with current practice, and offer clear advantage to key players will be most readily adopted.

· Project champions often focus debate and interest around change initiatives.

· Change requires both emotional and technical resources.

· Implementing change requires that several steps be undertaken. These steps include (a) establishing a sense of urgency, (b) generating communication around the initiative, (c) empowering staff to implement the change, and (d) consolidation.

· Many changes fail over time because they fail to be consolidated. Consolidation is the process of altering policies, systems, and procedures to make them consistent with the proposed changes.

References

Bechtell, M.L. (1993). *Untangling organizational gridlock*. Milwaukee, WI: ASQC Quality Press.

Berry, L. (1995). *On great service*. New York: The Free Press.

Buck, J. (1998). Managing change: The art of balancing. In *Harvard business review on change* (pp. 55-82). Boston: Harvard Business School Press.

Fisher, A.B. (1995, April 17). Making change stick. *Fortune*. 121-128.

Goodman, P., & Dean, J. (1994). Why productivity efforts fail. In W.L. French, C.H. Bell, & R.A Zawacki (Eds.), *Organizational development and transformation* (pp. 441-449). Boston: Irwin.

Grant, R.M., Shani, R., & Krishnan, R. (1994). TQM's challenge to management theory and practice. *Sloan Management Review*, (Winter), 25-35.

Hutton, D. (1995). *Managing the human aspects of organizational change: Management accounting guideline #34*. Toronto: Society of Management Accountants of Canada.

Judge, T.A., Thoresen, C.J., Pucik, V., & Welbourne, T.M. (1999). Managerial coping with organizational change: A dispositional perspective. *Journal of Applied Psychology*, 84(1), 107-122.

Kanter, R. (1985). *Managing the human side of change*. New York: The Free Press.

Kotter, J. (1998). Leading change: Why transformation efforts fail. In *Harvard Business Review* (pp. 1-20). Boston: Harvard Business School Press.

Mishra, A.K., & Mishra, K.E. (1994). The role of mutual trust in effective downsizing strategies. *Human Resource Management*, 33 (2) , 261-279.

Podsakoff, P.M., & MacKenzie, S.B. (1996). Impact of organizational citizenship behavior on organizational performance: A review and suggestions for future research. *Human Performance*, 10(2), 133-151.

O'Toole, J. (1996). *Leading change: The argument for values-based leadership*. New York: Ballentine Books.

Richardson, P., & Denton, D.K. (1996). Communicating change. *Human Resource Management*, 35(2), 203-216.

Rogers, E.M. (1983). *Diffusion of innovations*. New York: The Free Press.

Smeltzer, L.R. (1991). An analysis of strategies for announcing organization-wide change. *Group and Organization Studies*, 16, 5-24.

Steininger, D.J. (1994). Why quality initiatives are failing: The need to address the foundation of human motivation. *Human Resource Management*, 33(4), 601-616.

Strebel, P. (1996). Why do employees resist change? In *Harvard Business Review* (pp. 86-92). Boston: Harvard Business School Press.

Tabak, L. (1996, September). Quality controls: Improving corporate communications. *Hemisphere* 33-34.

Welch, R.J. (2000). *Monitoring conditions for staff acceptance of organizational change: A case study at St. Lawrence Islands National Park*. Unpublished master's thesis, University of Waterloo, Waterloo, Ontario, Canada.

Zeithmal, V.A., Berry, L., & Parasuraman, A. (1988). Communication and control processes in the delivery of service quality. *Journal of Marketing*, 52, 35-48.

1

Putting it all Together: One Successful Program

User and Community Preferences for Pricing Park Services:

A Case Study*

INTRODUCTION

Government agencies are showing increasing interest in applying fees for service. Municipal agencies, like park and recreation departments, have been increasingly involved in fees over the past decade (Brademas & Readnour, 1989; Crompton, 1994; Weissinger & Murphy, 1993). Recent initiatives like the U.S. Omnibus Consolidated Rescissions Act, which enables federal natural resource agencies to test fee programs, suggests that at least some federal agencies are not far behind their municipal counterparts. However, pricing represents one of the great ongoing challenges confronting public administrators. The challenge is one of ensuring supply, especially to low-income groups, while maintaining demand. Administrators adopt fees, in part, to gather resources so that they might provide

quality services to the larger community. However, as agencies implement fees, they must do so in a way that reduces the inherently exclusionary effects of those same fees (Brademas & Readnour, 1989; Goodale, 1985; McCarville & Smale, 1991; More, 1998).

Our understanding of pricing and user response to pricing has emerged largely from the study of users in publicly funded natural areas. Much of this research focuses on user reaction to fees once fees have been instituted. A recent report, prepared by Reiling, Cheng, and Trott (1996), is indicative of many of these studies. They asked campers at Maine State Parks if they would reduce their camping activity if prices were increased. Members of all socioeconomic groups indicated that higher fees would discourage participation, and this trend was even more pronounced among low-income campers. These results suggest inevitable negative consequences arising from potential fee initiatives.

While offering valuable insight to decision makers about user groups, this perspective offers only limited insight into pricing and pricing strategy, because it addresses the generally passive role of the agency setting the prices. The agency that charges a fee must then endure unpleasant consequences, ranging from complaint behavior to loss of customer base. It seems clear, however, that pricing efforts would benefit from agencies taking an active role in ameliorating the negative effects of pricing. This case study reports one agency's efforts to do just that. This agency, the Canadian Park Service, in particular, the Rocky Mountain Parks, embarked on a strategy designed to increase understanding for and acceptance of proposed fee changes *before* changes were undertaken. The agency used consultations with the community to improve pricing strategy before planned fee increases were implemented. This case study makes two basic contributions to the pricing literature. First, it reports many of the insights the agency gathered from extensive public consultations on pricing and pricing strategy. Second, it outlines the agency's application of these insights. Though the setting is that of a national park system, the strategies reported here will be of interest to any agency hoping to undertake pricing initiatives.

The Winds of Change

Like its predecessor in the United States, the Canadian Park Service was originally charged with the role of protecting dedicated areas for the ongoing benefit, education, and enjoyment of the nation. Funding for the agency has traditionally been straightforward. Parks and historic sites were considered to be national assets and a "contribution to the health and happiness of the citizens. Therefore all basic facilities . . . such as trails and campgrounds . . . [we]re to be provided out of public funds rather than being paid entirely by the persons who use the parks" (Laing, 1964). Within this context, fees were sometimes imposed, but resulting revenues were considered to be almost inconsequential by users and administrators alike.

Dramatic reductions in funding through the 1990s caused a rethinking of this approach. The agency lost almost one-third ($95 million Cdn.) of its operating resources over a three-year period; however, it was simultaneously granted the authority to retain revenues generated through measures like fees and charges. The challenge was one of establishing pricing practices which fulfilled the agency's

short-term monetary objectives while maintaining the agency's long-term service and protection mandate.

The agency decided that any change in fee structures should be predicated by consultation with users, private sector partners, and the nation at large. Staff assumed that the general public and potential users were both willing and able to suggest how pricing strategies might best be undertaken. As a result, the pricing process was underpinned by consultative efforts to gather public views regarding when fees should be applied, the way in which fees might best be applied, to whom they should be applied, and for what purpose they might best be used. These consultations were undertaken with both the general public and directly with park users. This study offers the results of these consultations, then reports how they were used to develop policy within the park system.

This report represents a single case study. The unit of analysis for this study is the Western Region of the Canadian Park Service. At the time these measures were instituted, this region was comprised primarily of four Rocky Mountain Parks. Case study methodology requires that evidence be gathered from a variety of sources (Yin, 1994). Consistent with Yin's recommendation, this report draws on a variety of sources, including agency reports, news releases, personal interviews, and promotional materials.

RESULTS OF CONSULTATIONS

Preliminary Consultations

As noted, fee implementation was viewed as an issue worthy of widespread consultation. A series of data-collection strategies were undertaken to gather the ideas and opinions from the general public as well as park users. Although description of the respective methodologies and setting-specific results gained from these strategies are beyond the scope of this paper, general observations are useful here. These observations should be helpful to any decision maker planning to develop pricing strategies that might best meet users' preferences and expectations.

A National Poll

A polling agency conducted a national survey on behalf of the agency. This poll was intended to gather input from a diverse range of citizens on park-related issues. Over one thousand (1,365) Canadians were polled on issues relating to use and awareness of parks and management priorities and concerns, including revenue generation and pricing (Angus Reid Group, 1993). Respondents included both those who had and had not recently visited national park sites. It should be noted that similar results have been reported in the context of the national park system in the U.S. (National Park Fees, 1995). As a result, both the discussion of the results and the resulting strategies discussed here should be relevant to both U.S. and Canadian settings.

The national poll suggested the types of pricing strategies that are more or less acceptable to the general public. Most believed that rising costs could be offset by "charging for specific services in the campground, for the use of firewood or showers and charging campers higher fees" (Angus Reid Group, 1993 p. 22). Predictably, local users of the parks did not share the general public's enthusiasm for such fees. The majority of local respondents were in favor of a nominal fee charged to all users rather than user fees for specific services. The poll suggested little support for charging senior citizens full adult entry fees. Nor was there support for measures that would reduce levels of service in order to cut operating costs. Finally, the poll suggested that more frequent visitors, typically those living closest to the parks, were more likely to use the parks during off seasons than those coming from or living at a greater distance.

Next, poll results suggested the public's preferences in terms of park policy. For example, over half (60 percent) believed that costs should be recovered. Apparently, the older the individual, the more likely he was to favor using gate proceeds to support parks and to favor limiting visitor access to protect plants and animals. These trends were of considerable importance when pricing (and related communication) strategies were developed.

The poll results also suggested that proximity to national parks was a critical factor in visitation levels and resulting price sensitivity. Those living closest to the greatest number of park sites were the heaviest users of national park facilities, reporting the highest number of annual visits to parks. This suggests that response to fee initiatives may vary in terms of proximity to the resource. These relatively heavy, local users may be most likely to resent changes in fee-collection strategies or in fee levels (McCarville, Reiling, & White, 1996). The pricing literature suggests that these users typically possess a narrow or restricted "latitude of acceptance" regarding price levels and policies (McCarville, 1996). As a result, they may be the first to recognize changes in policy and will likely be opposed to change in policy as a result.

On-site Survey

Given the discrepancy in views between the general public and park users, a survey was conducted to gather the views of visitors traveling through the parks. Staff conducted this survey with over one thousand (1,058) individuals, contacted at random, responding to questions regarding the quality of the facilities they enjoyed while visiting various national parks and their preferences regarding pricing practices (Parks Canada, 1995). Though this survey was concerned with many of the same questions posed by the national poll, it focused solely on park visitors. As suggested, these users' views were considered an important component of subsequent pricing deliberations. Further, it was reasoned that respondents who have actually visited a park site may view subsequent survey questions as less hypothetical and respond in more genuine terms. The survey format also offered respondents more specific scenarios than did the national poll instrument.

Results suggest that visits to parks are typically made by a small group or involve a family event. Groups of visitors tended to be comprised of fewer than three people. Although numbers differ from one park to the next, almost 75 percent of respondents reported having three or fewer people in the car when contacted by survey personnel. Approximately half reported only two visitors in the automobile. These respondents were generally travelling with family (83.1 percent) or friends (11.1 percent). Approximately 20 percent were visiting on a daily (20.2 percent) or an annual (21.9 percent) pass. Almost 40 (36.7) percent were visiting on a four day pass. This information suggests how various pass options might be designed and their potential popularity among this group of respondents.

In terms of pricing strategy, these respondents tended to favor paying one fee as they entered a park rather than paying a series of fees for access to services while in the park. Seventy percent of local visitors and 68 (68.4) percent of "other Canadian" users favored this general entry passport approach. However, there was considerable disagreement over the preferred fee type. Generally, as many respondents favored a per-person pass as favored a per-vehicle pass. This trend changed somewhat when the survey question offered a specific context for the respondent. When the question was presented in the context of a statement about fairness, ("Visitors travel in a variety of groups and party sizes. The fairest way to charge a park entrance fee would be on a per-person basis rather than on a per-vehicle basis") respondents were more likely to favor the "fair" alternative suggested by the survey statement (i.e., the per-person alternative). This suggests that many users may respond to messages offering a particular context in which to assess pricing practices. In other words, they may be open to suggestion when assessing fee policies. Consequently, it was decided that efforts to alter fee policies should be accompanied by messages which justify those changes in terms that users might find appealing.

Willingness to pay hypothetical fees declined as fee levels were increased from $3.00 per adult to $4.00, but little additional decline occurred when they were further elevated to $5.00. This pattern was also evident when per-party costs were increased from $7.50 per day to $10.00 to $12.50. Resistance to fee increases was most pronounced among local users. In

other words, local users were least likely to agree to pay increased price levels. Clearly, the parks' heaviest users were the most intransigent of the user groups in terms of acceptance of fees. Staff believed that more data were required from this group so a series of focus groups was arranged.

Focus Groups

A series of focus group sessions were scheduled throughout the region in which the parks were located. Each of these sessions brought together a small group of users, recruited based upon their common demographics or use patterns in the region's parks (The Advisory Group, 1994). Sessions were introduced by senior regional executives (directors and superintendents) who outlined existing challenges and policies, while offering background financial information. The sessions were conducted by moderators who guided participants through debate on fees and charges at national parks within their region.

Focus group members were typically comprised of repeat users of the region's parks. The term "user" was defined in its most general sense, so group members ranged from bus and tour operators to back country hikers. Given their seemingly disparate interests and activity patterns, they displayed a remarkable degree of agreement on a variety of issues. Participants in the focus groups seemed keenly aware that their tax dollars had already been allocated to support park initiatives and often believed that fees represented a "second charge" by that same agency. However, they seemed willing to pay fees if sufficient need, or benefit could be established. Group members suggested that any attempt to raise fees should be predicated by efforts to rationalize costs. They indicated that such efforts should be widely promoted to enhance community support for subsequent price changes. They also suggested that early promotional efforts be devoted to explaining upcoming pricing initiatives. They asked that promotions be undertaken months before any fees were instituted. This point was made most vehemently by private sector concerns whose profit margins were dependent upon price levels. They made it clear that increased fees were most problematic when these increases were levied too late to be passed along in their own promotional literature.

There was considerable support for a nominal entrance fee. Group members generally indicated that all those passing through or using the parks should be charged such a fee. It was considered as the most fair, efficient, and easy-to-understand means of fee collection. Group members were upset with current "free riders" who gained access to park resources but failed to pay entrance fees. Apparently, there exists a group of heavy park users who use their knowledge of park policy to gain access to selected park resources without making payment. This group both annoyed and discouraged those who agree to pay to enter these parks. They believed that their suggestion of "100 percent compliance" dealt with this issue of fairness and the free rider.

They offered a series of suggestions that would improve the sense of value, choice, and convenience now enjoyed by park users. In terms of value, several groups suggested that current offerings within the parks be enhanced. For example, they indicated that private sector providers might establish rental opportunities based on guidelines established by parks' personnel. Such efforts would provide an improved sense of value for visitors, and the resulting contractual arrangements could generate additional funds for the parks.

However, focus group members believed that promotions should not be restricted to justification of upcoming initiatives. These users suggested that every opportunity be taken to inform users about fees, fee options, and noteworthy opportunities while visiting parks. One group suggested that the backs of receipts might contain information about opportunities available while in the park, where passes or additional tickets might be purchased, and so on. These users seemed to long for information about all that was available in the parks. They asked staff to communicate more openly with their clientele regarding all facets of fees and agency programs.

Choice was also of considerable interest to these users. They suggested that a variety of time-based passes be made available. Such

passes, they suggested, should be available by the day, the week, the season, and so on. Differential fee systems also received support from these users. They indicated that more popular activities might be priced at higher levels to decrease crowding and increase revenue. Less popular sites, seasons, or activities could be priced at lower levels to both increase interest and to offer less expensive options for price sensitive users. These recommendations may also help solve a problem identified by the national poll. The poll suggested that more frequent visitors are likely to use the parks during off seasons than are their less involved counterparts. Therefore, season discounts or annual passes may have considerable appeal to this heavy user group.

There was general support for a fee system characterized by simplicity and speed in its processing of visitors at park checkpoints. Focus group participants offered suggestions that would enhance convenience levels while on-site. First, they indicated both a desire and a willingness to pay extra for a reliable reservation system. They even suggested that several sites could be excluded from that system so that "drop-in" visitors from distant locations would not be disadvantaged. They also indicated a desire for regional passes so that they could travel from one park to the next without the need to purchase multiple passes. In addition, they suggested that passes for in-park activities should be made available at multiple outlets like local businesses and park offices.

Taken together, these results suggest that, though users would prefer not to pay fees, several conditions can render payment less problematic. Generally, within the context of the public sector, the need for large fee increases should be established before increases are introduced. Further, fee increases suggest reduced value for the user. As a result, measures that enhance value (and reduce related costs) must accompany fee increases. Finally, fees are problematic because they offer an ultimatum to users. They are being told to either pay a fee or be denied the service. Such ultimatums are unpleasant and unwelcome for most users. Those surveyed during this consultation suggested that meaningful choices or options can reduce the irritation associated with fees. Choices enable users to pay only for programs they value at prices they find most acceptable. Although these insights are collected in a specific context, they offer considerable insight to any agency hoping to charge fees for its programs.

Implications for Practice

This case study now outlines the ways in which the Canadian Park Service integrated these insights into daily operations. Agency response is discussed in terms of preparation, communication with users, expanding the role of front line staff and establishing a sense of value.

Agency Preparation: Developing Categories of Service

First, agency personnel established principles intended to guide revenue decisions. These guidelines suggested that a relationship exists between level of subsidy and the identity of the primary beneficiary of a service. These guidelines are consistent with those set forth by Crompton and Lamb (1986). If the beneficiary is the immediate user, the service is classified as a "private good," and its fees are established on a cost-recovery basis. Services like hot pools, camping, or guided walks were believed to fall under the category of private goods and were priced on a cost-recovery basis. Activities that were inherently consumptive or that take place in over-utilized environments were to be charged even higher fees (cost recovery plus) in hopes of reducing levels of use.

Other services were offered on a partial cost-recovery basis. Such services benefit the user but are also beneficial for other park users. Such services, typically classified as "merit goods" (Crompton & Lamb, 1986), received partial funding from the tax base. Public safety services, general park information, and message services were given this designation. Finally, a few select services received the designation of

"public goods" and received full tax support. No fees were assigned to such services. These services were believed to benefit all Canadians, so all taxpayers were expected to contribute to their provision. For example, research devoted to monitoring endangered species or efforts to establish new parks qualified as public goods. These basic policies set the stage for all subsequent pricing strategies.

Efforts to Communicate with Users

Insights gathered from the various public consultations suggested that communication would play a key role in any pricing initiative. A strategy was developed to (a) communicate reasons for price increases long before those increases were instituted, and (b) change price expectations with new information so that expectations might rise with the new prices. This strategy, developed by a private communications firm, was comprised of several elements, including a documentary series, a multi-use "flagship" brochure, and radio blitzes prior to long weekends throughout the summer months (FWJ Communications, 1995).

Specifically, measures were taken to establish the agency's increased need for revenue. This was done through a documentary series developed through a regional cable television operator. This series, comprised primarily of interviews with park service staff, highlighted two points. First, a case was made for the decline in tax-based appropriations. Messages indicated the relatively small proportion of operational funds that originate with the tax dollar, as well as the importance of fees for all merit and private services.

Second, the consequences of fee payment, or failure to pay, were outlined. As suggested, the consultation exercise made it clear that users wished to be reassured that fees were not being wasted or allocated at the whim of bureaucrats. They preferred that their fees make a difference by either maintaining or improving valued resources, so the television series indicated that fee revenues remained in the parks so that services could be maintained or enhanced.

Expanding the Role of Front Line Staff

Management determined that staff members be fully involved in promoting the need for fees. They believed that users typically valued interactions with staff so it was likely that users would direct any questions or complaints regarding fees to staff. Such contact offered two important opportunities for the agency. First, it offered an opportunity for staff members to discuss the need for fees. As a result, staff members were briefed on the need for the fees, the benefits arising from the payment of fees, and the disposition of such fees. It was hoped that positive contact with staff members might generate considerable positive word-of-mouth communication among users. Second, ongoing discussions with users enabled front line staff members to gather information on public reaction to fees. Staff were therefore considered an important source of information on the impact of fees on visitation levels and on general perceptions of the fee program.

Staff members were considered more than purveyors of information, however. It was considered essential that, to improve service levels, front line staff should be empowered to respond to user concerns. As a result, responsibility for many decisions that had traditionally required managerial approval were turned over to staff. Preparation for this new-found authority included additional staff training, improved internal communication, and the allocation of additional resources to handle ongoing user concerns. Training was offered to help staff deal with jobs that were quickly evolving from "ticket sellers" to "compliance officers" to "visitor service representatives". Staff members were offered additional training in topics ranging from active listening to the history of the national park system. To improve communication, a series of staff meetings were arranged to share ideas and concerns among fellow staff members and with management representatives. Front line staff were issued 4"x 10" cards that described the new fee structures and the reasons for the changes. Staff were able to use these cards as "crib sheets" to help them answer user questions. These cards were also distributed to visitors while they waited in line at main entry points. In this way, the visitors were fully informed of the changes in fees before they were asked to pay those fees.

Flexibility was offered by providing staff with improved technical support and the authority to use agency resources when addressing users' concerns. In terms of technical support, staff were offered upgraded registration systems to support their on-site efforts. These upgrades included improved record keeping capabilities, as well as more user-friendly computing systems. These improvements enhanced the speed with which staff could process visitors and improved their ability to handle complaints. In addition, each staff member was authorized to allocate agency resources in order to resolve user problems and complaints. Staff were empowered, for example, to move campers who complained about the quality of a site. Further, they were authorized to give full refunds immediately to clients who were unhappy with their visit.

Staff members were also encouraged to offer a complimentary night of camping to campers who complained about some aspect of their visit. This free night represents a form of "symbolic atonement" used in many service industries as a tangible measure of the agency's regret over problems (Berry & Parasuraman, 1991). Though such measures cost the agency very little, they create what is known as "secondary satisfaction." Such satisfaction, which arises if problems are handled to the satisfaction of the user, is related to greater loyalty and positive word-of-mouth communication (Goodwin & Ross, 1992). Indeed, all of the Canadian Park Service has now adopted a "satisfaction guaranteed" policy, and staff are empowered to take whatever steps necessary to ensure visitors receive positive value for their fee. These measures were designed to help staff take control of their own service settings in order to improve service levels. This enlarged role for staff has generated an unanticipated benefit: end-of-season surveys among seasonal staff suggest that they were delighted with their new ability to solve obvious concerns before the issues escalated into problems for both staff and visitors.

Establishing Sense of Value

Public consultations also made it clear that the agency's efforts should also be devoted to establishing a sense of value. Value is generally defined as perceived benefits moderated by the costs the user believes he paid in order to enjoy those benefits (Monroe & Petroshius, 1981). In other words, the greater the benefits enjoyed or the lower the costs, the greater the value for the user. As a result, efforts focused on the number and quality of services provided with the purchase of a pass to the parks. This was achieved by (a) making clear the connection between payment and benefit, (b) outlining price and program alternatives, and (c) reducing non-monetary costs associated with the purchase of park passes.

Specifically, a full-color fold-out "flagship" brochure was created to guide users through a trip to the Rocky Mountain Parks and related attractions in the region. The brochure, called "Pathways to Past Ways: Canadian Rockies Heritage Tour," offers a welcome to the park user, accompanied by a fold-out map with suggestions on how to best enjoy a visit to each of the many sites in the area. The brochure includes the sites' characteristics (all expressed in terms of benefits offered to visitors), hours of operation, and $100 in discount coupons for use at these sites. Further, a newsletter is now distributed at all entry points. It advises users of upcoming events, points of interest, and any special information deemed appropriate by staff. This newsletter, coordinated through a private sector company, is funded entirely through advertising. Each of these measures is designed to enhance visitors' enjoyment of the sites as well as increase a sense of value during their visit.

Results of the public consultation suggested considerable desire for choice in the types of available fees. Consequently, the new pricing strategy included a variety of meaningful price alternatives. These alternatives were designed to ensure that users could exercise choice in the price they eventually paid to visit park sites. The tenets of pricing suggest that the best price alternatives recognize the user group's particular use patterns (Nagle, 1987). The consultations indicated that users hoped

fees might recognize temporal variation. On-site surveys suggested that users vary in the amount of time they remained on-site, the number of parks they visited over the year, the number of times they visited a park in a given year, and so on. Pricing schemes were developed accordingly. For example, in addition to a single park pass, a regional pass was developed. Purchase of the pass provided access to a variety of sites in the region.

Further, the amount of time a pass could be used was altered. Annual passes had traditionally followed the calender year, and ceased to afford access with the new year. This administrative decision discouraged the purchase of passes late in the year, because of the reduced value the purchaser received. Changes were instituted so that annual passes would be honored for one year from the purchase date. This initiative encouraged the purchase of passes throughout the year.

Provision of choice offers an added benefit in that it aids users in selecting a fee type or fee level that is most acceptable to them and their own personal resource levels. Staff members were instructed to, where appropriate, aid users in making price-related choices. For example, if campers indicated that they wished to spend several nights on site, staff immediately advised them that an annual pass offered the lowest overall cost. Staff members could issue the pass and coupon book immediately. Staff were also able to indicate whether or not any of the discount coupons applied to this visit. If so, they simply removed the coupons and offered an immediate discount to the users. Approximately $35,000 in coupons were redeemed last year. This represents considerable savings to visitors. Further, if visitors purchased a short-term pass, but later decided to purchase a more expensive annual pass, staff could credit the visitors for the amount already spent on the short-term pass. In effect, penalties were removed if visitors attempted to upgrade their passes.

Another issue related to value is that of overall cost reduction for visitors. These users expected convenience and simplicity when paying fees. Convenience, or more accurately lack of convenience, represents a nonmonetary cost (Monroe & Petroshius, 1981). Staff were aware that users were confronted with a myriad of hurdles to be overcome in order to visit a national park. The need to plan for travel, accommodation, and on-site activities represents considerable psychological cost for some users. Measures were put in place that minimized such costs. For example, the agency began to sell passes off-site. It was believed that off-site sales could reduce crowding at sale points, typically gates, at park entrances. Arrangements were made with retail outlets that specialized in outdoor clothing and equipment and gas stations located on all approaches to the park sites.

Although this measure has created extra work for park staff, since it seems particularly difficult to keep partners supplied with the appropriate number and types of passes, it has proven a useful alternative for many users. Thousands of visitors have avoided lines at the entrance kiosks by going, instead, to partner agencies for their passes. This program may be expanded to include entry points like airports and other partners that also serve park users (e.g., recreational vehicle rental agencies, tourist information centers, etc.). In a related initiative, the agency now sells passes at a 10 percent discount to anyone expressing interest in making volume purchases of passes. This offer may be of interest to hotels, travel agencies, car rental companies, or even companies who hope to provide additional benefits to their partners or employees.

The nature of fee-related concerns varied among user groups. While individual users were typically concerned with convenience while on site, private sector companies were most interested in the costs associated with last-minute fee changes. Indeed, the bus and tour company representatives indicated a need to be informed more than one year in advance to accommodate changes in their own pricing structures. In the focus groups they reported considerable dissatisfaction with "surprise" fee increases. They did not wish to learn of new price levels as they arrived at the park gate, presumably because they were unable to pass these costs along to their clients. The agency now provides these companies with 18 months' notice of changes in price levels or policy. They have established a system whereby up to 2,000 user companies can be notified within 48 hours of changes to fees or fee policies. In this way, these companies are planning with the most up-to-date information available.

User Reaction to These Initiatives

The question becomes, "What have been the results of these measures?" Though only very preliminary results are available, they are encouraging. Entrance fees at these parks doubled over three years, yet visitation levels remained constant over that same period. Further, the complexion of these visitors has also remained constant. In aggregate terms at least, neither local nor distant visitors have been displaced as result of this remarkable increase in fee levels. Neither has complaint behavior increased. Management established a toll-free number to respond to questions or concerns about the fee increases or other park policies. There continue to be calls about fees in general, but the number of these calls has not increased since these measures have been instituted. Finally, recall that visitors have been offered a "satisfaction guarantee," indicating that if they were dissatisfied with the value they received from their entrance fees, they could request a full refund. Last year, while one campground collected over $1 million in revenues, it paid out less than $2,000 in refunds! This pay-out represents less than one percent (.02 percent) of revenues for that campground. This number is surprisingly low, considering that satisfaction may be influenced by weather, the presence or absence of wildlife, other users, and so on. Staff attribute the relatively low number of refunds to their new-found ability to solve problems on the spot.

Conclusions

In conclusion, there seems little doubt that fees have become an important issue for administrators and users alike. Related studies suggest that fees are being applied to public leisure services at unprecedented levels, and this trend is unlikely to change in the short term. Clearly, however, the application of fees in the public sector is fraught with difficulties.

Fees are intrusive because no one wants to pay them (Leuschner, Cook, Roggenbuck, & Oderwald, 1987). Fees are symbolic because they represent a change in the way public agencies "do business." Fees are exclusionary, so their application by the public sector is problematic.

This case study offers administrators some insight into the pricing dilemma. It suggests that the key to successful pricing may rest with an agency's community of users. The thoughtful application of insights gathered from this community seems to offer profound dividends for all concerned. The agency described here reports that though prices have doubled, visitation rates have remained stable, and user complaints have been minimal. Though these results may be at least partially a function of conditions unique to the national park setting, it seems equally clear that the measures described here have been functioning as intended. The principles of choice, communication, the expanded role of staff, and more "user friendly" program policies seem useful and appropriate in any pricing context. Other public settings could benefit from their application.

References

Angus Reid Group. (1993). *A study of Canadian attitudes toward Canada's national parks*. Calgary, Alberta: Author.

Berry, L. L., & Parasuraman, A. (1991). *Marketing services: Competing through quality*. Toronto: The Free Press.

Brademas, D., & Readnour, J. (1989). Status of fees and charges in public leisure service agencies. *Journal of Park and Recreation Administration, 7*(4), 42-55.

Crompton, J. L. (1987). *Doing more with less*. State College, PA: Venture.

Crompton, J. L., & Lamb, C. (1986). *Marketing government and social services*. New York: John Wiley & Sons.

Canadian Park Service. (1995). *Parks Canada revenue policy*. Working Document.

FWJ Communications Ltd. (1994). *A communications strategy for the introduction of personal use fees*. Calgary, Alberta: Author.

Goodale, T. (1985). Prevailing winds and bending mandates. In T. Goodale & P. Witt (Eds.), *Recreation and leisure: Issues in an era of change* (pp. 195-207). State College, PA: Venture.

Goodwin, C., & Ross, I. (1992). Consumer responses to service failures: Influence of procedural and interactional fairness perceptions. *Journal of Business Research, 25*, 149-163.

Laing, A. (1964). *A statement on national park policy*. House of Commons, Ottawa, Canada.

Leuschner, W. A., Cook, P. S., Roggenbuck, J. W., & Oderwald, R., G. (1987). A comparative analysis for wilderness fee policy. *Journal of Leisure Research, 19*, 101-114.

McCarville, R. (1996). The importance of price last paid in developing price expectations for a public leisure service. *Journal of Park and Recreation Administration, 14*(4), 52-64.

McCarville, R. E., Crompton, J. L., & Sell, J. A. (1993). The influence of outcome messages on reference prices. *Leisure Sciences, 15*, 115-130.

McCarville, R. E., Reiling, S., & White, C. (1996). The role of fairness in users' assessments of first-time fees for a public recreation service. *Leisure Sciences, 18*(1), 61-76.

McCarville, R. E., & Smale, B. J. (1991). Involvement in pricing by municipal recreation agencies. *Journal of Applied Recreation Research, 16*, 200-219.

Monroe, K., & Petroshius, S. (1981). Buyers' perception of price: An update of the evidence. In H. Kassarjian & T. Robertson (Eds.)., *Perspectives in consumer behavior* (3rd ed.) (pp. 43-45). Dallas TX: Scott, Foresman & Co.

More, T. A. (1998). A functionalist perspective on visitor fees. *Proceedings of Society and Resources Management, Seventh International Symposium*, 238-239.

Nagle, T. T. (1987). *The strategy and tactics of pricing: A guide to profitable decision making*. Toronto: Prentice-Hall.

Parks Canada. (1995). [1994 Exit Survey of Visitors to the Rocky Mountain Parks]. Unpublished raw data.

Reiling, S. D., Cheng, H. T., & Trott, C. (1992). Measuring the discriminatory impact associated with higher recreational fees. *Leisure Sciences, 14*(2), 121-138.

The Advisory Group (1994, December). *Report on public consultation exercise for personal use fees in Alberta*. Calgary, Alberta: Author.

Weissinger, E., & Murphy, W. (1993). A survey of fiscal conditions in small-town public recreation departments from 1987 to 1991. *Journal of Park and Recreation Administration, 11*(3), 61-72.

Yin, R. K. (1994). *Case study research: Design and methods*. London: Sage.

* This case study first appeared in the *Journal of Park and Recreation Administration* Vol. 17(1). The full citation is McCarville, R., Sears, D. & Furness, S. (1999). User and community preferences for pricing park services: A case study. *Journal of Park and Recreation Administration*, 17(1), 91-105.

INDEX

place of residence, as a client group descriptor, 126
point of purchase, importance of communication at, 112
point-of-purchase displays and demonstrations, 140
political issues, identifying, 29
portfolio analysis
  cash cows, 42
  definition of, 41
  dogs, 42–43
  loss leaders, 43
  question marks, 42
  stars, 42
positioning
  attributes-based strategies, 46
  comparisons to competitors-based strategies, 46–47
  definition of market position, 45
  guidelines for adopting strategies, 47–48
  perceptual mapping, 48–49
  price-based strategies, 46
  product class-based strategies, 46–47
  questions to be answered by a positioning strategy, 46
  repositioning, 49–50
  role of, 45–46
  user-based strategies, 47
  use-related strategies, 47
presentation
  acknowledging the importance of staff members in, 197–98
  blueprinting the encounter, 202–6
  bringing backstage activities to the front, 197
  case study on, 213–14
  controlling ambient conditions, 208–9
  discovering clients' expectations and requirements, 200–201
  ensuring that supply matches demand, 210–11
  fixed position strategies for, 201–2
  involving clients in service production and delivery, 199
  managing social factors, 210
  as the moment of truth, 195–96
  organizational socialization, 206–8
  priority queuing, 211–12
  process-based strategies for, 202
  separating frontstage and backstage activities, 196–97
  service-based strategies for, 202
  supporting the encounter with appropriate systems, 199–200
  training clients to coproduce services, 206–8
  using design features to build a positive atmosphere, 209–10
  using staff name tags, 198–99
  waiting and the leisure experience, 212–13
  see also delivery; distribution
price incentives
  differential pricing, 139–40
  packaging/bundling, 139
pricing
  debate over, 148–49

determining when fees may be appropriate, 151–52
developing a safety net to ensure access to services, 153–55
and distribution, 183–84
equity models and, 150–51, 154–55
importance of, 147
moral systems of merchant vs. guardian, 149–50
public-merit-private classification system for fees, 151
safety net options, 153–54
understanding all of the costs to participants, 147–48
understanding the public's reaction to fees, 152–53
pricing strategy
  agency priorities as a price setting criterion, 170–71
  balance as a basic principle of, 164
  case study on, 175–76
  choice as a basic principle of, 163–64
  communication as a basic principle of, 164–65
  creating a matrix for, 173–75
  fairness as a basic principle of, 162–63
  managing pricing through policy statements, 161–62
  marketplace forces as a price setting criterion, 172–73
  neutral pricing, 167
  penetration pricing, 165–67
  pricing triangle, 170–73
  program characteristics as a price setting criterion, 171–72
  role of, 162
  skim pricing, 168–70
priorities, as a price setting criterion, 170–71
process-based presentation strategies, 202
process charting. see blueprinting the service encounter
product bundles
  augmentation categories, 81–82
  augmentation guidelines, 79–81
  core, actual, and augmented levels, 79
  value propositions, 82
product design, and distribution, 183
product families, 83
product life cycle
  basic shapes of, 70–71
  case study on, 83–84
  decline/extension phase, 72
  definition of product, 69
  diffusion of innovation (DOI), 74–75
  growth phase, 71–72
  introductory phase, 71
  linking products through product families, 83
  maturity phase, 72
  moving from a product orientation to a client orientation, 78–79
  problems with the notion of, 69–70
  product bundles, 79–82
  product characteristics that facilitate or inhibit diffusion, 75–78
  tactics to delay the onset of decline, 73–74